Paper Wars

DECLASSIFIED

Paper Wars

Access to Information in South Africa

Edited by Kate Allan

WITS UNIVERSITY PRESS

Published in South Africa by:

Wits University Press
1 Jan Smuts Avenue
Johannesburg
2001
http://witspress.wits.ac.za

First printed 2009

This publication has been supported by a generous donation from SAHA.

ISBN 978-1-86814-491-4

Cover design and layout by The Library Design
Edited by Alex Potter
Indexed by Elaine Williams

Printed and bound by Creda Communications

Contents

Abbreviations

AEB	Atomic Energy Board
AEC	Atomic Energy Corporation
ANC	African National Congress
ATI	access to information
BNFL	British Nuclear Fuels Ltd
BOSS	Bureau of State Security
CBW	chemical and biological warfare
CDRC	Classification and Declassification Review Committee
CEO	chief executive officer
COSATU	Congress of South African Trade Unions
CSVR	Centre for the Study of Violence and Reconciliation
DAC	Department of Arts, Culture, Science and Technology
DCC	Defence Command Council or Directorate for Covert Collection
DFA	Department of Foreign Affairs
DHA	Department of Home Affairs
DIO	deputy information officer
DME	Department of Minerals and Energy
DOD	Department of Defence
DOJ	Department of Justice
DTI	Department of Trade and Industry
EIA	environmental impact assessment
FOIP	Freedom of Information Programme
FXI	Freedom of Expression Institute
HEU	highly enriched uranium
HSI	head of staff intelligence/hoof staf inligting
IAEA	International Atomic Energy Agency
Idasa	Institute for a Democratic South Africa
JW	Johannesburg Water Pty Ltd
MOU	memorandum of understanding
NARSA	National Archives and Records Service Act
NCAC Act	National Conventional Arms Control Act
NECSA	Nuclear Energy Corporation of South Africa
NECTEC	Nuclear Energy Costs the Earth Campaign
NGO	non-governmental organisation
NIA	National Intelligence Agency
NIS	National Intelligence Service
NNR	National Nuclear Regulator

NPA	National Prosecuting Authority
NPT	Nuclear Non-Proliferation Treaty
ODAC	Open Democracy Advice Centre
OSI	Open Society Initiative
PAIA	Promotion of Access to Information Act No. 2 of 2000
PBMR	pebble bed modular reactor
PBMR Ltd	Pebble Bed Modular Reactor (Pty) Ltd
PNE	peaceful nuclear explosive
SAB	South African Breweries Ltd
SABC	South African Broadcasting Corporation
SADF	South African Defence Force
SAHA	South African History Archive
SAHRC	South African Human Rights Commission
SALRC	South African Law Reform Commission
SAMS	South African Medical Services
SANDF	South African National Defence Force
SAPS	South African Police Service
SFJ	Struggles for Justice Programme
TRC	South African Truth and Reconciliation Commission
TRC Act	Promotion of National Unity and Reconciliation Act
UDF	Union Defence Force
USD	US dollar
ZAR	South African rand

Acknowledgements

Paper Wars could not have been conceived and completed without the support, input and diligence of Verne Harris and Oliver Barstow. Their contributions were vital to framing the scope, content and objectives of the book. Special mention must also be made of Piers Pigou, Sello Hatang, Rolf Sorenson, Olga Pickover, Catherine Kennedy, Charlotte Young, Shadrack Katuu, Sam Jacobs, Esmerelda Dirks, Fritz Schoon, Jonathan Klaaren, Iain Currie, and Michele Pickover.

I would like to thank the numerous people with whom SAHA employed or worked closely with in its access to information work, in alphabetical order: David Banisar, Florencia Belvedere, Simon Delaney, Mukelani Dimba, David Forbes, Evelyn Groenink, Naeem Jeenah, Loren Landau, Dale McKinley, Teboho Makhalemele, Kgaogelo Nchaupe, Mashile Phalane, Laura Pollecut, Rob Thomson, Alison Tilley, Darshan Vigneswaran, and David Wallace.

Thanks also go to the staff of the following organizations, in no particular order: the Gay and Lesbian Archives (now known as Gay and Lesbian Memory in Action); the Law School, The Mandela Institute, the Law Clinic, Wiser, the Graduate School for Humanities and Social Sciences, the Forced Migration Studies Programme, Research Unit for Law and Administration, the University Archives, Historical Papers, and the William Cullen Library at the University of the Witwatersrand; Centre for Applied Legal Studies; the Nelson Mandela Foundation; Centre for the Study of Economic Crime at the University of Johannesburg; Lawyers for Human Rights; the Legal Resources Centre; the Institute for Security Studies; Earthlife Africa; the Freedom of Expression Institute; the Open Democracy Advice Centre; the Public Service Accountability Monitor; the Treatment Action Campaign; Khulumani Support Group; Izikho Museum; Switzerland's Apartheid Debt and Reparation Campaign; Biowatch; the Ceasefire Campaign; Anti-privatization Forum; the Coalition Against Water Privatization; Angola 2000; the Baragwanath Perinatal HIV/AIDS Research Unit; the Biko Foundation; the Centre for the Study of Violence and Reconciliation; Forest Group; Freedom Park Trust; Idasa; the Institute for Advanced Journalism; Jubilee South Africa; Robben Island Museum; the South African Society of Archivists; the Attridgeville Community Based Organisations (CBOs); the Media Institute of Southern Africa (MISA); Research Unit for Law and Administration (RULA); AIDS Consortium; Centre for Health Policy; Access to Learning Materials in Southern Africa Project; Justice for Animals; South African Institute of International Affairs (SAIIA), University of the Western Cape (UWC); COSATU; Southern and Eastern African Trade Information and Negotiations Institute (SEATINI); Xwe African Wild Life; Netherlands Institute of Human Rights (Utrecht University); the BioWeapons Prevention Project; Platform against Nuclear Energy (PLAGE); the East and Southern African Regional Branch of the International Council of Archives; the National Security Archives; the International Centre for Transitional Justice; the Institute for Justice and Reconciliation; UNESCO; the International Records Management Trust (IRMT); Queens College (City University of New York); the University of Michigan; International Research on Permanent Authentic Records in Electronic Systems (InterPARES); the Swiss National Scientific Research Foundation; and The Library Design.

I am very grateful to the attorneys who provided probono or other legal services to SAHA (Abheda Bhamjee, Crystal Cambanis, Kathryn Gawith, Aslam Moosajee, Richard Moultrie, Caroline Nicholls, Nasreen Rajab-Budlender, Lisa Thornton, Mark Wesley, Probono.org, Webber Wentzel Bowens, and Denys Reitz), to SAHA's funders (Atlantic Philanthropies, the Rosa Luxembourg Foundation, the Foundation for Human Rights, the Ford Foundation, The Charles Stuart Mott Foundation, and Australian Volunteers International), and to Wits University Press.

Thanks must go to the current and former members of SAHA's board of trustees: Nkosinathi Biko, Luli Callinicos, Jean de la Harpe, Horst Kleinschmidt, Ruth Morgan, Noor Nieftegodien, Dumisa Ntsebeza, Michele Pickover, Marlene Powell, Ciraj Rassool, Graham Reid, Raziah Saleh, and Noel Stott.

Last, but by no means least, my gratitude goes to my partner Darshan Vigneswaran for his unconditional support and patience, and to my family.

Contributors

Kate Allan is a human rights lawyer who has been involved in a diverse range of human rights initiatives. She completed a Masters of Law at Harvard University in May 2009. Prior to that she was a lawyer in the Rights and Equalities Unit at the United Kingdom Ministry of Justice, advising government on data protection laws. From 2005 to 2007 she was the Coordinator of the Freedom of Information Programme at the South African History Archive (SAHA) and was responsible for litigation and advocacy in relation to the South African Promotion of Access to Information Act of 2000. Prior to her appointment at SAHA, she was employed as a Solicitor at the Consumer Credit Legal Service in Melbourne, Australia and a sessional lecturer for Monash University's Post-graduate Diploma of Legal Practice. She has also worked for other organisations in Australia and South Africa on human rights issues including discrimination, refugee rights, mandatory sentencing and anti-terrorism laws. Kate has an LLB and a Bachelor of International Business from the Queensland University of Technology.

Richard Calland has for the past fourteen years been working in the field of democracy and governance in South Africa and the region. He is now Associate Professor in Public Law at the University of Cape Town, where he teaches constitutional and human rights law, and Director of its Democratic Governance & Rights Unit. He specializes in the law and practice of the right to access to information and whistleblowing protection; in administrative justice and public ethics; and in constitutional design – largely derived from his work as programme manager of the Political Information & Monitoring Service at Idasa which he led from its inception in 1995 until 2003. He is still serves as Programme Director of the Economic Governance programme at Idasa – Africa's leading democracy Institute and as part-time Executive Director of the Open Democracy Advice Centre (ODAC), a law centre based in Cape Town that specialises in the 'right to know', and which Calland founded in 2000. Calland has in recent years served as an expert consultant to the Carter Center, the foundation led by former US President Jimmy Carter, advising on various transparency projects in Bolivia, Jamaica, Nicaragua, Peru and Mali. He is a member of the International Advisory Group for the Medicines Transparency Initiative (MeTA) and provides regular strategic advice on politics and governance to a range of local and international corporates. In South Africa, Calland writes a fortnightly political column for the *Mail and Guardian* newspaper, 'Contretemps', and is a regular commentator in the media. His most recent book, *Anatomy of South Africa: Who Holds the Power?* was published in late 2006. He is a Senior Associate of the Cambridge University's Programme for Sustainability Leadership. Before coming to South Africa in 1994, Calland practiced law at the London Bar. He holds an LLM from the University of Cape Town, a Diploma in World Politics from the London School of Economics and a BA (Hons) Law from the University of Durham.

Dr David Fig is an independent environmental policy researcher specialising in areas of energy, technology, agriculture, trade, corporate accountability and biodiversity. He has monitored the nuclear industry in South Africa extensively and is the author of *Uranium Road: Questioning South Africa's Nuclear Direction* (2005). His career has included working for a number of research organisations including the Latin America Bureau (London), the International Labour Research and Information Group (Cape Town), Group for Environmental Monitoring (Johannesburg) and Southern Africa Resource Watch (Johannesburg). He taught sociology at the University of the Witwatersrand in Johannesburg. He is currently part of the TNC Working Group of Our World Is Not For Sale, and is a member of the international research network on Business Development and Society based at the Copenhagen Business School. He chairs the board of Biowatch South Africa and formerly served on the board of South African National Parks which involved the restoration of conservation land to communities which had been forcibly removed under apartheid.

Dr Chandré Gould is a senior researcher in the Crime, Justice and Politics Programme at the Institute for Security Studies. Between 1996 and 1999 she worked as an investigator and evidence analyst for the Truth and Reconciliation Commission (TRC) in the Western Cape. She was one of the investigators responsible for the TRC's investigation into the apartheid chemical and biological warfare (CBW) programme. She obtained her PhD from Rhodes University in 2006. She has remained involved in efforts to strengthen national and international bans on nuclear, chemical and biological weapons and to make life scientists aware of the risks of dual-use research. Her previous books include *Secrets and Lies, Wouter Basson and the South African Chemical and Biological Weapons Programme* (Zebra 2002), *Hide and Seek:Taking account of small arms in Southern Africa* (edited, 2004) and *Selling Sex in Cape Town: Sex work and human trafficking in a South African city* (Institute for Security Studies, 2008).

Verne Harris is a programme manager for the Nelson Mandela Centre of Memory and Dialogue at the Nelson Mandela Foundation, and an honorary research associate with the University of Cape Town. He participated in a range of structures that transformed South Africa's apartheid public records system — among others, the African National Congress' Archives Committee, the Arts and Culture Task Group, the Consultative Forum that drafted the National Archives of South Africa Act, the Truth and Reconciliation Commission, and the South African History Archive. Widely published, he is best known for the books *Exploring Archives: An Introduction to Archival Ideas and Practice in South Africa* (1997, 2000 and 2004), *Refiguring the Archive* (2002), *A Prisoner in the Garden: Opening Nelson Mandela's Prison Archive* (2005) and *Archives and Justice* (2007). He is also the author of two novels, both of which were shortlisted for South Africa's M-Net Book Prize.

Piers Pigou is currently director of the South African History Archive. He came to South Africa in 1992 to work for the Black Sash paralegal advice office in Johannesburg, before joining the violence monitoring organisation Peace Action in 1993. He joined the Independent Board of Inquiry in 1994 where he monitored and conducted research and investigations into political violence and police torture in the transition to democratic rule. He worked in the investigation unit of the Truth and Reconciliation Commission from 1996 to 2000, subsequent to which he joined the Centre for the Study of Violence and Reconciliation, where he was responsible for the coordination of its Violence in Transition Project. In 2003 and 2004 he worked on several projects in South Africa, Zimbabwe and East Timor dealing with transitional justice, reconciliation and human rights. In 2005 he helped establish the Zimbabwe Torture Victims Project based in Johannesburg, which provides medical, psychosocial, humanitarian and legal support to victims of organised violence and torture from Zimbabwe.

Laura Pollecut is an independent researcher, writer and advocacy specialist with a specific interest in access to information and the military. She was active in the anti-apartheid struggle, monitored the pre-election violence, and worked for the Truth and Reconciliation Commission. She tracked the passage of the Open Democracy Act from its inception until it was passed as the Promotion of Access to Information Act in 2000. She is currently involved in several research projects but also plays a coordinating role within the Ceasefire Campaign, an anti-war and demilitarisation organisation.

Preface

Conversations that result in new ideas or programme directions invariably occur in bars and cafés. This was predictably the way in which the idea for this book was discussed and decided upon. That it would, like many book projects, become a creature unto itself, providing a much broader and targeted analysis than originally intended, was not anticipated, nor was the length of time taken to complete it. The discussion among Oliver Barstow, the South African History Archives' (SAHA) special projects officer, Verne Harris, SAHA's former director and at that time consultant while the position of director was vacant, and I (Kate Allan), coordinator of SAHA's Freedom of Information Programme (FOIP), took place on a Friday afternoon in a local Melville bar at a time when the organisation was in a state of flux. There had been staff changes over the year, and FOIP needed revisiting to finalise or revive existing projects, and to imagine new directions and goals. Verne Harris, always one for ideas, proposed the book as a means to finalise and report on some of the projects undertaken by FOIP; disseminate its findings on the utility of South Africa's access to information laws as a tool of democratic governance in the unique historical subject areas in which the organisation operated and the political and cultural setting in which the 'regime' operates; and provide Oliver Barstow and me with a target on which to focus our energies in an organisation with endless and unbounded opportunities for engaging with discourses of conflict. So the decision was made.

In the following six months funding was allocated, contributors were secured, a publisher identified, and the institutional material for use by the contributors pulled together and passed over. A rather ambitious deadline of October 2006 was set for final drafts. It would not be until October 2007, after a few contributor changes, content restructures and multiple drafts, that the manuscript was submitted to Wits Press for review. Rather than the smaller 'report' on the various successes and failures of the organisation in using the Promotion of Access to Information Act over the previous five years, it has become a comprehensive report on FOIP's core projects, and an attempt to provide a commentary on the obstacles and issues involved in using access to information laws in South Africa.

Background

History of the South African History Archive

SAHA was established in Johannesburg in 1988 by representatives of the Mass Democratic Movement, including the United Democratic Front and the Congress of South African Trade Unions, as the first 'democratic' archive in South Africa. In the context of increasing state censorship and harassment of grassroots organisations and general information centres in South Africa, Harare was seen as the ideal location for the safe storage of SAHA's material. The holdings formed the basis of a unique collection of primary, grassroots material produced by people and organisations actively engaged in liberation struggles inside South Africa. Soon after the apartheid government's unbanning of many political parties, SAHA moved its collection to Johannesburg. In 1991 SAHA became a legally constituted entity managed by a board of trustees, and in 1994 moved to Historical Papers in the William Cullen Library at the University of the Witwatersrand, where its collections were placed under the control of the university's curator of manuscripts and were managed by an archivist.

In around 2000/01 the shifting realities of the transition to democracy introduced a new dimension to SAHA's work. It repositioned itself as a human rights archive and examined ways in which it could expand on its commitment to documenting and disseminating information about not only historical conflicts, but contemporary struggles for justice and participation in democratic processes. The organisation positioned notions of accessible archives and records as central components of the human rights and governance culture, discourse and practice. These goals underpinned the creation of two programmes in 2003: the Struggles for Justice Programme (SFJ)[1] and FOIP. When funding was received from philanthropic organizations SAHA expanded its operations. That it remained a priority to funding bodies was largely due to the unique position in which it is placed - its straddling of the archival sector, academia and the more activist human rights sector, and the significant outputs it has managed to achieve with so few staff.[2]

The Freedom of Information Programme

The flagship endeavour for SAHA's repositioning as a human rights archive was FOIP. The establishment of FOIP was necessarily preceded by the Promotion of Access to Information Act No. 2 of 2000 (PAIA), which shaped the constitutional right of access to information in Article 32 of the Bill of Rights in the South African Constitution, and was enacted 'on the unsuitable foundation of the authoritarian and secretive state'.[3] SAHA regarded archives and access to information as key components in the transition from a secretive and oppressive state to democratic governance, and PAIA's inception was therefore seen as an opportunity for SAHA to further its contribution to archival discourse, increase and complement its collections, test the boundaries of the legislation and its role in finding 'truth' in a society suffering from an ingrained culture of secrecy and decades of repression, and explore some of the more sinister histories of South Africa. FOIP has submitted around 900 requests for information to a range of (primarily national) government departments, parastatals and private entities. Just over a majority of the requests have been submitted on behalf of individuals, NGOs, activists and researchers.[4] It is ironic, given SAHA's roots, that much of FOIP's time would be spent negotiating and litigating for access to records from the incumbent government, a government formed out of the Mass Democratic Movement.

The book

Why this book and what is its point?

If truth be told, this book is nothing more than an attempt to achieve the goals and objectives of the original founders of SAHA: to document struggles for justice and human rights, to provide access to this information and to promote a more equitable way forward. Although what it also sets out to do, importantly, is to ensure that the insight gained through the work — the institutional memory, as such — is not lost to dusty archive boxes and the mental recesses of former staff, and to therefore serve as a resource for other practitioners, researchers and academics. That it is able to do this is largely due to its straddling of sectors and the expertise that it has attracted.

What makes the book a useful resource, and FOIP an effective tool for change, is that SAHA does not limit its exploration to PAIA requests. SAHA's positioning as a human rights organisation with archival competence in an academic setting gives it a comparative advantage that enables it to authoritatively speak to the broad range of issues arising from the use of and dialogue around access to information laws. It was founded by archivists, and in its 20 years has employed skilled archivists. This has afforded it an archival competence that informs its work on freedom of information such that it has a greater understanding of whether refusals, or indeed releases of records, are legitimate or not. This advantage has been boosted by the employment of lawyers through Australian Volunteers International, enabling it to pursue appeals in-house in a way that would ordinarily be briefed out to attorneys and advocates.[5] Its knowledge and resource base is wide and provides it with a holistic view of the right of freedom of information. It has engaged in and hosted training programmes, seminars and conferences; participated in law reform inquiries; lobbied for law and policy reform and greater access; and participated in international forums and activities. Its staff have published scholarly articles, books and conference papers, and been responsible for numerous poster exhibitions and books dedicated to human rights and archives. It regularly engages with the press and publishes opinion pieces and newspaper articles. Its expertise in the field was recognised in September 2006 when it was awarded the Golden Key Award by the South African Human Rights Commission and the Open Democracy Advice Centre for the 'best use of the Promotion of Access to Information Act by a member of the public or organisation'.

So what is it that this book tells us? Is PAIA an effective tool? Does it allow citizens to participate in democratic governance? Does it permit truth telling, particularly in the context of a transition in which so much weight was placed on truth? The answer, on the weight of evidence, is 'no, not yet'. There are significant cultural barriers, resulting from a long history of oppression and attempts to maintain the interests of the powerful. How do we come to this conclusion?

The book, through an examination of four projects[6] and a range of other case studies, illustrates both the frustrations and the ripening potential of access to information in South Africa. While doing so, a number of themes emerge. Firstly, the right of access to information is hampered by a lack of resources dedicated to preserving and making available historical records from the apartheid era and to ensuring that appropriate records management practices are implemented so that contemporary records are easily locatable. Interlinked with the issue is the mass destruction of records that took place prior to and shortly following the transition to democracy. Not only is this of concern for the right of access to information, but also for ensuring that government is able to make proper use of its own information for service delivery. Secondly, information and deputy information officers responsible for responding to access requests, and their superiors, rely heavily on broadly read and misapplied exemptions and the limited instances in which the public interest test may apply to refuse access to information. Similarly, public bodies benefit from the lack of cost-effective and efficient appeal mechanisms available to requesters, often pursing requests to the litigation stage in the hope that the requester will give up. That the South African Human Rights Commission and the public protector have failed to be proactive in promoting compliance with PAIA and in enforcement has aggravated the problem. Thirdly, the intersection of other legislation, in particular apartheid era legislation, has resulted in confusion about whether the right of access to information contained in PAIA trump provisions in earlier enactments that deal with access to public records. This has been exacerbated by the minister of justice's failure to participate in any way in efforts to resolve these difficulties.

What do these themes ultimately tell us? They all stem from a lack of support within government for the right of access to information and the right to engage in decisions that affect citizens. Political motivation for promoting and ensuring compliance with PAIA is clearly lacking; despite Thabo Mbeki's early role in establishing the Open Democracy Task Team, there are no political champions of the right and therefore no driving force for ensuring a top-down approach that could trickle through ministries to lower-level officials. The blocking of access to information that relates to decisions that government wants to make, uninhibited by citizen participation, and a cultural lack of transparency and openness and therefore structural reformation, can be mirrored in the defensive way in which government and political parties approach critical engagement by civil society. Treading on the outspoken and alleging disloyalty and subversiveness are becoming an acceptable means of maintaining support.

Before I go on to outline the content of the various chapters, it is important to put the book in its proper context. As Harris foregrounds in his conclusion, the implementation of PAIA sits against the backdrop of the country's transition from apartheid to democracy. There are universal dynamics at play — many of the issues identified are experienced in most other developed and developing countries — but local specificities play a role.

Further, it is necessary to emphasise that the book limits its discussion to public bodies, primarily because the majority of requests submitted by SAHA were to them. It cannot, with any authority, comment on the implementation of PAIA within private bodies or on the utility of PAIA in accessing information from private bodies. In addition to the added burden imposed on requesters to demonstrate that they need the information requested from a private body to exercise or protect an additional right, there are likely to be a number of factors impacting upon the right of access that do not apply to public bodies, for example, additional or differing legislative requirements regarding incorporation, the retention of records and the confidentiality of business dealings. The constitutional right of access to information from private bodies, and the resultant impact of PAIA on access, is an issue that needs to be explored and tested, as it has significant ramifications for a whole host of other socioeconomic rights. And finally, as Harris states, the authors write from the 'hurly-burly' of activism. The organisation, while having strong relationships with a number of governmental bodies and academia, has never been one to shy away from a good fight for justice.

Chapter overview

In chapter 1, Richard Calland examines the politics and practicalities of access to information and provides a framework for what lies ahead by setting out the legal and conceptual background, by putting South Africa's position in an international context, and by identifying the main political and institutional factors that determine the effectiveness of an access to information regime such as South Africa's. He examines the larger dimensions of the right of access to information: the extent to which it is the result of a global constitutionalism or a strong local imperative; the utility of access to information and the relationship between its effectiveness and its civil society roots and civil society use; the extent to which the right is a leverage right and part of an 'interwoven basket' of rights; and the broader political factors that have led to an effectual stalling of implementation and reform required to ensure full realisation of the right. Calland also raises some of the impediments to access and questions the approach taken by SAHA by asking whether it has inadvertently caused government to slam shut the door for everyone. Ultimately, he concludes that, despite its successes and failings, in the context of a robust judiciary, the rule of law prevails in that, even without access, secrecy must be justified.

In chapter 2, Piers Pigou discusses SAHA's use of PAIA to follow up on recommendations of the Truth and Reconciliation Commission (TRC) in relation to access to both hearing records and records of the security establishment and military uncovered by the TRC, and SAHA's targeted focus on records at risk of being destroyed or buried in shrouds of bureaucratic secrecy. The chapter commences with a discussion of the project's immediate uncovering of evidence to suggest that the custodian of TRC records, the Department of Justice, was uncertain about the whereabouts of the records.

The chapter examines access to the TRC archive and highlights the obstructive attempts of various public bodies, including the National Archives, the Department of Justice and the National Intelligence Agency, to follow the recommendations of the TRC and allow public access. It asks one primary question: Why, given that the key objective of the TRC was to uncover the truth about events occurring during apartheid in an effort to facilitate reconciliation, is the incumbent government blocking access?

In chapter 3, Dr David Fig discusses SAHA's collaboration with Earthlife Africa and the latter's Nuclear Energy Costs the Earth Campaign. The chapter provides an overview of the development of nuclear technology in South Africa, highlights questions about the nuclear industry and use of radioactive materials that remain unanswered, and considers the significance of responses received to requests submitted to the National Nuclear Regulator, the Nuclear Energy Corporation of South Africa, Eskom, the Department of Minerals and Energy, and the Pebble Bed Modular Reactor company. It details how the project aimed to address disparate views about the dangers involved in the use of nuclear technology by securing access to information that can inform dialogue and debate, and how access to information could be frustrated by a general ignorance about the importance of proper record-keeping practices and participatory governance. It also comments on how the project unexpectedly raised, through then President Thabo Mbeki's reaction to the work of Earthlife Africa, very real concerns about the government's attitude towards NGOs.

In chapter 4, Dr Chandré Gould discusses SAHA's Nuclear Weapons History Project, a project that was seen as necessary because neither the apartheid government nor the post-1994 government embarked on a systematic release of information relating to the country's nuclear weapons programme. The disclosures to the International Atomic Energy Agency were never published. The officials who worked in the programme believe that they are still bound by undertakings of secrecy. Unlike the case of the apartheid era chemical and biological warfare programme, the TRC chose not to place the nuclear weapons programme under scrutiny. Inquiring academics, journalists and freedom of information activists have been blocked by an official stance. The chapter examines the legitimacy of the three assertions informing the stance: firstly, that all the key questions have already been answered; secondly, that further disclosures would undermine South Africa's commitment to non-proliferation; and, thirdly, that most, if not all, relevant state documentation was destroyed. Gould identifies the extent to which the government responded to ten key questions about the nuclear weapons programme and to which records were able to fill the gaps in its history.

In chapter 5, Laura Pollecut discusses her work as a researcher in the joint SAHA and Gay and Lesbian Archives project Gays in the Apartheid Military, which aimed to uncover information regarding the programme of the apartheid South African Defence Force (SADF) for homosexuals. One of the primary aims of this project was to determine

SADF's official policy, if any, regarding gays and lesbians in the military. The project focused primarily on the work of Dr Aubrey Levin, a psychiatrist at 1 Military Hospital, where many alleged abuses took place. The project, unlike others, interviewed former military personnel and utilised declassified lists of military intelligence records to identify files that potentially contained information relevant to the research. As Pollecut shows, records revealed information about a range of other issues of significance during apartheid, including the monitoring of civil society organisations and conscientious objection. The chapter examines the request process; the response of the military archives to PAIA; the content of the records received; and, more critically, the relationship of these documents to the Levin case, SADF's policy on homosexuals, and the ensuing revelations regarding conscientious objectors.

In chapter 6, I consider the multiple factors that impact on the right of access to information: the disparate interpretation of PAIA provisions; the intersection of other legislation relating to record keeping and classification; the limitations of appeal mechanisms; and other external factors, including the impact of the mass destruction of records prior to and after transition to democratic governance, record management practices, and the culture of secrecy pervading public bodies. I examine these issues through a discussion of developments since the enactment of PAIA and various case studies.

Finally, in chapter 7, former SAHA director Verne Harris concludes by bringing us to a more ethical and rounded enquiry that examines why gatekeepers become gatekeepers, and questioning what it might take to 'get it right'. Harris frames his enquiry by reminding us that freedom of information rightly falls within the frame of democracy and justice, but that democracy and justice are undefined notions and are always in a state of becoming. Within this framework, he posits the following: we must believe in the notion of a legitimate secret, and to understand its role we must begin with the individual, as secrecy is the 'stuff of daily life'; our positioning within society informs our attitudes towards these concepts; and the notion of contract is embedded in the concept of secrecy, such that it is something we agree to and accept. Freedom of information therefore becomes a contest in which contextualised information, rather than information per se, becomes the resource in play, contextualised by the creator of the record, its owner and its archon, and by public discourse and political power. Contract, as Harris describes it, cannot therefore be held up as a substitute for contest. He goes on to argue that public institutions use contract as a substitute for contestation, confusing law with justice, and that this is the result of four cultures: record making, mediocrity and bureaucratic compliance, puerile democratisation, and secrecy. He concludes by holding that an ethics acknowledging the gatekeeper in us while reaching beyond gatekeeping is all that any of us can begin to aim for.

Kate Allan

1

Illuminating the Politics and the Practice of Access to Information in South Africa

Richard Calland

'Secrecy is the first essential in affairs of state.'

Cardinal Richelieu

'Do we have a right to information? Certainly. But we also have a responsibility to act on it.'

Al Roberts, associate professor of Public Administration in the Maxwell School of Citizenship and Public Affairs, Syracuse University

Introduction

Institutions and bureaucracies have a life of their own. Or so it seems. When they are under attack, they retreat; like tortoises, there is a tendency for the head to glide back under cover. This is one of the two central messages of this book: despite its constitutional obligations, the South African state has not yet cast off its historical tendency towards secrecy. Secrecy, the evidence suggests, remains its first essential. But the second message is as positive as the first is disappointing. When used diligently and with persistence, South Africa's new access to information (ATI) regime is capable of penetrating the tortoise's shell. That shell may be tough and the state's approach may be imperfect, but in many cases the information will emerge eventually. At the very least, the system now requires, and applies, the legal principle of *justification* — the principle that must underpin any human rights culture. As Professor Etienne Mureinik, one of the original architects of South Africa's ATI law, explains, the link between the right of ATI and the principle of justification is a profound one:

> Access to information is a matter of the utmost importance to any effort to bring about a culture of justification. A government which closes its files will be under much weaker pressure to justify its decisions than one which has to open them.[1]

Now, thanks to South Africa's new constitutional order, and the law that gives effect to the right of ATI that is enshrined in the Bill of Rights — the Promotion of Access to Information Act No. 2 of 2000 (PAIA) — the state must explain and thereby justify its retreat to secrecy, both in law and in fact. It is tempting to stop at this point rather than delay the reader, because this book contains a series of compelling stories, but my task is to provide a framework for what lies ahead by setting out the legal and conceptual background; by putting South Africa's own position in an international context; and by identifying in headline terms the main political, institutional and other fault lines that appear to be predominant in determining the effectiveness or otherwise of an ATI regime such as South Africa's.

South Africa's place in the global explosion of ATI law and practice

Stories are important because they bring life to the law. And the explosion in ATI law and practice around the world over the past ten years has two dimensions, one legal, the other one human. On the legal side, the facts are straightforward. Over 50 countries have passed some kind of ATI law in the past decade. There are now over 60 in total.[2] The principle of transparency appears to be more than a passing fad, introduced into the 'good govern-ance' lexicon in the early 1990s. While some of those 50 countries have responded cyni-cally to the call of the World Bank and other such institutions for greater transparency by rapidly passing ATI laws so as to look good and tick a box, others have done so as a result of social campaigns for the 'right to know'.

South Africa's case falls into this latter category; or, at least, it does to my mind. But it should be noted that this is not necessarily the predominant perspective of those that have considered the question. There are two divergent views. The first posits South Africa's case as one that coheres with the idea of a global 'constitutional' movement. The other places far greater emphasis on the domestic lobby for an ATI right and asserts that the origins of South Africa's right of ATI are 'home grown' rather than part of a global trend.

Thus, on the one hand, Arko-Cobbah,[3] for example, cites Darch and Underwood[4] in support of his contention that 'South Africa's introduction of PAIA was influenced by a global constitutional imperative rather than by a popular pressure'. Puddephatt's briefing paper to the 2008 'state of the art' international conference on the right of ATI convened by the Carter Center (the Carter Center Conference) noted that the substantial move to-wards openness legislation around the world seems to be 'tied to the wave of democrati-zation that followed the political events at the end of the 1980s and early 1990s'.[5]

Although it is probably true that the inclusion of a right of ATI benefitted from the influence of a 'global constitutionalism' that impacted on the overall process of constitu-tion making in South Africa, there was surely a strong local imperative as well. Secrecy,

STATUTES OF THE REPUBLIC OF SOUTH AFRICA–CONSTITUTIONAL LAW

PROMOTION OF ACCESS TO INFORMATION ACT
NO. 2 OF 2000

[ASSENTED TO 2 FEBRUARY, 2000]   [DATE OF COMMENCEMENT: 9 MARCH, 2001]
(Unless otherwise indicated)

(*English text signed by the President*)

This Act has been updated to *Government Gazette* 27406 dated 22 March, 2005.

as amended by

Financial Intelligence Centre Act, No. 38 of 2001
[with effect from 3 February, 2003—see title CRIMINAL LAW AND PROCEDURE]

Judicial Matters Amendment Act, No. 42 of 2001
[with effect from 7 December, 2001, unless otherwise indicated—see title COURTS]

Promotion of Access to Information Amendment Act, No. 54 of 2002

Judicial Matters Second Amendment Act, No. 55 of 2003
[with effect from 31 March, 2005, unless otherwise indicated—see title COURTS]

proposed amendment by

Judicial Matters Second Amendment Act, No. 55 of 2003
(provision not yet proclaimed)
[see title COURTS]

ACT
To give effect to the constitutional right of access to any information held by the State and any information that is held by another person and that is required for the exercise or protection of any rights; and to provide for matters connected therewith.

Preamble.—RECOGNISING THAT—

* the system of government in South Africa before 27 April 1994, amongst others, resulted in a secretive and unresponsive culture in public and private bodies which often led to an abuse of power and human rights violations;

* section 8 of the Constitution provides for the horizontal application of the rights in the Bill of Rights to juristic persons to the extent required by the nature of the rights and the nature of those juristic persons;

* section 32 (1) (*a*) of the Constitution provides that everyone has the right of access to any information held by the State;

* section 32 (1) (*b*) of the Constitution provides for the horizontal application of the right of access to information held by another person to everyone when that information is required for the exercise or protection of any rights;

* and national legislation must be enacted to give effect to this right in section 32 of the Constitution;

AND BEARING IN MIND THAT—

* the State must respect, protect, promote and fulfil, at least, all the rights in the Bill of Rights which is the cornerstone of democracy in South Africa;

(Issue No 40)   423

Figure 1: South Africa's current Promotion of Access to Information Act, introduced in 2000 to give effect to the constitutional right to access information. SAHA's Freedom of Information Programme was launched shortly thereafter to test the parameters of this legislation.

after all, had been a hallmark of the apartheid regime; black South Africans had been denied any right of access to governmental power; ignorance, including a lack of any decent educational opportunity, had been a central tenet of the apartheid regime's strategy of oppression. As Justice Kate O'Regan, one of the most progressive and influential members of South Africa's first Constitutional Court, has noted: 'The Right of Access to information should not be seen as an afterthought or optional extra in our constitutional dispensation. It is integral to our conception of democracy.'[6] Hence, my own perspective supports the alternative view, although it is also subjective, because I was a part of the Open Democracy Campaign Group (about which more is said below). This notwithstanding, it should not be forgotten that the lucid and potentially far-reaching right to ATI that appears in the South African Constitution at section 32 did not appear from thin air or as a result of external pressure. Firstly, there was a strong campaign for its inclusion in the Interim Constitution that emerged from the political negotiations that preceded the country's first democratic election in 1994. Secondly, there was an even firmer lobby for the inclusion of the right in the final Constitution; indeed, section 32 represents a stronger articulation of the right than the provision that appeared in the Interim Constitution. In the years that followed, the Open Democracy Campaign Group — a civil society lobby that included human rights, democracy and environmental organisations, as well as trade unions — advocated for a strong piece of legislation to give effect to the constitutional right (as required by section 32(2)).[7]

It could be argued that PAIA came about simply because the constitutional provision said that there had to be legislation to give effect to the right; and, indeed, that is certainly true. But the question is: would South Africa have ended up with PAIA — or a weaker version — had there not been the civil society coalition pushing for a strong piece of enabling legislation?

It was a protracted process, to say the least — Parliament took the full three years that the constitutional provision gave it to pass the law — and not one whose story deserves to be retold in detail here. In fact, Parliament itself should not be blamed for the slow progress towards the statute book; rather, the executive took control of the Bill and removed it from public view for long periods. The first draft of the Bill had, in fact, been drafted and published as early as 1995 by the Open Democracy Task Force established by the then deputy president, Thabo Mbeki. The group was headed by Mbeki's trusted legal advisor, Advocate Mojanku Gumbi, but included a prolific human rights lawyer, the late Professor Etienne Mureinik. Driven by Mureinik's idealistic instincts, the group had produced a far-reaching draft, culling various sections from what it regarded as the best freedom of information laws from around the world. The Open Democracy Bill included chapters on 'open meetings' (so-called 'sunshine law') and on whistle-blower protection that were subsequently excised, totally in the former case, or hived off into a separate law in the latter case.[8] Between 1995 and 2000 the Bill vanished for long periods into the nether regions of the executive, to emerge, months later, with further reductions to its overall reach; for example, after the Bill was discussed by cabinet, the exclusion of cabinet records from the scope of the Bill was introduced into the draft. Eventually, the Bill was tabled in Parliament, and in the second half of 1999 an *ad hoc* committee chaired by Advocate Johnny de Lange, then chair of the Justice Portfolio Committee, worked to finalise the Act (having first held a series of public hearings at which a wide range of civil society and business organisations made submissions).

Perhaps the main point that is of greatest significance for the future health of the ATI regime that can be extracted from the history of the passage of the law through Parliament is this: a number of organisations developed both an interest and a competence in ATI, and, moreover, the taste for using the law. There is empirical data in support of the assertion that where civil society organisations are involved in the implementation of the law, governments are likely to be more compliant.[9] Although the direct connections may appear vague now, there is no doubt in my mind that the fact that South African civil society is now willing and able to use the law that finally emerged from the elongated process (i.e. PAIA) is intrinsically connected to the fact that the law has civil society roots, although it could also be argued that those roots are neither deep enough nor wide enough, in that only a very small number of civil society organisations have been able to take up the challenge of not only using the law regularly, but contesting failures to comply with it by government and other information holders. The demand for the law that came from a very diverse and credible range of civil society organisations working together as the Open Democracy Campaign Group has not been subsequently fully matched by a similar appetite for using the law that was the fruit of their labours.

The quote from Professor Al Roberts that introduces this chapter — an academic who, as he puts it, 'uses as well as studies' ATI law — sums up this aspect of the challenge very well: an ATI law is useless unless it is actually used. Indeed, the usage is not only fundamental to its value; it is fundamental to its instrumentality. As many of the stories that follow this introduction show, the political will to comply with the legal obligations created by PAIA has only finally emerged as a result of unyielding pressure from civil society organisations such as the South African History Archive (SAHA). This replicates, in a South African setting, the experience of elsewhere — an experience that is being charted with increasing diligence by both the community of users and the academy internationally.[10]

Perhaps the three most significant aspects of the international trend — the state of the art, so to speak — are: first of all, the increased understanding of the relationship between the right of ATI and other legal instruments; secondly, the idea of the right of ATI as a human right with multiple dimensions, including the socioeconomic dimension; and, thirdly, the importance of the politics of the policy. These trends are reflected in the potentially watershed Carter Center Conference of February 2008. Each of these three aspects of the global ATI community's understanding of the contemporary challenge is pertinent to the South African experience; and, indeed, all are traversed at various points and in different ways in this volume, and are now considered briefly in turn.

Part of a family of laws

I will return to this driving theme later. But there is one additional framing issue that should be introduced at the outset. ATI law should not be seen — or assessed — in isolation. For one thing, by its very nature, it not only cuts across a whole range of institutional and political factors that may impact on its well-being, but, in legal terms, it is also not an independent vessel. Behind the sometimes complex facade of ATI lies a very simple idea: people want to know what is going on, and now, moreover, they have a right to know, enshrined in international law[11] and protected in many cases by a constitutional and/or statutory right. For the layperson, therefore, the legal instruments will be immaterial — they just want to know what is going on and why a particular decision was taken by those in power. Sometimes this involves a piece of paper — a 'record'; sometimes it involves a decision and the reasoning behind the decision; sometimes it may involve getting access to, or correcting, your own personal record held by a governmental or private body; and sometimes it may need someone on the inside to get the information out (a whistle-blower).

To cover this diverse ground requires more than an ATI right. Indeed, ATI — or its predecessor label, 'freedom of information' — is something of a misnomer. The right is not to information in a general sense, but to a record. Moreover, it is a right, therefore, to an existing record. Government is under no duty under an ATI regime to create a record or to scratch around to put together an answer to a question. The citizen has a right to request (to 'seek', to use the language of the international legal instrument, Article 19 of the International Covenant on Civil and Political Rights) a record; the state has a duty to respond to that request. Thus, in terms of access to written reasons for a decision — a so-called right to administrative justice — or to your personal records (a right to data protection) or to impart information as a whistle-blower, it is essential to develop an interwoven basket of legal rights and duties that will, together, comprise what the community of users is beginning with a growing degree of consensus internationally to describe as the 'right to know'.

Indeed, the initial approach of the Open Democracy Task Team in South Africa was to try and include as many of the component parts of what it conceived as 'open democracy' under the umbrella of the Open Democracy Bill, which in its first iteration included not just the provisions providing for a right of access to government information, but also public access to government decision making (so-called 'open meetings' law) and protection for whistle-blowing. In fact, although it may have appeared to be comprehensive at the time, the state of the art has moved on rapidly in the ten years that followed the first draft of the Open Democracy Bill; now, there are other aspects of the 'right to know' that the Open Democracy Task Team would probably have wanted to add to its already extensive draft law — including records management, data protection and a right to written reasons for executive action.

While this volume focuses solely on ATI, this notion of a 'family of laws' — what Kate Allan in chapter 6 calls the 'multiple faces of information governance', which is a very appealing way of putting it that also captures the modern complexity of information management driven by rapidly changing information technology — is significant to both our conceptual and our instrumental understanding and application of the right of ATI. Thus, South Africa has in section 33 of the Bill of Rights a right to just administrative action and, from this constitutional derivation, a statutory right to written reasons for an executive decision by virtue of the Promotion of Administrative Justice Act of 2000. So far as whistle-blowers are concerned, the Protected Disclosures Act of 2000 (an offshoot of the Open Democracy Bill that was the predecessor to PAIA) provides a legal remedy for employees who disclose information of wrongdoing and who suffer a reprisal as a result of having done so. On data protection, we await the implementation of the work of the South African Law Reform Commission, which has for a number of years been engaged with the task of producing an appropriate piece of legislation.

As hinted above, the questions of both record making and record keeping are very pertinent. A number of the cases canvassed in this volume illustrate why this is so. They also draw useful attention to the danger that laws such as the Key Points Act or the Protection of Information Act, which, however justified or reasonable the public policy and public interest considerations that may well lie behind them may be, have the effect of undermining the purpose of the right to ATI. So, necessary though this legislative patchwork quilt may be, it is also possible that it may cause a degree of confusion. PAIA is supposed to be the overriding law. But there is evidence that public servants are as aware of the other laws and that they are, naturally, anxious not to breach them when giving out information.

A prime example of this risk averseness came in 2006 and 2007 with a number of cases where public servants were disciplined for disclosing information to the media in breach of public service regulations, even though they may have been doing so in accordance with the scheme advanced by the Protected Disclosures Act. Similarly, one can well imagine how a public servant faced by a request for a record that may have a politically sensitive disposition may choose to defer to a competing law or regulation — whether the Protection of Information Act or else some internal system of classification — and be led to conclude that the 'safer' course of action would be to withhold the information.

In chapter 6, Kate Allan writes from the perspective of SAHA, an organisation that has certainly taken up and met the challenge posed by Al Roberts in admirable fashion. Her chapter is a thorough review of many of the most important aspects of implementation of PAIA since it came into force in early 2001. This introduction, which attempts to frame the issues and set the South African experience so far in a wider context with broader horizons, should be read in tandem with Allan's analysis. I write as a founder member of ODAC — the Open Democracy Advice Centre — a specialist law centre that, like SAHA, uses PAIA and supports its usage by communities in pursuit of socioeconomic justice; as a law centre, ODAC is also able to identify and launch test case litigation.

ATI as a human right with a multidimensional instrumental value

Civil society's approach has been in concert with what I would regard, and describe, as a paradigm shift in the understanding and application of the right to ATI around the world, which is worth noting in order to recall a major underlying purpose of the right. The paradigm shift has been viewed as being a shift away from seeing the right merely as a companion to the right to freedom of expression (which is its international law derivation) towards seeing it as a leverage right,[12] important in and of itself, but far more significant in terms of its value in helping to protect and exercise other rights, particularly social and economic rights. It is a subtle shift conceptually and legally, but in instrumental and practical terms, the consequences, especially in developmental states and societies, are potentially huge, although there is also now a growing consensus that the right to ATI is a fundamental human right with its own set of attributes and intrinsic worth, aside from its instrumental value.[13]

Either way, many of the most vivid stories that have emerged around the world in recent years have shown the human side — and the wider human rights potential of ATI — of the transparency explosion. For example, in early 2004, along with fellow members of the Institute for Policy Dialogue Transparency Task Team, I attended a *jun sunwai* (public hearing) at the rural village of Kumbhalgarh in Rajasthan, India. We watched, spellbound, as the MKSS (Mazdoor Kisan Shakti Sangathan) conducted a forensic examination with and alongside the community that exposed the corruption that had contaminated the state's food-rationing scheme. The use of Rajasthan's ATI legislation was fundamental to the methodology, in which information garnered from state records, from the records of the (private, licensed) ration dealers and from the community itself was triangulated so as to reveal the discrepancies in the ration dealers' records and, thence, the extent of the corruption.[14] As a result, many ration dealers lost their licences and/or were arrested, and the state scheme was overhauled.

In South Africa, work with various communities has shown how, when they are accompanied along the way by specialist organisations like SAHA or ODAC, community organisations can access information that enables them to leverage the right to access to adequate housing or to water or health care.[15] For example, in Ntambana, a small village in rural KwaZulu-Natal, a province of South Africa, ODAC's support of a community request for information about water access policy led to the community receiving clean water for the very first time — one of many stories in which the persistence and skill of the professional NGO when accompanying an equally determined local community organisation or activist individual will ensure that the relevant records are prised from government and used to claim other socioeconomic rights. Thus, in these circumstances, PAIA is helping ordinary poor South Africans regain their human dignity and achieve a better material quality of life.

This is the good news side of the story. The downside is the realisation that has emerged here and elsewhere that Rome was not built in a day, and that these success stories are perhaps the exception to the general rule, benefitting as they do from a special combination of factors that are not available to all. I have quipped previously that, in fact, the phrase should be 'Stockholm was not built in a day', since it is the Swedish model of habitual institutional openness to which we should all aspire.[16] But Sweden has had 300 years of practice to perfect its habit. It takes a long time to reorient institutional practice and culture to the point where openness is the default position. Platitudinous though these sentiments may be, they do capture the essence of the struggle for the full realisation of the right to ATI, which has a practical, implementation dimension, but also a political one.

The politics of the policy: Why is South Africa such a tortoise?

'Political? Why so?' many people might ask. Isn't this just a technical issue? Is it not simply a question of processing a request for a record: get the mechanics right and all will be well? But, to use another cliché, information is power. Hence, getting access involves issues of power relations and the insecurity that accompanies them. The politics of the policy is attracting new attention, both in South Africa and elsewhere around the world, as a wide variety of countries grapple with the challenge of implementing ATI law. The Carter Center Conference sought to recognise this by devoting two of the five commissions to which the 140 delegates from 40 countries contributed — one on the politics and economics of ATI, and the other on the structural and cultural context. As Andrew Puddephatt, the convener of the former commission, noted in his briefing paper:

> If progress is to be made we will need more rigorous analysis of the politics of the policy … [the politics] will include structural factors such as the level of socio-economic development, the strength or weakness of various institutions, the type of political system, and its stability, the perceived self-interest of political actors, specific national and regional histories and cultures, the wider international dimension, and certain contingent factors of both personalities and events.[17]

In response to this political challenge, the delegates to the conference produced a wide-ranging declaration that can safely be described as the 'state of the art' in terms of the current understanding and agenda for the international ATI community of practitioners.[18] The declaration has a very strong emphasis on combatting the political obstacles to effective implementation of the right, and can usefully stand as a call for action in any society, including South Africa's.

The cases in this volume illuminate both the politics and practice of an ATI policy. They reveal that two of the government agencies that one would hope and expect would be champions of the law — the Department of Justice and the National Archives — have, in fact, turned out to be at times two of the most obstructionist of government bodies. This is disappointing, to say the least. Admittedly, they have been faced by difficult requests, with potentially profound political consequences. When we (ODAC) took the information commissioner of the Republic of Ireland to visit the National Archives in 2006, she was told by the national archivist that there were certain documents in the Archives that must never see the light of day, because were they to be revealed, they would threaten the stability of the democratically elected government. One can speculate on the type and nature of such records, and it is likely that some of the requests about the past made by SAHA — concerning the relationship between the liberation movement and the apartheid regime, especially the existence of apartheid intelligence operatives amid the ANC leadership — have come very close to touching this particular nerve.

It may well be the case, therefore, that requests of this nature have the effect, whatever the intention, of turning people who otherwise might be, if not champions, then at least non-obstructionist in their attitudes to the Act, against it. When discussing possible reform with government, including the creation of an ATI commissioner, we were told by a senior government source that the minister of justice (Bridget Mabandla) had little or no appetite for pushing a reform agenda in cabinet, because 'when the cabinet looks out of the window, what it sees is the law being used by its political enemies to embarrass it'.

This is not to excuse this attitude; on the contrary, however sensitive the record, there is, as a matter of law, a right to access it unless there is an exemption that justifiably limits the right to ATI. But it does help explain the politics of the realisation of the right. If this is the case, does it raise questions about the strategy employed by SAHA and others in requesting such records at a time when the right to ATI is still 'bedding down' and PAIA systems are not yet firmly established? Would it, in the longer-term interests of the right and the usability of PAIA, have been better to have held off from their more politically awkward requests? In seeking to prise out some of the skeletons in the cupboard, has it inadvertently caused government to slam shut the door for everyone?

I used to take this view — that it was far more important to use PAIA in a tactically pragmatic manner in the first few years, to 'ease' government into the habit of a more open culture rather than to expect it to hit the ground running and to be willing and able

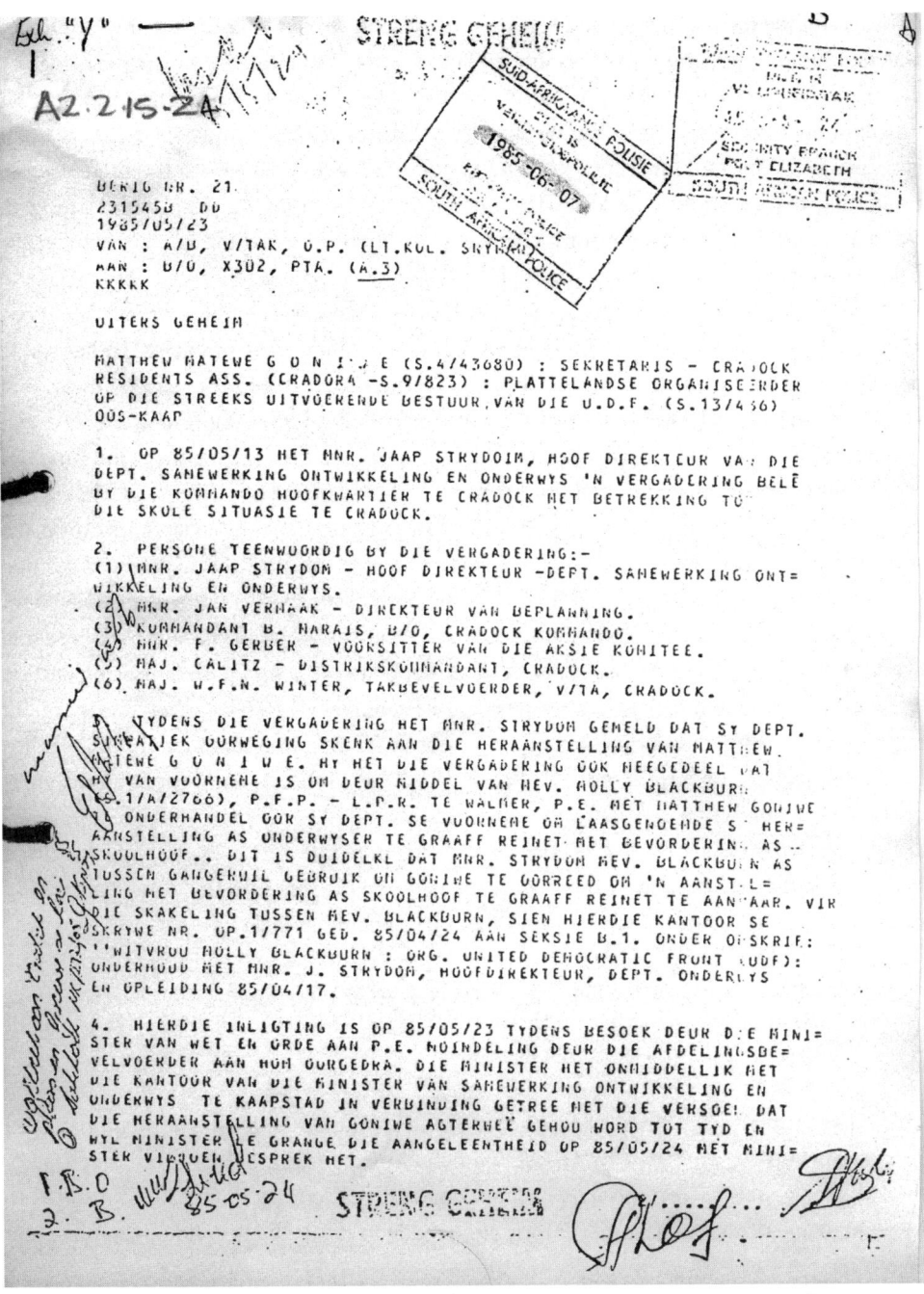

Figure 2: Top secret security police situational report from Lft Col Strydom to security police headquarters in Pretoria, dated 25 May 1985, six weeks before the abduction and murder of the Cradock 4. Strydom applied for amnesty in the Truth and Reconciliation Commission in this matter (Archived as SAHA Collection AL2878 – A2.2.15.24).

to deal with the most complex and sensitive requests from day one. Hence, my argument was that in order to achieve a workable ATI regime for the future — the primary goal — we needed to hold back and even sacrifice some openness in relation to the past. Part of this argument contained a utilitarian dimension: a key element in a viable ATI system is record keeping.[19] Often record keeping is not at a level necessary to facilitate access, prompting the question: should an administration spend time and resources putting in place a record keeping system for old records or should it invest the resources in establishing a new system that will ensure that future records will be properly kept?

Perhaps it was wrong to posit this question as a zero-sum game. Perhaps it is possible to do both at once. In any case, partly because of the requests that SAHA has made or supported, I have come to revise my view. Verne Harris is better placed to make this argument than I, as a historian and an archivist himself, but I have come to appreciate that the digging out of old records is not just of passing academic interest for historians, but also about establishing accountability for past deeds and abuse of power, and that part of the task of establishing accountability in the future is also, therefore, about settling the account of the past. The best example of this is the case study of the request for records relating to the murder of the 'Cradock 4'. As the writer says, with a note of surprise, there turned out to be 'great interest in the case'. Indeed, it was a notorious case. And it seems to me that accessing information about what happened is also about accessing justice for the family and comrades of those who fell in defence of liberty against the apartheid regime. In other words, in this context, the right to ATI is not a luxury right, a 'nice-to-have' add-on, but a core right, central to the overall constitutional quest for human dignity in the new South Africa.

This is a central theme of the current phase of implementation of the right to ATI in South Africa. As the delegate from the Presidency told the second annual indaba meeting of the Deputy Information Officers' Forum on 28 September 2007:

> PAIA is seen as something that is an 'add-on' to our other responsibilities and which is, frankly, seen as a nuisance. We need to understand that if people want to ask us about what we are doing, then we need to treat them with dignity and respond.

This comes from a government agency that has been one of the least compliant of all. In successive studies conducted by ODAC on behalf of the Open Society Initiative (OSI), the Presidency scored very poorly; in the second survey, conducted in 2004, it failed to respond to any of the requests for information made to it.[20] It did not, however, represent an outlier.

Overall, the scores attained by South Africa, in comparison to the other 14 countries surveyed, were lamentable. While the South African government's record in terms of denial of requests was no worse — or better — than the others, it was one of the worst performers in terms of what the survey branded as 'mute refusals' — that is to say, cases where there is no response by the information holder inside the statutory time limit (termed a 'deemed refusal' in section 27 of PAIA). Almost two-thirds of requests for information in the 2004 survey were 'mute refusals' (62 per cent).[21] In short, in South Africa, you are more likely to be ignored than responded to. Moreover, despite its ostensible linkage with the constitutional imperative of social transformation, noted above, not to mention the specific provisions in PAIA intended to ensure that socially disadvantaged people are assisted when seeking to use the Act, the OSI Justice Initiative methodology revealed how 'Ausi', an illiterate, non-English-speaking woman from a rural area was treated by a range of government departments. In nine out of ten cases, she was unable to even make the request for ATI.[22] South Africa's system is not delivering a service that respects a fundamental, constitutionally protected human right.

Enforcing the right of ATI

So, what to do? And, from the case studies presented in this volume, what is the diagnosis and what is the prescription? In this, one needs to distinguish between the challenges of implementation and the challenges of enforcement. At one end of this spectrum of challenges is the bookend of the law itself and, at the other end, the courts. In these two respects, South Africa is very well placed. PAIA is excellent in most respects and is underpinned by a constitutional right, as noted. Unlike many developing countries elsewhere in Africa, or in Asia or Latin America, the court system is both functional and mainly honest. One can say with a good deal of confidence that the rule of law prevails in South Africa. If you take a case to court, you stand a good chance of getting justice.

This is not to say that just because the court system operates in this way and rights can be enforced that there is necessarily access to justice. The greatest failing of PAIA is its enforcement mechanism — or, rather, the lack thereof. To appeal a denial, or a deemed refusal, an appeal must be lodged with the High Court. This represents, in many cases, a hammer to smash an acorn. As the *Ad Hoc* Parliamentary Committee, chaired by Professor Kader Asmal, appointed to consider the future of the Chapter 9 constitutional protection bodies noted: 'The complex and potentially expensive appeals mechanism provided for in the legislation places further obstacles in the way of ordinary individuals wishing to access information … it is significant that only a handful of cases reach the courts.'[23] Accordingly, the committee recommended that a dedicated information commissioner be appointed within the South African Human Rights Commission (SAHRC) (and that the appointment should be initiated 'immediately' with a 'ring-fenced' additional budget). As the report observed, the submissions arguing for an independent information commissioner mandated to receive appeals and make binding orders on access and disclosure resulted from impatience with the capacity of the SAHRC to provide real teeth in implementing PAIA. Certainly, as ODAC has discovered in the majority of its own cases, patience is a necessary virtue in pursuing PAIA requests. The cases reviewed in this book demonstrate unequivocally the same need.

Thus, there is some light at the end of the tunnel, although it remains to be seen how easy it will be for the SAHRC to move forward with the Asmal recommendation and the extent to which the proposal will be resisted or supported in Parliament (which, at the time of writing, was still waiting for the formal tabling of the report before beginning the task of processing its recommendations). If it happens, and the SAHRC itself adopts the more 'aggressive' stance that Asmal suggests may be appropriate, then potentially the scope for enforcing the right rises exponentially. In other countries, as diverse as Scotland, Australia, Canada, Thailand and Ireland, information commissioners have made all the difference in terms of permitting the volume of caseload that will, in turn, provide both the jurisprudence and thereby the guidance to government over how to deal with requests, and how, in particular, to interpret and apply the exemption clauses.

Figure 3: Members of the Abahlali base Mjondolo (Shack Dwellers) Movement show their receipt for the PAIA request submitted, with the assistance of ODAC, to Durban City Council for development plans in their area. Source: ODAC.

The implementation challenge: Is it worth the bother?

As far as implementation is concerned, there is a dual need. One is political, the other more technical, although the latter is largely dependent on the former because of the need for a resource commitment, both financial and human. On the political side, it is clear that government needs to reach a macro-level decision to respect the Constitution, and section 32 in particular. Moreover, implementation needs champions spread across the various agencies who are willing to develop best practice. To an extent, this is already happening. As is noted elsewhere in this volume, ironically it is the South African Police Service that is providing the best example of compliance — putting in place systems and respecting the need for sound procedural responses to requests under compliance. It is ironic because this was the hound dog of apartheid, yet perhaps because of the institutional hierarchies, and the culture of legal obedience that comes with them, it has proved to be far more compliant with its legal duties in the case of PAIA than many other ministries that one would expect a far less secretive approach from.

But this is also about deepening our collective understanding of transparency and how ATI law works in practice. It is an international process: all around the world, a variety of democracies — old and new — are having to learn how to handle new responsibilities for openness legislation. So South Africa is not alone in facing this difficult challenge. And there are reasons for optimism amid the tardiness and political blockages. The Deputy Information Officers' Forum represents an excellent opportunity not just to exchange views and share learning and best practice, but also to recognise the importance of the job and to attach greater kudos to the position, pivotal as it is to the effective working of the ATI system.

Furthermore, a body of jurisprudence is now growing usefully. Government has lost every single case that has reached the High Court.[24] Some of the cases are responding creatively to the challenge of both implementation and enforcement. The Supreme Court of Appeal in the Earthlife matter ordered that a small panel of experts be appointed, by agreement between the parties, to review the records and advise whether the records were exempt or not.[25] The Earthlife case (dealt with by David Fig in chapter 3) also shows the importance of coalitions — in that case, a specialist NGO working with a specialist ATI specialist organisation. This is a virtuous model. It is unreasonable to think that civil society organisations, even well-resourced NGOs, will take up ATI as a useful addition to their advocacy armoury overnight. They have many pressing concerns, and it is clear that to use PAIA effectively requires skill and experience. Thus, the role of organisations such as SAHA and ODAC is vital — as companions to other NGOs with socioeconomic justice and human rights agendas.

This point is affirmed by Dale McKinley's case study on water access rights (see chapter 3, Box 3.1). He concludes that despite the difficulty of the struggle, and the many obstacles, in the end it produced 'positive results'. In his study, Terry Bell expresses shock and disappointment at the response of government to his own requests for information (another of the stories recorded here; see chapter 2, Box 2.1). Yet, as he knows only too well from his own experience as an investigative journalist, when a government has something to hide, it will do its best to keep it hidden. The only question is whether the democratic system is good enough — and strong and robust enough — to force the information out in the end. This requires a collusion of institutions and social forces. One law does not make a democracy, and in this sense, PAIA should not be seen as a golden bullet.

Which throws up the final question: Is PAIA worth having? If it is like getting blood out of a stone to make PAIA work, why bother? The answer is twofold. Sometimes it works and sometimes it does not. When it does work, you get the information. Even if you do not get the information, the government has to then justify its secrecy. The rule of law bites and it must show that non-disclosure is not only lawful because it is covered by an exemption, but that the public interest in non-disclosure is greater than the public interest in disclosure. As the evidence accumulates, so society will be able to reach its own conclusion, and it is on that point that the argument comes to rest. In the end, it is only by meeting our individual and collective responsibility to act on it that we will be able to show the value of the right to ATI. If we do so, then the social demand for openness will grow to the point where the political costs of secrecy will be too great for any government to bear.

2

Accessing the Records of the Truth and Reconciliation Commission

Piers Pigou

Introduction

> Maybe the success of the Commission will be that we've created this incredible archive ... I would see our final report as a road map that will lead investigative journalists and scholars and politicians and critics and I hope — poets and musicians and everyone else into that body of material, so that they in turn will be able to critique it and address many of the issues that we in the commission simply do not have time to.
>
> Charles Villa Vicencio, head of the TRC's Research Department[1]

The mandate of the South African History Archive (SAHA) to collect and promote the preservation of records relating to the struggle against apartheid and the infrastructure of repression inevitably meant it would give special attention to the records of South Africa's Truth and Reconciliation Commission (TRC). SAHA was especially well placed to take on this role, given that two of its former directors, Verne Harris and Sello Hatang, previously worked for the National Archives. The former, in particular, was responsible for liaison with the TRC between 1997 and 2001 and was a member of the TRC team that investigated the availability and destruction of apartheid era state security and intelligence records. Its current director and author of this chapter is a former TRC investigator, and the SAHA board of trustees' chairperson, Dumisa Ntsebeza, was the TRC commissioner who headed the investigations unit. SAHA therefore has a unique vantage point regarding what records might and should be available.

The work of the TRC has received unprecedented global attention and is held up by many as a positive example of what can be achieved using a restorative justice approach when dealing with an authoritarian and repressive past. By its own admission, however, the commission's work was only part of a broader longer-term process of attempting to determine what happened and why in the struggle against apartheid; the commission ultimately recognised that much more could and should be done.

The TRC's processes generated an enormous paper, digital and audio-visual archive, both in terms of its own internal institutional records and an array of substantive information about violations and related contextual factors. These were collected and generated through interrelated processes of statement taking, investigation, submissions, hearings, document retrieval, research and analyses. The TRC, in its final report (1998), appropriately noted that 'this material represents one of the most remarkable collections in the country and belongs to the nation'.[2] It further stated that:

> one of the key aspects of the Commission's work has been its commitment to transparency and public scrutiny. Its records, which are in the form of documents, video and audio tapes, pictures and photographs, as well as a computerized database, are a national asset which must be both protected and made accessible.[3]

A series of recommendations with respect to the transfer of the archive and the subsequent facilitation of access were also included.[4]

It is over eight years since the TRC handed its final report to then President Mandela,[5] and four years since the Codicil was handed to his successor, then President Mbeki.[6] Between 1998 and 2003, over 3,000 cubic metres of TRC records were transferred from Cape Town to Pretoria.[7] The TRC archive, with the exception of the records of the Reparation and Rehabilitation Committee and the database of victims compiled by the Human Rights Violation Committee, is now housed at the National Archives in Pretoria, where it remains unprocessed and therefore largely inaccessible to the general public. The seven volumes of the final report have not been widely disseminated and are only available in electronic or hard copy versions at a prohibitive cost; the promised popular report has never materialised.[8] Needless to say, the findings and recommendations of the TRC have been accessed by very few South Africans. While a significant amount of material from the TRCs public hearings is available on the Department of Justice's TRC website,[9] this material is also largely unavailable to most South Africans who do not have internet access. Over and above this, the website does not provide a useful search engine and has not been updated for several years.

Despite assertions to the contrary, it has never been SAHA's intention to duplicate the TRC archive. It has, rather, aimed to test the parameters of South Africa's new access to information laws, and has therefore tempered its requests to certain types of records. This has deliberately included a cross-section of issues that sometimes involved requests for similar records made to different government agencies. In several matters, requests have been repeatedly submitted, and in a number of cases legal action has been taken. Requests did not usually follow a linear path, and most requests took months, or years, to finalise.

This chapter focuses on the work of SAHA's Freedom of Information Programme (FOIP)[10] in using the Promotion of Access to Information Act No. 2 of 2000 (PAIA) to secure access to the TRC archive and to records relating to its transfer and processing. In 2001 the TRC was still operational, and its date of completion had already been extended by over three years in order to finalise the amnesty hearing process. SAHA therefore initially focused on issues relating to the transfer of the archive, to its preservation and to maintaining the integrity of so-called sensitive records that were illegitimately severed from the main archive. Following the transfer of the archive in 2001, SAHA has increasingly focused its attention on efforts to access specific records. This chapter will therefore first consider access to records relating to the transfer and processing of the TRC archive; secondly, access to records of the archive; and, finally, requests for associated information.

Tracking the progress of the transfer and processing of the TRC archive

In its 1998 report, the TRC recommended that its records be transferred to the National Archives after the Codicil to the report was made public.[11] During that year, the TRC's regional office records were transferred to its Cape Town headquarters, where they could be used to facilitate the writing of the final report. Although the commission's records are legally the property of the Department of Justice (DOJ), it was decided, in accordance with the recommendations in the final report, that the physical records should be located at the National Archives. The bulk of the records were subsequently boxed up and sent to Pretoria. The detail of exactly what was transferred was hazy, especially given that records from the amnesty process were still being utilised, as were records used for the processing of reparations and the writing of the Codicil. Consequently, there was little, if any, public clarity on their status.

Requests for TRC records inevitably meant that some sort of protocol was required to process them. In late 2001 a committee of representatives of the National Archives, which had physical possession of the records, DOJ, which retained legal custody, and the National Intelligence Agency (NIA) was established under the chairmanship of DOJ's deputy information officer (DIO), David Porogo, to manage the records and deal with related matters, such as requests. It was this committee that made determinations on many of SAHA's earlier PAIA requests.

Access to TRC transfer lists

The National Archives generated a transfer list of the TRC materials that it had relocated from Cape Town to its repository in Pretoria. This provided a rough overview of the materials collected from TRC units and officials. In mid-May 2002, SAHA informed DOJ that it was launching a TRC archives project that would focus on using PAIA to access the

TRC's records. SAHA explained that its intentions were rooted in the spirit of the TRC's own recommendations and that the project was intended to supplement official initiatives in this regard. DOJ was specifically asked whether it had developed a policy on public access to the archive and whether it had identified records for voluntary disclosure in terms of PAIA.[12] Attached to the correspondence was a formal request for a copy of the transfer list.[13]

This request was subsequently refused on the basis that the transfer list could not be found within the department.[14] Given DOJ's position as custodian of the records, this admission was remarkable. No indication was given as to whether the department would rectify the situation. SAHA appealed in late August, but was refused, and by the end of the year had lodged an application in the High Court for access to the list and other records in which the internal appeal process had brought no relief. In May 2003, SAHA secured an out-of-court settlement with DOJ on several matters; this included an agreement to provide SAHA with a copy of the detailed listing of all TRC records transferred to the National Archives.[15]

Access to National Archives' records on the TRC archive and related recommendations

The National Archives was the primary role player in the physical transfer of the records, and had been tasked by the TRC to take several courses of action with respect to the records. In May 2001, shortly after FOIP was initiated, SAHA submitted a PAIA request to the National Archives for copies of correspondence files documenting the National Archives' dealings with the TRC and other parties (in particular, DOJ) in relation to the archive of the TRC.[16] Despite the recommendation that the archive be transferred after the Codicil was completed, SAHA was aware that work was already under way. It would be almost three years, however, before this PAIA request was finalised.

Although the National Archives was legally obliged to respond to the request by July 2001, the request was ignored. In late October 2001, SAHA submitted an appeal on the basis that a failure to respond was deemed a refusal in terms of the Act.[17] In early November the National Archives informed SAHA that access to non-classified records relating to the request would be granted.[18] No further detail was provided, and it was unclear on what basis some records would be made available and others would remain 'classified' (and therefore not available). SAHA appealed, invoking section 25(3) of PAIA and arguing that the reasons given for refusal were inadequate. The following week the national archivist, Dr Graham Dominy, informed SAHA that the records could not be released because they were in the process of 'being transferred to the National Archives in an operation that has implications for state security, the safety of staff and the security of assets'. Dominy also claimed that the appeal consequently fell away and suggested that the request be resubmitted at a later date.[19] SAHA responded, arguing that the explanation for partial refusal was inadequate, as relevant sections of PAIA had not been cited, and that consequently the appeal remained in place.[20] The national archivist responded, now pointing out that the refusal was derived from sections 37 and 38 of the Act, which related to issues of confidentiality and security. He repeated his suggestion that SAHA reapply for the National Archives' correspondence files after the transfer was complete.[21]

In a separate, yet related request, SAHA sought records documenting endeavours by the National Archives to follow up on the recommendations relating to archives and record keeping in the TRC's final report.[22] The Department of Arts and Culture (DAC)[23] decided to conjoin its handling of both these matters. In June 2002 the DAC director general, Dr Robert Adam, reiterated Dominy's position that the PAIA requests should be resubmitted once all the TRC records had been housed at the National Archives; he added that SAHA would not be charged for the reapplication.[24]

On 20 June 2002, SAHA met with the national archivist in an effort to clarify the objectives of FOIP and follow up on a number of issues relating to outstanding requests. In subsequent correspondence to the national archivist, SAHA's then director, Verne Harris, confirmed that Dominy had agreed to reconsider SAHA's requests for records documenting the National Archives' institutional endeavours to follow up on the TRC's recommendations.[25] In late June the National Archives informed SAHA that the committee managing the TRC records 'had identified a security threat and [had] embargoed all classified files on the TRC records until the move had been completed'.[26] In essence, this was the same reasoning that had been provided six months earlier in reaction to the first request.

In August 2002, SAHA submitted an internal appeal to the minister of arts and culture, Dr P.M. Maduna. In October the minister rejected the appeal, arguing that a security threat had been identified and that he would adhere to the advice of NIA and the reason for refusal put forward by the director general and the national archivist.[27] In late November, however, after consultation with NIA, DAC's Legal Services Directorate offered SAHA partial access to the records requested. In fact, what was offered were records relating to the completed movement of TRC records and an undertaking to consider requests for other records on a case-by-case basis. This certainly represented progress, although SAHA was puzzled that security concerns were again being invoked as a possible reason for not releasing these materials.[28] It was only later that SAHA appreciated how this reasoning was linked to another matter it was pursuing in relation to the severance of 'sensitive' records (see below).

The responses to both requests (i.e. for access to records relating to the transfer of the TRC archive and actions taken in relation to the TRC's archival recommendations) were still inadequate; SAHA therefore decided to litigate and filed papers in the High Court in January 2003. Thereafter, in May that year, an out-of-court settlement was reached with DAC in terms of which SAHA accepted that its request for these records could only be finalised once cabinet had formally accepted the TRC report.[29] The report was accepted later that month, but, despite its undertakings, DAC did not provide the documents as agreed.[30] On 13 August 2003, however, SAHA received a DAC progress report on the implementation of TRC recommendations from Dominy. The report alleged that the National Archives were responding seriously to the TRC's recommendations; that these had been scrutinised closely and that appropriate implementation action had been considered and in several instances undertaken.[31]

SAHA publicly raised concerns that the progress report was silent on several key TRC recommendations, including the need to document, secure and bring under archival supervision certain surviving apartheid era security establishment records; the need to determine the status of the security establishment records in relation to national (i.e. archival) legislation (in particular, the legal status of the South African National Defence Force archives); and the need to develop a plan to locate and retrieve documents removed by operatives of the apartheid security structures.[32]

SAHA also spent several months trying to determine the status of the progress report and other details, including its date, its author, whether it was approved and, if so, by whom.[33] SAHA argued that without contextual information, the document did not constitute a record. The national archivist responded, arguing that this was what was on file and that PAIA did not oblige him to create a new record in order to satisfy SAHA's request. Mediation by the State Attorney's Office finally led to the national archivist providing the contextual information and accepting liability for SAHA's costs.[34]

The TRC's 34 boxes and two files of sensitive records

As these cases proceeded, an even more contested and complex matter unfolded. In May 2001, SAHA submitted a request to DOJ for a 'list of all TRC records taken into [its] custody'.[35]

Locating the documents

In his previous employment at the National Archives, SAHA's then director, Verne Harris, had been informed during a meeting with the TRC about a grouping of documents contained in 34 boxes and two files that had been taken from the main TRC archive by the former chief executive officer (CEO) of the TRC, Biki Minyuku. He heard that the documents had been placed in the custody of NIA, and he had publicly raised concern about this at a conference convened in 2000, which prompted NIA to lodge a formal complaint against him.

As DOJ was the legal custodian of the archive, the request for the list was sent to it. PAIA obliged the department to respond by 16 August 2001, but it only did so in mid-December that year, claiming that it was unable to locate the records and suggesting that SAHA should instead approach the National Archives.

In October 2001 Harris had submitted a request for records in the custody of the National Archives and DAC head office that included the conference paper and the controversial reference to the severed documents. SAHA then submitted a request to the National Archives for detail on TRC records that had not been sent to it, but received no response. SAHA also wrote to NIA seeking clarification on the matter. NIA wrote back, stating that it believed that the records were in fact with DOJ. This was reiterated in correspondence dated 3 April 2002 from the minister of intelligence to independent journalist Terry Bell (see Box 2.1).

Box 2.1: Testimony of Terry Bell

Like so many historians, researchers and journalists, I celebrated when South Africa's freedom of information legislation came into force in March 2001. But, within months, I was disillusioned. I remain so, except that I now also celebrate the existence of SAHA, based at the University of the Witwatersrand. Without SAHA, many remaining fragments of our tortured past would have remained buried, perhaps never to surface.

Although PAIA is supposed to allow any citizen the right to seek and obtain documents of relevance to themselves or work they are doing, the process can be cumbersome, time-consuming, expensive and very often frustrating. In particular, SAHA has pursued the documentary fragments of the past that emerged because of the TRC process.

It has not been easy. Even documents that had once been in the public domain, although not properly scrutinised and analysed, disappeared. A classic case concerned 34 boxes of documentation and two files that had been secured by the TRC. According to the commissioners and the legislation governing the TRC, all this documentation should have gone to the National Archives. It did not. To all intents and purposes, 34 boxes and associated files simply disappeared.

Fortunately, the contents of the boxes and the files had been catalogued: there was a record of the general nature of the contents. I had seen some of these documents, but had not had time to examine them closely; there were several files I was keen to peruse. One concerned the murder of a former African National Congress (ANC) activist, Mziwonke 'Pro' Jack, in 1991, at the time of some bitter internecine feuding in the Western Cape. The little I knew of the contents indicated that with access to them it might be possible to establish the reason for the killing of Pro Jack and who might have suggested or even ordered it.

There were also 13 boxes containing the complete public record of the TRC hearings into the apartheid state's chemical and biological warfare programme. Although these records contained formerly classified documents, all had been vetted by the TRC and lawyers representing both the Department of Foreign Affairs and the Non-

Proliferation Council. They had cleared the documents — which had been quoted from extensively during the hearings — for release to the National Archives.

Also in the collection were copies of various published reports, including newspaper clippings and the file relating to the assassination in 1988 of the ANC's chief representative in Paris, Dulcie September. This included material supplied by the French security services, which had not been translated by the time the TRC mandate ended. It made for a bizarre collection.

In any event, all the documents had been in the public domain and were legally required to be transferred to the National Archives. And it was to the National Archives that I directed my initial inquiries in 2000. Verne Harris, then deputy director, confirmed that he had established in 1999 that the 34 boxes had 'gone missing'. He was informed that a set of 'sensitive' documents had been taken into custody by DOJ. But inquiries initially drew a blank, before he was eventually told by DOJ that NIA would need to be consulted about the whereabouts of the missing documents.

In October 2000 Harris spoke at a post-TRC conference in Cape Town and mentioned in passing his concern that NIA had apparently taken charge of a collection of so-called sensitive documents. The statement caused a major upset in certain government quarters. Within a week, a circular arrived on the desks of all staff at the National Archives: in future, all presentations or papers delivered by officials, even in their private capacity, should be vetted by DAC, which controls the National Archives.

But Harris avoided the gag by leaving the National Archives and taking up the post of director of SAHA. I saw this move and the pending implementation then of PAIA as heralding the end of the quest for the 34 boxes of missing TRC documents. Instead, it signalled the start of months and years of frustration and lengthy delays in official responses, peppered with official claims of ignorance and characterised by deliberate disinformation and downright lies.

I was able to establish that the decision to declare the material in the boxes and files 'sensitive' had been taken by the former TRC CEO, Dr Biki Minyuku. He admitted to me that he had not personally assessed the collection of material, but had relied on the opinion of a former TRC investigator whose reputation among his peers was, to say the least, controversial.

Minyuku was also unable to say under what authority he had acted and his replacement as acting CEO of the TRC, Martin Coetzee, admitted that Minyuku had 'acted without mandate'. However, Minyuku maintained that, as a 'matter of national security', he had arranged with the then minister of justice, Dullah Omar, to take charge of the documents. They had been removed from the TRC offices 'for safekeeping'.

But DOJ denied ever having had the documents. Yet I was able to establish that Omar had written to the TRC in April 1999 stating that he had personally taken charge of them. His then administrative secretary, Johan Labuschagne, subsequently informed some TRC officials that the boxes had been handed on to NIA.

The *Mail & Guardian* was prepared to publish the information I was able to dig up, and the pressure mounted. In May of 2002, in a statement issued by the national archivist, Dr Graham Dominy, and DOJ DIO David Porogo, an official investigation was announced. Dominy and Porogo stressed that the responsibility for TRC records rested with the National Archives, which would spearhead the investigation.

However, there had already been an admission by DOJ deputy director John Bacon that the department knew where the documents were. He also conceded that they had been sent to NIA 'for classification'.

What was not publicly known at the time was that Bacon, Dominy and Porogo had been at a meeting at the National Archives on 26 April at which it was decided to fob off my inquiries by announcing an official National Archives-led investigation. In what turned out to be an embarrassing oversight for the parties concerned, minutes of that meeting were released nearly a year later and I obtained a copy.

The minutes stated clearly that the documents were 'save (sic) in the offices of the Minister responsible for NIA' and detailed how the national archivist, DOJ and NIA intended to 'deal with the media'. However, only weeks before that meeting, the then minister 'responsible for NIA', Lindiwe Sisulu, had responded in writing to me that the missing documents 'are in the safekeeping of the Department of Justice'.

But until the minutes of the 26 April meeting became public, there was still confusion about where the missing boxes and files were being kept. In May of 2002 Intelligence Services spokesperson Lorna Daniels delivered this explanation: '[The documents] are technically in the possession of the Department of Justice, but physically held by NIA.'

Barely a month later, Sisulu told Parliament that the documents were being 'declassified in line with their status' by 'an inter-Ministerial task team'. Yet, on the same day, NIA's DIO, J.W. McKay, wrote to SAHA, explaining: 'All the TRC documents are the responsibility of the Department of Justice and are not in the custody of the agency.'

We now know that the documents were (illegally) in the custody of NIA; that they have undergone a classification process that appears not to have been properly authorised; that senior officials deliberately misled the media and the public; and that no satisfactory explanations have ever been given. Above all, some of that documentation, previously in the public domain, remains hidden.

However, the chipping away by SAHA, backed by sections of the media, has had an effect: we now know more than perhaps we might had the bureaucrats had their way completely. And some government departments have shown a degree of willingness to comply with access to information requests. In fact, the Department of Defence has received the warmest accolades in this regard, although I, for one, reserve my judgement.

After all, this was a department that kept most of the details of its murderous violations of human rights in a separate department, the Directorate for Covert Collection (DCC). And when investigators stumbled on the DCC's headquarters with its rows of computers and filing cabinets, they were instructed to withdraw with just three files. Twenty-four hours later, DCC headquarters was an empty shell; all the documents, files, computers and disks had vanished.[36]

Terry Bell

TRC 'dark secrets' will out

Leader Reporter

THIRTY-four boxes of "potentially sensitive" files - which could contain some of apartheid's darkest secrets collated by the Truth and Reconciliation Commission - may soon be available for public viewing following a dramatic legal breakthrough by the South African History Archive (SAHA).

The breakthrough came earlier this month when SAHA lawyers reached an out of court agreement with the Department of Justice, which undertook to release documents it received from the TRC or provide valid reasons for not doing so.

The documents in 34 boxes could reveal information which may expose some of the most bizzare and sinister operations of the apartheid era - and also expose the ANC government's attempts to keep them secret.

The deal sanctioned by the Transvaal High Court, ends a long-standing battle waged by SAHA for access to documents which government claim went missing after the TRC handed them to then Justice Minister Dullah Omar in April 1999.

SAHA director, Verne Harris, told "The Leader" this week, the costly legal battle for the files started in May 2001 but only reached a climax with an out of court settlement early this month.

The Government, according to Harris, has until June to fulfill its obligation to release the files.

He said the Government has formed a task team to inspect the files and report to SAHA every two weeks.

"We also have a full list of the contents of the boxes. If they fail to release the contents by the end of June, we will most certainly pursue the court action,"

Harris said these particular files were kept separately and secretly from the other records handed over by the TRC to Government.

"Our efforts to get access to these files were also stifled by the authorities but we have now established that these files are at the offices of the Minister of Intelligence, Dr LN Sisulu.

"We have taken this action as a matter of principle. The general public would have have had serious difficulty in getting access to these files. We believe the public has a right to know what is in those files because this right is entrenched in the South African constitution," said Harris.

"It is not clear why the Government wanted to block

(Continued on page 2)

(From page 1)
access to these files. Some of them could be "potentially sensitive" but according to our knowledge the majority of the flies are fairly innocuous and could not cause any embarrassment to the authorities."

Harris, a former employee of the National Archive, said the authorities could have been reluctant to disclose information collected by the TRC because of a "broader paranoia" within the government.

Meanwhile, it has been learnt there are more than 7 000 intelligence files on opponents of the apartheid regime collated by members of the former government's notorious security network.

The files contain details of jailed, banned, detained and banished activists.

According to former TRC chief investigation officer, Dumisa Ntsebeza, most of the documents have never seen the light of day, not even during the commission's hearing.

Included among the records of former Security Branch surveillance may be information provided by turncoats or informers that led to the assassination of high profile activists, such as the unsolved shooting of University of Natal academic Rick Turner in 1978.

Jody Kolappen of the Human Rights Commission, said there was strong argument for the disclosure of the information contained in the files because this would in the public's interest.

However, he was emphatic this needed to be balanced with what he argued as "unintended consequences" as to what this could emotionally and otherwise mean to those detained, their families and also to those connected with the informers and former intelligence operators.

However, Kolappen said the public had every right to know what happened to the detainees during the apartheid regime.

He added, however, that the issue needed to be "properly managed".

Kolappen also pointed out there were many factors which needed to be taken into consideration, including the possibility of "misinformation" that could be in the files to cause division amongst the anti-apartheid forces.

"There could also be legal implications involved but on the broader front there was a strong case against the prevention of disclosure," said Kolappen.

Figure 1: Press clipping, Leader reporter, *The Leader*, 23 May 2003.

The week of 3 April 2002, Bell published an article about the mystery of the severed documents, chronicling Harris's efforts initially at the National Archives and SAHA to locate the missing documents and the confusing and contradictory claims and denials being made by government officials from DOJ, NIA and the National Archives.[37] The following week DOJ claimed on national radio that the 'sensitive' records were in fact in the possession of NIA; later that week, NIA finally admitted that this was the case and undertook to return the records to DOJ.[38]

Despite having ostensibly cleared up the matter, subsequent utterances by public officials further compounded the confusion: the minister of intelligence, Lindiwe Sisulu, claimed that the documents were 'in the safekeeping of DOJ and that NIA's involvement with these documents is to advise the Department regarding their appropriate classification before they are forwarded to the National Archives ... [and] to provide security advice'.[39] Meanwhile, DOJ spokesperson Paul Setsetse said that NIA held the documents.[40] This was particularly disturbing, as there was no provision in the TRC Act for the *ad hoc* classification of TRC documents; it was assumed that the apartheid enacted Protection of Information Act No. 84 of 1983 was being relied upon to justify the classification process.

Two weeks later, in late April 2002, Harris wrote in the *Natal Witness* and raised a series of disturbing questions about the whereabouts of these TRC records, the bizarre sequence of events that marked SAHA's efforts to locate the documents, the absence of accountability of responsible bureaucrats and the eventual forced admission that NIA had the documents.[41] Resorting to a play on words, a senior NIA official would subsequently explain that the documents were 'technically in the possession of DOJ, but physically held by NIA'.[42] A few days later, and after consultation with various NGOs, the Cape Town-based Institute for Justice and Reconciliation, headed by the former TRC director of research, Charles Villa-Vicencio, submitted a request to the Office of the President for clarification as to what had actually happened to the records.[43]

In early May 2002 the national archivist informed SAHA that an official investigation led by the National Archives would determine where the records were and what had happened to them.[44] The investigation confirmed that the records were being held by NIA; the Ministry of Justice subsequently admitted that it had sent them there for classification purposes because of their purported sensitivity.

On 19 May 2002 Minister of Justice Maduna informed the Institute for Justice and Reconciliation that he was not aware of a new request to access the contested documents. He claimed that 'as far as [he] could establish', only one request had been submitted to access these documents, and that the applicant had been asked to 'identify the document for purposes of tracing it', but had not come back to the department. He dismissed the 'wild allegations' about the alleged obfuscation around identifying the documents' whereabouts, asserting they were 'totally off the mark'. He confirmed, however, that Minyuku had moved the documents because he feared that 'journalists, and perhaps others, wanted to get hold of [them] even before Government itself had seen [them]'. Maduna asserted that his predecessor, Dullah Omar, had agreed that the documents be transferred 'to protect the integrity of the process, even against journalists'.[45] In response to Maduna's claim that there was no pending request, SAHA submitted a PAIA request the following day to DOJ for copies of 'all records in your possession documenting the chain of custody of the records described in [an] attached list from the time they were transferred from the TRC in 1999'.[46] A parallel request was also submitted to NIA, which was subsequently transferred back to DOJ.

Confusion about the documents mutated into a semantic debate over who was actually in control of them. At the time that the documents were sent to Minister Omar, his portfolio was officially minister of justice and intelligence services. The two competencies were subsequently separated into distinct ministries. In early June 2002 the new minister of intelligence, Lindiwe Sisulu, reportedly confirmed that the documents were safe, telling Parliament that they were being 'assessed ... and declassified in line with their status' by an inter-ministerial task team (the Classification and Declassification Review Committee — CDRC).[47] No detail was provided about their whereabouts or as to why the documents were being treated separately from the main TRC archive.[48] On the same day, SAHA received correspondence from NIA that 'all the TRC documents are the responsibility of DOJ and are not in the custody of the agency'.[49] A senior DOJ official explained that 'the TRC stuff may be locked away in one of our buildings, but only NIA has the key'.[50] The whereabouts of the documents remained unknown.

The relevant government departments had effectively dismissed SAHA's concerns and consistently failed to provide adequate answers, raising suspicions about the motives of those involved. Apart from finding out exactly where these documents were, SAHA wanted to determine whether the contested records had been severed legally, and if so, on whose authority. SAHA was also worried that the records had been sent to NIA, which, it submitted, had no legal authority to remove TRC documents for classification. On top of this, SAHA was now very concerned that the responsible government departments appeared unwilling to adhere to the timelines and other provisions set out in PAIA. Former TRC commissioners and senior staff members of the commission also expressed concern that there was no legal provision for these documents to be classified by NIA or its CDRC.

SAHA had already obtained a list of what was contained in the documents and knew from interactions with former TRC staffers that many of the documents mentioned in it were not sensitive and were already in the public domain. Other files contained useful leads relating to incidents and investigations that the TRC had been unable to follow up.[51]

SAHA approached the National Archives in May for any information it might have, but in June 2002 it also refused a request for records that documented the chain of custody of the records that had been severed by Minyuku. National Archives referred SAHA back to DOJ, pointing out that the records requested were 'currently the subject of an investigation as to their exact status and location'.[52] SAHA submitted an internal appeal, noting that the national archivist had failed to follow the correct PAIA procedures in terms of transferring the request and citing the relevant section/s of the Act in relation to the refusal. SAHA also noted that it was not asking for the TRC records, but the National Archives' own records relating to the severed documents.[53] The response from the national archivist reiterated concerns about a 'security threat' that had been identified by 'the inter-Departmental committee responsible for the secure movement of the records' and refused access.[54]

Exasperated, yet still unwilling to pursue litigation, SAHA submitted a complaint to the South African Human Rights Commission (SAHRC) claiming that both NIA and DOJ were flouting the law and blocking access to the constitutional right of access to information.[55] Inexplicably, no assistance was forthcoming from the SAHRC. Meanwhile, public pressure was mounting, and in June 2002 the Johannesburg-based NGO the Centre for the Study of Violence and Reconciliation (CSVR) wrote to Archbishop Tutu as the TRC chair proposing that clear recommendations be made to ensure that all TRC files were made public as soon as possible. CSVR urged the TRC to undertake its own assessment of section 29 files to determine what could be released for public scrutiny. In addition, CSVR requested the TRC to locate the missing boxes of documents and make recommendations regarding access to their contents.[56]

In mid-August 2002, almost three months after receiving the application, DOJ re-fused SAHA access to the records documenting the chain of custody of TRC records, claiming that they could not be found.[57] An internal appeal was submitted to the min-ister of justice in late August, to which the state should have responded within 30 days. In early October, the Ministry of Justice acknowledged receipt of the appeal, dated 26 August, pointing out that it had only been received on 19 September 2002.[58] Meanwhile, SAHA had still received no official response from the minister of arts and culture, Dr Ben Ngubane, to the appeal that it had submitted to the National Archives and DAC in June, prompting it to alert the minister that it would be forced to make an application to court for review.[59] An out-of-court settlement was subsequently reached, with the result that certain National Archives' records relating to the TRC archive were released to SAHA in the first quarter of 2003. No further light, however, was shed on the whereabouts of the missing records.

Amongst the 45 pages of documents received was a copy of minutes from a meeting convened at the National Archives in April 2002 at which representatives of NIA and DOJ were present, which revealed that the 34 boxes had indeed been located in the office of the minister of intelligence. No apparent progress had been made in the 11-month 'investiga-tion' that had been launched to locate the documents. SAHA made the document public, prompting journalist Terry Bell to raise questions as to why both the national archivist and the DOJ DIO, David Porogo, had announced the launch of an investigation into the whereabouts of the documents when they knew perfectly well that they were in the office of the minister of intelligence. The national archivist vehemently denied that he had lied, pointing out that there had been an investigation that had been subsumed into the work of CDRC.[60]

Dominy described Bells' article as 'mischievous in deliberately misrepresenting the fact[s]', and argued that the minutes referred to had been misinterpreted. He acknowl-edged that a senior official from DOJ had made the assertion at the meeting that the files were at NIA, but that an investigation had been subsequently launched to determine whether this was indeed the case. Dominy also queried comments contained in the article that had been attributed to SAHA's director, Verne Harris, pointing out that Harris had never raised his concerns with the National Archives, and that he could not have been searching for the missing 34 boxes of documents for more than three years, because he had been employed at the National Archives only two years previously.[61]

SAHA was deeply distressed by what it perceived as the national archivist's cavalier response to its legitimate concerns. Harris reminded the national archivist that he had spent over a year trying to locate these records when still employed at the National Archives before taking up the same quest as director of SAHA. Harris also pointed out that when he had expressed his concerns at a conference in 2000, he was attacked by NIA, which denied having the records, and was threatened with disciplinary action by his superiors, something which, Harris argued, was instrumental in his decision to leave the National Archives. SAHA and Bell pointed out that it was almost a year since the 'investigation' had been launched and that, given the lack of conclusion, something was evidently amiss.[62]

Despite acknowledging receipt of the appeal submitted in August 2002, the Ministry of Justice did not respond. By December 2002, SAHA decided to litigate and filed an application in the High Court claiming that neither DOJ nor its DIO had applied their minds properly to the matter, and that the exemptions, in particular that the disclosure of these documents would 'prejudice the defence, security and international relations of South Africa', had not been reasonably applied.

In late January 2003, SAHA's attorneys were informed by the State Attorney's Office that it was in possession of the transfer lists, as well as other documents relating to the chain of custody of the TRC records. At this stage, the state had not filed a notice of its intention to oppose in the case lodged against DOJ and was now requesting further time to 're-analyse' the actual records.[63] While this represented some progress in terms of the transfer lists, SAHA was concerned that the state was still resisting access to the so-called sensitive records. Although SAHA was legally entitled to play hardball, it recognised the importance of being flexible if this could facilitate movement towards its principle objective of access.[64]

In May 2003, SAHA secured out-of-court settlements with DOJ and DAC. In terms of the settlement with DOJ, SAHA was given copies of records that confirmed that the sensitive TRC records had been moved to the Ministry of Intelligence in 1999. The settlement with DOJ required a final handover of the documents to SAHA by the end of 2003 and the submission of an interim progress report in the meantime. If the matter were not finalised by that date, SAHA reserved the right to pursue action in the High Court.[65] The agreement confirmed that the contested documents would be transferred to the custody of DOJ, which would release the documents or provide valid reasons for not doing so.[66] In terms of the settlement with DAC, SAHA was given copies of National Archives' records documenting the custody of the sensitive records.[67]

SAHA had proved its point with regard to its rights of access to records detailing the custody issue and had eventually forced some level of action and transparency, albeit reluctantly, from the responsible departments. The final capitulation by government on these matters through an out-of-court settlement had, however, ensured that no legal precedent had been set.

Access to the 'sensitive records'

Having located the records, SAHA's focus now shifted to accessing the content of the contested boxes. The settlement applied not only to documents, correspondence and other records relating to the provenance, custody and movement of the records, but to the actual records themselves. The settlement also directed that the documents contained in the 34 boxes would be delivered to the National Archives in three batches, the first of which would be in late September 2003.[68] On the eve of the first handover, SAHA warned that if the deadline were missed it would by forced to take further legal action. The documents were subsequently released by NIA to the National Archives, but they remained unavailable to the public. SAHA accused DOJ of failing to honour the terms of the settlement. The department's chief director of communications and DIO denied that the department had reneged on undertakings to release the documents.[69]

Among the documents referred to in the settlement was an inventory; one entry in the inventory was entitled 'List of informers'. Not surprisingly, the media were particularly interested in the contents of this file.[70] As the TRC process had failed to lift the lid on the informer issue (a concern that resounded in the post-TRC period),[71] interest in this particular file was considerable. SAHA was not confident, however, that this listed document would be released;[72] DOJ subsequently denied there was such a list.[73]

In November 2003 the national archivist confirmed that the records were indeed at the National Archives, where they were being processed and scrutinised by a multi-agency team that was formulating recommendations about which records could be released and which required continued protection. SAHA was incensed that a further delay regarding access was now in the offing and another vetting process of the documents was being undertaken. The national archivist accused SAHA of overreacting, and of not contributing to the debate on access in a balanced and professional manner.[74] SAHA hit back, accusing the state of reneging on three access agreements and of consistently reneging on its legal obligations.[75]

SAHA felt that it had no choice but to return to court to seek a final resolution regarding access. Shortly before Christmas 2003 the State Attorney's Office tried to pre-empt a court battle by offering SAHA sight of the review committee's worksheet, detailing its findings and recommendations. SAHA rejected the offer, as it would have been prohibited from publishing the contents of the worksheet, which included the committee's reasons for non-disclosure.[76]

In mid-January 2004, shortly before the case was scheduled to be heard in the Pretoria High Court, DOJ filed a related affidavit in which it confirmed that a TRC file catalogued as 'List of informers' no longer existed.[77] The department strongly defended the non-disclosure of the files and the related classification processes it had embarked on.[78] This time, however, government departments broke ranks when NIA's information officer asserted that the documents were 'not in the custody of the agency' and Porogo accused NIA (its co-respondent) of misleading him in June 2002.[79] Porogo explained that in January 2003, at a meeting between officials of the two departments, it became clear that NIA 'would not summarily release the documents' to DOJ.[80] He claimed that DOJ was then informed that the minister of intelligence, Lindiwe Sisulu, felt that these documents were 'sensitive'. She purportedly stated that NIA 'can only approve that the courts can come and inspect the documents. Once they are delivered to the courts we have no jurisdiction over their safety'.[81]

This disclosure provides a remarkable insight into NIA's approach to PAIA and its interpretation of its legal responsibilities. Porogo claimed that the situation was only rectified with the establishment of CDRC, which by January 2004 had declassified 658 of the 1,684 documents for immediate release, had given partial disclosure for another 198 documents, and was reviewing a further 512.[82] In its responding affidavit, SAHA accused DOJ of dealing with its request for access to the files 'with contempt and total disregard' for the Constitution. SAHA accused Porogo of 'shamelessly' lying about the CDRC review and breaking many other promises.[83] SAHA asserted that the classification process had no legal basis. Despite this, the state was granted a further postponement to respond to SAHA's most recent affidavit.[84]

The case was scheduled for 11 May 2004, but was postponed again until 17 August to allow the new minister of justice, Bridgette Mabandla, an opportunity to familiarise herself with the case. The courts granted the department a further postponement from August until 15 November 2004, and in early November the department requested another ten-day extension. Evidently, the 'classification' process had not been finalised. Exasperated, SAHA pointed out that there were several outstanding issues relating to the case, including an undertaking from DOJ that it would provide an affidavit confirming that the 'List of informers' referred to in the inventory could not be found. SAHA also pointed out that the state attorney had agreed to provide details on new documents that had been declassified by 15 October, but had failed to do so. Not surprisingly, SAHA was reluctant to accede to a further postponement, especially as the matter was now likely to be pushed over to 2005.[85]

On 15 November 2004 the director general of DOJ, Vusi Pikoli, wrote to SAHA's lawyers and provided a 335 page annexure that listed details on all the documents under consideration, setting out in each case whether the document could be disclosed fully, partially or not at all, and reasons for any refusals or severance of information. In addition, another affidavit was provided in relation to the 'missing' list of informers. The department had also been specifically instructed by Pikoli to assist SAHA to access the required documents.[86]

After a three-year battle, it was a remarkable result — the documents were reunited with the main TRC archive in the custody of the National Archives, and over 60 per cent of the contested documents had been placed in the public domain. It was now possible to scrutinise what all the fuss had been about. Not surprisingly, the bulk of contentious documents related to the records gathered by the TRC during its investigations into Project Coast, the apartheid military's chemical and biological warfare (CBW) programme. The South African government had put tremendous pressure on the TRC not to proceed with its public CBW hearings and, in some respects, the barriers put in the way of access to these records resonated with the problems of access experienced by the TRC during its own inquiry.[87]

Indeed, most of the documents that SAHA was ultimately refused access to related to the CBW programme, and included details on the production and deployment of substances, as well as details on individuals involved in Project Coast. Other documents related to specific criminal investigations (i.e. the murders of Dulcie September,[88] Pro Jack[89] and Alan Kidger[90]), gun running, investigations by General Pierre Steyn,[91] and several internal ANC documents, including some relating to its military tribunals.

Although SAHA believes that there are grounds to successfully challenge the ongoing refusal of access to some of these documents, it decided not to take the matter any further, believing that the point of principle had been made — namely, that government departments could not unilaterally impose blanket restrictions on access in terms of PAIA. Although SAHA had not ensured that these departments adhere to the letter or spirit of PAIA, it had forced them to employ a transparent process that ultimately compelled disclosure. Once again, no legal precedent had been set, but SAHA's actions had provided a platform from which others could begin their own inquiries. SAHA's concern regarding the legality of the classification process was, however, never resolved, and the role of NIA in assisting to determine what TRC records are in the public domain and what are not appears to be firmly entrenched.

Access to other TRC records

Between 2001 and 2004 SAHA submitted 38 PAIA requests relating directly to the TRC archive. FOIP intended to test access to certain types of records, some of which were clearly already in the public domain and others whose status was less clear. Following the launch of its TRC project in 2002, SAHA submitted a range of requests to DOJ and the National Archives for specific files believed to be contained in the archive. At this stage, SAHA was already in dispute with DOJ, DAC and NIA regarding the matters detailed above. Rather than waiting for these matters to be resolved, SAHA undertook to submit requests that would test PAIA with respect to different types of documents. It was also SAHA's intention that the submission of requests would contribute to a decision to expedite the processing of these important records.

Amnesty records

The TRC's conditional amnesty process required applicants to provide details of and justification for the perpetration of gross human rights violations. Applications were submitted to the commission's Amnesty Committee, which conducted an administrative process to determine whether the application was germane in terms of the set criteria for eligibility, and whether the matter constituted a gross human rights violation and therefore required a hearing. Hearings were conducted in public, and in a number of incidents, testimony was supplemented by the submission of documents and other evidence in support

Figure 2: When the Truth Commission handed over the final segment of its report to President Mbeki in March 2003, it acknowledged there was much unfinished business to be attended to. Although the Truth Commission confirmed that many apartheid era intelligence and security documents were destroyed, it revealed that many had not been. Consequently, it recommended that government undertake an archival audit of remaining documents to determine exactly what remained. To date, no such audit has been carried out. Copyright: Zapiro / *The Sowetan* (Archived as SAHA Collection AL3129 – H2).

of or in opposition to the application. Transcripts of the 255 public hearings and 1,632 hearing days are available on the TRC website.[92]

SAHA made several attempts to access copies of amnesty applications and other documentation submitted during the public hearing process. These efforts also met with mixed results. Among the 34 boxes of sensitive documents, it emerged that there were a number of copies of amnesty applications. Having reviewed these documents, however, the director general of DOJ granted access to some and refused access to others. In general, the rationale provided for the former was that the documents were already in the public domain.[93] SAHA certainly agreed with this, having argued that all amnesty applications that resulted in public hearings had been put into the public domain.

In incidents of refusal, however, the director general put a variety of reasons forward. In some instances, it was argued that disclosures would be unreasonable in that they would constitute an unreasonable disclosure of personal information.[94] Interestingly, in some of these matters, the director general argued that the information had been provided to the TRC on a confidential basis.[95] It is not clear whether these applications resulted in public amnesty processes, although it is stated that the information in the applications is not in the public domain, implying that these matters were dealt with in chambers. SAHA has yet to contest the notion introduced by the director general that the applicants and other implicated persons would have to give consent before the records can be released. In other matters, the director general asserted that non-disclosure was necessary to protect the integrity of law enforcement and legal proceedings, citing section 39 of PAIA. Other reasons included the mandatory protection of individuals whose security would be compromised by disclosure (section 38). All of these reasons, or a combination thereof, were proffered in a number of applications relating to the CBW programme, gun-running activities and certain ANC applications.[96] The inference that these matters are still subject to criminal investigation and possible prosecution is obvious. Nevertheless, it remains to be seen whether the politics of prosecution determines whether these matters are taken forward or left unattended.

Some of the reasoning provided for refusing access to certain 'sensitive' documents was contradicted by the fact that the document was provided elsewhere. In one instance, access to an amnesty application was refused in one section of the settlement and granted in another.[97] This was also the case regarding the controversial 'Staff report to the Steyn Inquiry', which had large sections redacted in the Afrikaans version, but was provided without excision in the English version.[98] This understandably raises questions about the integrity of the decision-making process.

Amnesty materials relating to the murders of the Cradock 4

In June 2004 David Forbes, a local documentary filmmaker, submitted a PAIA request for a full transcript of the amnesty hearings into the murder of the 'Cradock 4'[99] and copies of all documents (annexures) submitted during the amnesty hearing process (see Box 2.2). He believed it was self-evident that these documents were already in the public domain, as the documents had been formally submitted during a public process. SAHA intervened when DOJ failed to provide a full response. The department denied access in the first instance and on appeal, arguing that the provision of these documents would constitute an unreasonable disclosure of personal information, violate third-party confidentiality protections and prejudice ongoing legal proceedings (i.e. sections 34 and 39 of PAIA). SAHA applied to the High Court for review, arguing that the state was placing an incorrect reliance on the stated sections and had failed to take into account PAIA's provisions for upholding the public interest (i.e. section 46). Prior to filing its answering affidavit, DOJ granted access to the transcripts requested; SAHA responded that access to the transcripts was not sufficient and advised the department to file its answering affidavit. It was not until the department did so that the requester was provided with a listing of documents that purportedly related to the request and reasons for refusal in relation to each. The department expanded its reasons for refusal and relied in addition on two other exemptions that protected the life and safety of third parties and agreements of confidentiality. The listing, however, was not clear: some documents were referred to simply as 'memo dated 16 June 1985' without any contextual information. This prompted SAHA to review the transcript, which was around 2,500 pages; SAHA discovered that the department had in fact listed just over half of the documents that applied to the request. SAHA followed up with the department's DIO, Marlyn Raswiswi, seeking clarification, and received a short response alleging that the documents were 'privileged'. Some 16 months later, on the morning of the scheduled hearing in the Pretoria High Court, the state capitulated and in an out-of-court settlement acquiesced by agreeing to give SAHA full access to all the records requested. This was an important victory, but also a frustrating one, as once again it allowed the state to prevent the setting of a legal precedent in terms of access to TRC records.

Box 2.2: The case of the Cradock 4

In 2003, after many years of deliberation, I began making a film about the murder of the Cradock 4 by the security forces on 27 June 1985.

Imperative to the film were two things: the participation and support of the families of the Cradock 4, in particular the widows, and access to all records that make up the story of the murder of the four men.

The widows of the Cradock 4 gave their blessing and provided support to the film. In return, I set up a fund to ensure that profits from the film would be distributed to the community through a trust managed by the widows.

With the assistance of Zenzile Khoisan, former TRC investigator, and funding secured from the National Film and Video Foundation, we set about perusing the files and photographs at the Times Media Library and SAHA. Many of SAHA's collections were donated by the Legal Resource Centre, which represented the widows at the inquests and TRC hearings into the murders.

On 2 June 2004 Zenzile and myself went to the Pretoria offices of DOJ to submit a PAIA request for access to records relating to the case. Both the inquests and the TRC hearings had been open to the public. At the time, we thought that requesting the records of these hearings would be a mere formality.

What followed was a period of obstruction and what I can only describe as incompetence and arrogance by DOJ officials. I was confronted with silence; lies; a failure to return telephone calls, faxes and e-mails; and a failure to deliver on promises; it seemed that the DOJ did everything in its power to deny us access to the records.

In short, the DOJ's behaviour stood in direct contravention of PAIA. Left with no option, I resorted to writing a letter to the director general of DOJ, but this too went unanswered.

In January 2005 I happened to be going to Port Elizabeth and decided to drive down via Cradock and visit two of the widows who still live there, Mrs Nomonde Calata and Mrs Sindiswa Mkonto. Imagine my surprise when Nomonde told me that DOJ officials had been there just two days before and intimidated them into signing affidavits that stated that they did not consent to the release of the Cradock 4 records.

Nomonde told me that the Cradock mayor's office had called and told her that 'National Intelligence(!)' required the telephone numbers of all the widows.

Shortly afterwards, a man and a woman arrived at her house with Mrs Mkonto in tow, and said they were from the DOJ. They sat with the widows for two hours and told them that for their own protection they should not cooperate with me.

Nomonde said she felt frightened and intimidated. At no stage did DOJ representatives tell her that she had a right to legal representation at the meeting, or a period of time in which she could consider her options, as required by PAIA. The DOJ officials then gave both widows a Notice to Third Party, which had previously been signed by Advocate Pikoli on 18 January 2005, and instructed them to come to the police station to make statements that would be used to deny any access to the files of their deceased husbands.

DOJ's tactics are hard to believe and appear to be the work of incompetent officials. The third-party regulation of PAIA requires that an individual whose personal information is contained in a record must be consulted before the record is released so that the individual has an opportunity to argue against release or express his/her consent to access. The fact remains, however, that the widows have few rights under PAIA to make any representations, as they are not third parties as contemplated by PAIA. Was the error a result of incompetence on behalf of the department, or an attempt to avert any further pursuit of the records?

I discussed the situation with Nomonde, who felt that she had been unfairly pressured and intimidated, and wished to continue cooperating with me. I told her to take her time in making a decision and to consult her family.

After several weeks, both widows made a second affidavit laying out the scenario as it had occurred and repudiating their earlier statements to the DOJ lawyers. This new statement stipulated that I should have complete access to all the files concerning the Cradock 4. While these statements would not be influential in a determination of access, they constituted a clear demonstration of the lengths to which DOJ was willing to go, lengths that were unlikely to be viewed favourably by the court in our future proceedings.

I finally enlisted the help of SAHA, which had legal experience in these matters, and which set legal action in motion in June 2005. Faced with court action, DOJ released copies of the hearing transcripts, most of which were, ironically, already publicly available on its website. To bolster our case, we closely read through the thousands of pages that made up the transcripts, making a note of every document utilised as evidence in the hearings.

Filming was delayed beyond the day of the twentieth anniversary of the activists' deaths on 27 June 2005. At the outset of the project, this had been set as the date on which we had planned the release. By this stage, completing the film against all odds had become a matter of principle.

The date marked another interesting progression in the case, at which the privacy interest of the deceased men, and therefore the widows, ceased. The affidavits obtained by DOJ were, as a consequence, no longer of any value.

The legal process dragged on through a protracted filing process, and despite all efforts by SAHA to obtain clarification of the reasons for refusal and the ill-conceived answering affidavit raised in their defence, no response was forthcoming. A court date was finally set for 14 September 2006; more than two years had passed since I had made the initial PAIA request to DOJ.

Less than 24 hours before the High Court hearing, DOJ indicated that it wished to settle out of court. I was not keen to settle, and wanted the legal process to take its course so that our case could set a precedent for future PAIA requests.

On the day of the hearing I discussed my concerns with our advocate; as DOJ was finally offering us everything we requested, we were forced to accept. In the five minutes prior to the scheduled hearing, DOJ agreed to the terms of our settlement and we entered the courtroom only to leave five minutes later with a settlement that ordered that DOJ give unrestricted access to the records within 30 days. Left with no choice DOJ showed the first signs of cooperation.

There was wide media interest in the case, which was reported in the Pretoria News, The Star, The Sowetan, The Citizen, EP Herald, Weekend Post, SA Press Association, South African Broadcasting Corporation (SABC) TV and SAFM (the English-language SABC radio station).

It was disappointing that following settlement, SAHA was told by the State Attorney's Office that DOJ was seeking counsel's advice as to the validity of the terms of settlement. We were never told of the outcome of this advice and were given full access to the records as agreed in court.

I was amazed at the interest in the murder of the Cradock 4. Our court order was a victory for democracy, for free speech and freedom of information, and a victory for the principles for which the Cradock 4 died.

David Forbes
Independent South African film producer/director

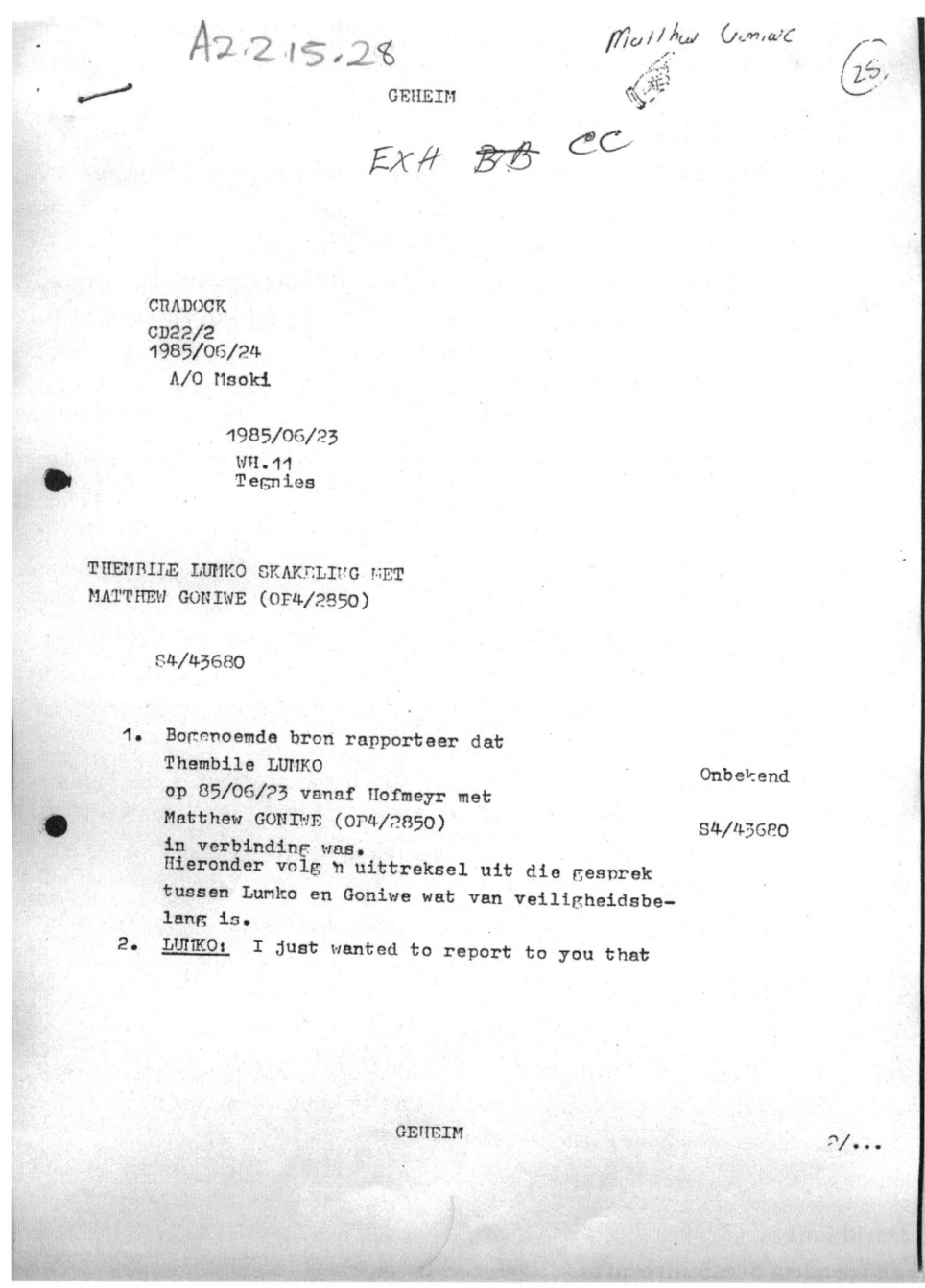

A2.2.15.28

Matthew Goniwe

(25.)

GEHEIM

EXH ~~BB~~ CC

CRADOCK
CD22/2
1985/06/24
A/O Msoki

1985/06/23
WH.11
Tegnies

THEMBILE LUMKO SKAKELING MET
MATTHEW GONIWE (OP4/2850)

S4/43680

1. Bogenoemde bron rapporteer dat
    Thembile LUMKO   Onbekend
    op 85/06/23 vanaf Hofmeyr met
    Matthew GONIWE (OP4/2850)   S4/43680
    in verbinding was.
    Hieronder volg 'n uittreksel uit die gesprek
    tussen Lumko en Goniwe wat van veiligheidsbe-
    lang is.

2. LUMKO: I just wanted to report to you that

GEHEIM

2/...

Figure 3: Secret security police report including transcript of telephone conversation by Matthew Goniwe, compiled by Major Eric Winter, commander of Cradock Security Police, the week before the abductions and murder of the Cradock 4 (Archived as SAHA Collection AL2878 – A2.2.15.28).

GEHEIM

- 2 -

the boers and the police were provoking us so we stoned them, they ran to town. We chased another black policeman here in the township, he could not run and we caught him. We've beaten him up and took his service revolver.

GONIWE: Where is the revolver now?

Lumko: It is here with me.

GONIWE: Hey man you'll be shot there by the police. I don't know what advice to give you, but as I say you are busy with a difficult battle which you will not win. What you can do try and restore peace there.

3. UITKENNING

3.1 PERSONE

Matthew GONIWE (OP4/2850)   S4/43600

Thembile LUMKO - s/man van Hofmeyr.   Onbekend

Die Afdelingsbevelvoerder
Veiligheidstak
AFDELING COSTELIKE PROVINSIE

1. Vir u inligting.

2. Die Takbevelvoerder, Veiligheidstak, Middelburg(Kaap) was op 1985/06/23 telefonies ingelig van bogenoemde inligting.

```
                              MAJOOR
TAKBEVELVOERDER    :    VEILIGHEIDSTAK
CRADOCK            :    E.F.H. WINTER
```

GEHEIM

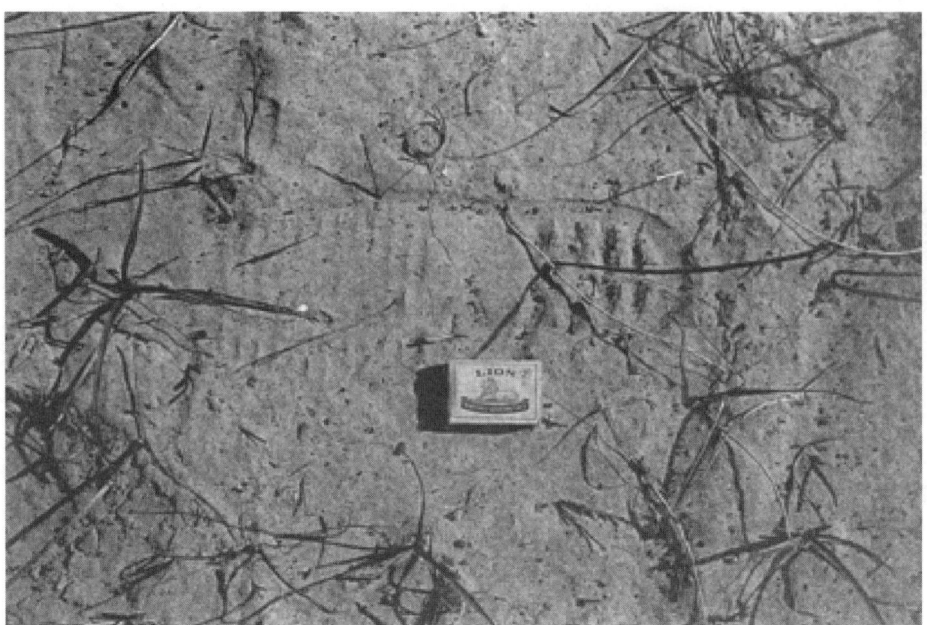

Figure 4: Scene photographed in bushy area near Bluewater Bay, Port Elizabeth. Photographer: Warrant Officer Leerink. Original album prepared by Warrant Officer Els. Shows footprint as observed at the scene where Sicelo Mhauli's body was found.

Figure 5: Scene photographed on 28/6/1985 at 15h30 in bush on the Veeplaas road, Port Elizabeth. Photographer: Warrant Officer A McKay. Shows close-ups of area at the scene were an apparent blood spot and a shoe were observed. This was discovered at the scene where Sparrow Mkonto's body was found, near Redhouse.

Amnesty application of Eugene de Kock

SAHA's inability to secure legal precedents in the Cradock 4 matter has allowed DOJ to employ similar tactics in other matters, resulting in further unnecessary obstruction and obfuscation. In 2006 SAHA submitted a request for access to the entire amnesty application presented by Eugene de Kock to the TRC.[100] Colonel de Kock had been the commander of the security police's crack counter-insurgency unit during the 1980s and had been arrested in March 1994, charged, and convicted of multiple murders and other crimes. In late 1996, as the TRC was getting settled into its operational mode, De Kock released a flood of allegations against colleagues and former commanders during the hearings on the mitigation of his sentencing. These allegations, coupled with other revelations that surfaced during the trial and related investigations, resulted in security police officers from all over the country submitting their own applications for amnesty.

As in so many other instances, the DIO failed to deal with the request within the time period prescribed by PAIA and requested an extension, arguing that the application was contained in various different collections and was not collated in one submission (as it had been when lodged by De Kock's lawyers in December 1996). SAHA disputed this fact, as it had been privy to viewing of boxes containing the record in the Cradock case and was aware that the record was in fact not separated as the DIO alleged, but, rather, contained in a number of boxes that were stored together. The request unfolded in much the same manner as the request for access to the Cradock 4 records. In a complaint submitted to the SAHRC in July 2007, SAHA stated:

> The DIO again failed to consider that the contents of the application were aired in public hearings held by the TRC, that the application as far as we are aware was not subject to any *in-camera* hearings, and that the TRC Act states that the confidentiality of all investigation materials and amnesty applications lapses once a public hearing is held. We submitted an internal appeal to the Minister in that same month setting out grounds upon which we relied in the Cradock case and raising our serious concern with the failure of the Department to consider the substantial similarity of the records subject to the request. Aside from several other attempts to elicit responses from the Department, we called the [DIO] on 9 May 2007, then followed up with an email confirming her advice that she would follow the matter up with the Minister. When we still did not receive a response we sent a letter to the Minister on 14 June 2007 advising her that we would commence legal proceedings if we did not receive a response. On 29 June 2007 we received a response from the Minister stating that she upholds the decision of the [DIO] on the bases that disclosure will breach the privacy of third parties (section 34(1)), may compromise the safety of third parties (section 38(1)), and may impede prosecution by the National Prosecuting Authority (section 39(1)(b)(iii)(aa)). These same grounds were utilised in the Cradock case in relation to a portion of Eugene de Kock's and other individuals' amnesty applications which we ultimately gained access to.[101]

Eugene de Kock's amnesty application represents the most comprehensive submission by a former security force member of the former government. As such, it provides an unprecedented window into the world of a senior foot soldier of the regime. De Kock's activities traversed the country and the region, where he and his unit were responsible for a significant number of counter-insurgency operations. While SAHA appreciates that there may be aspects of the De Kock application that can be legitimately redacted, the organisation rejects the notion of blanket refusal, and at the time of writing was again preparing for litigation to establish a precedent in this regard. In many instances, aspects of the De Kock amnesty application are already in the public domain. Indeed, SAHA has secured fragments of the application from legal representatives of victims mentioned in some of these matters, as well as from the department itself as a result of the settlement in the Cradock matter. SAHA has made this very clear to the department and the minister, but such reasoning has apparently fallen on deaf ears.

Section 29: *In-camera* records

Section 29 of the TRC Act allowed the commission to subpoena individuals to appear before it to answer questions *in-camera*. Several dozen persons were subpoenaed by the Human Rights Violation Committee during 1996 and 1997 — a comprehensive listing has not been published — and the information gleaned was subsequently utilised in further investigations, research and analyses. The process also successfully solicited amnesty applications in several instances.[102]

In June 2003 SAHA submitted five requests to DOJ for copies of transcripts of section 29 hearings.[103] These included the hearings of former 'superspy' Craig Williamson, testimony from several security police officers involved in the 1988 death in custody of Mamelodi activist Stanza Bopape, the testimony of former askari[104] Joe Mamasela, the testimony of Winnie Madikizela-Mandela and the testimony of members of the Khumalo Gang who were involved in terrorising the East Rand community of Thokoza in the early 1990s. Five months later the department responded, denying access to all records and, citing section 37(1)(b), arguing that the testimonies had been given with undertakings of confidentiality from the TRC. SAHA immediately appealed, but the minister of justice upheld the rejection, citing the same grounds.

In March 2006 SAHA once again submitted an application for section 29 transcripts.[105] In its application, SAHA listed a number of transcripts that had been aired in subsequent public hearings. In April the DOJ responded, stating: 'The documents contain information that was supplied in strict confidence by various third parties. The information was supplied after their confidentiality was guaranteed, so we are unable to breach our undertaking'.[106] In June SAHA submitted an internal appeal, arguing among other things that DOJ did not hold a duty of confidentiality to third parties, and that some of the records were already in the public domain. The following month, the rejection was upheld by the Ministry of Justice.[107] SAHA contested the notion that the TRC made any agreements of this nature and subsequently submitted a PAIA request for records confirming such an undertaking.[108] As expected, no such records could be located. In a meeting with the DIO of the department, SAHA again pointed out that transcripts of certain *in-camera* testimonies were already in the public domain, having been utilised in other hearings; these included the testimony of Madikizela-Mandela (disclosed in the November/ December public hearings into the activities of the Mandela Football Club), as well as testimonies from amnesty applicants involved in the Bopape and Khumalo Gang cases. In addition, the Mamasela transcript was successfully secured by former security policeman Dirk Coetzee, who took the TRC to court to access the transcript as part of his criminal defence on murder charges. The DIO agreed to conduct further inquiries regarding these transcripts, but responded shortly thereafter by rejecting the application without having done so.

SAHA recognised that the transcripts of these hearings may contain sensitive information and consequently was not calling for blanket access, as has been assumed in some quarters. Instead, it argued that the records should be reviewed on a case-by-case basis. As with the records contained in the 34 boxes saga, there may well be cogent reasons for withholding certain information, but there is no justification for a blanket refusal. Such blanket refusals are contradictory to the spirit of PAIA; the TRC never intended that restrictions on access should continue for an undefined period.

In June 1998 the TRC agreed that '[a]ll information gathered by the TRC, including [section 29] hearings, remained confidential until such time as the Commission decides otherwise'.[109] In August the commission acknowledged that the issue of access to these records 'was a sensitive matter' and that 'all the transcripts need[ed] to be scrutinized in terms of the naming of persons etc.' There was a caution 'against a blanket policy on access', and three senior staff members were tasked with drawing up a recommendation.[110] No such recommendation was forthcoming at that stage, and no mention was made about access to section 29 transcripts in the TRC's November 1998 report presented to Nelson Mandela. In effect, a decision on how to proceed with this was put to one side.

In June 2002, CSVR wrote to Archbishop Tutu as TRC chair, urging him to make recommendations to ensure that all TRC files were made public as soon as possible and for the TRC itself to undertake its own assessment of section 29 files to determine what could be publicly released.[111] No such review was undertaken, but a decision on access to the transcripts was taken at the TRC's final meeting in March 2003.[112] Unfortunately, the minutes of this meeting were captured on a laptop that was subsequently stolen.[113]

Access to the report of the auditor general

Several other requests submitted by SAHA to DOJ for records that were also deemed to be 'sensitive' were subsequently handled as part of the '34 boxes' case. These included, for example, the request to access the Dulcie September case file and the report of the

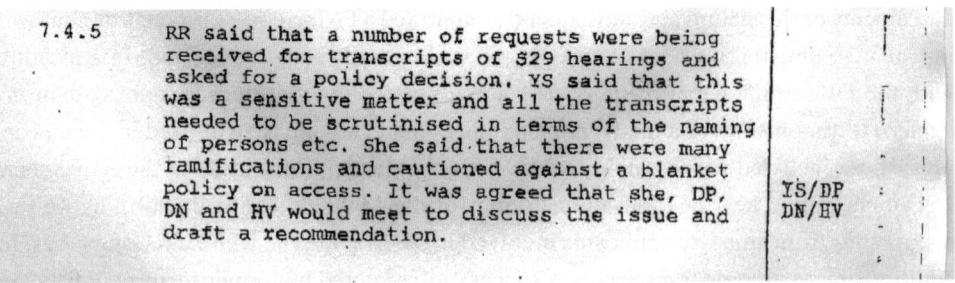

7.4.5   RR said that a number of requests were being
received for transcripts of S29 hearings and
asked for a policy decision. YS said that this
was a sensitive matter and all the transcripts
needed to be scrutinised in terms of the naming
of persons etc. She said that there were many
ramifications and cautioned against a blanket
policy on access. It was agreed that she, DP,
DN and HV would meet to discuss the issue and
draft a recommendation.   YS/DP
                                                     DN/HV

Figure 6: Extract from TRC commissioners' minutes, dated 6 August 1998, stipulating a recommendation that a policy of access to section 29 *in-camera* transcripts be developed. What the commission ultimately recommended remains contested as the minutes of the final commissioners' meeting in March 2003 are missing.

auditor general to the TRC entitled 'A Review by the Auditor General of the Secret Funds for the Period 1960–1994'.

The Kahn Commission had been set up in July 1991 by then President F.W. de Klerk to review active covert projects that were being run by the security and intelligence community. Where possible, cabinet was apparently keen to close these operations down, but where they were to continue, it was stipulated that 'they should not benefit from any particular political party or organization [and] they should serve the broader national interest in countering of violence, intimidation, sanctions and international isolation'.[114] Kahn's report provided details of funding of secret projects run by the intelligence and security community. Given the limited public disclosures relating to this aspect of security operations and its potential import for developing our understanding of specific violations and the infrastructure of apartheid repression, this was a particularly important document. SAHA made requests for this document to DOJ, NIA and the auditor general's office.

Having at first failed to locate the document, it was eventually found with related correspondence among the 34 boxes being held by NIA; once 'reviewed' by CDRC, access was refused by the director general of DOJ on the basis that:

> the disclosure [of] the documents referred to will reveal information pertaining to expenditure incurred with respect of military tactics or strategy or military exercises or operations undertaken in preparation of hostilities or the connection with the detection, prevention, suppression or curtailment of subversive or hostile activities as well as expenditure incurred in respect of the obtaining of information from confidential sources.[115]

Access was therefore denied in terms of provisions contained in section 41 of PAIA, i.e. in the interests of the 'defence, security and international relations of the Republic'. This blanket refusal is revealing, as it suggests that disclosure of apartheid era covert funding could compromise contemporary operations, which in turn raises a number of interesting questions about the extent of the continuities from past operations in terms of strategies and tactics employed by post-1994 security agencies involved in covert operations. Curiously, SAHA received correspondence from NIA six months after Pikoli had refused access to the document, stating that the report contained information on third parties (i.e. other state departments) and that NIA was going through the process of third-party notification in terms of section 47 of PAIA. NIA undertook to revert back to SAHA on this matter, but never did.[116]

The TRC's human rights violation database

The TRC developed a relational database as a way of capturing and analysing the array of data generated and collected by it. It included 'testimony from victims' statements, testimony taken at hearings, investigation material, transcripts of section 29 hearings, submissions made by institutions and individuals, and research and corroborative material'.[117] As with other intellectual property generated by the commission, the database is the responsibility of DOJ. As far as is known, since being handed over to the department, no effort has been made to preserve this valuable resource or make it publicly available.

In March 2006 an application for access to the database was submitted.[118] SAHA specifically stressed that it did not want access to any personal information, but rather to fields of data, such as types, locations and dates of violations. This would provide an opportunity for further quantitative analyses that had not been undertaken by the TRC. SAHA made it clear to DOJ that it was in contact with the individuals who had designed the database and who could advise on how to mask fields containing personal information.

The request was refused on the basis that the database contained personal information. SAHA immediately submitted its appeal, pointing out that the department had failed to apply its mind in terms of exercising this exemption, as SAHA had specifically stated that it did not want personal information. Remarkably, DOJ did not contact SAHA to discuss the request. Instead — allegedly on the advice of technical 'experts' within the department — it decided that masking these fields of data was either not possible or could jeopardise the integrity of the overall database. The DIO, Marlyn Raswiswi, proceeded to issue over 22 000 third-party notifications to everyone whose name appeared on the database. SAHA became aware of this following a series of irate communications from victims demanding to know why SAHA wanted their personal information. When SAHA subsequently secured a copy of the letter sent out by DOJ, it was shocked to find that it stated that 'Kate Allan of SAHA requests access to all your personal information'. This was, of course, in complete contradiction to the request submitted. The minister never provided a formal response to the appeal, but noted around one year later upon a complaint to the SAHRC that the request was not granted because the 'masking of information … entails creating a new customer-tailored record which is different to severing parts of the record'. DOJ had not contacted the individuals who created the database.

When SAHA contacted the DIO, she alleged that she had sent the notices some six months earlier in response to SAHA's original request; it was apparent that this was not the case, because, although she had dated the notices March 2006, they were in fact not received by the individuals until August of that year. SAHA secured a meeting with the department in late 2006, at which it was apparent that the official concerned knew that she had seriously erred, and she indicated that she would take steps to facilitate removal of the personal information with a view to providing access. Nevertheless, SAHA highlighted its concern about the ramifications of the misrepresentations contained in its third-party notifications and requested that she contact those persons who were likely to have received the notices (some thousands of notices were returned to sender as the addresses utilised would have been collected by the TRC up to ten years previously); the DIO alleged that this would be an unreasonable diversion of resources. Despite requests for the department to rectify this situation, no action had been taken almost a year after the misleading letters were sent out and no final decision with regard to accessing the database had been communicated.

Individual TRC case files and other TRC materials

Ahmed Timol, Steve Biko, the Gugulethu 7, Boikie Thlapi and Dulcie September

The TRC made clear recommendations that victims and families of victims should have unfettered access to their own files, 'regardless of whether they are publicly available or not'.[119] SAHA's experience in this regard has been somewhat inconsistent. In 2002 it submitted requests on behalf of victims' families for the TRC's case files on two high-profile activists, Ahmed Timol and Steve Biko, who died in the custody of the security police in 1971 and 1977, respectively.[120] The file on Timol could not be located, and was refused in terms of section 23 of PAIA; this raised further concerns about the integrity of the collection. In the Biko matter, full access to over 8,000 pages of records was granted, which included comprehensive case files on Biko from DOJ's Directorate of Security Legislation.

Subsequent requests for individual case files have also had mixed results: a request for access to the case file on the murders of the Gugulethu 7[121] was conditionally granted, allowing SAHA to view the files and submit more specific requests for the records. A request for the case file of Boikie Thlapi, a young activist who was last seen beaten and bleeding on the floor of a police station in the Western Transvaal, was also submitted. As with the Timol case, the TRC files could not be located and were refused in terms of section 23.[122] In both matters, the requests were made on behalf of interested organisations and not the victims' families.

A request for access to the TRC investigation file on Dulcie September on behalf

11/09/06 11:41 FAX 0466227122   Spirals Trust   ☑01

justice

Ks Third party notification

Department:
Justice and Constitutional Development
REPUBLIC OF SOUTH AFRICA
Private Bag X81, Pretoria, 0001 – Tel: 012 – 315 1730, Fax: 012 – 357 8004
Momentum Building, 329 Pretorius Street, Pretoria, 0002
Please quote our reference number in all correspondence

Our reference:	7/6/9 Allan K (2)
Enquiries:	Ms M M Raswiswi
E-mail:	MRaswiswi@justice.gov.za
Date:	24 March 2006

Dear Sir/Madam

NOTICE TO THIRD PARTY OF A REQUEST IN TERMS OF SECTION 47 OF THE PROMOTION OF ACCESS TO INFORMATION ACT, 2000 (ACT NO. 2 OF 2000)

I refer to a request to have access to information in terms of the Promotion of Access to Information Act, 2000 (Act No. 2 of 2000):

a. You are hereby informed that the Deputy Information Officer is considering a request for access to information. This notice serves to confirm our correspondence with Ms K Allan from the South African History Archives.

b. The description of the record(s) requested are as follows:
    • All your personal information that is on the Truth and Reconciliation Commission's Victims database.

c. The name of the requester is:
    • Ms K Allan from the South African History Archives.

d. You may within 21 days after receipt hereof inform the Deputy Information Officer at the abovementioned address/fax number/telephone number or via e-mail by:
    (i)   Making a written or oral representations to the Information Officer why the requester for access should be refused; or
    (ii) Give written consent for the disclosure of the information to the requester.

Regards

M M RASWISWI (Ms)
DEPUTY INFORMATION OFFICER

HIV/AIDS is a murderer ✂ bring it to justice

Figure 7: Correspondence sent by the Department of Justice to 22,000 South Africans who submitted statements to the TRC, claiming that SAHA wanted access to their personal data in the TRC database – something SAHA had explicitly stated it did not want.

of the September family was rejected[123] on the basis that information contained in the files had been supplied in confidence (in terms of section 37 of PAIA); this was a direct reference to the materials supplied to the TRC by the French authorities. The matter was subsequently dealt with as part of the '34 boxes' saga and, once again, a decision was taken as part of the out-of-court settlement to deny access. It is evident that the materials requested did indeed include statements and other evidence collected during the official French police investigation, which includes statements containing untested allegations. Whether or not this justifies the blanket refusal to access all the documents in the TRC, however, remains moot.

In another case, SAHA was initially refused access to a TRC case file relating to the murder of an Umkhonto we Sizwe member in KwaZulu-Natal in the early 1990s.[124] In this matter, the related criminal investigation remains (at least in theory) live. Details of the criminal investigation were divulged to the TRC investigators, and it was this information that family now wanted to access. However, as in the September matter, the investigation file allegedly contained information and untested allegations about third parties, and the request was rejected in terms of sections 37 and 38 of PAIA (i.e. the protection of confidential information and the protection of the safety of individuals). SAHA appealed the case and, to its surprise, in late June 2007 the Ministry of Justice overturned the appeal, granting access to the file. It is not clear what sections of the file (and investigation materials) have been withheld or whether access to the file can be interpreted as indicative that no further investigation will be conducted into the murder.

Listing of video recordings of TRC hearings

In October 2001 a request for a listing of video recordings of TRC hearings that were in the custody of the National Archives was submitted. Some eight months later, SAHA was informed by the director general of DAC that the lists had been compiled by TRC staff, but that SAHA should approach DOJ for these records.[125] The request was not transferred by DAC as required by PAIA, and relevant sections of the Act were not quoted in correspondence. The national archivist subsequently undertook to provide a more detailed response in writing,[126] which he did. He pointed out that DAC was not refusing the request, but advised that an approach be made to DOJ. He also pointed out that this request touched on 'difficulties with the intellectual copyright claims of the South African Broadcasting Corporation'.[127] As an aside, five years later, questions about copyright and the related utilisation of the TRC's audio-visual records remain contested and unresolved.

In late July 2002 SAHA submitted an internal appeal to Minister Ngubane, pointing out that DAC had responded to the initial request five months after the due date and had failed to transfer the request as required (even though SAHA contested that the matter should have been transferred). SAHA insisted that the National Archives was the competent authority to deal with the request, as the materials requested were located there.[128]

No response was received within the stipulated time period, prompting SAHA's attorneys to warn Minister Ngubane that SAHA would be forced to litigate in an instance of a 'deemed refusal' (i.e. if the Ministry of Arts and Culture did not respond) and urged him to deal with the appeal.[129] The Ministry responded in early September 2002, saying the minister had referred the matter to DAC,[130] which in the following week informed SAHA that the matter had been referred to the Office of the State Attorney.[131]

In early October 2002 the minister responded, granting SAHA full access to the video listing. By doing so, he implicitly acknowledged that the decision to access these records was vested in the National Archives and that the suggestion to approach DOJ in this instance was unnecessary. This would accord with the TRC's own recommendations that only 'in the case of record categories identified as requiring protection, [should] the National Archivist refer requests for access to the Department of Justice'.[132] The minister, however, defended the national archivist's initial response, pointing out that while technically his failure to use the correct procedure could be interpreted as a refusal, this was not the intention.[133]

TRC administrative records and testimony and submissions to public hearings

It is important to note before concluding that, while the restrictions were minimal, SAHA did gain unfettered access to records contained in the TRC archives. Several requests for TRC administrative records were submitted by SAHA during 2002; these included a request for access to the first sets of minutes of TRC commissioners' meetings[134] and a request for the human resources policy adopted by the commission. These requests were granted in both instances, albeit not within the stipulated decision-making time frames. SAHA also secured access to records that were generated through public hearing processes. These include testimonies made at the human rights violation hearings into the January 1991 Sebokeng night vigil massacre,[135] as well as submissions that were made to the TRC during the public hearing processes.[136] This includes a full set of submissions made to the business hearings.[137]

The 'politics' and practicalities of accessing the TRC archive

In line with TRC recommendations, SAHA has consistently promoted an opening of the TRC archive and called for widening access to related apartheid era records that have remained undisclosed. The records of the commission and its report provide a framework for further engagement, for taking the work of the TRC and its recommendations forward. Efficient and effective access to the archive is in the national interest and of critical importance if South Africa is to deepen its understanding of what happened in the past and why.

Despite its importance, there has been remarkably little support for this call, which in turn reflects a general disaffection towards dealing with the TRC's unfinished business. Some aspects of this, especially those relating to reparation and prosecution, have generated considerable public attention and debate. In terms of the archive, however, there has been only very limited interest; most of the attention in the immediate post-TRC era has come from foreign academics and researchers.

SAHA's efforts in trying to access TRC records have had some positive results, but have too often resulted in unnecessarily lengthy, hostile and litigious engagements. In all such instances, SAHA has secured favourable settlements, forcing DOJ and DAC to provide records that they had previously refused to disclose. Despite this, last minute out-of-court settlements have ensured that no legal precedents have been set, enabling continued employment of the blocking tactics. In each settlement, it was understandable to assume that, at least, some clear guidelines had been established on access to particular categories of documents; however, recent decisions indicate that little progress has been made. Problems experienced with several access requests to DOJ constitute the bedrock of an official complaint about the department submitted in July 2007 to the SAHRC. Given the department's role in mainstreaming access to justice throughout government, these shortcomings in relation to how it handles requests for TRC records suggest DOJ is not currently competent to fulfil this role.

DOJ retains primary control over decisions regarding access. The committee established under David Porogo no longer meets, but it is clear that although decisions are now taken without meetings, DOJ officials continue to rely on interactions with both the National Archives and NIA for advice and assistance. This experience suggests that the department is not competent to manage the access process, and SAHA supports a call for this responsibility to be officially delegated to the National Archives.

The National Archives will ultimately be responsible for processing and preserving the TRC archive. The absence of a clear mandate to proceed with this (and requisite resourcing) has left the archive in a parlous state, which in turn has clearly compounded problems in terms of determining and facilitating access. The situation is further compounded by the absence of detailed finding aids, which perhaps inevitably results in delays and failures to locate certain documents.

In October 2006 the national archivist confirmed that additional resources will be made available to revamp and resource the work of the National Archives. This will include the construction of a new building and facilities. Although this process will include the processing of the TRC archive, it is unlikely that we will see an improved access regime until 2011 or 2012 at the earliest.[138] The legacy of South Africa's TRC continues to be eroded.

Work carried out by SAHA for the newly published biography of Desmond Tutu, *Rabble-Rouser for Peace*, shows that although meaningful access to the security files of the apartheid era is difficult, the National Archives can still produce unexpected nuggets for researchers. The author of the book, John Allen, tells the story.

Box 2.3: Researching Desmond Tutu

When I began work on my Tutu biography, one of the questions I most wanted answers to was how many attempts the security forces had made on Desmond Tutu's life and why they had not pursued them more seriously. The archives did not get me the answers I wanted — which was not unexpected. What was unexpected was finding that Tutu had come under the scrutiny of South Africa's principal intelligence agency — the Bureau of State Security, or BOSS — a decade earlier than either he or anyone in the church had known.

The then Bishop Tutu first rose to prominence after he became general secretary of the South African Council of Churches, and during 1979 and 1980 increasingly began to confront the apartheid state. He became the target of security force harassment of various kinds, but the first clear evidence of his life being threatened was during a visit he paid to the Venda bantustan in 1981, when he and the Methodist leader, Peter Storey, were forced into the bush and roughed up while being expelled from the territory.

The best evidence I had for later attempts to kill Tutu were the sabotage of a car at Johannesburg airport in 1987, telephone calls to Tutu's office in early 1989 — during which an ex-convict said that he had been offered money to assassinate him — and a possible attempt after the funeral of Communist Party general secretary Chris Hani in 1993.

Encouraged and guided by the staff of SAHA — to whom I was pointed by the Department of Historical Papers at Wits University — I asked SAHA to submit requests for any material in security force archives that mentioned Tutu, his movements or security force activity around him in the relevant periods. I followed up with an inquiry that I thought had an even more remote chance of turning up anything useful: did the National Archives have any record of how Tutu was once refused, then granted, a passport long before he became a public figure?

We drew a blank on the first requests. SAHA told me that the archives of the old South African Defence Force (the apartheid army) 'work on requests diligently, but under-resourcing means it still takes a long time'. The South African National Defence Force eventually reported finding nothing. SAHA reported that NIA was 'hopelessly slow', and nothing came of that request. But SAHA was able to determine for me that there had once been at least three separate security police files on Tutu. If they still existed, they have not been found. SAHA emailed to me that:

The police records (which included the Security police ones) were in such a bad way that they were transferred to the National Archives and when we saw the National Archivist … he told us that it would probably take a couple of years to get them in order … but that if we drew our specific requests to their attention again as a group, they could take a look to see what the prospects were of recovering individual files before they've all been comprehensively organised.

In the end, the principal Tutu security files SAHA accessed were DOJ's files on Tutu, apparently kept for the purposes of determining whether he should be put under restriction orders.

The surprise came when SAHA sent me a rare find from the files of what used to be known as the Department of the Interior. I had told SAHA:

You may recall that one of the issues I was looking into was why, after Tutu was refused a passport to work for the World Council of Churches in 1971, the government changed its mind when he wrote to [prime minister John] Vorster and asked him to reconsider the decision. I have just dug up a file I received on a visit to the National Archives in 2000, which indicates that he applied for the passport on July 21, 1971, in Ladybrand in the Free State, and Pretoria refused the application on August 20. Of most interest is that the Bantu Affairs Dept recommended the issue of a passport, but Interior refused it after the application was sent for a police report. It seems from the record that the police issued an 'unfavourable report' on Tutu between July 20 and mid-August. Tutu then wrote to Vorster later in the year, the matter was referred to the Interior Minister, and he got his passport early in 1972.

The document that SAHA's inquiries turned up in the Department of the Interior's archives was a letter of 22 December 1971 from Vorster's intelligence adviser at BOSS. It revealed that BOSS had advised against the issue of a passport in August. In response to Tutu's letter to Vorster, BOSS reiterated its opposition:

Tutu wants to give the impression in his letter to the Honourable Prime Minister that he can be an asset to South Africa if he is allowed to take up the TEF post [the Theological Education Fund was associated with the World Council of Churches]. Given his political attitude to the South African system so far, I very much doubt he will employ his energy in favour of the Republic of South Africa.

There was no indication of what BOSS believed Tutu's 'political attitude' to be or how it had established his views. However, as I write in *Rabble-Rouser*, it appeared that summer holiday fever came to Tutu's rescue — the letter arrived at the Department of the Interior between Christmas and New Year, and by the time it received attention, the interior minister had approved Tutu's passport.

The discovery of the BOSS letter added useful perspective to how the apartheid government saw Tutu, long before he developed a high-profile political role. More than that, it showed how diligent work in archives can produce the most unexpected evidence from the most unlikely sources, which, when pieced together with material from other sources, can provide vivid insights into the past.

John Allen
Author of *Rabble-Rouser for Peace*

3

In the Dark: Seeking Information about South Africa's Nuclear Energy Programme

David Fig

Introduction

The nuclear industry is, by its nature, secretive and opaque, wherever it is found. The South African industry is no different. A major element of this climate is the secret proliferation of nuclear weapons during the apartheid period (see chapter 4). Other elements promoting secrecy include the need to safeguard fissile materials, the need to curb trafficking in equipment that may lead to proliferation, and the need to ensure the integrity and security of nuclear facilities. However, the climate of secrecy has also been used to mask the economics of the nuclear industry, its safety record, the health and safety history of its workers, and the good governance (or lack thereof) of its controlling and regulatory bodies.

With plans for the expansion of the nuclear energy industry currently under way, it is essential for the public to ensure that any departures from transparency are addressed.[1] Under apartheid, the state had no accountability to its citizens in this regard. However, with the new democratic state striving to extend and enhance the values of consultation, participation and openness, secrecy militates against public involvement in fair decision making. The expansion of nuclear plants and facilities threatens to return citizens to the era in which they faced an intransigent security state, one that had little regard for building democratic political culture or respecting the rights of all citizens.

The nuclear energy industry in contemporary South Africa cannot shake off the tendency to defy democracy and transparency. Implicated in this are a number of state institutions. These include the energy utility Eskom, the Nuclear Energy Corporation of South Africa (NECSA),[2] the Department of Minerals and Energy (DME), the Department of Public Enterprises, the National Nuclear Regulator (NNR),[3] and the National Electricity Regulator. Pebble Bed Modular Reactor (Pty) Ltd (hereafter PBMR Ltd), which is developing new-generation nuclear technology, is a company with a majority shareholding by state institutions (Eskom, the Industrial Development Corporation and the government). The documentation initiated by all these bodies should be available to requesters and, like the documentation of other state bodies that are subject to the Promotion of Access to Information Act No. 2 of 2000 (PAIA),[4] should be in the public domain.

Why would the public want access to such documentation? The provision of electricity in South Africa is a highly politicised issue. Citizens require information to understand how the country's energy policy is being implemented, particularly in relation to choices of technology. A nuclear revival — at the expense of alternative technologies — is one that requires intensive public scrutiny. This is particularly the case when the state intends to support the nuclear revival with tens of billions of taxpayers' rands, and where the risks are a cause of public concern.

Citizens are also being faced with electricity outages, which were said by government to be the result of power shortages or even sabotage. While it is true that South Africa's electricity demand is rapidly approaching its supply, at the time of writing this had yet to happen. When the cuts affecting Cape Town during the summer of 2005/06 — related to problems mainly experienced at the Koeberg power station — were investigated by the National Electricity Regulator, they were instead attributed to inadequate maintenance, negligence and failure by Eskom to conform to operating procedures.[5] Nevertheless, power shortages have been offered as the reason for scaring consumers into accepting further nuclear power.

Nuclear energy has also been promoted as 'clean' and carbon friendly, despite the intractable problems of nuclear waste and the fact that the entire nuclear fuel cycle, a series of operations from uranium mining through to reactor decommissioning, makes a considerable contribution to carbon emissions.

There has yet to be a formal national debate interrogating the industry's claims and determining why, of all forms of electricity provision, nuclear has almost privileged access to government and decision makers. The potential of renewable forms of energy has yet to be unleashed in full. The comparative economics of each technology needs to be verified through full disclosure, enabling the public to have a greater ability to make informed choices.

The health of former nuclear industry workers has come under closer scrutiny in recent years. Around 2000 former Pelindaba workers are concerned that their deteriorating health may have occupational causes.[6] Many were subjected to radiation and harmful chemicals. In attempting to follow up, the individual workers have had to obtain their medical records from NECSA. This process has resulted in many delays, as NECSA claims not to have centralised medical files on its employees.

With each proposal for new developments in the industry, changes have been subject to public scrutiny in the form of environmental impact assessments (EIAs), which allow for participation by interested and affected parties. Participation has not always been taken seriously by government, resulting in legal and other challenges to the EIA process. These challenges are indices of the highly controversial nature of the industry. Its claims are contested by a range of civil society organisations, which act as public watchdogs in securing rights to information and good governance in a climate in which 'energy security' is becoming increasingly politicised.

The story told here is one that analyses the history and politics of the nuclear energy industry. It attempts to give some understanding of the current revival of interest in the expansion of this industry. It then relates the difficulties faced by civil society in its insistence that there be full disclosure on a range of relevant issues like health and safety, economics, and corporate governance.

In pursuing these issues, civil society organisations such as the South African History Archive (SAHA), the Freedom of Expression Institute (FXI) and others have been at the forefront of pressing state institutions to reveal information to which the public should be entitled under the law. Their role as champions of the right to know is essential in the democratic process.

A history of nuclear energy in South Africa

Origins of the nuclear energy industry in South Africa

South Africa was drawn into the first phase of the development of the nuclear industry in the United States and Britain immediately after the Second World War. During the war, the Allies had secretly developed nuclear weapons at Los Alamos in New Mexico. Known as the Manhattan Project, the weapons research was initially aimed at beating Nazi Germany in the race to harness nuclear fission to a deliverable weapon.[7] It was believed that the first side to develop such weapons would have an overwhelming advantage in the outcome of the war. However, by the time that the Manhattan Project scientists had tested their weapons in the Nevada Desert, the war in Europe was over. Instead, the weapons were deployed at Hiroshima and Nagasaki in August 1945.[8]

When the war came to an end, there was a short-lived debate about what should happen to these weapons. Many of the physicists who had worked on the bomb felt that they should be placed under the control of the newly formed United Nations Organisation. However, the onset of the Cold War, a result of the deterioration of relations between the emergent superpowers, the United States and the Soviet Union, put paid to any multilateralist sentiments. The burgeoning tensions created the opportunity for the United States and Britain to retain control of the weapons technology, which was never internationalised. As the Cold War intensified, so it became imperative for the Soviet Union under Stalin to obtain its own nuclear weapons. By 1949 this had become a reality, and the nuclear arms race had begun.

The Manhattan Project struggled to source supplies of the fissile material. Of a number of options, uranium seemed to be the most suitable. The uranium for the bombs had been sourced from the then Belgian Congo (now the Democratic Republic of the Congo), but further supplies were limited.[9] The continued interest in developing weapons after the war required the acquisition of substantial and reliable sources. Local scientists were asked to comb the geological literature for any clues, and came up with a field report dating back to 1923 in which it was recorded that substantial amounts of uranium were present as a by-product of the Witwatersrand gold mines.[10] Since there had been no prior commercial value for this mineral, the ore was simply added to the mine dumps and slime dams characteristic of the region.

The US and British governments initiated a USD 46 million programme for uranium exploration. In May 1944, and again late in 1945, geologists were dispatched to South Africa's gold mines to verify the earlier reports. It was concluded that 'present evidence appears to indicate that the Rand may be one of the largest low-grade uranium fields in the world'.[11]

The prime minister at the time, Jan Christian Smuts, was elated with these findings and took a personal interest in following the progress of verifying the extensive presence of uranium. In February 1946 he drafted the relevant scientists and officials into a Uranium Research Committee, which set about monitoring the commercialisation of the mineral. Links were established with experts at various scientific institutions in the United States and Britain. Smuts encouraged the export of uranium samples to laboratories in these countries, and went on a personal mission to meet with General Groves, former head of the Manhattan Project, as well as metallurgists located at the prestigious Massachusetts Institute of Technology who were examining the samples.

The American and British governments were overwhelmed by the results of these investigations, which showed that there were enormous reserves of uranium in the South African gold mines. The recovery of uranium was not regarded as a difficult technology, and it became very easy to establish separation plants at the mines. The governments of the United States, Britain and South Africa entered into a secret agreement that allowed the weapons-owning states to import almost all of South Africa's uranium output. Two-thirds would be bought by the United States and one-third by Britain. A fixed price was agreed on that would take into account the costs faced by the mining industry in separating the uranium, the repayment of loans covering this work and the guaranteed margin of profit.[12]

The gold-mining companies were extremely happy with this arrangement. The mining industry had been dislocated by the war, as the rail system had to prioritise the movement of war materiel, and there were bottlenecks in the steel industry. At the same time, the mining industry was keen to develop important new goldfields in the northern

Orange Free State. The windfall from the exploitation of uranium resources, which lasted for a decade, made this more economically feasible.

Smuts was eager to capitalise further on the role of South Africa beyond being simply a supplier of uranium. The mandate of the Uranium Research Committee was to oversee the use of uranium for export, but Smuts conceptualised a broader institution charged with the country's nuclear research programme. Instead of placing it within the existing Council for Scientific and Industrial Research, which specialised in applied research, Smuts felt that the model used in countries like the United States, Britain and Canada of a separate entity should apply in South Africa. He piloted legislation through Parliament foreseeing the establishment of the Atomic Energy Board (AEB) on 1 January 1949.[13] Ironically, in the whites-only general elections in May 1948, Smuts lost his seat and his party lost its majority. The era of apartheid was ushered in under the premiership of D.F. Malan. The launching of the AEB thus coincided with the coming to power of the apartheid government.

Figure 1: Aerial photograph of the Nuclear Energy Corporation of South Africa.
Source: supplied by NECSA

The nuclear industry during the apartheid era

The offices and workshops of the AEB first occupied buildings in downtown Pretoria. The operations of the board were then relocated to a farm west of Pretoria called Pelindaba (a Zulu term meaning 'the discussion is over', signifying the industry's secretive nature). Pelindaba became the home of the first research reactor acquired by the AEB. This occurred as a result of the 'Atoms for Peace' programme initiated by US President Dwight

D. Eisenhower, whose efforts to spread nuclear research technology were aimed at distracting certain allies from proliferating nuclear weapons. The reactor became known as SAFARI-1, and has largely run on weapons-grade uranium (90 per cent enriched) since being commissioned in 1965.[14]

The industry received strong support from all apartheid prime ministers, especially H.F. Verwoerd and B.J. Vorster. It was Vorster who announced in Parliament in 1970 that South Africa planned to develop its own uranium enrichment capacity. This involved splitting the AEB into two corporations: one involved in broad research (the Atomic Energy Corporation—AEC), the other dedicated to the enrichment project (the Uranium Enrichment Corporation). The latter was established at Valindaba ('the talking has ceased'), a property neighbouring Pelindaba. This became the site of conversion, pilot enrichment and, ultimately, full-scale enrichment plants. Vorster stressed that the logic of the programme was to enable South Africa to create value through local beneficiation of the uranium, and that the programme would be dedicated to the peaceful use of nuclear energy.[15]

The training of South African scientists was conducted in countries like the United States, Britain, West Germany, France and Sweden, and there was considerable nuclear cooperation with Israel and Taiwan. Most of the accolades for collaboration on reactor research went to the United States. Dr A.J.A. 'Ampie' Roux, the first AEB president, explained:

> We can ascribe our degree of advancement today in large measure to the training and assistance so willingly provided by the USA during the early years of our nuclear program. [South Africa's research reactor] is of American design, [and] much of the nuclear equipment installed at Pelindaba is of American origin, while even our nuclear philosophy, although unmistakeably our own, owes much to the thinking of [American] nuclear scientists.[16]

Yet much of the inspiration for the enrichment project was a result of extensive nuclear collaboration with West Germany, despite later denials by South African scientists, who claimed that the enrichment process they used was entirely home-grown.[17]

On the surface, the state was putting into place a number of the key components of the nuclear fuel chain. It would not take long before the electricity utility, Eskom, bought coastal land within 28 kilometers of the city of Cape Town in order to construct the country's first nuclear power station. Different European consortiums vied for the construction contract, but with increasing misgivings about apartheid, the Dutch-led consortium was forced to withdraw after an unfavourable parliamentary vote. The prize went to a French-led consortium instead, because parliamentarians in Paris had done nothing to disturb the progress of the project, and construction was initiated in 1977.[18]

Using a Westinghouse-based model, the French built two pressurised water reactors on the Koeberg site, each with the capacity to generate 965 MWe. These came on-stream in 1983 and 1984 respectively, and to date represent Africa's only nuclear power station. The reactors have reached almost half their operating life, and should be decommissioned around 2030.

To accommodate the radioactive waste from the power station, a disposal site was identified at Vaalputs in the Northern Cape province, over 450 kilometers from Koeberg.[19] At Vaalputs, only the low- and intermediate-level wastes are stored in drums buried in pits close to the earth's surface. The highly radioactive waste — mostly consisting of spent fuel — is kept on site at Koeberg in storage ponds. Initially, this measure was an interim one, meant to last for 10–15 years in order to cool the spent fuel efficiently so that it could be stored in silos at Vaalputs. However, this has not happened. Instead, the holding racks in the storage ponds have continually been rearranged in order to accommodate further spent fuel rods. The national policy on radioactive waste management took a further 20 years to materialise, and remains agnostic about solutions for high-level radioactive waste. Vaalputs itself was forced to close for a period in 1996, when the NNR discovered over 40 deviations from licensed procedures.[20] The AEC built a fuel fabrication plant at Pelindaba and also attempted to develop plans for what might have become a reprocessing facility at Gouriqua on the southern Cape coast. Reprocessing is the technology used for removing the plutonium and other radioactive elements from spent fuel used up in nuclear power stations. It was clear that South Africa was aiming to put in place all stages of the nuclear fuel chain.

There are two vulnerable moments in the fuel chain: the enrichment stage and the reprocessing stage. If these technologies are available, it may be possible to divert fissile material into weapons proliferation. With the completion of the enrichment facility at Valindaba, apartheid South Africa did precisely this, diverting enriched uranium into a systematic programme to manufacture nuclear weapons. This came at a time when the apartheid state was under increasing pressure both internally and externally. From the 1973 Durban strikes, which initiated the rebirth of a long-dormant trade union movement, to the June 1976 Soweto youth uprising, the capacity of the state to repress rebellion had begun to reach its limits. The growth of the black consciousness movement under the charismatic leadership of Steve Biko, the swelling of the membership of exiled liberation movements by an exodus of young activists and extensive student unrest added to the state's vulnerability. In 1974 the Portuguese dictatorship fell, and by the following year the neighbouring ex-colonies of Angola and Mozambique had won independence under the Marxist leadership of liberation movements. Wars of liberation were also under way in Namibia and Zimbabwe.

The apartheid state's response was not only greater internal and external militarisation, including murderous raids on neighbouring countries, but also the decision to build nuclear weapons: 'We'll have the bomb if we want,' intoned cabinet minister Owen Horwood at an election meeting in 1977. The bravado masked the fact that the weapons were crude and the air force lacked suitable means to deploy them. The question arose as to the identity of the potential victims — would the bomb be dropped on Luanda, Lusaka, or even Soweto? Any of these options would have been disastrous, given the ongoing Cold War and the potential for retaliation from the Soviet Union or China. Later, the bomb makers justified their manufacture as a deterrent. The plan was that if apartheid ended up under grave attack or threat, possession of the weapons could be demonstrated as a means to extend the power of white rule.

In the end, as Chandré Gould shows in chapter 4, some rationality prevailed and the weapons of mass destruction were dismantled at the turn of the 1990s. President F.W. de Klerk was still in power when he announced in March 1993 that the programme had been ended, the weapons decommissioned, the uranium returned to Pelindaba under safeguard and all the documentation destroyed. South Africa rejoined the International Atomic Energy Agency (IAEA), signed the Treaty on the Non-Proliferation of Nuclear Weapons, and allowed for the full international inspection of its nuclear facilities.

The nuclear policy of the ANC

On coming to power, the African National Congress (ANC) government generally upheld the stance assumed by its predecessor on non-proliferation. It drew on the kudos obtained from South Africa being the first state to renounce its nuclear weapons status. It resumed the Africa seat at IAEA in Vienna and went further in introducing domestic legislation safeguarding its non-proliferation policy. It also promoted the Treaty of Pelindaba, aimed at making the African continent a nuclear weapons-free zone. However, the state apparatus has, especially from 1998, actively promoted the expansion of the nuclear energy industry.

A few months before the first democratic elections, the ANC Science and Technology Desk in the Western Cape, together with a local NGO, the Environmental Monitoring Group, promoted a conference on the future of nuclear policy in South Africa. The conference was addressed by Trevor Manuel, then head of the ANC's Department of Economic Planning. Speakers included opponents and proponents of nuclear energy. Officially, the ANC took no policy position on the question, leaving it open to future debate. However, Manuel promised that 'we shall not tolerate circumstances in which policy on issues as critical as a nuclear programme be confined to experts in dark, smoke-filled rooms. The debate must be public and the actions transparent'.[21]

Two years later, DME hosted an Energy Summit, with wide attendance by a number of stakeholders, including civil society organisations. The Energy Summit was one of the steps taken in catalysing a White Paper on Energy, a document signalling the direction of policy and legislative intentions arising from this policy. By the time of the summit, the state nuclear research entity, the AEC, had significantly scaled down its operations and staffing. The future of the Koeberg nuclear energy complex was also somewhat uncertain. In the final White Paper, published in July 1998, it was explicitly stated that any expansion of the industry would occur within 'the context of an integrated energy policy planning process with due consideration given to all relevant legislation, and … subject to structured participation and consultation with all stakeholders'.[22]

Other signalled intentions were that there would be restructuring of the nuclear industry 'necessary to ensure the environmental sustainability and cost-efficiency of South Africa's energy economy, while seeking maximum benefit from historical investment'.[23] It was also indicated that restructuring would be done in 'a participatory fashion', and that there would be a thorough investigation into Koeberg's technical and financial performance, which 'will be made available for public scrutiny and comment before a final decision is made on the future of Koeberg'.[24]

In practice, none of the promised consultation or participation has materialised, and the nuclear policy continues to be crafted in the 'dark, smoke-filled rooms' that Manuel supposedly rejected. The drafting of the Nuclear Energy Act No. 46 of 1999 and the National Nuclear Regulator Act No. 47 of 1999 was designed in DME by officials whose primary consultation was with the Chamber of Mines. The period allotted for public comment on the National Radioactive Waste Management Policy and Strategy was so short that the minister was forced to extend it for an extra 90 days to accommodate public comment.[25] Very few of the concerns expressed by the public were reflected in the final policy document.

There has been no broad stakeholder consultation on the future of the nuclear industry; neither has this applied specifically to the future of Koeberg, as promised in the 1998 White Paper. Most of the decisions about nuclear development have occurred within DME and the Department of Public Enterprises, without wide consultation with other departments. Much of the decision making has been from the top down, without any stakeholder participation. What appears to be government policy has bypassed even the policy processes within the ruling ANC.[26]

This lack of transparency indicates how, in the space of the last decade, the executive branch of government has come to dominate national policymaking. Cabinet has become susceptible to the special pleading and some of the false claims of the industry, securing for it a highly subsidised place in the sun at the expense of more sustainable technologies, human health and the environment.

The revival of the nuclear industry in South Africa

In practice, the local renaissance has been led by those promoting the pebble bed modular reactor (PBMR). This is a high-temperature reactor using helium gas as a coolant. The fuel takes the form of small particles of 10 per cent enriched uranium encased in graphite spheres approximately the size of billiard balls. These 'pebbles' are introduced to the reactor and removed when spent. The reactors are designed to produce a small amount of energy (165 MWe) and therefore in most cases would only be viable when more than one module are grouped together. Its promoters foresee them being built alongside a factory or in a residential area. The waste would be stored on site for the life of the reactor. Claims have been made by the developers that the reactor is 'inherently safe'. Similar reactors have operated in the United States and Germany, but in both cases research into this model was discontinued. The South African version has been based on the German prototype and royalties continue to be paid to German companies. Plans for a Chinese rival high-temperature reactor will provide the South African manufacturers with considerable competition.

Ironically, the idea for a PBMR was mooted by a group of researchers who had originally worked on the South African nuclear bomb. Their first task was to persuade Eskom to support the project. In 1998, the company PBMR Ltd was formed. Initially, this was a full subsidiary of Eskom, but gradually other investors were drawn in. These included the state Industrial Development Corporation; the US reactor operating company Exelon; and British Nuclear Fuels Ltd (BNFL), the almost bankrupt state-owned reactor company. Exelon subsequently decided to withdraw its investment, while BNFL sold its reactor-building operation (Westinghouse) to Toshiba, which currently acts as the only foreign partner.

As in most cases of nuclear development, the prototype has been subjected to numerous design changes, huge cost overruns and extensive delays. The industry's intention is to build a demonstration plant on the Koeberg site and a fuel-manufacturing plant within the Pelindaba complex. In 2005, PBMR Ltd announced that the costs of these two developments would amount to ZAR 14.9 billion (USD 2 billion), most of which would have to be public investment. This figure does not include any operational costs, nor does it cover decommissioning at the end of the reactor's life. The aim was to have the plant operating by 2008, with commercial replication starting in 2013.

By March 2007 the EIA was still far from complete, as was the licensing of the demonstration model by NNR. The EIA has had to be scrapped and restarted, partly because of challenges from civil society[27] and partly because the company had substantially altered the design. Despite being incomplete, PBMR Ltd awarded tenders for the construction, the provision of turbines, the delivery of graphite for the fuel and other functions.

One of the key institutions safeguarding good governance in the industry is NNR. Created as an independent statutory body, the functioning of the regulator depends on its impartiality. In 2005, when there was a vacancy for the position of the regulator's chief executive officer (CEO), the cabinet appointed Maurice Magugumela over the heads of the regulator's board. Magugumela had been the former safety and licensing manager of PBMR Ltd. The credibility and independence of the regulator are therefore now at issue.

Although Eskom has signed a letter of intent to purchase the first 24 production models of the PBMR, there has been disquiet about this within the Eskom board. The letter of intent is qualified by a statement requiring Eskom to opt for the least-cost technology. It is doubtful whether the PBMRs will ever be the lowest cost option, yet the support of the cabinet for the technology may neutralise these provisos, forcing the utility to purchase these reactors. After the state has invested so heavily in the technology, it will be difficult to write it off for economic reasons.

Why has South Africa chosen to develop a technology already abandoned by more sophisticated nuclear industries in the North? Both the United States and Germany have desisted from this path. The South African programme seeks to take advantage of the so-called nuclear renaissance, whereby, after a long period following the accidents at Three Mile Island and Chernobyl, orders for nuclear reactors dried up completely. Nuclear energy programmes became unpopular in most of Europe, with referendums or laws reversing nuclear developments in countries like Germany, Austria, Sweden and Italy. No orders have been placed for new reactors in the United States. However, since the turn of the century, there have been new reactor orders in the Russian Federation, China, Japan, South Korea, India and Finland. The South African industry is confident that it can tap export markets in places like Turkey, Indonesia and the rest of the African continent. PBMR Ltd has also been linked to a venture aiming to produce PBMRs in the United States if approved by that country's regulator. President George W. Bush is busy implementing an energy strategy that will offer government subsidies to reactor builders. Without considerable state support, the economics of the pebble bed make little sense.

While South Africa is hoping to take advantage of any niche demand for small third-generation reactors, it is also bearing most of the development risk. This could backfire, something that Exelon realised in its decision to disinvest. If so, the experiment would have occurred without considerable financial burdens for the North.

Ultimately, even South Africa may become impatient with the PBMR's tardy delivery. Pressures already exist for the building of further pressurised water reactors, and the minister of public enterprises, Alec Erwin, a staunch advocate of the pebble bed, felt that future large-scale electricity needs can only be met through ordering a reactor that can deliver an output of around 1,000 MWe. Having teamed up with Westinghouse in the PBMR project, the government is considering the feasibility of ordering one of Westinghouse's new AP1000 reactors.[28]

Questioning the logic of the nuclear renaissance

The state has offered various arguments in support of the nuclear revival: (i) nuclear power is clean, green and carbon friendly; (ii) South Africa's future electricity needs cannot be met by renewables or energy saving; (iii) the nuclear industry is evidence of the country's technological advancement; and (iv) there is no risk of weapons proliferation. However, these points are all based on mythology rather than hard facts.

Nuclear power generates radioactive waste, whose most lethal component, plutonium, has to be insulated from the environment for approximately 244,000 years, the time it would take for its radioactivity to be diminished to safe levels. When we consider that human beings (*homo sapiens*) only emerged 35,000 years ago, have only been engaged in agriculture for the past 10,000 years, and have only been urbanised for the past 5,000 years, questions arise as to how these long-lasting radioactive residues are to be managed over their hazardous lifetime. The problem of managing the highly radioactive waste has not been fully resolved anywhere in the world.

On the question of carbon emissions, it is true that the reactors themselves emit little carbon dioxide. However, if one considers the entire fuel chain, without which power cannot be generated, it turns out that nuclear energy makes a positive contribution to carbon emissions. This can easily be seen in the very energy-intensive uranium enrichment process, as well as emissions from the mining and milling, reactor construction and decommissioning, and reprocessing stages. It is worth noting that nuclear energy is not recognised as a technology that can earn carbon credits under the provisions of the Kyoto Protocol. This indicates that scientists and politicians linked to the UN climate change negotiations felt that, in order to protect the climate, we should not replace the use of coal, oil or gas with nuclear plants.

Renewables, unlike fossil fuels, are not depleted with use, and are therefore a much smarter long-term option than nuclear. Prices have fallen and many processes have been commercialised, making it possible for those generating renewable electricity domestically to sell surplus power back to the grid. However, in South Africa, state investment in renewables to date has been derisory, despite imminent breakthroughs in the affordability of solar energy (developed at the University of Johannesburg with German support). The new South African National Energy Research Institute has established tertiary training in renewable energy at Stellenbosch University. There is a small commitment on the part of the state to increase the share of renewables in South Africa's energy mix, but this may be a case of too little, too late. Countries like Germany, Spain and Denmark lead the way in terms of the extent to which renewable energy sources are part of their energy mix. German jobs in the renewable energy sector now far outnumber those in the nuclear industry.

While countries may bask in the status of having nuclear technology, we need to ask whether this is the most appropriate path for Africa's development. It certainly generates far fewer jobs than an equivalent investment in renewable energies. It employs a small number of very highly skilled operators and scientists, in comparison with lower-tech energy solutions that can be generated in a decentralised manner throughout every community and where fewer skills are required for maintenance, repair and installation.

The patriotic glee with which certain cabinet ministers have supported the extension of the nuclear power industry is an expression of a technological nationalism. While the current politicians have supported a non-proliferation stance, this same technological nationalism could one day be extended to the reacquisition of nuclear weapons. In September 2006 the intelligence community received with some acclaim an academic presentation that argued for the option of holding nuclear weapons in reserve to face an increasingly dangerous and uncertain world.[29] South Africa's democracy is young and fragile, and there are no guarantees that our current constitutional values will be upheld indefinitely.

Finally, government proponents of the nuclear renaissance argue that this will be a quick fix for the power shortage likely to be experienced by the economy, based on current electricity capacity. Electricity cuts have been intermittent all over the country in the last few years, particularly in cities where the utility has been placed on a commercial footing, and too little has been spent on upgrading and maintaining old equipment. During 2005 a series of incidents, including a fire under a pylon, caused one of the two nuclear reactors at Koeberg to trip. When this happens, power to the grid is disrupted. More seriously, on Christmas Day 2005 it was discovered that the rotor of a generator linked to the second reactor had been damaged by the presence of a misplaced bolt. The plant had to be shut down for some time, pending the sourcing and shipment from France of a replacement rotor in April 2006. This led to more substantial power disruptions throughout the Western Cape, affecting households, industry, services and agriculture. The summer harvests of fruit and wine had to be destroyed. Electric pumps operating sewerage systems failed, and sewerage leaked into wetlands and freshwater bodies important to biodiversity, ravaging their ecosystems for at least the next decade. The growing tourism industry feared that its clients would select other destinations because of the unreliability of the electricity supply. The second unit at Koeberg had to be shut down for some weeks between March and July because its nuclear fuel needed routine replacement. While both plants were shut simultaneously, there were severe electricity cuts at the beginning of the local winter.

On the eve of municipal elections on 1 March 2006 the minister of public enterprises, Alec Erwin, held a press conference during which he stated that the damage at Koeberg had been the result of sabotage. During the same meeting, the minister of minerals and energy, Lindiwe Hendricks, alleged that the actions were an attempt to affect the outcome of the elections. The ministers announced their intention to have the matter investigated by the National Intelligence Agency. The media and trade union response was one of outrage. Minister Erwin went on to deny he had implied sabotage, despite repeated running of the television news clip in which his allegations were audible to all. The major trade union federations, the Congress of South African Trade Unions (COSATU) and Solidarity, sharply criticised ministers Erwin and Hendricks. The regional secretary of COSATU in the Western Cape, Tony Ehrenreich, stated: 'The sabotage accusations were clearly absurd and incorrect. After the minister was heard on radio and television making the accusation, he further discredited himself by denying it.'[30] The elections in the metropolitan area of Cape Town were hung, and the opposition Democratic Alliance went on to form a coalition administration without the ANC.

While police and intelligence operators are still to report on the bolt incident, the National Electricity Regulator of South Africa in August 2006 issued a damning report on the outages. Its findings accused Eskom of inadequate maintenance, breaches of licensing conditions, inappropriate risk assessment, negligence, failure to conform to operating procedure, inadequate implementation of corrective measures and complete failure to notify supervisors of abnormalities. It further declared that the six incidents resulting in shutdowns could have been avoided.[31]

All this points to the problems arising from gross mismanagement by Eskom, despite it being aware that electricity demand is rapidly reaching full capacity. Belated plans to add capacity to the system include recommissioning some coal-fired power stations that had been mothballed when supply exceeded demand, adding new coal-fired and gas-turbine power stations to the grid, and looking to the Democratic Republic of the Congo to supply hydroelectric power from the Inga Falls complex. Demand-side management and energy conservation measures have been stepped up. Instead of an increased reliance on centralised electricity generation, the lesson should have been learned that the answer is one of greater decentralisation and dissemination of multiple energy sources throughout the country.

Further, the new head of NECSA, Rob Adam, formerly director general of science and technology, is a great proponent of the idea that South Africa should enrich its own uranium. The country's enrichment capacity was closed down after its abandonment of the bomb programme. Bomb-grade uranium can be used inside the SAFARI-1 research reactor at Pelindaba, although there are plans to change to much lower levels of enrichment. Enrichment is expensive and highly energy intensive. It makes economic sense only if South Africa is to add a further ten Koeberg-sized or over 50 PBMRs to its existing energy plants. Conversion and enrichment would add 100 per cent value to that of the mined ore.[32] Will the drive to set up enrichment facilities spur on the expansion of the civilian nuclear programme in South Africa and the rest of the continent?

With enrichment facilities, proliferation of weapons of mass destruction would become an option. The discussions within the intelligence community, mentioned earlier, have broken through the earlier political taboo about using nuclear technology for peaceful purposes only. The genie is now out of the bottle.

Civil society takes on the nuclear industry

Over the years, a number of civil society organisations have been active in challenging the nuclear industry. During the apartheid years, the key organisation was the voluntary Cape Town-based Koeberg Alert. At one stage this campaign had six area committees in the Cape Peninsula and Atlantis. Koeberg Alert organised public meetings, monitored emergency tests, distributed information, researched the industry, held street theatre and organised demonstrations. Active mostly in the 1980s, the organisation was hampered in its activities by apartheid legislation such as the Key Points Act, as well as state of emergency legislation.[33] Nevertheless, it had informal links with groups all over the country and was able to operate as the anti-nuclear conscience of the people of Cape Town.

By the 1990s anti-nuclear activism had been absorbed into broader environmental activism exemplified by another volunteer organisation, Earthlife Africa. Earthlife Africa was formed in 1989, and by 2006 had active branches in Johannesburg, Cape Town, Durban and Windhoek (Namibia). At times the organisation also had a presence in Pretoria, Pietermaritzburg and Kampala (Uganda). The organisation was governed by an annual inter-branch congress and a Statement of Beliefs. Between congresses, branches operated autonomously, but with extensive mutual consultation. By 2004 the active branches had formed campaigning structures called Nuclear Energy Costs the Earth Campaign (NECTEC), managed by full-time campaign coordinators engaging in training and advocacy work. The NECTEC campaigns have involved interventions in the media and lobbying parliamentarians, canvassing for alternatives to nuclear energy (such as renewables), contesting the EIA for the PBMR, and supporting former nuclear workers to obtain access to records on their health status with a view to securing compensation for damage caused. NECTEC has also worked with a range of community-based organisations, local municipalities, faith-based groups, representatives of trade unions and trade union federations, land claimants, and other activists. Earthlife Namibia has focused its efforts on questioning the rights given to mining companies to extract uranium inside national parks.

In Johannesburg, Earthlife Africa's NECTEC campaign formed an alliance with SAHA in 2004 to help it obtain official documents through the provisions of PAIA.

The struggle for information on worker health

During 2003 Earthlife Africa Johannesburg's NECTEC was approached by a number of former workers at Pelindaba. These workers complained that they were suffering from health problems, which could be related in some way to their exposure to radioactivity and dangerous chemicals while previously working for AEC/NECSA. The workers sought to have their medical status verified in order to obtain workers' compensation funds from the state.

One such worker, James Mcephe, now 69, suffers from painfully itchy skin and is prone to bleeding after the slightest impact. His eyes burn, making it difficult to see, and he complains of other bodily aches and pains. Mcephe maintains that he was healthy prior to working as a labourer for NECSA at Pelindaba:

> I was fine at the beginning [in 1986,] but we used to load chemicals onto tractors and do a lot of maintenance work on broken pipes that funnelled liquids around the complex. We were never

told about the risk of radiation contamination and there was never any safety training given to us — my protective clothing consisted of a pair of overalls. Now I am consumed by diseases. Things are bad, so bad I have to go to the clinic every month for treatment.

Retrenched in 1999, Mcephe's complaints to NECSA about his health status went unheeded.[34] He was one among many who ultimately approached Earthlife Africa to intercede.

Earthlife Africa engaged Dr Murray Coombs, a toxicologist with expertise in occupational diseases, to develop a report on the background and health status of the affected workers. Coombs was at this time operating as a private consultant with Health Gap Network, a Pretoria firm. In order to conduct the study, Coombs needed to examine the complete medical records of the former workers. Initially, NECSA was unprepared to grant access. Earthlife Africa therefore turned to SAHA to provide expertise in acquiring the official medical files on the affected workers. Initial requests for 23 personal records were submitted pursuant to PAIA in July 2004.[35]

Victor Motha's files were part of the original 23 requests. Victor was a Pelindaba worker, who joined NECSA soon after qualifying as a chemical engineer at Pretoria Technikon. While working in a fluorine plant in November 2001, Motha fell ill. His father, Clive, recalled that Victor said nothing about having inhaled fluorine: 'He ate his dinner as usual, and started vomiting. We rushed him to hospital, and there he died.' He was 21 years old. His death certificate, still in his father's possession, claimed that his death is under investigation. Shortly thereafter the family received correspondence from the then minister of minerals and energy, Phumzile Mlambo-Ngcuka (later the deputy president), promising the family that NECSA would investigate Motha's death: 'No stone would be left unturned in this investigation,' she stated. Yet to date this is where the correspondence with the family ended. Later, DME officials claimed that the report on the investigation was available from the Department of Labour.[36] Immediately after the case was aired in the press, Clive Motha received a cheque for R6,000 from the Department of Labour, ostensibly to cover funeral costs (of four years previously). Clive Motha felt that this might have been issued to 'keep the family happy so that we don't talk to outsiders'.[37]

Figure 2: Clive Motha at home, standing beneath a graduation photograph of his son Victor. Copyright: *The Star.*

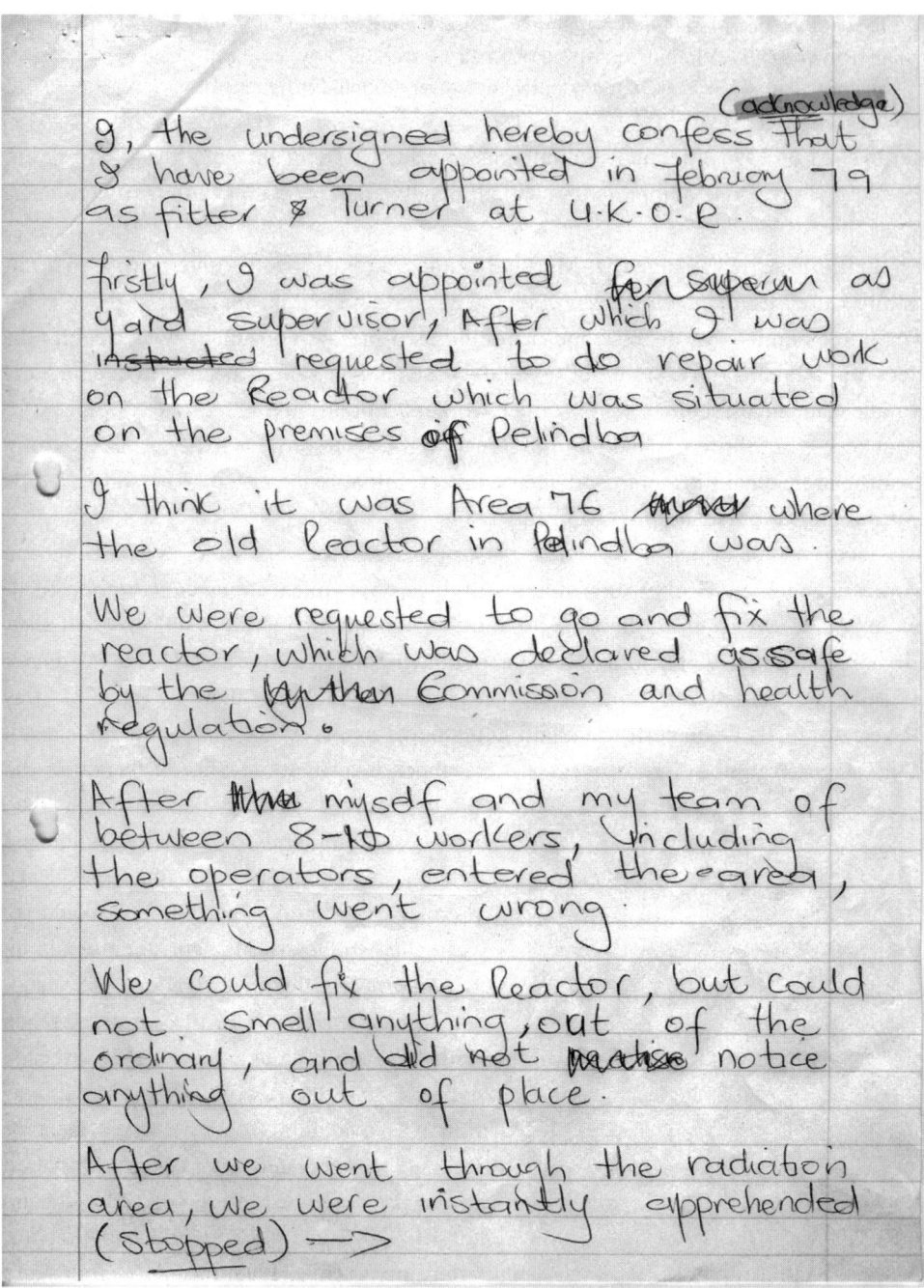

(acknowledge)

I, the undersigned hereby confess that I have been appointed in February 79 as fitter & Turner at U.K.O.R.

firstly, I was appointed for super as yard supervisor, After which I was instructed requested to do repair work on the Reactor which was situated on the premises of Pelindba

I think it was Area 76 where the old Reactor in Pelindba was.

We were requested to go and fix the reactor, which was declared as safe by the Commission and health regulation.

After myself and my team of between 8-10 workers, including the operators, entered the area, something went wrong.

We could fix the Reactor, but could not smell anything, out of the ordinary, and did not notice anything out of place.

After we went through the radiation area, we were instantly apprehended (stopped) —>

Figure 3: Statement submitted together with a request for medical records by former employee of Pelindaba contracted to work on nuclear reactor which is alleged to have leaked. The statement outlines the employee's physical ailments after exposure.

Mr VonK de Ridder, the official and
health inspector, as well as other health
inspectors, immediately started to
monitor us, after which a blood
Count was taken.
After which our clothes were taken
away from us and burned.

We were given clean overalls on
our way home.
We were about 4 workers who were
instructed to report at Pelindaba the
~~the~~ following day. After which the following
5 days ~~we~~ were required to be
at Pelindaba for +- 35 mins. We
had to lie in the ~~teadease~~ leadbox
~~box unit to receive the chemotherapy~~ to
ensure that the radiation which we
were exposed to, would leave our
bodies.
After the instruction was Signed and
U·K·O·R handed us our packages,
did we not realise what awaits us.

After all these years, I first experienced
burn pains in my ~~fingers~~ toes & thumbs
In 2003, I felt I could not
be in the sun, and should not be
in it, even though I am a nature
lover. I then went to the Academic
Hospital in Pretoria, where I was

examined by our Specialists
A Copy of the specialists report
is included!
Last year December we were flying
from Cape Town to Port Elizabeth
At Cape Town International, we were
~~scanned~~ monitored, and the
Scanner went off profusely.
I was told to remove my hat,
but the scanner still went off.
Fortunately, I was allowed to depart
to Port Elizabeth
On the 27th December 2004, we ~~to~~ again
took a flight from P.E to C.T
In P.E, ~~the~~ security guards took
me to a private room to monitor
me, I had to remove everything
from my watch, to my ring and hat,

They even searched between my balls,
but found nothing.
The Scanner just Continued Beeping.
I was ~~informed~~ instructed ~~to sit~~
still in the plane, on ~~seeing~~ Count
that I could immobilise the instruments
on the plane. As I am writing this
letter to you, every bone in my body
is on fire, it burns like hot coals
in a fire.

It took until mid-November 2004 for NECSA to respond with releases of records related to the formal request. By the time these files were released, four workers (one of whom had been Victor Motha) were already dead. Of the remaining 19, 13 workers presented themselves for medical examinations. Of these 13, Coombs revealed that ten ex-employees (77 per cent) 'have been exposed in the course of their employment to a hazardous substance which could cause adverse health effects'. The hazards referred to included radioactivity, chemical exposure and noise. Eight workers (62 per cent) needed immediate medical investigation and treatment. Four of these workers (31 per cent) had illnesses 'very likely to be occupationally related'.[38]

Coombs, in assessing the nature of the information released, reported that the records were incomplete in relation to statutory requirements governing nuclear worker health, as laid out in the National Nuclear Regulator Act No. 47 of 1999. Coombs suggested that the records be requested again, but with a more specific description of what was required. NECSA was now called upon to provide full medical and human resources files, the results of all tests conducted for radiation exposure, compensation claims records, death certificates and post-mortem records. This request for additional information was intended to close the gap in relation to the 23 original requests.

Between November 2004 and June 2005 SAHA put in a further 224 requests relating to NECSA's knowledge of the health status of individual workers. Under PAIA, government agencies are given 30 days to respond; NECSA failed to conform. It refused to respond to SAHA in writing, and gave no timelines suggesting when the documentation might be made available. Workers, some of whom were by now in a serious condition, were faced with continued stalling by the authorities. With no formal response, NECSA issued contradictory verbal assurances to SAHA and Earthlife. Eventually, NECSA's designated information officer claimed that she could 'not estimate the delay as she was not working directly with the employees responsible for copying the files'.[39] Nevertheless, in September NECSA provided SAHA with records relating to 30 requests. Fourteen of these related to requests for additional information under the original 23 requests. In the face of the continued and unexplained delays in the provision of information, SAHA approached the public protector, the South African Human Rights Commission (SAHRC) and NNR for support.

Was NECSA deliberately being intransigent or simply incompetent? On a visit to NECSA on 6 October 2005, SAHA ascertained that there were a number of reasons for the corporation's extremely slow response:

· Records relating to individual employees were distributed across a number of internal NECSA departments.
· Record collections were catalogued in different ways. Injuries were listed by year, whereas human resources listed employees by their personnel numbers;

medical files were in order of the employee's identity number; and compensation claims were arranged by the employee's name.[40]

· For each collection, different requirements applied. For example, the human resources records had to be retained for seven years, whereas medical records had to be kept for 40 years. Some information requested had therefore been destroyed.

NECSA claimed that, faced with such challenges, it was in the process of regrouping and re-sorting records relating to all 25,000 past employees. It estimated that this process would take until the end of 2005, and had required the full attention of a team of eight; four extra officers would be appointed. NECSA estimated that the cost of reorganising the records would be ZAR 4.5 million. Priority would be given to the release of requested records, which would occur in batches.

NECSA also provided assurances that records would be released pursuant to the 210 outstanding requests by the end of 2005. The assurances were not tantamount to any kind of refusal of information, making it difficult for SAHA to argue a case for litigation in order to effect the rights of the requesting individuals under PAIA. The assurances also made it difficult to engage the public protector and the SAHRC in any intervention.

By the end of 2005 NECSA had released many of the requested medical records in batches; over the course of 2006 SAHA continued to pursue the remaining records, without much success. The first batch released in 2006 arrived in January, without any explanation of the intended release of the remainder as requested. Some of the records continued to contain gaps. Nevertheless, having achieved broad access to the records of most of the concerned individuals, Earthlife agreed to take over SAHA's role in submitting further requests to NECSA for the records.

Despite NECSA's failure to provide written advice as required by PAIA or to comply with its own guarantees on timelines for release, the public protector and the SAHRC failed to take any significant steps to intervene. The public protector requested an explanation from NECSA, which merely reiterated the conversation between itself and SAHA in October 2005,[41] and took no steps following SAHA's response setting out the multiple failures to comply with not only NECSA's own guarantees in relation to medical record requests, but with requests for non-medical records (dealt with below), some of which had been outstanding for over two years. Further, despite a meeting with the SAHRC in October 2005, it did not contact SAHA regarding the latter's complaint until January 2007, at which time it attached a letter from NECSA that misrepresented the 2005 agreement and stated that it (NECSA) had continuously provided access to records over the 2005/06 period. SAHA again responded that the 2005 agreement had not been complied with and that NECSA had failed to respond to the non-medical record requests, which had now been outstanding for almost three years. The SAHRC did not respond.

The initial Coombs report stimulated concern about the fact that a public body like

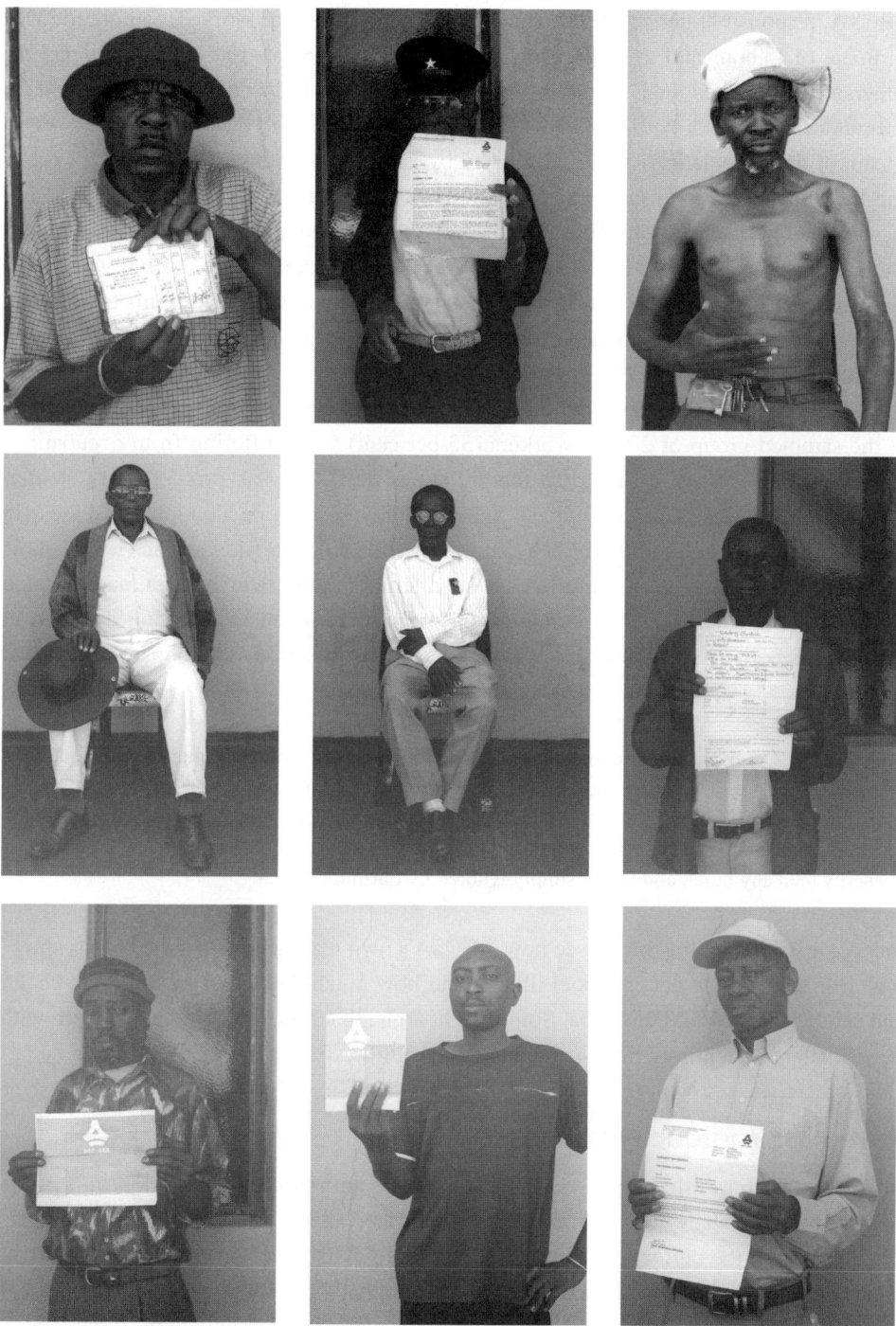

Figure 4: Former NECSA workers living in Attridgeville who, together with Earthlife Africa, submitted PAIA requests for their medical records in order to claim compensation for occupational illnesses.

NECSA, responsible under the law for the health and safety of workers to both the Department of Labour and to NNR, should have paid such belated attention to its poorly integrated record keeping. To offset reputation problems in an industry that should be scrupulous about its duty to protect its workers, NECSA decided in August 2005 to set up a team of five 'specialists' — all nominated by NECSA — to investigate Motha's death and the allegations of unsafe practices at NECSA resulting in the hazardous exposure of some workers. Efforts by Earthlife to propose representation of its own experts on the team were all rejected, leading to fears that the NECSA nominees would whitewash the institution.[42] Earthlife was offered a chance to make submissions to this committee, chaired by Mogwera Khoathane, a former NECSA radiation protection officer who now runs his own consultancy.[43]

The final Coombs report, published in September 2006, claimed that 72 members of the sampled group of 208 ex-workers (35 per cent) were suffering from occupation-related illnesses. 'If we even accept that 50 out of the 72 present problems of potential occupational diseases, it may indicate 5 100 employees with occupational diseases [in the historical pool of 30 000 NECSA employees since the 1960s],' Coombs wrote in his report. NECSA's response was to refer to its internal inquiry, which it claimed was due to report in January 2007.[44] It is interesting to note the defensiveness and delusion in the comments of NECSA's spokesperson, Chantel Janneker, in relation to the Coombs report:

> Dr Murray Coombs, in his report, makes assumptions that cannot stand interrogation and is misleading Earthlife Africa, and is supporting it in its drive to put any nuclear related matter into a negative light. Recent international opinion, prevalent even among environmental groups, is that, on balance, nuclear power is a more environmentally friendly option to produce energy than any other, and this is simply ignored by Earthlife Africa.[45]

Indeed, it will be interesting to see how NECSA's own team deals with the claims showing clear evidence of occupational illness, and how much this is attributed to lax health and safety standards at Pelindaba. Some might argue that NECSA's belated concern with these matters has entirely been a response to Earthlife Africa's use of PAIA.

Revealing radioactivity

In April 2004 Earthlife publicised the existence of an unfenced calibration unit in the vicinity of Pelindaba whose radioactivity was elevated above legally recognised dosages. The purpose of the unit when set up in 1979 was to assist with the calibration of instruments used by geologists. The existence of this unit had been made known by a group of former residents of the area, who are currently engaged in a formal claim to the land at Pelindaba. Claimants felt fearful that NECSA was taking no steps to safeguard the public

Figure 5: Award-winning cartoonist Zapiro's interpretation of Mlambo-Ngcuka's reaction to the fact that NNR had confirmed Earthlife Africa's readings of radiation levels of ten times the legal limit at an unfenced calibration centre located 20 metres from low-cost housing. Copyright: Zapiro.

from radioactive releases. The calibration centre was located 20 metres from a low-cost housing development. Earthlife's readings at the unit measured 20 to 30 microsieverts per hour, as opposed to the legal limit for ionising radiation measured outside a storage facility for radioactive materials that emissions should not exceed 2.5 microsieverts per hour.[46]

Earthlife's whistle-blowing, timed to coincide with the nineteenth anniversary of the Chernobyl accident, attracted the ire of the president and the minister of minerals and energy (then Phumzile Mlambo-Ngcuka): President Mbeki denounced the NGO for recklessness, untruth and 'scaremongering', while the minister announced that she would pursue the introduction of legislation to curb this kind of whistle-blowing. The matter was dropped after NNR confirmed that Earthlife's readings of the radioactivity levels were accurate. However, the incident revealed that the politicians were capable of knee-jerk reactions to complaints, probably emanating from the industry, about NGOs voicing legitimate concerns.

The FXI went on record as being deeply alarmed by government's statement of intent to introduce legislation to make individuals and organisations 'speak responsibly' on sensitive matters. Ironically, the minister had chosen World Press Freedom Day to make her remarks, which further incensed FXI:

> These threats place a blot on [South Africa's record of free media] on the very day when this freedom is being celebrated, and underlines the tenuous nature of this freedom. Earthlife has since been vindicated by the National Nuclear Regulator about the excessively high levels of radiation in the area. They have also clarified the fact that their initial statement never alleged the existence of a toxic site, but had termed it a calibration site. Therefore, if any institution can be accused of making baseless statements, then it is the government itself ... Earthlife should therefore be congratulated for its watchdog role, not attacked for it by the government.[47]

Not only do the threats fly in the face of national framework environmental legislation, which is sympathetic to whistle-blowers,[48] but they foreclose precious political space for civil society to raise public interest issues. What was also noticeable was that the basis for the attack on Earthlife was a set of false statements attributed to the organisation and clearly drawn to the president's attention, presumably by the nuclear industry, without any attempt to verify them.

4.5.4 Radiation dose limitation

The *normal operational exposure* of individuals must be restricted to ensure that neither the *effective dose* nor the *equivalent dose* to relevant organs or tissues, caused by the possible combination of *authorised actions*, exceeds any relevant *dose limit* specified in Annexure 2. In order to comply with these regulations holders of *nuclear authorisations* must, as a precondition for engagement of occupationally exposed workers who are not their employees, obtain from the employers, including self employed individuals, the previous *occupational exposure* history of such workers.

4.5.5 Medical Surveillance and Health Register

4.5.5.1 A comprehensive medical surveillance programme and health register must be established and maintained for all occupationally exposed workers in a form approved by the NNR. All entries in the health register must be made by an appointed medical practitioner or a person so authorized in writing. The holder must retain the register for a period of 40 years from the date of last entry.

4.5.5.2 An employee must have right of access to his medical records and health register at all times.

4.5.5.3 After consent has been obtained from the employee, the holder must provide the NNR with access to the employee's medical records and health register. The NNR may, with the consent of the employee, appoint an independent medical practitioner to assist in the conduct of a review of said records.

Figure 6: *Government Gazette*, 28 April 2006, Act passed by the National Nuclear Regulator stipulating the record-keeping requirements for the nuclear industry for all workers.

Casting the first pebble

SAHA assisted Earthlife Africa to request a number of key documents related to the nuclear energy industry, apart from health records of former NECSA workers. Many of these requests were to place documents in the public domain that dealt with different aspects of the industry, both historical and contemporary. A number of these documents had to do with the secrecy surrounding the development of the PBMR.

Earthlife Africa had long been aware of certain studies, especially on the economic feasibility of the PBMR project. It was widely known, for example, that in 2001, a macroeconomic study on the PBMR and the fuel plant had been conducted, but never placed in the public domain.[49] When approached under PAIA to reveal this document, Eskom claimed it was with PBMR Ltd rather than with Eskom. In turn, PBMR Ltd acknowledged that it had the document, but refused to release it on the grounds that, among other factors, it would harm the company's commercial and financial interests.[50] SAHA launched an appeal on the grounds that some of the information in the report was already in the public domain.[51] Release of the information was not aimed at strangling competition, as commercially confidential sections could be masked should they be deemed to cause any harm. However, it is suspected that some of the information may reveal substantial departures from legal compliance, in which case disclosure in the public interest would outweigh the harm envisaged. The appeal was ignored.

In March 2000 consultancy firm PriceWaterhouse had issued a due diligence and business case report on the PBMR. When SAHA requested this document under PAIA,[52] Eskom gave an outright refusal, claiming that 'commercial' and 'research' information would be disclosed. Eskom did, however, release a report entitled 'Detailed Feasibility Report: Report on the Commercialisation of the PBMR', dated April 2002. On 8 September 2005 Eskom announced that the results of the internal appeal on the PriceWaterhouse document would be released 'subject to severance of the parts of the report that are considered not to fall within the disclosure provisions of PAIA and are exempted from disclosure'.[53] Detailed motivations for the masking followed, mostly citing commercial confidentiality. Kate Allan, who coordinates SAHA's Freedom of Information Programme, commented: 'Given the excessive severance of figures and recommendations in the report, it is difficult to ascertain exactly what the findings say.'[54] It is clear that this document, crucial in assessing the economic viability of the PBMR project, was not being permitted to inform public debate, implying that PBMR Ltd had something to hide.

Submissions of requests to DME have, by and large, proved fruitless, and are still pending. In February 2005 SAHA was referred to the Department of Labour[55] in the case of the request for documents relating to the investigation into the death of Victor Motha. This was despite a public assurance given by the minister to the Motha family that there would also be a 'high level investigation' at NECSA.[56] In November 2005 three outstanding internal appeals and the outcome of two requests to the DME were being awaited.

Who regulates the regulator?

NNR has also been the recipient of a number of requests under PAIA. NNR is the custodian of public health in relation to the nuclear industry and is involved in the licensing of nuclear facilities. It has board representatives from a number of stakeholders, including government, industry, the community and trade unions. The regulator emerged from a history of being part of the industry — the licensing branch of the AEC — to independence in 1988 in the form of the Council for Nuclear Safety. With new legislation, the council formally became NNR in 1999.[57] While it should regulate even-handedly, NNR has been hampered by a number of defects: insufficient resources for carrying out its mandate; political control by the very government department that promotes nuclear energy, DME; and a weighting of its board in the interests of the industry rather than the general public. Nevertheless, the regulator monitors all nuclear facilities and both its information and its governance practices are of interest to a wide range of citizens.

NNR is also meant to collect and report annually on the number of breaches of safety at nuclear plants. It has a responsibility to guarantee that the operators of nuclear facilities are protecting the health of their workers, particularly where there have been operational problems and unplanned releases of chemicals and ionising radiation. More specifically, it is important that the licensing requirements of new facilities be placed in the public domain. Of special interest is the rationale used by NNR for terminating the licence held by the AEC to operate the Vaalputs radioactive waste site. After some time, this licence was reissued. If there were serious violations of the conditions of the licence, the public should have the right to know what went wrong.

On the question of governance, the allegedly irregular appointment of Maurice Magugumela, a former employee at PBMR Ltd, as CEO of NNR, was also of public interest. In particular, there was a suspicion that the NNR board had been sidelined — contrary to legal procedure — in the making of this appointment.

These issues informed the requests for documentation that Earthlife and SAHA submitted to NNR, which included:

- records relating to mining accidents and injuries, to violations of safety measures and safety regulations, and worker safety in relation to releases of cyanide and sulphuric acid;[58]
- records related to the licensing of the PBMR by NNR;[59]
- the report on the termination and renewal of the Vaalputs licence (violations of the licence led to temporary closure at Vaalputs of the national radioactive waste disposal facility);[60]
- records documenting exposures to dangerous substances of workers at Pelindaba, Koeberg and Vaalputs;[61]
- technical safety records issued by NECSA and Koeberg;[62]
- the report of the investigation into Ron Lockwood's complaints against Eskom (non-disclosure by the company of occupationally related illness);[63] and
- minutes of the NNR board and any other records during the period December 2004 – March 2005 regarding the appointment of Magugumela as CEO of NNR.[64]

Constant difficulties were experienced in getting NNR to respond to these requests. In February 2006 SAHA met with the CEO of NNR and was assured of cooperation. The list of outstanding requests was resubmitted. In a response in May, NNR claimed to have referred the matter of the CEO's appointment to the consideration of its own board. On the question of mine acids, the request was referred to NECSA, because 'NNR [had] no jurisdiction in this area'. Other requests would, it was stated, be commented upon within one calendar month.[65]

After the NNR board met, it communicated to Mashile Phalane of Earthlife Africa Johannesburg that the board's minutes were confidential, but that 'if there [were] any specific items on which [he required] information on Board decisions, then this may be made available to [him]'.[66] Clearly, the board was being somewhat cavalier with the law and was prepared to reveal the circumstances around how the CEO was appointed over its members' heads.

After a further meeting with NNR in August 2006, a number of reports were released, including the licensing requirements for PBMR, safety regulations contained in the legislation and the report on the termination of the Vaalputs licence. The last of these had not previously been in the public domain. It outlines the results of an inspection visit to the Vaalputs nuclear waste disposal facility in September 1996.[67] The inspection recorded that there were 55 violations of compliance with the licence. The operators of the facility, the AEC (now NECSA), failed, among other things, to implement quality controls and training programmes, to develop emergency planning, to maintain records, to control radioactive effluent, to maintain personnel radiological protection, to check instrumentation and to audit safety procedures. Worst of all, the process of backfilling the trenches that house the nuclear waste drums was inadequate and there were no arrangements to store or retrieve records on the disposed radioactivity. The document noted that there was a 'general lack of management and supervision at all levels of the AEC organisation responsible for Vaalputs' and that there was no 'effective mechanism to ensure compliance with the undertakings in the Vaalputs licence'.[68] The Council for Nuclear Safety then halted further waste from being received at Vaalputs until there was proof of compliance with licence conditions.

This document took a decade to reach the public domain. By accessing NECSA's own website soon after its receipt, and coinciding with Vaalputs' twentieth anniversary, one could read the following:

> Happy is the land that has no history. And happy is the nuclear facility that makes no news. The Vaalputs nuclear waste depository, in sparsely populated and near-desert Namaqualand, has for fifteen uneventful years (against an annually negotiated fee) been receiving low and medium level nuclear waste from Eskom's Koeberg nuclear power plant near Cape Town.[69]

Clearly, NECSA was erasing entirely the historical memory of its poor nuclear safety management record. Without the use of PAIA to obtain the documents from NNR, no one could begin to question either its poor practices or its distortions of history.

Despite some reasonable successes, NNR's credibility remains battered in relation to the appointment of a PBMR Ltd official as its CEO. It is reluctant to deal openly with this matter, which further affects its need to have an open-handed reputation. Interestingly, when the problems at Koeberg needed official investigation, this was given to the National Electricity Regulator to do, rather than to NNR. It will be necessary for NNR to rebuild its reputation and public trust, but it can only do this by acting firmly to assert its independence from the special interests attached to the nuclear energy industry. Reform of NNR, particularly its need to be answerable to a department that does not promote the nuclear industry and its need for better community-driven oversight, is something that civil society organisations have been promoting.[70] Perhaps the work done by SAHA and Earthlife in getting NNR to take its public responsibilities seriously might help the institution to recognise its historic task. This is ever more essential to all citizens, who require protection against ionising radiation, especially if the industry is to expand in the near future.[71]

Conclusion

The use of PAIA has played an important role in getting the nuclear industry to respond to an array of public concerns about failures in corporate governance. For many years, the activities of the industry were shrouded in secrecy. This can no longer remain the case. However, this requires public vigilance and the valuable monitoring role of the relevant NGOs. In this case, the hero(in)es are SAHA's Freedom of Information Programme and the NECTEC of Earthlife Africa's Johannesburg branch.

Clearly, most of the relevant medical records are now with the former employees of NECSA, but the road to claiming compensation will be long and will remain fraught with bureaucratic obstacles. The high incidence of former workers whose health deteriorated for occupational reasons means that many others may step forward to claim their compensation. The in-house investigation into health and safety conditions at Pelindaba is unlikely to be too critical of past practice at NECSA. However, the results may trigger an important dialogue with other health professionals who have a strong justice agenda.

There are still a number of outstanding documents that have defied efforts to effect their release. The process of encouraging release is of necessity a dogged one, sometimes bringing early results, but mostly requiring the exercise of great patience in prompting the institutions to realise their legal obligations to divulge.

Information is a tool, and greater information on the nuclear energy industry would, of necessity, be critical to decision making around South Africa's energy future. To date, the industry has — first under apartheid, and more recently under a democratic dispensation — gained privileged access to the state, as well as retaining control over much information that should have been in the public domain. The public is being asked to bankroll the industry, which has not sought to raise its own capital, to the tune of tens of billions of rands. The public needs to feel confident that the decision to expand the industry is justified by its viability and feasibility. The studies undertaken in this regard need to be placed squarely in the public domain, instead of being kept under wraps, citing commercial confidentiality as a reason to suppress their findings.

Whistle-blowing is now recognised under South African law, and yet our decision makers are keen to limit civil society interventions. The sterling work of civil society groups in supporting whistle-blowers is a key contribution to the building and safeguarding of our rather fragile democracy. The important work of groups like Earthlife Africa is essential to our self-knowledge as a society faced with a series of risks that need to be understood, assessed and managed with rigour.

Box 3.1: A parallel case: The Coalition Against Water Privatisation and Johannesburg Water

A brief history of resistance to water privatisation

The ANC government's adoption of the International Monetary Fund- and World Bank-influenced neo-liberal macroeconomic policy (in its Growth, Employment and Redistribution policy — generally known as GEAR — of 1996) made water — and all basic needs/services — a market commodity, to be bought and sold on the basis of private ownership and the profit motive. Since then, South Africans have witnessed the gradual privatisation of water (in various forms).

As a result of the privatisation of water provision over the last several years, poor communities in and around Johannesburg have found themselves unable to access and/or afford water and have responded with active resistance. One of the new social movements that arose to lead such resistance is the Anti-Privatisation Forum (APF), an umbrella organisation for grassroots community groups mostly located in Gauteng Province (which includes Johannesburg and Pretoria). Formed in 2000, the APF's guiding principle has been that basic needs, such as water, are a fundamental human right, not a privilege to be enjoyed only by those who can afford it.

As a result of these struggles, the Coalition Against Water Privatisation (the Coalition) was formed in late 2003, bringing together a range of community organisations and progressive NGOs in a collective effort to turn the tide against water privatisation.

In 2004 the City of Johannesburg's corporatised water service provider, Johannesburg Water Pty Ltd (JW), initiated the roll-out of pre-paid water meters in Phiri, Soweto, as part of Operation Gcin'amanzi ('Operation Conserve Water'), which was its 'cost-recovery' programme to enforce payment and ensure continued profit margins. This was accompanied by a huge public relations campaign by JW in which it made repeated claims about widespread community consultation and choice over the introduction of pre-paid meters; argued that the poor would benefit by being able to 'own/manage' their water consumption; and declared that the free 'lifeline' provision of 6,000 litres of water per month, per household (after which the meter automatically cuts off supply) is more than enough to meet the basic needs of a majority of poor households. JW also instigated an intense 'law and order' crackdown on community dissent/resistance to the pre-paid meters, which saw scores of Coalition activists and community members being arrested and imprisoned.

Accessing information in support of community struggles

In the heat of ongoing resistance to Operation Gcin'amanzi, the Coalition realised that there was a need to utilise PAIA to access crucial information from JW (and its legal owner, the City of Johannesburg) for a number of reasons, including:

- · to access the results of JW's own community surveys, meetings and progress reports, in order to ascertain whether the results of these were consistent with JW's claims of widespread community acceptance of and support for the installation of pre-paid meters;
- · to access JW directives and correspondences with individual households in Phiri, thus allowing the Coalition to test whether or not residents were being provided with freedom of choice around the pre-paid meters and the extent to which JW was using threats and intimidation;
- · to access the management/business contracts between JW and the French water multinational Suez Lyonnaise des Eaux to see what in-built provisions there might be in direct relation to the installation of pre-paid meters in poor communities (and in other communities), as well as pricing structures for water delivery in such communities; and
- · to access correspondence and minutes of meetings involving JW, the City of Johannesburg, the public prosecutor and the South African Police Service in order to determine the character and extent of JW's response to community protest/dissent.

With the assistance of SAHA and the Centre for Applied Legal Studies, the Coalition then submitted an extensive PAIA request to JW (and the City of Johannesburg) in late 2004. It was not until mid-2005 that the City of Johannesburg began to release the first trickle of documents to the Coalition. By the end of the year, and after numerous follow-ups and threats to take the matter to court, the City, and finally JW, released a substantial number of documents related to the initial PAIA request.

What was gained?

The Coalition's experience of utilising PAIA was, despite the long delay in the release of information, a positive one. SAHA proved to be of immeasurable value and assistance, not only in formulating and submitting the initial request, but in ensuring that JW and the City of Johannesburg were constantly followed up on and hounded. The resultant relationship forged between the Coalition and SAHA is exemplary of the kind of partnerships that should be found between progressive NGOs and social movements/community organisations.

The information gained has gone a long way in helping the Coalition to counter JW's public claims and arguments around the character and content of Operation Gcin'amanzi and to expose the more general lack of transparency surrounding basic service delivery by public sector institutions and, more specifically, in relation to public–private partnerships. Additionally, the information has provided crucial facts and figures that have strengthened the Coalition's ongoing constitutional rights to legally challenge the use of pre-paid water meters, especially as regards illegal water cut-offs, the sufficiency of the allocated 'free water' amount and discrimination against poor households.

The Coalition was also able to use the information in strategising around its activities and campaigns. Subsequently, the Coalition embarked on its own research survey/project in Phiri, informed by the gaps/omissions in JW's surveys and the claims/arguments flowing from them. A more vigorous and focused media and information campaign against the organised repression faced by resisting residents was undertaken and the tactics adopted by community residents were shifted accordingly. Information gleaned from the management contracts and internal reports was used to launch a more concerted domestic and international campaign against the partnership between JW and Suez Lyonnaise des Eaux.

While it would be incorrect to argue that the accessing of information in this case has resulted in significant practical 'victories' for the Coalition, there can be no doubt that the information has been extremely useful in assisting the Coalition to take forward its activities/campaigns. Our experience has also highlighted the importance of using the PAIA as a tool to further inform and empower the struggles of poor communities around basic services, as well as to place more pressure on public authorities and elected officials to be accountable and transparent to those they work for and represent.

Dale T. McKinley
Founding member of the Coalition

4

The Nuclear Weapons History Project

Chandré Gould

Introduction

The past seldom allows the luxury of neat stories with clear beginnings, middles and ends. History and its documentation are, rather, a reflection of the complexities of human relationships, interaction and (mis)communication. To expect that the enactment of the Promotion of Access to Information Act No. 2 of 2000 (PAIA) would result in researchers, academics or members of civil society being able to gain access to information that would allow us to sew up bits of our history into neat packages would be to have an incorrect expectation of the Act. How we record our lives and how states record their processes are necessarily imperfect. There is no Rosetta stone, no single source of information that will provide the answers to the multiplicity of questions we may have about aspects of our past. Indeed, knowing what questions to ask and who to ask them of is often the most difficult and most important part of finding information, as this chapter shows. In 2003 the South African History Archive (SAHA) embarked on an extensive process to determine the right questions, and who to ask them of, in pursuit of answers about South Africa's nuclear weapons programme.

Wits University academic Professor Garth Shelton was commissioned to identify the key unanswered questions about the apartheid nuclear weapons programme and to identify the government institutions from which the information could be requested. In that period, a total of 65 requests for information were submitted to ten institutions: the Department of Foreign Affairs (DFA), Armscor, the Department of Defence (DOD), the National Energy Commission of South Africa, the Office of the President, the Department of Trade and Industry (DTI), the Council for the Non-Proliferation of Weapons of Mass Destruction, the National Nuclear Regulator, Denel and the University of the Free State. The scorecard of responses by these institutions presents a dismal picture that inspires a number of questions. Was SAHA asking the right questions of the right institutions?

If so, were the negative responses the result of reluctance by the institutions to release documents in their possession? Were the institutions unable to process the requests because of a lack of capacity, or because officials were unfamiliar with the subject matter and the records contained in their archives? Or, was the lack of response because all the documents relating to the nuclear programme were in fact destroyed, as claimed by those involved in the nuclear programme and its termination?

This chapter considers a selection of key unanswered questions about the nuclear weapons programme. It refers to information that is already in the public domain that may provide answers (or where they may be found) and assesses the requests for information and the responses received. On that basis, it draws tentative conclusions about the usefulness of PAIA as a tool for uncovering and recording the past.

Finding the questions

Unlike the apartheid chemical and biological weapons programme that was scrutinised by the Truth and Reconciliation Commission (TRC), and, in even greater detail, during the marathon trial of its head, Dr Wouter Basson, the nuclear weapons programme has never been the subject of close public attention. The TRC did not investigate the nuclear weapons programme because of the former's very specific mandate — to investigate and make findings about individual cases of human rights abuses. In instances where there were no recorded human rights abuses related to a particular programme, or, more specifically, where there were no statements by victims or applications for amnesty by perpetrators (as was the case with the nuclear weapons programme), the TRC did not have an obvious or clear mandate to investigate. This resulted in the TRC failing, on the whole, to reveal the systemic nature of apartheid; although, to a large extent, it did succeed in revealing the aberrations and horrors perpetrated by apartheid's foot soldiers.

As a result, very little detailed information is available in the public domain about the apartheid government's nuclear weapons programme. There is information to suggest when and how the programme was initiated and the nature of the process that informed the change from a civilian nuclear programme to a weapons programme. Academics have considered the role of scientists and technicians in the development of the nuclear strategy, largely on the basis of the testimonies of those involved. The location of the facilities where uranium enrichment took place is known, as is the duration of the programme and the reasons for its termination. As a result of the successful application of the Freedom of Information Act of 1966 in the United States, there are also a significant number of documents revealing what US intelligence knew about the programme.[1] There are principally six categories of information about the nuclear programme:

· testimonies of those involved, including a short book self-published in 2003 by three of the men involved in the programme;[2]

- academic analyses;[3]
- US intelligence assessments made available through the National Security Archive;
- public statements by South African officials;
- press reports; and
- official accounts (such as that produced by the Atomic Energy Corporation [AEC]).

Following a review of the available material, Shelton identified a list of almost 30 unanswered questions that ranged from technical issues about the amount of highly enriched uranium (HEU) South Africa produced to the nature of foreign assistance provided to the programme. For the purposes of this chapter, it would be impossible (and unnecessary) to provide a thorough audit of all of these; instead, I consider ten of the questions most likely to be of interest to a broad range of individuals and institutions. These are:

i.   When was the project to build nuclear weapons initiated, and who was responsible for making the decision to militarise the programme?

ii.   What were the key elements of South Africa's nuclear strategy?

iii. Were targets identified for the use of nuclear weapons?

iv. Which foreign countries were involved in the nuclear weapons production process or related activities?

v.   What was the nature of the nuclear weapons that were produced, and how many were there?

vi. Was the Kalahari (Vastrap) nuclear test site ever used for a 'cold test', and why was the site reopened in 1987?

vii. Did South Africa conduct a nuclear test in 1979?

viii. Why did F.W. de Klerk decide to reveal South Africa's nuclear weapons programme in 1993, and did he make an honest declaration about the programme?

ix. How did the International Atomic Energy Agency (IAEA) verify the termination of the weapons programme, and what were the details of the reports South Africa made to IAEA?

x.   Were all the documents relating to the nuclear weapons programme destroyed?

In the following section I consider the requests for access to information made between 2003 and 2005 in relation to these ten questions, the responses received from the various institutions, and the information in the public domain that may shed light on these issues.

Looking for answers

i. When was the project to build nuclear weapons initiated, and who was responsible for making the decision to militarise the programme?

In the foreword by Professor Gideon de Wet to the self-published book by three men who were involved in the programme, Hannes Steyn, Richard van der Walt and Jan van Loggerenberg, the claim is made that no official documentary evidence of the programme was archived.[4] Indeed, it was the absence of such a documented history that led the authors of this book to record their own versions of events.

The book provides insight into the thinking of the South African government in regard to industrial and technological growth and development from the 1970s, when it was recognised that these processes were essential to the long-term economic prosperity of the country. It thus provides a context in which the decision to develop nuclear weapons was made. The authors argue that the implementation of a strategy to boost skills and knowledge in key technologies,[5] including nuclear technology, coincided with South Africa's isolation. South Africa felt abandoned by Western powers to deal with what was believed to be a formidable threat posed by the Soviets in the region. Steyn, Van der Walt and Van Loggerenberg state that the rationale for the development of nuclear weapons was that, since the country was unable to meet its security needs through the production and use of conventional weapons, '[a] more cost effective way had to be found to reduce the threat of a conventional conflict in the sub continent with the USSR as the major sponsor of one of the parties'.[6] While this provides perhaps some understanding of the factors influencing the decision to establish a nuclear weapons capacity, it does not answer the very specific question about when the decision was taken and who was responsible for making it.

In 2005 requests for information were made by SAHA to Armscor, the arms procurement agency, for the answers to these questions. The first request was for 'records regarding the initiation of nuclear weapons development';[7] the second was for 'nuclear weapons feasibility study/studies'.[8] In the case of both requests, Armscor stated that it had conducted a search, but concluded that the documents did not exist in its archives.[9]

As a result of the research conducted prior to submitting the requests, SAHA was in possession of an excerpt from a book entitled *A Will to Win* that had been commissioned by Armscor to record its achievements. According to the authors of this book, it was the outstanding achievements of the scientists working on the nuclear explosives programme that 'caused the government to consider the possibility of producing nuclear warheads'.[10] The committee that did so, called the Witvlei Committee, was chaired by P.W. Botha (the prime minister), and included the minister of mining (F.W. de Klerk), the minister of

Figure 1: Kentron Circle Nuclear Weapons Facility at Gerotek's Elandsfontein Vehicle Test Range.
Source: Institute for Science and International Security

Figure 2: Storage vaults for nuclear materials and nuclear warheads at Kentron Circle.
Source: Institute for Science and International Security

foreign affairs (R.F. 'Pik' Botha), the ministers of finance and defence, the chairman of Armscor (Commandant Marais), Dr Wally Grant (succeeded by Dr Wynand de Villiers) of the Atomic Energy Board (AEB) , and the director general of foreign affairs (Dr Brand Fourie) as secretary. It was this committee, according to *A Will to Win*, that was responsible for all nuclear-related decisions. Indeed, it would appear that the Witvlei Committee may have made the decision to pursue nuclear weapons in 1978: 'At the beginning of 1978 this Committee had to reflect on the progress and continuation of South Africa's nuclear capability. They voted for the continued development of the bomb.'[11] Steyn, Van der Walt and Van Loggerenberg also refer to a cabinet committee established by P.W. Botha to oversee the military programme in 1978:

> [W]ithin a month of coming to power at the end of September 1978, the new South African Prime Minister, Mr P.W. Botha, set up a Cabinet committee to oversee the military aspects of nuclear devices. At a meeting held on 31 October of that year it was decided that Armscor, the Defence Force and the Atomic Energy Board should start to work together intimately and prepare a program to initiate a nuclear weapons programme. This program was immediately classified as Top Secret.[12]

In any event, with the exception of one reference to the minutes of an *ad hoc* cabinet committee in 1990 that advised on the termination of the programme,[13] all other information contained in the Armscor document appears to be publicly available. Nevertheless, the reference to these minutes suggests that similar documents of relevance to understanding the decision-making process with regard to the nuclear weapons programme may still be in existence.

Peter Liberman identifies the problem of pinpointing a date and motive for the shift from a civilian explosives programme to a military programme in his article entitled 'The rise and fall of the South African bomb'.[14] He suggests that the difficulty in doing so may be a result of the shift from a civilian to a military programme having been gradual. He analyses the decision-making processes involved in the nuclear programme, drawing from open source information and interviews with key figures involved in the programme. One such person is Professor Andre Buys, whose recollection of the decision-making structures was as follows: 'The chief of the defence force, the minister of defence and the prime minister were involved in the decision-making. Authority to go ahead with the weapons programme was obtained from the minister of defence, at that time P.W. Botha.' Asked whether the prime minister, B.J. Vorster, would not have had to give approval for the shift, Buys said he believed that Vorster would have been consulted.[15]

The question for this book and this chapter is whether the application of PAIA resulted in the release of new information about the weapons programme. In this case, it did not. Nevertheless, the release of the excerpt from the Armscor publication adds a little more detail to what was known already and is therefore valuable. However, a huge effort and a great deal of time was invested by the requester to obtain the information. In this case, the requester did not have a fixed or limited deadline by which the information had to be obtained. This is seldom the case for researchers, who usually work to tight deadlines set by publishers or by funders. It is seldom that a researcher can afford to wait for three years for information that may or may not provide new insights.

ii. What were the key elements of South Africa's nuclear strategy?

Much has been written about South Africa's nuclear strategy, based almost entirely on the testimonies of those involved in its development. Without any official documentation against which to measure these accounts, it is impossible to know whether the version of the strategy as recalled by the scientists and politicians is an accurate account of that adopted by P.W. Botha's government.

In August 2003 Armscor was asked for 'records regarding nuclear strategy, plans for nuclear future, and analysis of past approach to nuclear programmes'. In 2005, when no results were obtained, the request was refined to ask specifically for 'Armscor's nuclear strategy document', believed to have been authored by Professor Buys. In response, Armscor submitted an affidavit by Gideon Smith, general manager: acquisition of Armscor, stating that the documentation relating to the nuclear programme had been destroyed *after inspection by IAEA* to ensure that it could not be used for purposes of proliferation in the future. Quite how the strategy document could contribute to proliferation is unclear. In addition, there is no evidence to confirm that IAEA inspected this document.

SAHA rejected Armscor's claim on the basis that other nuclear-related documents had been released by the DOD and that there was no need to destroy strategy documents to prevent future proliferation; however, no further information was forthcoming from Armscor.[16] The 'Armscor nuclear strategy document' does no more than describe, in somewhat vague terms, the shift in South Africa's nuclear programme from a focus on the development of non-military explosive devices to the development of the weapons programme.[17] In other words, it takes us no closer to a measure against which to assess the memories of individuals about the details of the strategy.

Professor Buys, an author of the nuclear strategy document approved by the minister of defence,[18] has explained the development of the nuclear strategy as he recalled it. He remembered that while the point of the nuclear weapons programme was to create a credible deterrent, there was much debate and disagreement between the AEC and scientists about what exactly constituted such a deterrent. Some argued, he said, that a civilian explosive device that could be exploded on demand was sufficient. Others argued that this strategy amounted to a bluff and was not a credible deterrent. This was an ongoing debate throughout the project. Buys stated that the scientists and engineers argued that a credible deterrent had to involve a functional system: 'The military agreed with this argument and that's the basis on which we developed the programme.'[19] But a coherent nuclear strategy came later. This final strategy, according to Buys, was developed by the scientists and engineers who were concerned by the apparent lack of clarity about the nature of the deterrent on the part of politicians and military leaders. Buys also recalls there being some resistance to the nuclear weapons programme from the military, who saw it as a drain on military funds that did little to assist troops and commanders who were fighting in Angola.

While Buys is very clear, his memory of events and inter-agency tensions will inevitably be subjective. Indeed, the release of a document (see below) that shows that the South African Defence Force (SADF) was considering purchasing a system capable of delivering a nuclear warhead suggests that the SADF's resistance to the nuclear weapons programme may not have been as emphatic as Buys remembered, or that there were differences of opinion within the military about the utility of nuclear weapons. These are nuances that have historical relevance, but which will not be adequately understood and recoded in the absence of official documents.

Ultimately, as is well documented by academic scholars on the basis of interviews with scientists and engineers, the strategy that was adopted was aimed at gaining diplomatic leverage if Soviet or Soviet-backed forces threatened South Africa. Gradual disclosure of South Africa's nuclear capability, it was believed, would bring Western nations to the country's aid. A former IAEA assistant director for external relations, David Fischer, has questioned the notion that a nuclear deterrent would have brought the United States to the aid of South Africa in the event of the country being substantially threatened by a foreign military power. He argues that in the 1960s and 1970s South Africa was of geostrategic importance as a result of its location on the sea routes and its mineral resources. Reactions to information about the 1977 test site showed that there was international concern about South Africa's nuclear capabilities, but, he argues, 'within a few years, a South African threat to test would surely have been empty and indeed self-defeating'.[20] By the mid-1980s, at the height of visible resistance to apartheid, the United States was more likely to react to a test by increasing pressure on Pretoria to change rather than to act in support of the government:

> [O]nly in the event of a direct Soviet invasion of South Africa (and only if that was seen as threatening an important US strategic interest) was the nuclear test tactic likely to have succeeded — and in such a case it would probably have proved unnecessary. Test, or no test, the United States would have intervened.[21]

While this calls into question the reasoning of those responsible for determining the nuclear strategy and shows that they may have been deceived by their sense of South Africa's strategic importance to the United States in particular, it is not to say that the account given by the South African scientists is not an accurate reflection of their thinking at the time. Nevertheless, if, as Armscor and Buys allege, the nuclear strategy document was destroyed, it is unlikely that proof that this was indeed the strategy adopted will be found. The problem remains that the organisation that was the custodian of the strategy document, Armscor, has denied its existence and the reasons given for the document's destruction are not entirely credible. Application of PAIA has not brought us any closer to knowing what the official position was.

iii. Were targets identified for the use of nuclear weapons?

If the nuclear strategy were indeed as described above, it would make sense that no targets were identified against which nuclear weapons would be used. That is because at no stage was the actual use of nuclear weapons part of the strategy. Yet, in the absence of documentary proof that this was the case, questions persist about whether targets were set by the military.

In an attempt to find answers, DOD was asked for 'records regarding Angola (Luanda) and nuclear strikes',[22] and 'records that refer to potential, and/or intended targets for nuclear strikes (whether defensive or offensive)'.[23] A request was made to the Office of the President for the same records.[24] Again, this is information of historical value, but which would have no obvious relevance to proliferators. In other words, if such documents existed, there would have been no need to destroy them in order to meet the non-proliferation objectives of the post-1993 governments. In terms of the first request, DOD responded that, despite extensive searches, no relevant documents could be found. The second request, however, resulted in the release of a document entitled 'The Jericho weapon system', which was arguably the most significant to be obtained by SAHA during the course of the project.

Dated March 1975, the document is an analysis and advisory note to the chief of the defence force from the chief of staff.[25] It reveals that the SADF was considering delivery systems for nuclear warheads in 1975, two years before the nuclear programme apparently shifted focus from peaceful nuclear explosives (PNEs) to military development. It also suggests an acceptance by the SADF that if South Africa did not produce nuclear warheads itself, they may be purchased elsewhere. In 1975 the SADF was engaged in an intense military campaign in Angola; a nuclear threat was believed to be a real danger. The SADF expressed particular concern that China may provide a tactical nuclear weapon for use against South Africa. Interestingly, in light of far more recent threat perceptions, the document notes that 'the Director of the United States "Arms Control Agency" maintains that nuclear weapons will become available to sub-national groups such as terrorist organisations within the next ten years'.[26]

The reasoning in this document differs markedly from that of those who developed the nuclear strategy. Indeed, while the Soviet Union or Soviet-backed forces were identified as the most serious threat by the Nuclear Strategy Working Group, the SADF's analysis was that Western solidarity had been 'shattered'; that 'confrontation between the Free World and the Socialist Block has been replaced by consultation, thus lessening the danger of nuclear escalation'; and that the greatest threat was from sub-state groups supported by China. Despite the apparently differing assessment of the threat, the conclusion reached by the SADF was that a nuclear deterrent was necessary. The Israeli Jericho weapon system was considered an important addition to the SADF's arsenal because of its range and ability to deliver nuclear warheads. This is made clear from the conclusion reached by the chief of staff:

> In spite of the considerable cost involved in acquiring even a limited number of missiles with the Jericho weapon system, in view of the potential threat which faces the RSA in the foreseeable future, the possession of such a system will greatly add to our ability to negotiate from a position of strength.[27]

The release of this document raised hopes that other records dealing with issues relating to South Africa's nuclear posture, if not the nuclear weapons programme directly, had not been destroyed and could be located if the right questions were asked of the right institutions. However, it does not directly answer the question of whether South Africa had identified targets for the use of nuclear weapons. According to information obtained by Liberman through interviews with those involved in the nuclear programme, the strategy never went further than to 'detonate a nuclear bomb 1000 kilometres south over the ocean' or a '*threat* [emphasis added] to use a nuclear weapon in a battlefield situation'.[28]

The requests made to the Presidency met with no success. Indeed, failure by the Presidency to respond within the legally determined time frame resulted in SAHA issuing an internal appeal against the deemed refusal for records. This too met with merely an acknowledgement of receipt from the Office of the President, and no documents were forthcoming in the more than two years the matter was pursued. Indeed, it was not clear whether any attempt was made to find relevant records. It would appear as though the Office of the President brushed off the requests and did not regard them as warranting serious attention.

iv. Which foreign countries were involved in the nuclear weapons production process or related activities?

Records alleging that foreign governments assisted the South African nuclear programme date back to the mid-1970s. One such document is a complex organogram that appeared in the African National Congress'(ANC) publication *Sechaba* in November/December 1975 linking German businesses to the supply of nuclear equipment to South Africa.[29] In 1993, shortly after De Klerk's announcement that South Africa had manufactured

Figure 3: The ADVENA Nuclear Weapons Facility completed just before the termination of the nuclear programme. Source: Institute for Science and International Security

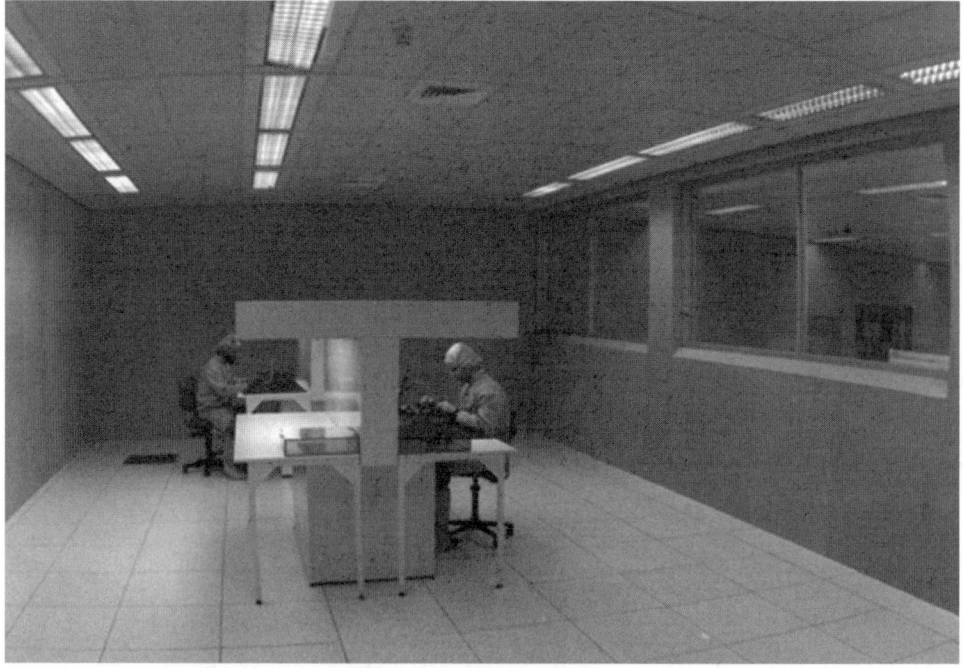

Figure 4: Clean room in the ADVENA Nuclear Weapons Facility.
Source: Institute for Science and International Security

nuclear weapons, it was reported in the South African press that researchers at the Stockholm International Peace Research Institute believed that Israel had helped the nuclear programme by providing expertise in exchange for uranium and permission to conduct nuclear tests in South Africa.[30] The same report referred to US assistance in the form of training for South African nuclear scientists. News reports in 1994 about the trial of Brigadier Johann Blaauw raised further questions about whether De Klerk had been honest in stating that South Africa had not been assisted by any other country in the development of its nuclear weapons programme. At issue was a series of deals brokered by Blaauw between Israel and South Africa that involved the exchange of nuclear materials and know-how.[31] In 1995 the *Washington Report on Middle East Affairs* reported that Israel and South Africa had cooperated for 30 years on nuclear weapons matters and referred to the natural alliance between two countries that were politically isolated and existentially threatened.[32]

In an attempt to obtain records relating to foreign assistance or involvement in the nuclear weapons programme, 11 requests were made to four different institutions: the DFA, DTI, DOD and Armscor.

DFA was asked for 'communications between Israel and South Africa regarding nuclear programmes and/or nuclear weapons'[33] and 'records pertaining to nuclear testing and Israel'.[34] DFA responded to these requests, noting the tremendous difficulty in obtaining records. An affidavit from Johan Kellerman, deputy director: nuclear and non-proliferation, described the steps taken to obtain records, which involved tracing the records from one archive to another. These efforts finally resulted in the discovery of a large cache of files that '[were] so voluminous it would require weeks — if not months — to adequately study all the documents contained in them'.[35] By March 2004 these problems had not yet been overcome; however, DFA made a number of documents available to SAHA, of which some referred to the nuclear collaboration between South Africa and Israel. While initially the documents provided to SAHA were masked in such a way as to make it impossible to determine their context, following a request by SAHA for clarity on the source and dates of the documents, a full set of unmasked documents were made available.

One of these documents is a telex (the author and recipient are not clear from the document) reporting on a question and answer session between Mike Richardson and US Ambassador Vernon Walters in Singapore in June 1986. Walters defended American policy towards South Africa, stating:

> We believe that by continuing the pressure rather than packing up our baggage and saying, 'to hell with you' — I personally happen to believe that if we did that the South Africans, in accordance with their traditions, would form their wagons in a circle and probably try to develop nuclear weapons and say, 'to hell with the world'.

He went on to refer to Soviet satellite information about the Kalahari test site and said that he would not be surprised if South Africa had developed a nuclear weapons capability, correctly speculating that South Africa's strategy would be to use the nuclear weapons to force foreign intervention: an interesting snippet of information, but nothing that takes us any closer to answering the question that SAHA had posed. Indeed, a good portion of the documents made available by DFA are news clippings that are of limited utility because several are not dated and the publication name does not appear on the records.

Only one of the documents, a telex from the South African embassy in Tel Aviv to DFA, hints at the furore that must have resulted from a news report that appeared on the front page of the Israeli newspaper *Yediot Ahronot* on South African–Israeli nuclear collaboration in 1989. The report claimed that large numbers of Israeli experts and military officials had been cooperating with South Africa in the conduct of nuclear tests from 'Bofat' Island in the Antarctic since 1985. The report also alleged Norwegian involvement in the collaboration.[36] Yet, in the absence of any more information, this too is nothing more than an interesting aside.

DTI was asked for 'records pertaining to nuclear devices exported',[37] 'records relating to agreements between Israel and South Africa relating to technology transfers relevant to nuclear weapons'[38] and 'records relating to technology transfer and assistance between South Africa and Germany relevant to nuclear weapons'.[39] DTI responded that it did not have any records of relevance to the requests, and it referred SAHA to the Department of Minerals and Energy (DME), which then failed to provide a response. SAHA lodged an internal appeal against the initial refusal by DTI on several grounds, about which it informed DME. Despite numerous efforts to get DME to address the requests, no response was forthcoming.

The one indication that documents revealing the relationship between Israel and South Africa still exist came from the refusal of DOD to provide 'records related to agreements between South Africa and Israel regarding co-operation in nuclear weapons and related areas',[40] 'navy records regarding Israel and use of/interaction with Simonstown Naval Base'[41] and a '1974 military cooperation agreement between South Africa and Israel'.[42] Not only were the requests refused, but DOD also refused to confirm or deny whether relevant documents existed.[43] The department relied on section 41 of PAIA to deny access to documents, which allegedly required protection because they contained information supplied in confidence to South Africa by another state and related to information held for intelligence relating to another state used by South Africa in the conduct of international affairs. What remains unclear is why the current South African government felt bound to honour confidentiality agreements made by the apartheid government. Certainly, the current government has been very concerned to show itself to be a fair and honest player in international affairs. Nevertheless, it seems inexplicable that it would feel bound to protect nuclear dealings between South Africa and other states that were made more than 20 years ago. According to Defence Intelligence, a memorandum of understanding (MOU) between South Africa and Israel defines what information could be released and what could not.[44] SAHA obtained a copy of the MOU in 2007 pursuant to a request; however, masking ensured that it revealed little about the substantive issues being protected.[45]

Some years following the refusal of access, SAHA was approached by a researcher requesting assistance to pursue records that he had independently requested from DOD regarding substantially similar subject matter. Interestingly, a large proportion of these requests were granted to him without masking. In discussions with DOD officials, they could not provide any clear explanation as to why SAHA's requests had been refused some years earlier; however, they conceded that they could not now prevent access. One factor that may have led to the release was that the researcher had identified from DOD's lists which files he wished to access.[46] Nevertheless, the documents failed to reveal any substantial information relating to the key questions pursued by the project.

Box 4.1: Obtaining records of the nuclear weapons programme

Obtaining records concerning the South African nuclear programme remains one of the most difficult tasks facing any researcher interested in apartheid era history. Finding documents relating to South Africa's alleged nuclear collaboration with other countries is even more difficult. Many of the key figures involved in the nuclear programme claim that all records were destroyed prior to F.W. de Klerk's 1993 announcement of the programme to Parliament and South Africa's eventual accession to the Nuclear Non-Proliferation Treaty.

However, some documents do still exist. At the central repository of the National Archives of South Africa there are several boxes of records detailing Pretoria's uranium sales to a variety of countries during the 1960s, including Israel. These documents are unclassified and available to researchers willing to wade through pages of extraneous information; they provide an early glimpse of South Africa's nuclear policy prior to the advent of the nuclear weapons programme. The DFA archive in the basement of the Union Buildings contains a smattering of documents that touch on the issue of nuclear cooperation. These files do not include any discussion of nuclear weapons collaboration, but there is a wealth of information on Israeli–South African scientific partnerships and exchanges under the auspices of the Council for Scientific and Industrial Research, including visits by nuclear scientists. These archives, up to the year 1986, were made available to me for extensive perusal without a PAIA request.

Another key source is the South African National Defence Force (SANDF) Documentation Centre. Unfortunately, access to SANDF files is far more difficult, and a PAIA request is no guarantee that they will be released. In 2005 I was permitted to consult a series of indexes listing military intelligence files by subject. I used these indexes to create a spreadsheet, which formed the basis of the PAIA request I filed in March 2005. Numerous redacted files were finally released to me in July 2006 after many complaints and a substantial reduction of the scope of my request. Other files were subsequently shipped to me in September 2006. These files cover a range of subjects, and the vast majority focus exclusively on conventional armaments and military intelligence cooperation between Israel and South Africa. However, there are a few unredacted documents discussing South Africa's chemical and biological weapons doctrine, as well as a set of documents detailing the initial arms deals negotiated by the Israeli and South African governments in 1974 and 1975, including references to nuclear weapons. Armscor refused to provide actual contracts or other records beyond raw financial data. This data is not specific enough to discern whether nuclear transactions occurred.

The fact that two major documents (the 'Jericho memorandum' of 31 March 1975 and the 1987 judgment from *The State v. Johann Blaauw*) are now in the public domain make it easier to write a coherent, albeit incomplete, narrative of this intensely secretive and controversial relationship. Ultimately, any scholar interested in this topic will have to cross-reference his or her declassified written sources with oral history interviews and other existing documents in order to piece together the puzzle of South Africa's nuclear cooperation with Israel and other countries.

Dr Sasha Polakow-Suransky
Author of The Unspoken Alliance (New York: Pantheon, 2009)

Requests to Armscor for 'records relating to technology or assistance between South Africa and Germany relevant to nuclear weapons',[47] 'records relating to commercial dealings with foreign countries and nuclear weapons'[48] and 'records related to Jericho Missile'[49] met with the same answer noted before: Armscor no longer had any documents relating to the nuclear weapons programme.

Although it is clear from DOD's response that the South African government is concerned that revelations about international links to the nuclear weapons programme could have a negative effect on current foreign relations, the argument has been rejected by critics. The same concern was raised by DFA during the TRC investigation into the chemical and biological warfare programme. In that instance, documents were discovered (and subsequently provided to SAHA) that revealed the nature of interactions among the United States, the United Kingdom and South Africa about the termination of the programme. While for a short time these revelations may have had uncomfortable consequences for South African diplomats, they did not cause permanent damage to foreign relations.

If, as is suggested by the DOD response, there are documents still in existence that reveal the nature of foreign involvement in the nuclear programme, it is vital to the histor-

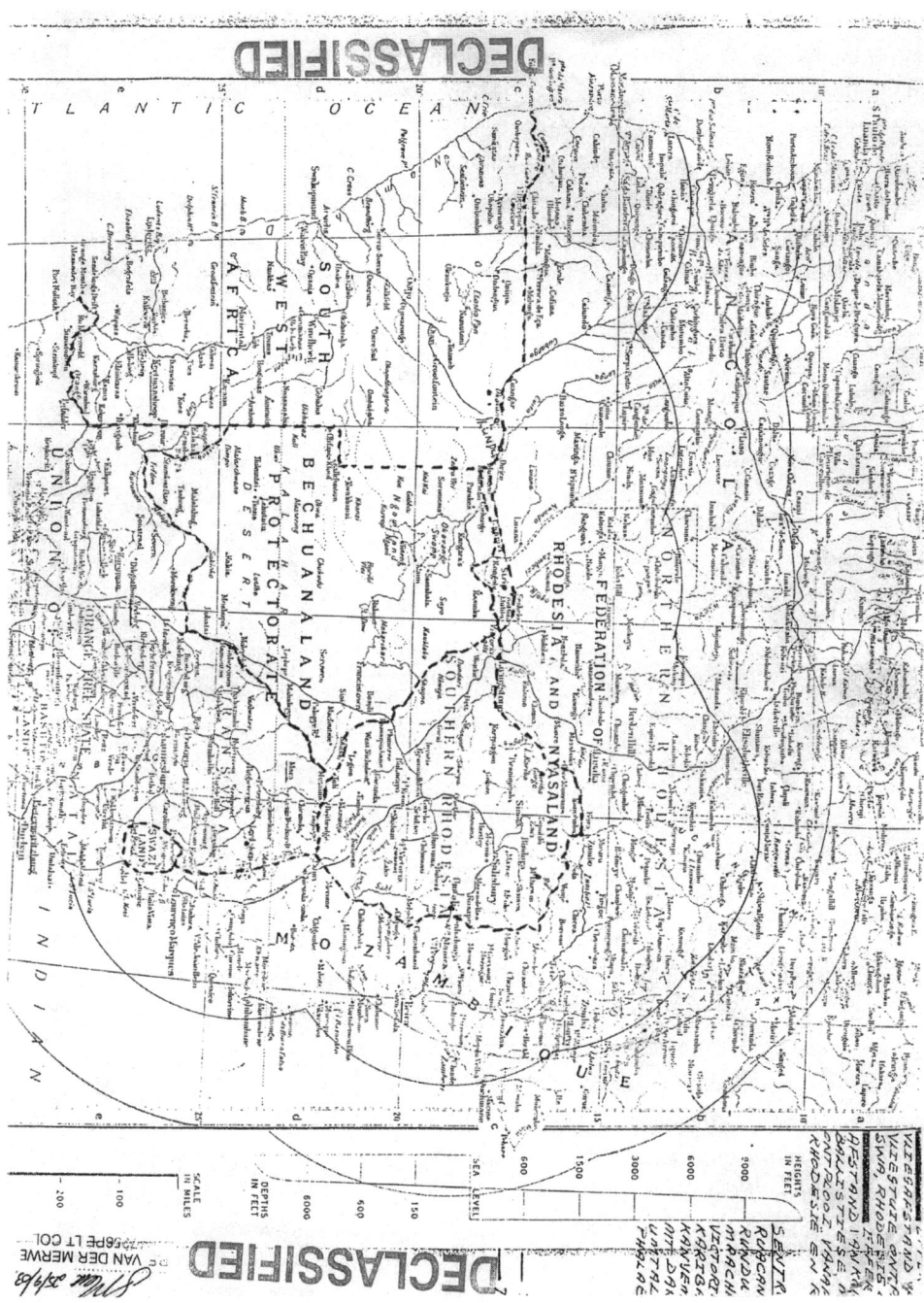

Figure 5: A map that is part of the first official record documenting South Africa's former nuclear weapons programme to be released since the apartheid government's pre-1994 disclosures. It concerns South Africa's consideration in the mid-1970s of acquiring the 'Jericho Missile' and potential launch trajectories (Archived as SAHA Collection AL 2878 – A3.2.1).

ical record that some arrangement is made for their release. The existence of documents confirming Israeli assistance to the South African nuclear weapons programme was given further credence in a statement made by Deputy Minister of Foreign Affairs Aziz Pahad to an Israeli newspaper, *Haaretz*, in 1997 that he had 'numerous reports on relations between academics from the two countries and on [nuclear] cooperation between the two to develop specific equipment'[50] of a military nature. Given Pahad's candidness about the cooperation and his admission that he had documents to prove it, the responses from government departments to requests for information are even more difficult to comprehend.

v. What was the nature of the nuclear weapons that were produced, and how many were there?

Figure 6: RSA-3 Missile, South African Air Force Museum, Swartkops AFB, Pretoria.

In 1993, when De Klerk made the announcement that South Africa had developed nuclear weapons, he spoke of the existence of six devices. Yet there remained suspicion in some quarters that smaller, tactical nuclear weapons had been developed and not revealed. There were even allegations that one or more of these smaller devices were unaccounted for and had landed in the hands of extreme right-wing groups. While these allegations are unlikely to have been true, they will persist in the absence of evidence to the contrary. SAHA attempted to locate records relevant to this question from four institutions: Armscor,[51] the Nuclear Energy Corporation of South Africa (NECSA),[52] DOD[53] and Denel.[54]

Armscor's response was the same as for all previous requests submitted: that all documents relating to the nuclear programme had been destroyed. This was despite the refusal being followed by a letter from the Wits Law Clinic rejecting the grounds for refusal, and letters from the requester following up. In 2005, after gaining no ground towards resolution, Armscor stopped responding.

NECSA's response was no less frustrating, but certainly more revealing. Asked for a report by Dr N. von Williegh to IAEA about the programme, NECSA stated with some measure of irritation:

[A]s you were previously informed, this confidential report by Dr N. von Williegh was submitted to the International Atomic Energy Agency in terms of international nuclear safeguards agreements. I herewith confirm that we are still awaiting clearance from the IAEA to make this report available to you. We have also, in the mean time, received instructions from the Department of Minerals and Energy that all requests about the weapons programme must be cleared with the Minister as well. Such clearance with regard to your request will be requested as soon as we receive a positive reply from the IAEA.

By August 2004, following letters from SAHA, there was still no response from NECSA, not even confirmation or denial that the document was in its possession. A formal letter of complaint about NECSA's failure to respond was sent by SAHA in July 2005 to the South African Human Rights Commission and to the public protector; this too failed to yield any positive results.

NECSA's shifting of responsibility to IAEA is curious. The document in question was written by South Africa to satisfy the requirements of the IAEA safeguards agreement. It is therefore curious that permission would need to be granted by IAEA for the release of the document. It is hard to imagine that IAEA would be required to grant South Africa permission to release its own document, particularly one that does not contain detail that could be seen to pose a proliferation risk. Indeed, the document is already in the public domain. This would suggest that NECSA's response was nothing more than a cynical attempt to delay the release of the document. Whether this was because the agency is honestly concerned about violating its international obligations is not clear.

What made the request particularly interesting is that SAHA had already obtained a copy through the research it conducted prior to submitting the requests. In submitting the requests, it aimed to ascertain what NECSA's position on the document was. Given that NECSA failed to substantively respond to the request, the request revealed little about NECSA's position in regard to the transparency of the nuclear weapons programme.

Denel responded to all requests with a standard refusal on the basis that all documents were destroyed, although attempts to obtain records about the destruction process also met with no success, despite extensive follow-up.

Ultimately, the question about the number and nature of weapons produced is answered in some detail by the Von Williegh document of May 1993. It refers to seven nuclear weapons devices. The record is as follows:

[T]he first nuclear device produced by the AEB in 1978 and provided with HEU in November 1979 under the code name VIDEO, was transferred for temporary storage on the 15th of that month to Ammunition Depot 92 of the SA Defence Force … The device was transported to the

Circle facility in April of 1982 where the HEU was replated. It was renamed MELBA. The first Armscor device was completed in December 1982 at the Circle facility under the code name HOBO, which was later changed to CABOT.

Table 4.1, which lists the seven devices, provides a little more detail.

Table 4.1: South Africa's nuclear devices

Name of device	Front or rear part	Date of production of device	Remarks
Video/Melba		November 1979	Replated 1982
Hobo/Cabot		December 1982	HEU later reused in 503[55]
306	Rear Front	June 1988 June 1989	Upgraded, pre-production model
501	Front Rear	August 1987 June 1988	Production model
502	Rear Front	November 1988 October 1988	Production model
503	Front Rear	November 1988 March 1989	Production model
504	Rear Front	March 1989 March 1989	Production model

Source: N. von Williegh, 1993, 'A brief overview of the development of nuclear explosive devices in South Africa', Atomic Energy Corporation of South Africa, May, p. 6

In the document, Von Williegh also addresses the issue of whether South Africa considered the development of a cannon and implosion-type fission device and a thermonuclear device with a fission detonator. It is stated that while ministerial approval was granted for development work on both types of devices, the nuclear strategy and the decision to limit the number to seven fission devices meant that the implosion technology remained underdeveloped.

In light of the information contained in this document, the response from NECSA is confusing. Is the agency being overcautious in its responses to requests for information because it is worried that it may inadvertently or consciously violate international agreements, or is there some other reason for its recalcitrance?

vi. Was the Kalahari (Vastrap) nuclear test site ever used for a 'cold test', and why was the site reopened in 1987?

One of the key questions in relation to the South African nuclear programme is whether the Kalahari test site (known as Vastrap) was intended for testing a nuclear weapon device. The answer to this question appears to be answered in the document by Von Williegh, who asserts that the test site was established to test a full-scale explosive device (not with HEU) that had been completed in 1977. According to Von Williegh, and confirmed by Steyn, Van der Walt and Van Loggerenberg, the test site had been identified and approved between 1973 and 1974. By 1977 two test shafts had been drilled and were ready for the tests. Since at that time no HEU was available for the test, SADF decided to go ahead with a cold test to establish the effectiveness of the 'logistic (the device was 4.4m long, had a diameter of 610mm and weighed 3 450kg), diagnostic and data acquisition systems'.[56] However, international attention on the site led to it being abandoned in August 1977, when the shafts were sealed. Confusion about whether the site was developed to test weapons or civilian explosive devices was understandable, given that the decision to change the nuclear programme's focus from the development of PNEs to the development of nuclear weapons for deterrent purposes took place in the same year, 1977.

According to Steyn, Van der Walt and Van Loggerenberg, the 1977 underground test was of an explosive device for civilian application in mining, rather than a test of a military nuclear device. Indeed, the authors appear to suggest that had the test site not been detected and the programme towards the development of civil nuclear devices not been halted, the military programme might not have started at that point.[57] Fear of detection of this first test detonation also resulted in a programme to reduce the size and yield of a device, such that:

> [it] could be shipped to the site and detonated in a very short period of time. The only data that could be obtained by these tests were the measurement of the explosive yield and the detection of a possible radio-active release … Preparations for a first fast deployment test were ready within six months of the detection of the site.[58]

Professor Buys recalled his own opposition to the Kalahari test on the basis that it was not necessary and would create the impression that South Africa had a weapon at a time when it did not, and thus create the possibility of a nuclear response from the Soviet Union.

Requests for information about the test, and particularly for information about whether Israel was involved, made to DFA,[59] Armscor[60] and NECSA[61] were fruitless, bringing us no closer to an official version of events. Once again, non-proliferation concerns in relation to the documents seem baseless.

vii. Did South Africa conduct a nuclear test in 1979?

In 1979 one of the satellites deployed in support of the Limited Test Ban Treaty of 1963 to detect nuclear explosions in the atmosphere detected a flash over the Indian Ocean that suggested that South Africa may have exploded a nuclear device. The evidence was, however, inconclusive, and those involved in the nuclear programme vehemently denied South African involvement in any such explosion. In 1993 Waldo Stumpf told the *Saturday Star* that '[i]f there was a nuclear explosion [in 1979], South Africa was definitely not involved'.[62] There is no reference to the alleged test in the Von Williegh document, suggesting that it was not reported to IAEA. Yet scientists from the US Los Alamos nuclear facility were convinced by the satellite data and released a press report in 1997 claiming that their view that South Africa did detonate a nuclear device had been vindicated by a statement by Aziz Pahad in which he confirmed that a nuclear test had taken place.[63]

Despite Pahad's statement, it is obviously important for historical reasons to obtain documentation that could affirm or refute the truth of these claims. Again, in light of the openness that Pahad demonstrated about both the test and Israeli cooperation, the refusal of documents seems inexplicable. Yet the documents obtained in response to several requests to DFA fell far short of the documentary confirmation sought. SAHA obtained:

· a letter dated 6 June 1985 from the South African ambassador to the United Kingdom's director general of foreign affairs enclosing newspaper articles about the alleged nuclear test in 1979;

· a letter dated 24 May 1985 from the South African ambassador to the US director general of foreign affairs regarding '[r]enewed allegation of SA nuclear explosion in 1979';

· a one-page letter dated 24 June 1985 from the executive chairman of the AEC of South Africa to the South African director general of foreign affairs regarding the '[r]enewed allegation of SA nuclear explosion in 1979';

· a letter dated 7 January 1987 from the general secretary of the Scottish Campaign for Nuclear Disarmament to the South African consul in Glasgow regarding Marion Island, indicating concern about a report of a runway planned for the island for use as a South Atlantic nuclear weapons testing base and alleged visits of South African and Israeli military advisors to the island; and

· a response to this letter from the South African consul in Glasgow on 19 January 1987 denying that such a runway was planned or that the island would be used as a testing base.

While each of these documents is relevant to understanding the history of the nuclear weapons programme, the fact that there was no indication of whether the documents formed part of a series held by DFA made it almost impossible for researchers to take the matter any further through requests for additional information.

viii. Why did F.W. de Klerk decide to reveal South Africa's nuclear weapons programme in 1993, and did he make an honest declaration about the programme?

On 24 March 1993 De Klerk admitted to Parliament that South Africa had stockpiled nuclear weapons that had been dismantled prior to the country's accession to the Nuclear Non-Proliferation Treaty (NPT) on 10 July 1991 and its signature of a Comprehensive Safeguards Agreement with IAEA on 16 September 1991. Tienie Fourie, a former DFA official, is recorded as telling Shelton that the timing of De Klerk's announcement was determined by a planned 'surprise' inspection by IAEA during which inspectors would have discovered evidence of the weapons programme. Such a discovery would have been extremely embarrassing for the South African government. This information led SAHA to request from DFA 'documents President De Klerk used to make [the] decision regarding revealing/dismantling the nuclear weapons programme',[64] and 'communications between Tienie Fourie and SA revealing the nuclear weapons programme and/or IAEA inspections'.[65] SAHA also requested 'communications between SA and the USA regarding dismantling of nuclear weapons'.[66] SAHA's requests to DFA (not limited to the requests noted above) resulted in the release of 21 documents (or parts of documents), but none provide or even suggest an answer to this question.

Buys and Fischer provide some detail. Fischer answered the question by referring to the obvious fact that by 1989 the security threat to South Africa was no longer sufficient to warrant a nuclear deterrent and, indeed, the existence of the weapons posed a threat to South Africa's international relations. He describes the closure of the programme in some detail, and appears to conclude that the programme ended in an honest fashion:

> De Klerk ordered the decommissioning of the pilot enrichment plant that had made the fissile material for the devices and the conversion to civilian use of the factory that had manufactured the devices. When all the fissile material had been recovered from the devices, and returned from Armscor to the custody of the South African Atomic Energy Corporation, South Africa formally acceded to the NPT, on July 10, 1991. By September 16, it had promptly concluded the required full-scope safeguards agreement with the IAEA. Since then the IAEA has carried out 115 inspections in South Africa in order to verify the completeness of the initial report submitted by South Africa on the amount and location of all nuclear material in the country. The IAEA Board of Governors and the general Conference have been informed that the inspections 'found no evidence that the list of facilities and locations of outside facilities provided by South Africa in its Initial Report ... was incomplete'. Nor was the IAEA Secretariat 'in possession of any other information suggesting the existence of any undeclared facilities or nuclear material'.[67]

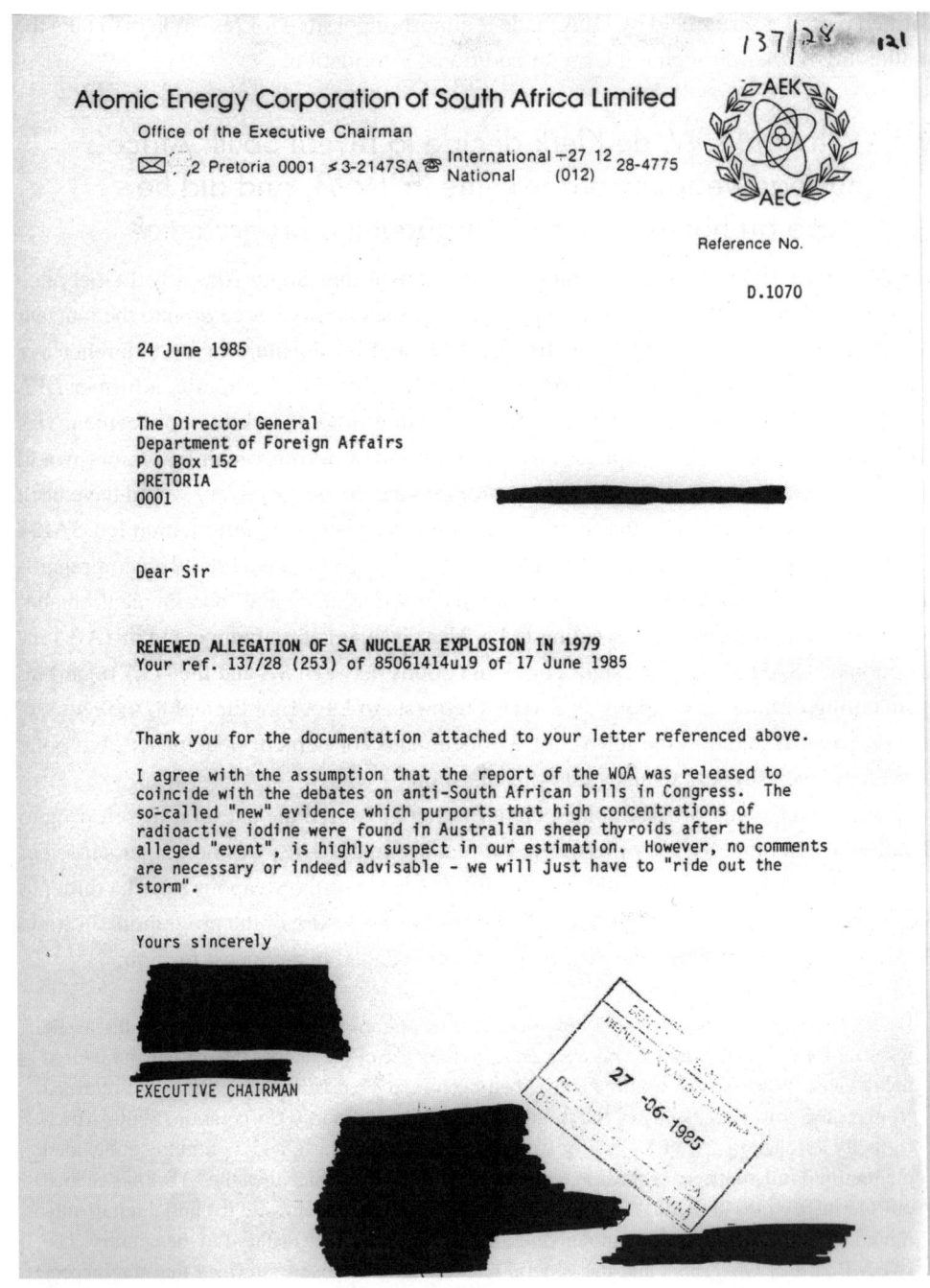

Figure 7: Correspondence dated 24 June 1985 from South Africa's Atomic Energy Corporation to the director general of foreign affairs, with respect to 'handling' allegations relating to South Africa's nuclear weapons programme in the broader context of international efforts to secure comprehensive sanctions against South Africa.

Buys' recollection and analysis were more nuanced. He argued that, given the reality that a significant number of people knew about the programme in detail, destroying the documents was no guarantee that someone would not eventually speak out and thus undermine De Klerk's credibility. He said that the scientists advised De Klerk to invite the international community to verify and audit the closure of the programme.[68]

On the question of whether the South African government held back information about the nuclear weapons programme, Fischer concludes that the only point one can make is that IAEA was:

> reasonably assured that the inventory of nuclear material declared by South Africa [was] complete; the IAEA's 115 inspections have not discovered anything that would suggest otherwise, and it's difficult to see what incentive the government, knowing that its hour was coming, would have had in concealing any HEU.[69]

In a speech made by the South African ambassador to Japan at the Second United Nations Conference: Towards a World Free from Nuclear Weapons, the process of dismantling the nuclear weapons programme was laid out:

> Events leading to De Klerk's 1993 announcement were preceded by the establishment of a steering committee of senior officials who were appointed by the then State President of South Africa in November 1989 to investigate the possibility of dismantling the nuclear programme. The officials were, inter alia, tasked to:

- dismantle the devices under controlled and safe conditions;
- melt and recast the High Enriched Uranium (HEU) from these devices and return it to the AEC of South Africa for safekeeping;
- decontaminate facilities fully and return severely contaminated equipment to AEC;
- destroy all hardware components of the devices as well as technical design and manufacturing information;
- advise the government of a suitable timetable of accession to the NPT, signature of a Comprehensive Safeguards Agreement with the IAEA and submission of a full and complete national initial inventory of nuclear material and facilities as required by the Safeguards Agreement; and
- terminate the operation of the Pilot Enrichment Plant at the earliest opportunity.[70]

The reasons given in this speech for the termination of the nuclear weapons programme are those echoed throughout the literature. They include the changing political circumstances both in South Africa and internationally that resulted in a dramatic reduction in the threat perceptions of the government, the tremendous cost of the programme, and (not mentioned in this speech) concern that the nuclear weapons would end up in the hands of an ANC government. Ironically, it could be argued that the moral advantage gained by South Africa through the voluntary termination of the nuclear programme has given the ANC government the basis on which it can play a prominent and important international role as far as nuclear weapons control is concerned. Augmented by the credibility of those in the ANC who lobbied against the apartheid nuclear weapons programme during the struggle against apartheid, South Africa is an important international voice on nuclear issues and has played a significant role in the establishment of Africa as a nuclear weapons-free zone. Perhaps the present government is concerned that additional details about the programme could undermine its hard-earned credibility.

ix. How did IAEA verify the termination of the weapons programme, and what were the details of the reports South Africa made to IAEA?

Of all the questions posed in this chapter, the question of verification by IAEA is perhaps the one that could have been expected to result in the most substantial responses. While reports by states to the IAEA remain confidential, it is difficult for analysts to understand why details of the verification process would be secret at this stage. Yet requests for documents from NECSA, Armscor and Denel met with the same results as those recorded above.[71] Only a query to DFA met with a positive result in the form of a letter dated 29 June 1993 from the Permanent Mission of South Africa to Dr Hans Blix, director general of IAEA, regarding verification of South Africa's nuclear weapons programme.[72] This letter reiterated South Africa's request for IAEA to verify that the nuclear weapons programme had been terminated. It noted that two teams of nuclear weapons experts had already visited South Africa, and requested that the verification process be completed by the September 1993 meeting of the IAEA board of governors. It contains no details of what was involved in the verification exercise. It is clear from the letter (authored by Jannie Roux) that South Africa was intent upon having the verification exercise completed as soon as possible. Once again, the existence of this document strongly suggests that other similar documents do exist, and there appears to be no convincing reason for them not to be placed in the public domain.

x. Were all the documents relating to the nuclear weapons programme destroyed?

There are several answers to this question — certainly, there are strong indications that the documents held by former members of the programme that related to the details of the programme and the devices, as well as the nuclear strategy, were in fact destroyed in a process described by Buys in some detail in an interview in August 2006 that is reproduced in full in

PERMANENT MISSION OF SOUTH AFRICA
TO THE INTERNATIONAL ATOMIC ENERGY AGENCY

SANDGASSE 33, 1190 VIENNA
TELEPHONE 32 64 93 SERIE

137/10/26.

9/2/2
JEF/ems
29 June 1993

On 24 March this year I wrote to you on the instruction of
my Government, inviting the IAEA to verify inter alia that
South Africa has fully terminated its nuclear weapons
programme, and that all the nuclear material has fully been
accounted for.

Since then, two teams of nuclear weapons experts visited
South Africa as part of this exercise. As was the case
since South Africa acceded to the NPT and signed the
Safeguards Agreement with the IAEA, South Africa offered
all possible assistance to these teams. This was done in a
spirit of ongoing co-operation and transparency and in
acknowledgement of the sometimes difficult task the IAEA
has in ensuring nuclear non-proliferation in the world

Today, in the same spirit of co-operation, I wish to invite
- and indeed urge - the IAEA to complete its verification
exercise in South Africa as soon as possible, and at the
latest in time for the September meeting of the Board of
Governors. South Africa therefore expects a final report on
both its terminated weapons programme, as well as the
completeness of its nuclear inventory, to be presented to
the forthcoming Board Meeting which is due to start on 21
September 1993.

Director-General
International Atomic Energy Agency
P.O.Box 100
1400 Vienna

Figure 8: Correspondence dated 29 June 1993 from the South African Mission of the IAEA to the IAEA requesting finalisation of the verification process confirming South Africa had terminated its nuclear weapons programme, the only country ever to do so. It is unclear why the names of the sender and recipient have been masked.

the annexure to this chapter. However, the fact that the application of PAIA resulted in the release of several documents of relevance suggests that others still exist and managed to escape destruction. What remains most confusing is the apparent inability of Denel, Armscor, NECSA or DOD to provide confirmation or details of the destruction process: DOD confirmed in 2006 that it was not able to locate the disposal authority ordinarily required prior to destroying documents, but alleged that the person responsible for destroying them had taken it.[73]

Conclusion

The fact that South Africa voluntarily terminated its nuclear weapons programme has provided the basis for the current government to engage internationally in discussions about nuclear non-proliferation and to play the role of honest broker in Iraq and to some extent in the controversy around the Iranian nuclear programme. This may mean that, as far as the Mbeki government is concerned, the information that is already in the public domain, however limited in detail, is sufficient to meet its foreign policy requirements. Indeed, it could be argued that any more detailed revelations, particularly about the nature and extent of foreign assistance to the South African nuclear weapons programme, would not necessarily serve the best interests of current foreign relations.

Nevertheless it would seem obvious that a detailed analysis of the factors resulting in the decision to develop nuclear weapons, as well as to terminate the programme, would allow for an even more positive role to be played by the country in international nuclear affairs. Indeed, analysts would be justified in believing that if South Africa is to play a useful role internationally in sharing its nuclear weapons experience in support of the voluntary termination of other nuclear weapons programmes, documentary evidence of the nature of the strategy would be important, but this has not proved to be the case.

This chapter has shown that the application of PAIA has resulted in very little new information being placed in the public domain. Indeed, the value of documentation obtained in terms of revealing important new details of the nuclear weapons programme required a disproportionate investment of time and energy by the applicants. The unfortunate conclusion, therefore, is that PAIA is a blunt instrument for researchers attempting to obtain documents from government departments. There are a number of reasons for this being the case. The experiences of SAHA suggest that there are few government institutions that have, since the demise of apartheid, expended time and resources on archiving and indexing documents from the past. Capacity constraints certainly play a role in making it difficult for institutions to trawl through what must be large caches of documents from the past. The fact that DFA has moved from one building to another added to the difficulty it faced in finding the information sought by applicants. Yet, this did not appear to be the problem faced by Armscor, DME, the Office of the President or DTI. While DME and NECSA appeared to be concerned about the political implications of releasing documents in their possession, their strategy and that of the Office of the President appeared to be to obfuscate and delay their responses until the applicant ran out of steam. Unless there is a clear political advantage to be gained by the institutions in searching for and making documents available, or unless requesters have considerable resources to litigate requests, it is unlikely that PAIA will become an effective tool for those attempting to analyse and record the past.

Annexure A: Approved notes from an interview with Professor Andre Buys

University of Pretoria
14 August 2006

The intention of this interview, conducted by Chandré Gould, was to obtain clarity on the status of the official documents of the South African nuclear weapons programme.

Buys: During all phases of the programme, from the explosives programme to the weapons programme and finally the dismantlement, all the documents relating to the programme were top secret. Top secret security clearance was required of the staff. When the programme changed from a civilian explosives programme to a weapons programme, security became more comprehensive. During the explosives programme at AEC, security clearance [of staff] was done through the police. The process was much less comprehensive than the security clearance process later, when it became a military programme. Then, the security restrictions were far more serious.

As an aside, Buys said that he believed that in the 1970s the United States had a South African informant in the civilian nuclear explosives programme.

In 1970 we started with the nuclear explosives programme. At that time, all the documents and reports were classified top secret, a record was kept of all documents and these were kept on file by the nuclear engineering division of the AEB. I am not 100 per cent sure, but the records were probably physically kept by the secretary of the head of that division of the AEB. But document control was also left to the discretion of individuals who were working with them, and the documents were kept in their offices. That was before it became a nuclear weapons programme. In retrospect, one could say that the documents were treated casually, especially in comparison to the very strict system that followed later.

Interest in nuclear weapons came after the disclosure of the test site in 1977. In 1974 we started preparing the test site. The test site was in the Kalahari, miles away from anything else, and the AEB had no security personnel out there. There was a need for some security at the site, and that's the first time that the SADF was informed about the nuclear explosives programme. At that stage, the contact was not at the highest level; it was the quartermaster general whom the AEB dealt with to get security personnel at the test site. The military provided the protection and personnel control on site. The SADF only became directly involved with the programme when we moved to the Circle site. That's when questions started about document protection. Then we were far more security conscious. Armscor security personnel were responsible for document control; some of them were civilians and some had military backgrounds. But there was full-time staff to look after security. Now security became a major priority.

At the beginning, when we started talking about a nuclear weapons programme for deterrence, some people at the AEC said that we already had a deterrent, that a civilian explosive that could be exploded on demand was sufficient, so there was no need to go any further. But by taking that approach, you are asking the government to bluff, and that bluff could be exposed. In other words, we would not have a credible deterrent taking that route. That was an ongoing argument throughout the life of the programme — when was the deterrent sufficiently credible?

When we started to work [at Circle], we argued that to be credible there must at least be a functional system, even if we knew that we were never going to fight with the weapons. The military agreed with this argument, and that's the basis on which we developed the programme.

When it became a military programme, it was run from the highest level. The chief of the defence force, the minister of defence and the prime minister were involved in the decision making. Authority to go ahead with the weapons programme was obtained from the minister of defence, at that time P.W. Botha.

Gould: Would Vorster not have had to give the go-ahead?

Buys: He would have been consulted.

Gould: At what level, or where would the meetings about the programme have taken place? Would it have been in the State Security Council?

Buys: Probably not at the Security Council level, because the Security Council kept minutes and not all Security Council members would have known about the programme. It was only an inner group of cabinet members who would have known about it, right up to the end. It would have been the minister of defence (P.W. Botha), the minister of foreign affairs (Pik Botha), the minister of finance (Barend du Plessis) and the minister of minerals and energy affairs, at that time F.W. de Klerk.

Gould: So De Klerk knew about the programme from the start?

Buys: Yes, he knew about it from the early 1980s.

As engineers we had to design something. Usually the first step in the design process would be to sit with the user and develop a user requirement specification. For us, that was quite unusual, though, because we had been working for the AEB [which was its own client for the nuclear explosives programme]. Now, for the first time, there was an external client. We were from the AEB, and Armscor was represented by Kentron. The Kentron people taught us how the process would work. There was a user specification requirement needed, but at that stage there was no user, because it was just intended as a deterrent. The military thought that the programme was unnecessary to the fight they were having in Angola and were worried that the programme was drawing funds from the military budget. They were not convinced about this programme at all. So we had to turn to the politicians, but they didn't know what they wanted. So it was left to the scientists. When the facility was first opened, we had a sense that something was missing. Brigadier John Huyser from the SADF's strategic planning division was asked to liaise with us. He had an insider relationship with P.W. [Botha] and could go to him directly without going through official channels. He told us: 'Don't ask too many questions, just make a bomb.' When we asked how big, he said 'very big'. When we asked other questions, we didn't get any satisfactory answers. I was worried; in fact, I was quite panicked, because here we were developing a very serious weapon that we felt nobody knew how to use. That was why I made the statement to P.W. [Botha] when we unveiled the weapons that is quoted in the book by Steyn, Van der Walt and Van Loggerenberg:

[Mr President, we are proud, today, to show you and your colleagues these sophisticated products of South African ingenuity. By placing these weapons in your hands, we are placing a terrible responsibility on your shoulders. We want you to know that we, who understand the consequences of these systems, regularly pray for you and your colleagues. We pray that you will have the wisdom and the necessary understanding of your accountability when you consider their use.]

My recollection of my statement is somewhat different. I think I said:

Mister President, I and my colleagues working in this facility are constantly aware of the huge potential for destruction of these systems. We therefore assure you that we will constantly pray for you and the government that you will have the wisdom to use this capability to the benefit of South Africa and ALL its people.

After that statement, P.W. [Botha] ignored me for the rest of the evening, throughout the cocktail party. But F.W. [de Klerk] came up to me and said that he had thought I was right, and brave to have said that.

When there was no leadership coming from the top, we had to go ahead and design the system. We took the initiative ourselves as engineers and scientists. We developed the nuclear strategy ourselves. The Nuclear Strategy Workgroup initially included Huyser, but he was like a bull in a china shop. I was then chair, and tried to draw up a sensible nuclear strategy for the country. The first strategy document was written by Huyser; that one was signed by P.W. [Botha], but it was ambiguous and spelt out various options: (i) that the weapons could be used as a political tool with no accompanying physical support [the 'bluff' option], (ii) that a nuclear weapon is built and kept secret — covert option, and (iii) once we have a minimal capability — in other words, one weapon — we would disclose it strategically — overt option. In his argument in support of the options, he recommended that we go overt with this. When P.W. [Botha] signed, he wrote on the document, 'I approve but we will wait until we are ready to go public.' But it was not clear what constituted 'ready'. Did it mean when the bomb was ready or when the political situation demanded disclosure? We saw the ambiguity and were concerned that the document was not clear enough. Then we went ahead and developed a strategy that was signed by Magnus Malan [the minister of defence]. We didn't have P.W. [Botha]'s signature on that document. It was a big document, properly bound, a top secret document.

There were three categories of documents relating to the programme: technical documents, strategy documents and technology development documents that related to other work that we did to keep the scientists busy — advanced warhead types and delivery systems.

The document management system was very comprehensive. It was illegal for us to copy any documents, unless we obtained permission and were authorised to do so. Then when copies were made, they were signed for and numbered. Information, including the numbers of the documents and all copies and who had them in their possession, was kept in a formal documents register. Every document and every copy had a unique number. Audits of the documents were done regularly, about once a year, by the security people. Now security clearance was very thorough and included a psychological profile, the person's habits and so on. We were interviewed by professionally trained interviewers. Relatives and friends were also interviewed and personal records checked.

All documents were listed in a register. The physical documents themselves were kept by the people who needed them. When you no longer needed a document, it was returned. When the extra copies of documents were no longer required, they were immediately destroyed.

When F.W. de Klerk took over from P.W. [Botha] in 1989, the decision was made to terminate the programme. One of the first things F.W. [de Klerk] did, in the first week as president, he called in the people from the AEC and Armscor and spoke to them about the programme. He told them, we are now going to negotiate the future of the country and we don't want the nuclear programme to become a red herring — an issue that could affect the negotiations — so we would rather get it out of the way. The deterrent was no longer necessary. That was a view that we generally shared. In fact, that was consistent with the nuclear strategy — when there was no threat, there was no deterrent needed. There were one or two people who were concerned about their futures after the closure of the programme, but there was no one who did not want closure. F.W. [de Klerk] was clear: he didn't want the nuclear [weapons] programme to be a negotiating point for other parties. He wanted it wiped out as if it had never existed. Dr Stumpf interpreted that to mean that we must try to destroy everything in such a way that we could say that there was never such a programme. Its existence could be denied. Stumpf thought that De Klerk was going to want to deny the existence of the programme. Stumpf then called in Armscor, Advena and the AEB and said, 'the existence of the programme will be denied by the government therefore we must destroy all traces of the programme'. That was his interpretation of De Klerk's order. So, starting in 1989, there was a total clean-up of all materials, facilities and documents.

By that time I was no longer in the programme; I was a senior manager at Armscor. At that time, though, I still had some documents, including the original strategy document that had Malan's signature on it. One day, it must have been in 1989, some security guys came to see me about the termination of the programme. They knew, from the record, exactly which documents I must still have had. They told me I had to give them the documents for destruction. I argued with them, because I didn't agree that all the documents should be destroyed, specifically not things like the strategy document. In the end, I was forced to hand them the documents or face prosecution. They left with the documents. I tried to complain, but got the same answer from everyone. The security guys were from Armscor Information security.

I heard that the documents were taken to Advena or the old Circle plant, where they were put in the furnace and burned. That process was also audited. They wanted an independent audit to show that everything was destroyed, so Professor Mouton, who was at that stage at Stellenbosch and highly regarded at the top political level, was appointed to audit the destruction. There was a problem with the building where the uranium furnace had been: it was slightly contaminated still, so they pulled up the floor and recast it so that no radiation would be detected.

So why was the existence of the programme eventually declared? We said that you can destroy the physical stuff, but you cannot destroy people's memories. It would be stupid to deny the existence of the programme, anyway, as it will inevitably leak out at some point. Rather, we advised, go for open verification of termination and let them [the international community] approve of the audit. I think F.W. [de Klerk] also realised that there was an advantage to be gained from disclosure in 1991. Anyway, it had to be disclosed before it leaked out.

There is every reason to suspect that every single document was destroyed. But there is human nature. People do keep things, but one has to be careful in trying to find this out, because if anyone kept copies of the documents, they would have been illegal copies, unofficial copies. I have tried to use my position of trust with people to try to find some documents, but I have not come up with anything substantial. I have found bits and pieces, but nothing of real value — for example, I would find a table of weights of materials, but that's it. Even the Jericho missile document that SAHA had released comes from a different area. John Huyser from strategic planning was asked to consider whether Jericho missiles would be of any use to us, probably because Israel had approached South Africa with an offer for them. But this document pre-dated the development of our nuclear weapons. It was not in any way related to the nuclear weapons programme.

In the programme, we were very cautious. We rather over-classified documents than risked them being under-classified. That is why no documents had any classification other than top secret. That is also why they were all destroyed. All there is now is an oral history.

I don't believe that there is still an attitude [in government] that we have to hide things. There are still sensitivities — commercial confidentialities — equipment that was purchased from other countries and these are relationships that people don't want to compromise. For example, if a company in the U[nited] K[ingdom] sold us a high-powered X-ray machine and that were to come out now, it would serve no purpose other than to harm the company. Let me give you an example.

In Armscor we wanted to have a history written about the armaments industry. So the Contemporary History Department at the University of the Free State was tasked, paid and given access to the Armscor archives. They even got permission to publish, but in the early 1990s, just before it was ready for publication, it was asked if it was really prudent to publish. It was felt that the timing would be inappropriate. We held the book back then, because it seemed a bit irrelevant to publish then, or even politically insensitive. In fact, it has still not been published.

During the TRC, Armscor was asked to make a presentation. I said that we should see if there was anything that we ought to confess, so we had an internal investigation. But we could not find any human rights violations. We could find violations of laws — the laws of other countries — but nothing of value to submit to the TRC. The TRC was not happy with that and sent their own team to the archive, but they didn't know where to start. It's a huge archive with many documents. We told them about the manuscript [described above] and officially presented it to them — that should still be part of the TRC records. Today, it would be silly to publish it — in any case, it would be more about how we beat sanctions, and that could look like bragging.

Prof. Buys' final comments: You must remember that in the 1970s, science was king. It was a pursuit of technology. The philosophy was to do the R&D [research and development] and the applications would follow — don't let the market dictate what you should do. I disagreed; I felt that we should be more pragmatic. I later also opposed the Kalahari test because I thought that by doing the test (which wasn't really necessary) we would increase the threat to South Africa, because we would create the impression that we had a weapon before we in fact did. That could have brought Russian nuclear weapons into the region. The world would never have believed that it was a civilian test. Remember that for this programme, because we were under sanctions, there was no information about how to build nuclear weapons. We had to reinvent the wheel, and people were completely absorbed and motivated by the science. They didn't always think of the bigger picture.

5

Unlocking South Africa's Military Archives

Laura Pollecut

Introduction

And it was terrible ... I couldn't believe that her body could survive it all.

Trudie Grobler, intern psychologist at No. 1 Military Hospital, on observing an aversion therapy session where a woman was subjected to such severe shocks that her shoes flew off her feet[1]

The mantra no doubt found throughout this publication is that the apartheid era was characterised by censorship and secrecy, particularly in the areas of defence and security. Despite laudatory objectives, the South African Medical Services (SAMS) of the South African Defence Force (SADF) carried its fair share of secrets and abuses. Although the Truth and Reconciliation Commission (TRC) unlocked some of these secrets, the truth revealed was miniscule in relation to what remains unknown. Despite consistent claims that thousands of documents have been destroyed or lost, many still exist, but are difficult to access in the archival maze in which they are buried.

In the same year that the Promotion of Access to Information Act No. 2 of 2000 (PAIA) came into being, the South African History Archive (SAHA) board approved the repositioning of SAHA as a human rights archive dedicated to documenting and contributing to the continuing struggle for justice in South Africa.[2] In 2001, SAHA and Gay and Lesbian Archive, an independent SAHA special project, embarked on a project to proactively seek records and build on research already published on gays in the military by requesting access via PAIA to documents held by the Department of Defence (DOD). The project, because of funding availability, had two distinct periods: the first resulted in a report published in 2003, and the second in a report still to be published at the time of writing.

In the first phase of this project, SAHA secured finding aids in the form of filing systems, lists and other information from the DOD archives that would help facilitate requests. Although seeking to uncover more information on gays in the military was central to the project, the work was by no means confined to this.

Gays in the military: Background

It became clear that the practice of psychiatry in the SADF was closely wedded to the preoccupation of the military authorities with eliminating patterns of behaviour that did not conform to SADF discipline and the apartheid war effort.[3]

Reports of the mental abuse of conscripts first surfaced in an article entitled 'The abuse of psychiatry in the SADF' in *War Resister*,[4] published in the 1980s by the London-based Committee on South African War Resistance. The article reveals information about the psychiatry ward at the No. 1 Military Hospital in Pretoria, where the then head of psychiatry was Dr Aubrey Levin. Although it explains that there were some genuinely disturbed people in the ward, a percentage of them were so-called drug users or gay. War resisters were also seen by the SADF as being disturbed. The article includes information on Greefswald, a notorious SADF drug rehabilitation camp in the then northern Transvaal, which Levin was purported to run.

The article devotes a section to the treatment of gays who were admitted to the hospital. It says that under Levin's regime, homosexuality was regarded as an aberration, and gays were subjected to electroconvulsive aversion therapy, a behavioural therapy supposedly used to correct their deviance. *Behavioral Psychology* states that:

> This therapy is essentially the opposite of desensitisation therapy. The object of aversion therapy is for the patient to dislike a stimulus that is currently perceived by the patient often as 'pleasurable' in some aspect. Aversion therapy is traditionally used for smoking cessation, alcoholism, gambling, obesity and sexual deviation. Stimuli associated with the behaviour to adjust/remove are paired with unpleasant/painful stimuli such as an electric shock or nausea brought about by administering emetic drugs.[5]

Accusations of this nature arose again in submissions to the health sector hearings[6] of the TRC concerning ethical issues and human rights abuses in the psychiatric services of the SADF.[7] Levin, working in Canada at the time, was summoned to appear at the hearings to answer accusations about unethical treatment of members of the SADF. In a response directed to the TRC in June 1997, Levin confirmed that he practised and advocated aversion therapy in the SADF, but defended his actions by saying that 'aversive therapy was an established form of behavioural therapy much in vogue in the 1960s and early 1970s, used at the time in the treatment of patients who could not accept their homosexuality'.[8] The TRC, however, did not have an opportunity to question Levin further. Levin received the letter from the commission containing the allegations three or four days before the

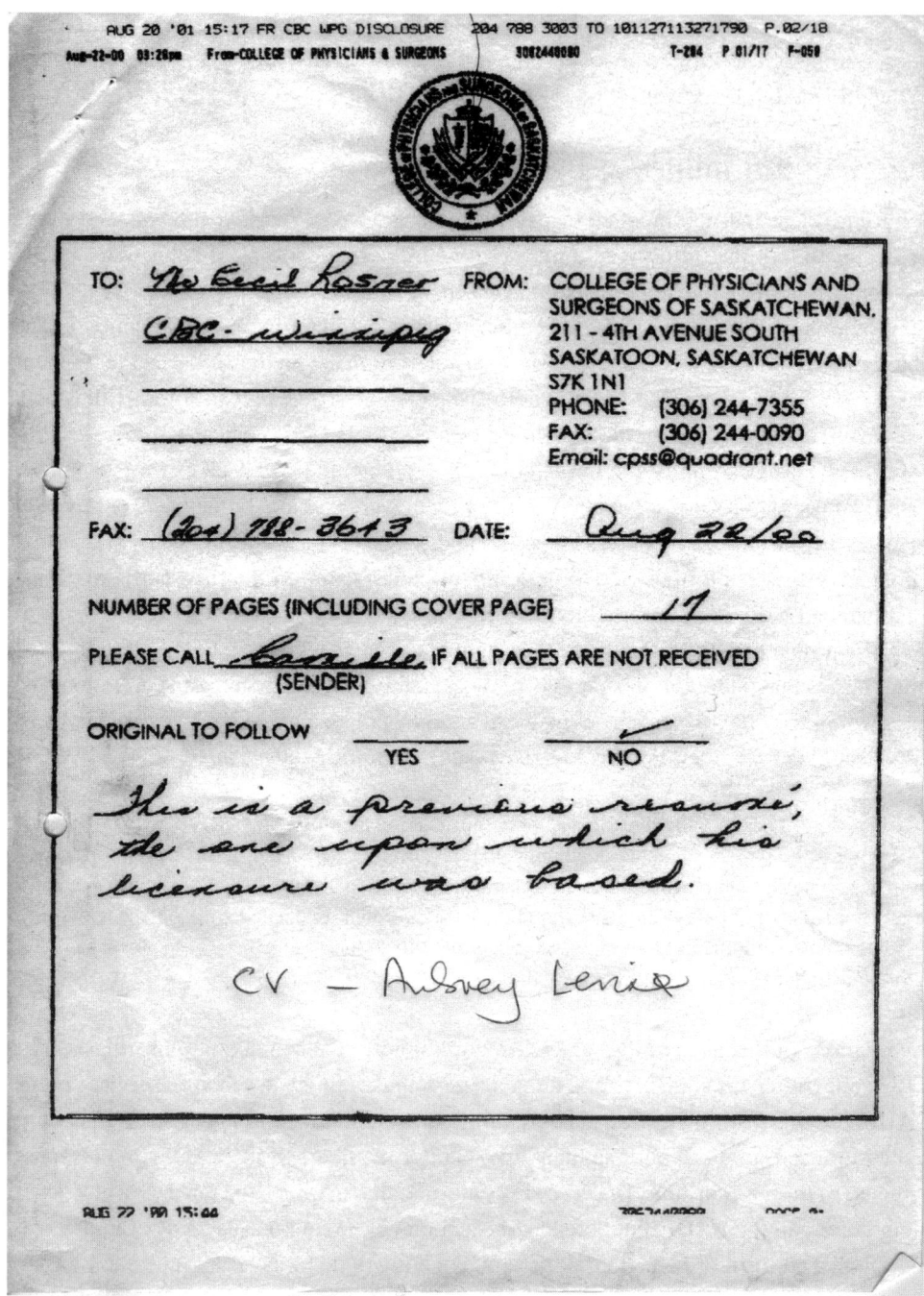

Figure 1: Cover letter of fax transmittal of the CV of Dr Aubrey Levin, the SADF doctor responsible for the SADF's controversial aVersion Project (Archived as SAHA Collection AL 2878 – A1.3).

hearing was scheduled to take place. In his written response, he argued that it would be impossible for him to 'drop everything, find large amounts of money for travel and legal expenses, instruct counsel, prepare a rebuttal, obtain documents and be able to attend the hearing'. Although the health sector hearing took place, Levin did not appear before the TRC.

The SAMS of the SADF did, however, appear before the TRC; the input was disappointing. General Knobel, surgeon general of the SADF from 1988 and the then surgeon general of the South African National Defence Force (SANDF),[9] delivered a presentation that set out to show SAMS in a very positive light, emphasising its reconstitution into a medical corps serving the defence force in a new South Africa. Very little of his presentation addressed the failures and racism of the past.[10] This prompted the chair of the hearing, Dr Wendy Orr, to say: 'General Knobel, I am sorry to interrupt you but we are very pressed for time, so could I please ask you to sum up within the next few minutes so that we can move into questions, because we do have many of those.'[11] When Knobel finally did conclude, another panel member, Dr Ramashala, said:

Sir, we have to face our past, and this submission has to address the past, in particular the past abuses. The omission at the centre of this submission is the complete silence around the war in which the SADF was involved. We are told by you, and through your submission, of policies, structures, achievements and the war is mentioned almost tangentially now and then.[12]

In defending the submission, Knobel said he had expected to get a set of questions that SAMS would be required to answer at the hearing, but that these questions were only received at lunchtime that day. He therefore asked for time to prepare answers. Among these questions were some relating to homosexuality:

- What was the SADF's policy with respect to sexual orientations, specifically homosexuality?
- Did SAMS play any role in the deployment or implementation of this policy, that is, did it contest or support this policy?
- Was SAMS' Director of Psychology involved in treating homosexuals?
- What methods were used: for example, was aversion therapy used, etc.?[13]

The final TRC report, in its section on the health sector hearing, was highly critical of SAMS. It held SAMS responsible for putting health workers in the position where strategic needs were given priority over the health of the patients treated by military medical personnel, and where, as a result, it was almost impossible to uphold international ethical and professional standards.[14] The report also confirms that the panel at the hearing felt that SAMS was evasive and that it made no attempt to consider the possible involvement of health professionals in human rights abuses, either through acts of commission or omission: 'The quality of the SAMS responses to the very extensive and probing list of questions posed at the hearing merely entrenched this perception.'[15]

The TRC's findings on SAMS did not include a specific reference to the treatment of homosexuals in the SADF. However, they did say that SAMS failed to provide adequate mental health support for SADF members, particularly conscripts exposed to violence.[16] The TRC also found that:

> The Department of Health, the SADF and the South African Police and Prisons failed to provide adequate training, support and ethical guidance to those health professionals in their employ, who were working in environments in which there was a conflict of interest between employer and patient. The interests of the patient/client were thus frequently subjugated to those of the state.[17]

After the TRC: The aVersion Project

In 1999, *The aVersion Project: Human Rights Abuses of Gays and Lesbians in the SADF by Health Workers during the Apartheid Era* was published by a consortium of organisations.[18] The research recorded in this publication took over where the TRC left off: it sought to investigate and document alleged abuses experienced by those serving in the SADF between 1960 and 1991 because they were or were perceived to be homosexual or to have same-sex partners. Research was conducted by interviewing survivors of medical abuse and their families or friends, as well as other individuals who could cast light on particular aspects of the research. The project also examined the institutional context, including explicit and implicit policies within both the military and the health professions, that allowed abuses by health professionals to occur.

Although many practitioners considered aversion therapy to be an authentic means to change a person's behaviour, it was always questionable as a treatment. The rather dry definition of aversion therapy provided earlier does not convey the pain and degradation experienced by patients who underwent it. An extract from an interview detailed in the aVersion Project report illustrates this:

> I found the therapy itself terribly painful, very disorientating.

> How did it make you feel?

> Oh complete depression. Ja, very down. It wasn't like I now suddenly found I'd turned into some hetero pussy hunter or something. I was actually just completely freaked out … and confused. It certainly didn't do much for my impulses of attraction for other boys, of which there were plenty of handsome specimens running around 1 Mil.[19]

Regarding practice in the treatment of homosexuality, King, Smith and Bartlett conclude:

> Only a small minority believed that current practice denied people distressed by their homo-

sexuality an effective means to change their sexual orientation. Our data shows how assumptions about public morality and professional authority can lead to the medicalisation of human differences and the infringement of human rights.[20]

Figure 2: Still from Gerald Kraak's 2003 film *Property of the State: Gay Men in the Apartheid Military.* Copyright: Gerald Kraak.

The aVersion Project was holistic and thorough. The personal accounts in the report of the project confirmed the electric shock and drug treatment doled out in Ward 22 of No. 1 Military Hospital, as reported in *War Resister.*[21] However, PAIA was not available to the researchers of the project or the TRC had they wanted to access more documentation from the DOD archives. The right of access to information was included in both the Interim Constitution and the 1996 final Constitution, but the enabling legislation was only enacted in 2001. Any right of access would have to be invoked in terms of the Constitution and was likely to encounter challenge.

The aVersion Project report did include SADF policy directive no. HSAW/1/13/82, which instructed staff during recruitment to identify those with behavioural problems and ensure they were not admitted to the permanent force. Evidence of whether or not aversion therapy was official policy within the SADF, however, was not established. Access to records would not only clarify whether or not medical personnel conducting therapy of this nature were acting within or outside that policy, but would also reveal complaints against SADF medical personnel in connection with discrimination or other human rights abuses.

Although a number of records were open at the DOD archives, the majority of them are still classified. Requests through PAIA would provide impetus for declassification and the release of records previously unseen.

Where to start? Using PAIA

The various filing systems in use in the DOD archives, as well as numerous lists of records held by both the military and military intelligence secured by SAHA at the start of the project[22] were consulted to gain an insight into what records were available and how best to word requests. Dr Aubrey Levin practised psychiatry at 1 Military Hospital during the period 1969–74; this period was perceived as being pivotal to the research. As mentioned earlier, the search was not confined to the issue of gays in the military, and research was extended from the 1960s into the 1980s. Records related to the SAHA archives[23] would also be requested in the hope that more information on this period of our history would be revealed. These included records relating to a number of NGOs, such as those involved in opposing the system and in conscientious objection. Lists of overarching collections were requested, including of heads of the army, the minister of defence, the surgeon general and the chaplain general, and from these lists files were requested for perusal.

Department of Defence archives

During apartheid, South Africa was a highly militarised society.[24] Militarisation reached its peak in the 1980s under President P.W. Botha, who was previously minister of defence in the National Party government. The use of extreme repression and censorship was inevitable, given the scenario of a minority government attempting to hold onto power in the face of a vast majority bent on liberation. The government controlled the flow of information, and those attempting to assert their right to know were labelled unpatriotic and the enemy.

DOD records date from 1912, when the Union Defence Force (UDF) was established. The archival records for the period 1912–69, which reflect the main business activities of all the components of the UDF and the SADF, are automatically available. The operational records relate to the First and Second World Wars, the Berlin Airlift and the Korean War, as well as military exercises and mobilisation during internal uprisings such as the industrial strikes of 1914 and 1922, the 1914–15 rebellion, and the unrest in the 1950s and 1960s.[25] The archives also hold the non-current records of the present-day DOD, including those of the SANDF.

Although the DOD archives, in particular the archives relating to the two World Wars, have been accessible to the public in the past, the notion of allowing citizens access to military documents of any description would have been abhorrent to the apartheid regime. Given this history, it was pleasing to note the willingness of the military to implement PAIA and to cooperate with organisations such as SAHA. Nevertheless, despite being staffed in the main by long-serving members with appropriate qualifications, the lack of streamlined and computer-based systems for access led to considerable delays. Harris and Pickover relevantly note: 'Traditional paper-based systems tend to be poorly resourced, managed by junior officials with little status and subject to high turnover rates, and imperfectly connected — if at all — to parallel or related electronic systems.'[26] As a result, the staff often lament that there is no money to improve efficiency and access. Given the breadth and density of the documentation retained at the archives, it is difficult to see how a digital environment could be implemented without considerable financial outlay.

PAIA requests

To ensure the requests encompassed what we were looking for, they were generally couched fairly broadly. This led to both positive and negative results. Requests were made, for example, for 'all SADF records of 1 Military Hospital Psychiatric Ward — period 1970 to 1990', and 'all SADF records relating to policy on homosexuality and to treatment of homosexuality'. The former were sought in an attempt to find records of patients who had been treated for 'sexual deviance', homosexuality and other alleged abuses that had surfaced regarding the mental treatment of members of the SADF. With the broad request on the policy and treatment of homosexuality, we were hoping to find other policy documents that would confirm the attitude apparent in SADF policy directive no. HSAW/1/13/82, which was already in the public domain. There was also the possibility that these documents would implicate policymakers in discrimination against and treatment of homosexuals or even of young, sensitive men who did not fit the army's stereotype.

The requests were submitted in batches and assessed by the staff at the DOD archives in terms of the right of access and the need for declassification.[27] This takes considerable time, as staff at the archives have differing security status and not all documentation is accessible to all staff; requests are therefore rarely responded to within the time periods prescribed by PAIA. Nevertheless, once a record has been declassified, future access by other requesters is a given.[28]

The first batch of requests was made in 2001 and the next followed in 2002. This constituted 26 requests in all, including nine requests for personal files. As time went by, framing of requests and a better understanding of the system made it possible to be more targeted in our search. Unless the requester knows the exact file he/she is looking for, a request may generate lists of records to be perused, and boxes of possibly relevant records for identification and request. Gaining access to indexes of specific bodies of files, such as surgeon general, chaplain general and minister of defence files, assisted in formulating more specific requests, but also, unfortunately, transferred the burden of finding pertinent information to the researcher. Whether or not this saves costs in terms of paying the archives for the search is questionable. It does, however, provide an opportunity to closely examine records and uncover valuable documentation that may otherwise have been overlooked. Another financial saving is that one requests perusal only until one locates something of relevance, which is then copied and paid for.[29]

By the time the first Gays in the Apartheid Military project report was produced in 2003, thousands of records had been perused, but the search was by no means exhausted. In addition, because of long delays by the DOD archives, records were still outstanding from the requests made in 2002. Days were spent at the DOD archives perusing lists of chaplain general files, as well as those of the surgeon general that had to be declassified.[30] Possible sources of information were identified and lists of requests submitted.

It became clear early on in our efforts that the DOD archives were working with limited resources and that there would be a degree of discretion in terms of the turn-around time frames stipulated by PAIA.[31] Regular meetings between SAHA and the staff at the DOD archives to discuss progress on all requests were helpful. At each meeting, DOD tabled a list of requests and the progress being made on each. If archives staff felt they needed further information to find a record, they were able to articulate this before declaring that the records could not be found. Senior staff were always present and, whether true or not, this tended to make us believe that they were treating the requests with the necessary commitment, despite the passing of time. While still in excess of the allowable extensions of time contained in section 26 of PAIA, it was necessary to concede to long delays to enable searches through large numbers of records; compliance with the original period would have unreasonably interfered with the activities of the public body concerned and may have resulted in raising of the exemption that allows a body to refuse access if it would result in an unreasonable diversion of resources.[32] DOD was also on a learning curve. All-encompassing requests such as 'all records relating to the treatment of homosexuality' would obviously take more time than a request for a specific file.

In retrospect, the records retrieved as a result of these early requests were limited, insofar as SADF policy on homosexuality, Dr Levin and aversion therapy were concerned. This is particularly so, given the number of hours spent perusing lists and records. A request related to the surgeon general records during this period hoped to turn up further policy documents similar to the policy memos of the 1980s, but none came to light at this point.[33] More success was achieved with records pertaining to the drug rehabilitation facility Greefswald. As a result of SAHA's first request seeking files on the camp in 2001,[34] lists were provided for perusal and records were identified and requested. Access was refused to five of them. This suggests that the more knowledgeable the researcher is regarding the filing systems, the better the chances are for success. PAIA is undoubtedly a powerful tool for digging deep, but does have its limitations. Military intelligence had to be involved in the declassification process and it is here that a large backlog exists; acceptance of a place in the queue with other requesters plays havoc with the legal requirements of stipulated times for dealing with requests and determining whether an internal appeal should be submitted.

In terms of expanding our project to other anti-apartheid records related to conscientious objectors, the Black Sash and the Institute for a Democratic Alternative in South Africa (Idasa), a certain degree of success was achieved. A substantial body of records on the SADF and conscientious objection came to light.[35] Due to the volume of files, not all were copied and archived at SAHA; they have been declassified and are available to the public at the DOD archives.[36]

Unnecessary masking

Redaction of information was not common in early requests; access was often simply refused. This could have been due to a number of factors, including that the concept of transparency and openness was new for bureaucrats and that PAIA was a relatively new piece of legislation. However, with pressure from requesters, including through litigation, the realisation that a document *could* be released with certain information masked led to releases with redactions from 2003. This was also problematic.

In 2005, after several years of waiting, the records of Minister of Defence P.W. Botha became available.[37] SAHA had requested perusal of these files in the hope of locating records relevant to the project objective of gaining additional information on policies regarding homosexuals and on whether the minister himself had sanctioned or was aware of the psychiatric treatment of members of the SADF. However, instead of providing inspection of the records, thousands of pages were copied and released.[38] The copying came about as a result of what the DOD archives saw as a need to mask all third-party names; in order to provide us with the records, they had to be copied to be masked. This had significant consequences.

Firstly, SAHA was charged for the copying, a cost researchers who are merely seeking perusal of the records ordinarily do not incur. Secondly, although DOD archives retained both the original *unmasked* documentation and the masked declassified documentation, a subsequent researcher wishing to peruse the records would be confronted with the masked copies without knowing what had been redacted. Of real concern, however, was the basis of the masking. Although SAHA appreciates the need to protect the privacy of individuals, the bulk of the masking was inappropriate, and at times appeared arbitrary and careless. For example:

- The names of people writing letters in an organisational or institutional capacity were masked. For example, the name of the author of a letter from the Civil Rights League that queried how the board that considers conscientious objection applications was set up was masked, as was the name of the official to whom the letter was addressed.
- The name of an official on a letter from parents wanting to know about the circumstances of their son's injury was masked.
- A letter from the attorney representing the Jehovah's Witnesses has all details concerning the attorney blanked out, although the advocate is mentioned by name.
- Names of people in correspondence with National Party officials, members of Parliament, and provinces and municipalities are masked, although they are writing and receiving correspondence in their official capacities.

Section 34(2) of PAIA states, among other things, that access to a document may not be refused on the grounds of unreasonable disclosure of personal information insofar as the information is in the public domain, is about a person who could not reasonably expect the information to be private, or relates to the position or functions of an official of a public body.[39] Where the exception applies, masking of the name may be appropriate if the individual does not consent to the document's disclosure or he/she cannot be located. However, where the exception to the exemption applies, masking should not be undertaken. In the instances raised above, one or more of these exceptions to the privacy exemption could have applied.

The excessive masking was raised subsequently with the DOD archives, the staff of which were apologetic and explained that due to limited resources, an inexperienced contractor had been employed to undertake the masking; it would be reconsidered. Obligations in terms of PAIA are not seen as a budget priority, and personnel are often contracted on a temporary basis. As a result, a lack of consistency in executing severance obligations is evident.

Box 5.1: The Black Sash

Records released about the anti-apartheid organisation known as the Black Sash[40] mainly cover the period 1985–87. They give insight into how anti-apartheid organisations were infiltrated. The sheet covering the information provided from a meeting, for example, has the source's name excised. This was presumably the name of the agent who infiltrated the group.

Mundane general circulars, such as those for the morning market, were obviously valuable, as they provided telephone numbers of some of the more active members.

Individuals talking at meetings also appear to be protected — masked, possibly to protect them or to prevent anyone isolating the name of the informer — although more prominent members, e.g. then office bearer Sheena Duncan, are not masked. Documentation comes from all regions, except the then province of Natal.

The gaps in the sequence of the documents suggest that some of the documentation was considered too sensitive to be included. Because of limited resources and the fact that the Black Sash was not the central focus of the research, these gaps were not challenged.

The released records

Policies regarding homosexuality

On policy and homosexuality, one of the earliest records SAHA received, dated 5 March 1979, is located within the minutes of the Defence Command Council (DCC) and is entitled 'Item 14 (confidential) — treatment of homosexuals in the SADF'. It states that, after discussion, DCC approved:

· disciplinary action against offenders; and
· the handling of matters internally rather than through the civil courts.

The subtext of this record is an implicit instruction to punish homosexual members of the SADF for their sexual orientation. It also suggests that there was a strong possibility of human rights abuses that had the tacit approval of DCC.

The major discovery at this point consisted of policy directives on homosexuality, dated about a decade after Levin conducted aversion therapy.[41] They were replicas of policy directive no. HSAW/1/13/82, referred to above; it would seem that each year the same memo was revised and circulated. These memorandums, labelled 'discipline/immorality/homosexuality (onsedelikheid)' and circulated among senior commanding officers, dealt with how homosexuals (or suspected homosexuals) should be handled on enlisting. They illustrate quite clearly that homosexuality was seen by those in authority as an obscenity. The reasons proffered for dealing with it as a disciplinary matter included that it could damage the name of the army, undermine discipline and expose certain leaders to extortion. The documents are clear that recruiting officers were to discourage candidates for the permanent force from joining where there were grounds for suspicion that such a candidate was homosexual. Further, existing members were to be discouraged from these practices, and those under suspicion were to be under constant supervision.

Access to incident reports

Access to files regarding injuries were sought to see whether any reports or complaints had been made that related to aversion therapy.[42] Nothing relevant emerged from this track either, because most of the records reflect injuries incurred in service in the field or in motor vehicle accidents. Recruitment files and records relating to exemptions and postponements, as well as administration complaints and irregularities, were accessed for similar reasons. None of the files perused indicated that an exemption had been sought due to a complaint made about the aversion programme.[43] Files relating to pensions were also accessed to see if documentation could be located that might have been expunged from Levin's personal file. Some of these records provide interesting insight into how apartheid resulted in different criteria for the different race groups and in the establishment of separate departments. However, we were unable to locate information relating to aversion therapy practised by Levin, or to any information that would reveal the experiences of servicemen.

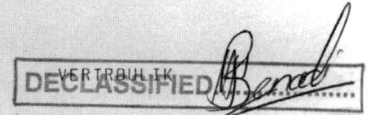

AANHANGSEL A BY BELEIDSDIREKTIEF
NR H SAW/   GEDATEER
JANUARIE 1982

DISSIPLINE : ONSEDELIKHEID : HOMOSEKSUALISTE

1.   Volgens informasie beskikbaar wil dit blyk dat die verskynsel
van homoseksualiteit onder lede van die SA Weermag al meer en
meer sy kop uitsteek.

2.   Homoseksualisme is geen nuwe verskynsel nie.   Dit is deel van
elke samelewing en dit was deur die eeue die geval.   Dit fluktueer
in voorkoms ; in tye van spanning en onsekerheid in die wêreld is
daar altyd 'n toename.   Dit moet aanvaar word dat 'n toename vir die
burgerlike bevolking ook 'n toename in die SA Weermag sal meebring.
'n die huidige tydstip van groter permissiwiteit, asook die feit
t sekere instansies homoseksualisme wil kondoneer of probeer goed=
praat, kan die verskynsel slegs afbrekende en ondermynende gevolge
in die samelewing hê.

3.   In die SA Weermag kan dit nog erger gevolge hê : nie net kan
dit die beeld van die SA Weermag skend nie, maar dit kan dissipline
direk ondermyn en kan betrokke lede ook blootstel aan afpersing,
wat vanselfsprekend ook 'n groter sekerheidsrisiko meebring.   Dit
is dus baie duidelik dat in die militêre milieu gedragsafwykinge
van hierdie aard onder beide geslagte totaal onaanvaarbaar is.

4.   Dit word besef dat dit nie altyd maklik is om die gevalle
van gedragsafwykinge te identifiseer nie.   Baie van hierdie mense
sal in die meeste gevalle nie erken dat hulle hul aan misstappe van
homoseksualisme skuldig maak nie, en buitendien slaag die grootste
gros daarin om hul probleem baie doeltreffend verborge te hou.
Te alle koste moet vermy word dat daar 'n heksejag van stapel
gestuur word, want dit kan slegs tot groter verleentheid vir die SA
'ermag lei.   Waar daar egter enige redelike gronde bestaan om
t vermoed dat 'n lid hom/haar aan gedragsafwykinge skuldig maak,
moet so 'n saak sonder versuim verder ondersoek word.   Alles moont=
lik moet gedoen word om die probleem te bekamp.

5.   Hoewel dit geensins die bedoeling is om aan Weermagsdele, Staf=
afdelinge en Ondersteuningsdiense gedetailleerde voorskrifte te
gee nie, veral in die lig van die feit dat elke geval op sy eie
meriete hanteer behoort te word, moet die algemene riglyne soos
hieronder aangedui gevolg word.

6.   Staandemag

     a.   In die eerste geval moet sover moontlik gepoog word om te
          verhoed dat lede wat 'n homoseksuele neiging het, in die
          Staandemag opgeneem word.   Hoewel alle gevalle nie geïden=
          tifiseer sal word nie, sal party gevalle wel aan die lig
          kom as gevolg van persoonlike onderhoude.

     b.   Met die keuring van dames moet daar gepoog word om 'n kun=
          dige persoon beskikbaar te hê om voorlopige evaluasie te
          doen en enige afwykende neigings te identifiseer.

Figure 3: SADF correspondence from 1982 entitled *Discipline: Promiscuity: Homosexuality* suggesting ways in which testing can be undertaken on potential soldiers to identify and weed out homosexuals (Archived as SAHA Collection AL2878 – A1.5.1).

GG/106/19/16/1

Telefoon	:	21-3611
Byl	:	36
Telegramme	:	SURGEN

SAGD Hoofkwartier
Privaatsak X202
Pretoria
0001

DECLASSIFIED

Julie 1981

Hoof van die SA Weermag (HSP)

GEDRAGSAFWYKINGS BY NDP'S/S MAG LEDE

1. U skrywe HSP/DPA/106/19/16/1 van 27 Mei het betrekking.

2. Homoseksualisme is deel van elke samelewing en dit was deur die eeue die
geval. Selfs in die Bybel word daarvan melding gemaak. In die SA Weermag is
dit geen nuwe verskynsel wat nou eers sy kop uitsteek nie. Ook is deur onder-
soekers getoon dit fluktueer in voorkoms. In tye van spanning en onsekerheid
in die wêreld is daar altyd 'n toename. Dit moet aanvaar word dat 'n toename vir
die burgerlike bevolking ook 'n toename in die SAW sal meebring.

3. Of daar huideliglik 'n toename in gevalle is, kan moeilik bepaal word. Daar
is geen vorige statistiek waarna verwys kan word nie. Om die persentasie gevalle te probeer bepaal sal ook nie veel waarde hê nie, want hierdie mense sal
in die meeste gevalle dit nie érken nie en buitendien slaag die grootste gros
homoseksualiste daarin om hulle probleem baie doeltreffend verborge te hou. Uit
informasie tot die SAGD se beskikking wil dit nie voorkom of daar wel 'n buite-
gewone toename in die SAW is nie.

4. Die SA Weermag is in breë verband 'n weergawe van die Suid Afrikaanse volk.
Dit geld ook wat betref die voorkoms van homoseksualisme en lesbinisme, hoewel
ook in die algemeen gesê kan word dat die SA Weermag minder aantreklik is vir
homoseksualiste is dit ook waar dat die instrukteurs- en verpleegberoepe baie
aantreklik is vir lesbiërs. Baie van hierdie lesbiese dames lewer uitstekende
diens en is dikwels uitstaande in hulle vakindelings, veral wat sport en instruksie
aanbetref. Ook beskik baie van hulle oor sterk leierskapeienskappe.

5. Alhoewel hierdie afwykings nie goedgepraat mag word nie, moet dit aanvaar
word dat sulke gevalle wel in die SA Weermag sal voorkom. Baie van hierdie
gevalle sal waarskynlik ook geen probleme veroorsaak nie en nie onder aandag
kom nie,

6. Daar sal egter die gevalle wees wat probleme gaan veroorsaak en wie se ge-
drag en optredes onaanvaarbaar en 'n verleentheid vir die SAW sal wees. Teen
sodaniges moet streng dissiplinêre stappe geneem word. In die Suid-Afrikaanse
strafreg word daar onderskeid gemaak tussen homoseksualisme en lesbianisme. Eg
is strafbaar en lg nie. Dit word voorgestel dat beide afwykings oor dieselfde
kam geskeer en strafbare oortredings gemaak word tov die RvD. Vertoë moet ook
aan die Dept Justisie gerig word vir soortgelyke aksie op die strafreg gebied.

7. Opsommenderwys dus die volgende :

    a. 'n Formele ondersoek gaan geen doel dien nie. Die resultaat sal on-
    betroubaar wees en kan slegs verleentheid vir die SAW veroorsaak.

    b. Dit moet aanvaar word dat sodanige gevalle in die SAW sal voorkom, dog
    ten alle koste moet 'n heksejag vermy word.

...../2

DECLASSIFIED

9480351PE MAJ.

Figure 4: SADF correspondence from 1981 warning that tests aimed at identifying homosexuals may be
potential source of embarrassment for SADF in terms of public perceptions (Archived as SAHA Collection
AL2878 – A1.5.2).

Greefswald

Volume 47 of *War Resister* describes Greefswald thus:

> In the 1970s and early 1980s habitual users — or people who were unfortunate enough to
> be caught more than once — were sent to Greefswald, a farm in the Northern Transvaal[44] ...
> Conditions were particularly brutal. The idea was to isolate and keep the inmates perpetually
> on the go and through strenuous exercise exhaust them to keep their minds off drugs.[45]

Access was gained to three substantial files on the drug rehabilitation facility that was
named as Levin's project in volume 47 of *War Resister*. SAHA was initially given access
to 'Greefswald Works Committee GG521/3/5/2/2 Jan–Nov 1977', but this file was returned at the request of DOD archives. An internal appeal was submitted, but was turned
down in terms of section 34(1).[46] Aside from the records in the file that included names
of individual conscripts and that could easily have been severed, access should not have
been refused. It is apparent that, as this was one of the early PAIA requests, SAHA was
overly cautious in terms of interpretation of the Act. SAHA did not have the resources
to litigate this request. The file may be released today subject to severance of names of
conscripts or permanent members of the force.[47]

An early Greefswald file,[48] numbered 3MH/104/10/14/1/1, consists mainly of combat
company reports. Included in these reports are addendums listing the regular visitors to
the facility. Although Colonel Aubrey Levin's visits are only recorded from November
1971, there is a reference to him in the body of an earlier report that leads one to the
presumption that he had visited the facility at an earlier date. Apart from being recorded
as a visitor in almost all the addendums from November 1971 onwards, in many of the
actual reports, reference is made to him and often to his team. Levin is generally the only
person mentioned by name, confirming that he was central to the project. The research for
Levin's dissertation[49] was done while he was at 1 Military Hospital. In his dissertation he
confirms that the programme was not his brainchild,[50] and states that Cocky Cockcroft,
the surgeon general at the time, directed the establishment of the programme through a
multidisciplinary team of which Levin was a member.

Another common denominator in these reports is the high number of servicemen
booking in sick. At one point, a report notes that 'although it is not yet a matter of concern, there do appear to be too many ill servicemen'.[51] In another it is blatantly stated
that the number is too high. This tends to offer weight to the allegations in volume 47 of
War Resister that conditions were particularly brutal. Also included is a song obviously
written by one of the conscripts. It reveals how they were treated and how they disliked
the camp:

> You pushed us around
> and expect no backchat

But let us tell you now
it won't always be like that
You brass ain't gonna count hereafter

You make us run
you teach us to hate
I think you are
creating your fate

Box 5.2: Individual service records

With a view to finding other conscripts who suffered human rights abuses during their national service (outside of those whose experiences were included in the aVersion Project report), an advertisement was placed in the media (a gay publication and a mainstream publication) offering to assist ex-conscripts and service personnel who had suffered human rights abuses in the SADF to acquire their service records using PAIA. A handful of men responded; only one of these declared his sexual orientation as homosexual.

In terms of the procedure, the servicemen would give SAHA permission to access their files, which we would then request. SAHA would treat these files as confidential and pass them on to the applicant without perusing them. One applicant was not keen for the file to be given to SAHA, and his file was sent directly to him. Another said he burnt the contents after reading it.

One applicant's file appears to be completely missing from the archives, while at least two others believe that critical information is missing. Although we seem to have reached the end of the road in terms of the missing file, we have not given up entirely. The applicant's history suggests that this is one file that might embarrass SAMS because of the treatment he received.

One of the requesters was a permanent member of the navy for 15 years, when his security clearance was suddenly taken away from him. He believes he lost the clearance because of his homosexuality. Hoping to resolve this mystery, his personnel files were accessed. SAHA has not had access to his records, as they are in his possession, but he says it provides very little insight into the removal of his security clearance. However, the ex-navy member does say that there is one record that suggests that there was an anti-gay movement in the SADF at that time.[52]

Of course, another explanation lies in the ongoing idea that homosexuals who were still fighting for acceptance in the broader society, never mind the security forces, feared being found out and exposed. They were therefore more vulnerable to blackmail. This is confirmed in 1980s policy documents and South Africa's bible on security matters, the Minimum Information Security Standards. Regulations have hardly changed since the 1980s, when they were at their most vigorous. At that time, sexual orientation was a specific issue, apparently, because gays and lesbians were more susceptible to blackmail. Although the document has been updated and it currently does not specifically mention gender orientation, it does not rule it out either. Section 2.2 of the guidelines with respect to security vetting for determining a person's security clearance states: 'Aspects such as gender, religion, race and political affiliation do not serve as criteria in the consideration of a security clearance, but actions and aspects adversely affecting the person's vulnerability to blackmail or bribery or subversion and his (sic) loyalty to the State or the institution do.'[53]

Policy advocated the rejection of homosexuals from the permanent force, but the attitude was different with regard to conscripts. A related SADF memo says that it is obvious that a conscript cannot be dismissed or allowed to use his homosexuality to duck service.[54]

P.W. Botha files

The P.W. Botha files turned up some fascinating records, particularly the file labelled 'Advice: tip-offs and inventions'.[55] This is an extraordinary file consisting of correspondence between P.W. Botha as minister of defence and 'patriotic' South Africans, some proudly stating that they are new immigrants. The correspondents offer new inventions, strategies, books, support and, in one case, congratulations to the National Party for its recent election win. Some of the inventions offered come complete with drawings. One contributor suggests that wild indigenous birds where 'terrorists are suspected to be operating be trapped and minute radio transmitters be implanted into them'.[56] Some of the ideas were passed on to the Armaments Board and the Committee for Inventions, Patents and Armaments. Unfortunately, because of the masking, it is not always possible to connect the response with the correct correspondent.

Another insight into the apartheid mindset comes from a record in an injuries and claims file.[57] Correspondence consists of complaints received regarding injuries and deaths and the surgeon general's responses. One complaint includes a letter from a parent whose son had died in an accident in a military vehicle. In the letter, the parent complains that the vehicle was driven by a 'coloured'. In his response, the minister states that he is not sure what all this has to do with apartheid, because coloureds are used in the army and were used before he was minister. He does, however, go out of his way to reassure the parent that there is no mixing with the whites, and that coloureds are not used in positions of authority, but in ordinary positions such as drivers of vehicles. He points out that it is much more difficult managing a large army than people realise.

Records relating to an incident involving assaults of new trainees by 'so-called old boys' are important in that they confirm anecdotal information of this nature.[58] The perpetrators were brought to court and newspaper cuttings plus letters from the public expressing concern are contained in the file. There is also a response from the minister to a parent

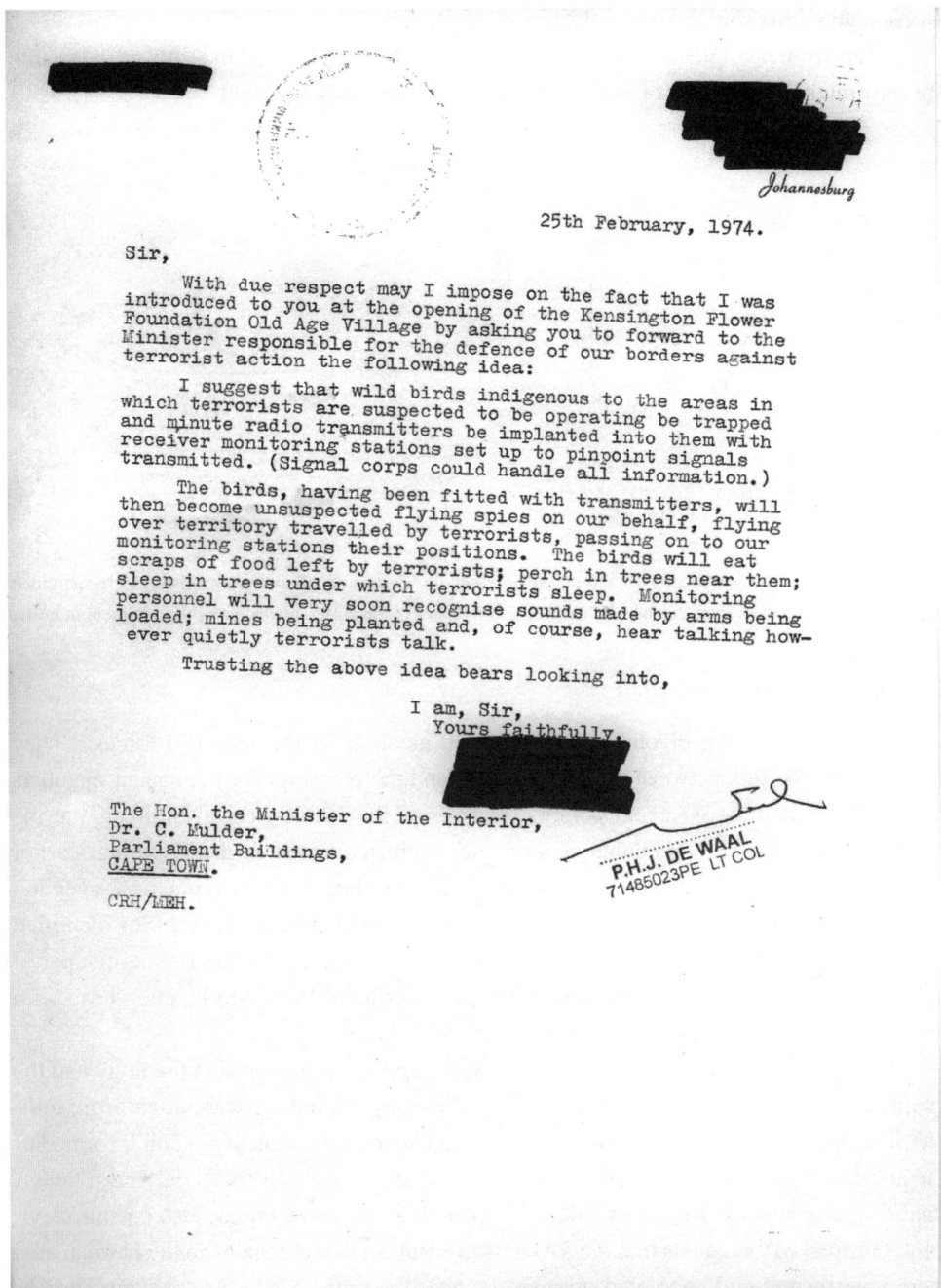

Figure 5: From the file 'Advice: Tip-offs and inventions', an example of an unnecessary, random classification of a submission to the Department of Defence by an amateur militarist in 1974. This document had to be declassified in order to be released in terms of PAIA from the DOD's Documentation Centre.

worried about his son serving in the army.

Apart from a single and unrelated reference to Colonel Levin, in terms of the search for information on the use of aversion therapy, nothing was revealed.[59]

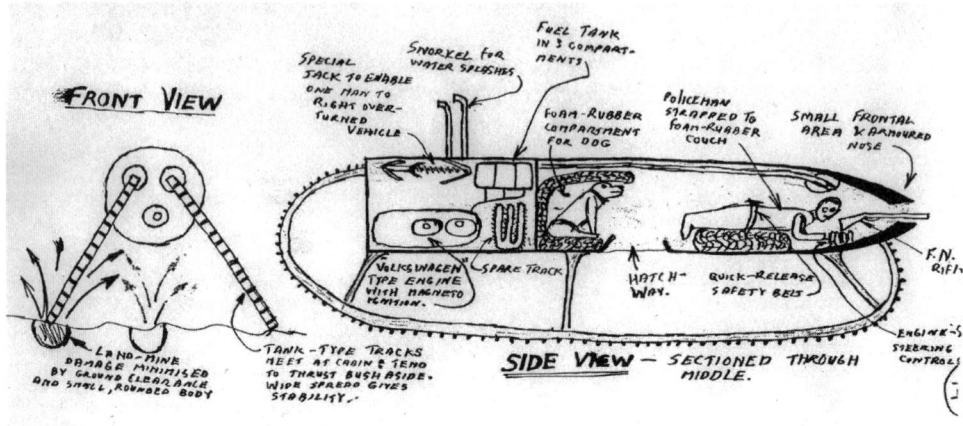

Figure 6: From the file 'Advice: Tip-offs and inventions', an illustration of an anti-terrorist vehicle submitted to P.W. Botha, then minister of defence, by a concerned member of the public indicative of the apartheid mindset.

Chaplains general files

Chaplains general were pivotal in the ethos and ideology of the apartheid forces.[60] They were seen as the link between the commanders and the conscripts or permanent members of the force.[61] The homosexual policy directives of the 1980s were also directed at the chaplains general. The chaplains general files were requested in the hope that earlier more explicit policy directives, particularly during the time that Levin practised aversion therapy, would be located. In January 2006 most of the chaplains general files identified in November 2004 were declassified and released.[62] Getting a handle on the manner in which the army chaplain service was run is quite difficult. Peter Moll's interviews with army chaplains for his thesis were helpful and revealing.[63]

The chaplains general files exposed the vast gap between liberation theology and the chaplaincy. Correspondence from the head of the army (including a document from military intelligence) warns against Bishop Tutu[64] and keeps the chaplain general informed of the anti-apartheid activities of the churches.[65] The importance of the N.G. Kerk (Nederlandse Gereformeerde Kerk — NGK — the Dutch Reformed Church) also becomes evident. One record[66] suggests that the SADF was ensuring that chaplains in the Durban area were investigated and appointed through the NGK or other Afrikaans-speaking churches.[67] The files also contained records relating to applications and approvals of chaplains' security clearances. One record is a query from a chaplain who had been working for two years when his security clearance was taken away from him. No response was recorded.

Box 5.3: Conscientious objection

The DOD conscientious objection files are rich in content. Documentation is found in many different files, and there is a degree of duplication. The individual conscientious objector files provide insight into the young white South African that stood up against the system and into how their efforts over the years changed the laws and contributed to the dismantling of apartheid.

A collection of files relating to the Gleeson Committee (mandated to investigate conscientious objection in 1991) contain a report on a workshop conducted by the Centre for Intergroup Studies on Alternatives to National Service (1989). In the report, Justice J.W. Edeling, chair of the Board for Religious Objection, traces the history of conscientious objection back to 1957, although it seems that his service and the establishment of the board goes back to the amendments to the Defence Act in 1983.

The files trace the changes in the approach of the apartheid government to conscription and community service and contain submissions from churches and NGOs on the Defence Amendment Act in 1985. They also contain policy documents on postponements and exemptions. The applications and arguments of various religious objectors are a feature of the files.

The records on the London-based Committee on South African War Resistance give an insight into how the South African government kept track of war resistance outside the country.[68] They show that this group was watched very closely by the apartheid regime and had willing informants. A meeting addressed by Laurie Nathan from the End Conscription Campaign was reported on by an unnamed person in attendance who was also a guest of the South African government.

One file[69] is a mine of information on how Jehovah's Witnesses were treated and what they endured in detention barracks. Personal testimony to this effect is included. The lengthy response from the detention barracks staff is also in the file.

A degree of success: Defence Personnel Advisory Committee files

The Defence Personnel Advisory Committee[70] files contained something of what we were looking for. A number of records reflect the policy dilemmas facing the conservative officials and suggest the evolution of later policy documents.

A letter from the surgeon general dated 13 June 1977[71] to the head of personnel referred to previous correspondence from the head of staff intelligence (hoof staf inligting — HSI) in which the need for policy regarding homosexuals in the investigation and selection of personnel was discussed.[72] The letter referred to a paragraph in the minutes of the Defence Personnel Advisory Committee in which HSI asked if there was a position on the issue. It needed to be discussed, HSI said, because of its serious implications and the need for a directive to come from the right committee. The surgeon general responded by stating that homosexuality was a legally punishable crime[73] and consequently was not accepted as an illness. Exceptional cases, where physical or psychological deviation could be determined, should, said the surgeon general, be handled on merit, and conscripts declared unfit for military service. The surgeon general noted that they were not in a position to draft policy. The matter was then taken up by the Defence Personnel Advisory Committee and the response noted in the minutes of 29 June 1977.[74] The chairperson of the committee referred firstly to earlier steps in this regard where homosexuals were dismissed and national servicemen had seized the opportunity to dodge service. A proposal that homosexuals be treated in the same way as Jehovah's Witnesses was also rejected, because of the security risk.[75] The committee therefore resolved to accept what the surgeon general had put forward: the practice of homosexuality was a crime and a member of the SADF found guilty as a result was to be dealt with accordingly; that in exceptional circumstances when physical and psychological deviations were noted, these servicemen were to be exempted from military service; and that civilians found guilty of this crime or similar deviations were to be summarily dismissed.

This documentation dated 1977 would suggest, as do many of the policy documents accessed on homosexuality, that the SADF did not officially sanction conversion therapy of any nature. The 1979 document, located within the minutes of the DCC referred to earlier, reflects a more hardened approach. It encourages 'disciplinary action against offenders' through its own channels.[76] Was aversion therapy part of this punishment? Did the powers that be turn a blind eye to this blatant discrimination against and condemnation of homosexuality? This is not clear.

Thousands of pages later

Has the exercise of digging for information in DOD archives' files accessed via PAIA been successful? On the implementation of PAIA, the Gays in the Apartheid Military project encountered many of the same problems already recorded in this publication. The DOD archives' lack of resources and budgetary constraints have contributed to long delays between requests and access. When PAIA was in the making, other countries with access to information legislation in place warned of the delays that would be encountered as more researchers sought access to records. This has certainly been the case in terms of the DOD archives and offers good reason for proactive declassifying. It has also shown that accessing information can be a costly affair. Unless more detail is known about the record and consequently a more precise request is drafted, the requester could be faced with a hefty bill for searches conducted by the body being queried. PAIA regulations state that a fee will be charged for each hour 'reasonably required for search and preparation'. Fortunately, the interpretation of the word 'reasonably' provides grounds for a challenge if costs appear excessive. Challenging refusals is also problematic. Once taken on internal appeal, funding is needed to take a failed request to court. Judging whether or not litigation is worth the time and effort is difficult. Without sight of the record, one can never be sure whether the content is worth the effort.

With specific regard to the DOD archives, more resources (human and equipment) are needed to improve access and shorten turnover times. Declassification is time consuming, making a strong argument for allocation of more resources to undertake the processing of requests and proactive declassification. It would also be of tremendous advantage to researchers if the DOD archives had a more comprehensive website. The fact that the *PAIA Manual* is on the DOD website is to be applauded; however, without information concerning file plans and records previously declassified, the requester is not in a position to assist the DOD by drafting specific requests.

In terms of the objective of unravelling more about aversion therapy and gays in the military, success has been limited. This is partly due to the nature of PAIA, as well as the organisation of the archives. The project will, however, continue to be a work in progress. There are still avenues that can be pursued; many more documents can be requested from the DOD and the TRC archives through the Department of Justice. Other institutional archives may also hold records that offer further insights. These will certainly confirm some of what we already know and perhaps take us a little further; however, there are no guarantees, given the random nature of the process of finding records.

From another perspective, the requests have unlocked many records that would have remained classified had these requests not been lodged. Many of the documents released through the course of this project have revealed a history of the SADF that has not been told and, more specifically, a history of those who through conscientious objection and other methods fought an inhumane system. Often, it has been the simplest documentation that has exposed the absurdity of apartheid, the ambivalence of the responses of officials when ordinary white South Africans egged them on in their racism, and the iron fist that sought to keep a majority powerless.

6

Applying PAIA: Legal, Political and Contextual Issues

Kate Allan

Introduction

In 2001 the South African History Archive (SAHA) uncovered the existence of 38 groups of military intelligence records that had been withheld from the Truth and Reconciliation Commission (TRC) by the Department of Defence (DOD).[1] The revelation immediately generated suspicions that the bulk of DOD's intelligence files had been deliberately withheld from the commission.[2] The military denied culpability and (former) TRC officials insisted that DOD had misled them,[3] but no call was made from any quarter for an examination of the records by the TRC, which was still operative at the time.[4] When SAHA sought access to the lists of records and the records referred to therein, a dispute ensued regarding the interpretation of the provisions of the Promotion of Access to Information Act No. 2 of 2000 (PAIA) and the intersecting operation of the Protection of Information Act No. 84 of 1982. The records were disclosed only after a protracted court battle challenging the notion that release would prejudice the defence, security and international relations of South Africa. The South African Human Rights Commission (SAHRC) and the minister of defence, who publicly stated that he would conduct an inquiry, did nothing. Access was granted only after the institution of court proceedings.

This case reveals that a number of factors hamper access to information, factors that are reflected in the chapters of this book. Pigou discusses the intersection of the Promotion of National Unity and Reconciliation Act No. 34 of 1996, the misconstrued application of exemptions, the inability of the bodies concerned to appoint competent decision makers, and the deflective approach of officials, which led to costly and lengthy disputes and, in some cases, court battles. Fig discusses the decentralised record-keeping practices of the Nuclear Energy Corporation of South Africa, which, coupled with that body's inherent secrecy and defensiveness, resulted in long delays in the provision of medical records, avoidance of requests, and little access to records regarding the environmental impact of nuclear energy. Similarly, the alleged destruction of records relating to the nuclear weapons programme of the apartheid state, discussed by Gould, meant that PAIA yielded little information. In locating information regarding the treatment of homosexuals in the military, Pollecut was required to trawl through thousands of pages of lists and records in order to locate fragments that gave minute insights into the experience of persons labelled as deviants or with principled objection to the military programme, and into the mindset of the apartheid government.

What these chapters do not discuss in any detail, however, is the extent to which technical issues regarding the intersection of legislation and the use and interpretation of PAIA provisions have impacted on the utility of the Act and access to records. What I therefore aim to do is to discuss: firstly, the extent to which disputes regarding the interpretation of PAIA provisions have been used to avoid disclosure; secondly, the capacity for pre- and post-transition enactments to impact upon PAIA exemptions and access; and, thirdly, the extent to which prescribed appeal mechanisms have been facilitative in upholding the right of access to information. Before concluding, I will briefly consider the impact of record-keeping practices and the destruction of documents prior to and after the transition to democratic governance, and the lack of a shift from the culture of secrecy that pervaded the government during apartheid.

Before moving on to a consideration of these factors, it is important to put the work of SAHA into context. Its origins lie in documenting struggles against apartheid, a foundation that pervades and informs its contemporary work. Its points of focus are mostly historical inquiries relating to both human rights violations committed by the apartheid state and the activities of those in opposition to it. Where it steps into the contemporary arena, it does so on the basis that the issues about which it, or those it represents, needs to be informed are ones that more often than not relate to an infringement of constitutional rights. These issues around which it focuses its work tend towards sensitive, contested and controversial territory. The lens through which it views the achievement of transparency is therefore coloured by this terrain.

This chapter and this book, then, present a picture of contestation that is specific. While the experiences of SAHA will certainly be shared in many respects by other requesters and civil society organisations working in the field, I do not intend through this discussion to purport to provide a whole and finite picture of the problems encountered in exercising the right of access to information; organisations such as the Open Democracy Advice Centre (ODAC), which focuses primarily on the use of PAIA to facilitate the exercise of contemporary socioeconomic rights, will have their own specific experiences. It is also important to note that I do not attempt to provide clear recommendations for reform; the intersections of these issues are complex and require a range of interventions at parliamentary level and within public bodies. What I aim to do is to discuss the areas of influence raised throughout this book and elucidate starting points for reform that will lead to greater enjoyment of the right of access to information.

The truth commission has been horrified to discover that the SANDF hid thousands of military files crucial to its investigations

Army file shock for the TRC

Evidence wa ka Ngobeni

The South African National Defence Force (SANDF) hid key apartheid-era military intelligence information from the Truth and Reconciliation Commission (TRC).

The commission had investigated the wholesale disposal of apartheid-era information and concluded that all military intelligence had kept was three series of files. Each series contains thousands of pages of records kept of military operations inside and outside South Africa during apartheid.

Last week, in answer to an archivist who submitted a Promotion of Access to Information Act request to the Department of Defence, a list was provided of 38 series of top secret documents still in the SANDF archive.

Verne Harris, director of the South African History Archive, attached to the University of the Witwatersrand, asked the department for a list of files contained in three "series" which the SANDF told the TRC was all that was left after the mass destruction of sensitive documents before 1994.

The 38 series contains thousands of classified documents on covert operations conducted by the apartheid-era government. The covert operations targeted anti-apartheid organisations in South Africa and abroad.

SANDF spokesperson Louis Kirstein said on Thursday he was unable to provide the *Mail & Guardian*

with comment as the chief of military intelligence was away.

"We have taken note of the allegations and the response is ready. But it cannot be sent to you because it has to be approved by the chief of military intelligence," Kirstein said. "The answer will come next week as we have already studied the allegations."

The South African History Archive's list of secret files still kept by the SANDF records the dates when the files were compiled. The oldest series file covers the period 1941 to 1977. One of the files was compiled from 1977 up until 1997, fuelling speculation that some apartheid-era covert operations carried on even after the 1994 general elections.

Former TRC officials expressed shock this week after being told about the new files. The TRC, they said, was only aware of three series files. This is reflected in the TRC's final report.

The report reads: "Although subjected to close scrutiny during the 1993 destruction exercise, a large volume of military intelligence files survived. The joint investigative team identified three discrete files groups from the SANDF archive."

This revelation is likely to buttress public belief that the TRC never managed to get to the truth of the apartheid-era atrocities.

Former TRC researcher Charles Villa-Vicencio, who led the TRC research team into the SANDF, said the new information shows that the

146

SANDF "deliberately misled the TRC".

Villa-Vicencio said the SANDF had told the TRC at the time that the three files series were the only ones that survived the systemic erasure of "sensitive" documents by the previous government.

"If these new files exist we believe that we were decidedly misled by the military. Their actions were morally reprehensible and are legally indefensible," he said.

Harris's response from the Department of Defence includes the number of boxes in which the files are kept. There are thousands of box numbers on the list.

It is highly unlikely that the South African public will ever know what is in those boxes, says Harris. The TRC, he says, "was the only window of opportunity to have access to those files".

The Promotion of Access to Information Act, he says, is one option the public can use to access information from the government. But there will be a problem. As the series files are classified "top secret" the SANDF will only release a "declassified" version to the public.

Villa-Vicencio said the TRC final report recommended, among other things, that a comprehensive audit of the military intelligence information be conducted.

This new information, he says, "demonstrates the necessity of such

an audit. We cooperated with the military in good faith and from this it seems that they did not do so. Maybe they were seeking to hide the information, which of course undermined the TRC's objective to make the truth available to the public."

Villa-Vicencio said the three files, which were given to the TRC, did not "have pertinent information" and failed to serve the commission's objectives.

"The question one should be asking is; why did they hide the information?" he asked, adding the information allegedly concealed by the SANDF could have helped the TRC to present a "far more extensive report".

"The SANDF was obliged to disclose all the files to the TRC according to the law. The military did not assist the TRC in this regard."

A senior TRC researcher, who did not want to be named, said the SANDF consistently "stonewalled" the commission's requests.

"The unfortunate reality is that the SANDF always created problems for the TRC. When they granted us access to those three series files it was too late and meaningless.

"Instead what we did was check whether files were still intact. We could not do anything as we had to deal with constant difficulties created by the SANDF."

State info not easily available, Page 51

Figure 1: Press clipping, *Mail & Guardian* (2001, 12 to 18 October). Copyright: *Mail & Guardian*.

The application of PAIA

This chapter appropriately starts by considering PAIA itself. Its provisions can be separated into two primary areas: substantive clauses that determine access, and procedural clauses that provide for review and enforcement. In regard to the former, I will discuss case studies in which the provisions have been broadly or incorrectly interpreted or applied, resulting in undue restrictions on access. In regard to the latter, I will discuss the limitations of the available enforcement mechanisms, as well as proposals for reform.

Interpretation

The legislation is largely unambiguous, however, there has been little consistency in the approach followed by public bodies, and disputes about what the legislation intended have resulted. These disputes fall into three key areas: the distinction between public and private bodies, the application of exemptions, and the public interest override. It is not the aim of this chapter to offer a comprehensive analysis of the provisions, but to present a selection of case studies that demonstrate that a number of external factors determine whether the application of PAIA provisions achieves the constitutional objective of access.

Public versus private bodies

We tend to think of 'public' and 'private' as mutually exclusive, as contrasting, as opposites. The Act has blurred this clean division by imposing a grey area in which a private body can be a public body or a public body private in certain circumstances. The distinction has also become distorted with the development of privatised utilities and contracted services. Not only is this confusing to requesters, but also to many recipients of requests.

In 2002 SAHA assisted Mondli Hlatshwayo, a master's student at the University of the Witwatersrand, to request access to minutes of meetings held between 1965 and 1973 at Iscor's steel manufacturing plant in Vanderbijlpark.[5] Iscor refused to process the request on the basis that it did not comply with procedural requirements in that the form submitted was for a public rather than a private body. When the Wits Law Clinic argued on the student's behalf that the records sought were from the period when Iscor was a public body and therefore the public body provisions applied, Iscor responded the following day by stating that no records could be found. Wits Law Clinic rejoined that Iscor could not have conducted a search for records almost 40 years old in one day.[6] When ODAC agreed to represent Hlatshwayo and applied to the High Court for intervention, Judge van der Westhuizen held that, while Iscor had been privatised, the meetings in question occurred during the period of Iscor's exercise of power or performance as a public body. In reaching his decision, he considered the objectives of the company and the power wielded through government by virtue of its large shareholding and the provisions of the Iron and Steel Industry Act No. 11 of 1928 and the Conversion of Iscor Limited Act No. 57 of 1989. Iscor was unsuccessful in its appeal in the Supreme Court of Appeal.[7]

In early 2007 SAHA submitted requests to Bosasa Operations (Pty) Ltd[8] in the belief that it was contracted to manage the operation of the Lindela Detention Centre for undocumented migrants. In response, the head of Bosasa's legal group alleged that Bosasa had not been responsible for management at any time (despite numerous media reports regarding allegations of corruption in the awarding of the contract to the company in around 1996), that Leading Prospect Trading 111 (Pty) Ltd was the contracted party, and that SAHA could not obtain information from it because it was a private body and the records were subject to a contract with the Department of Home Affairs, which determined that they were confidential. The head stated that she did not have the contact details for Leading Prospect Trading.[9]

When SAHA rebutted that Leading Prospect Trading was privately incorporated, but was contracted by a public body to fulfil a public function, and therefore its records were regarded as being records of a public body,[10] and threatened legal action, the head of Bosasa's legal group revealed that she was in fact the legal representative for both Bosasa and Leading Prospect Trading, and that the records belonged to the Department of Home Affairs, which would be responding to the requests. No further mention was made of the company's private body status or that she had made misleading statements about her knowledge of Leading Prospect Trading's contact details. Following SAHA's letter of demand and expression of its intention to pursue the matter in court, Bosasa and Leading Prospect Trading agreed to provide access to records they had in their possession.[11]

In both of these cases, the bodies concerned have attempted to exploit the subtleties of the division between public and private bodies, and they have attempted to hide behind private body provisions despite their clear present or past engagement in public operations. Iscor in particular presents a disturbing case of a body so intent on preventing access that it appealed to the Supreme Court. In all fairness, it had a right to do so. However, given its initial response that it could not find records from the 1960s and 1970s after searching for all of 24 hours, the intent behind its pursuit of judicial interpretation is questionable. Could it have been an attempt to deter a student from litigating against a well-resourced company? In any event, both bodies failed to consider that requesters have a right of access if they 'require' the information to exercise or protect another right.[12] The confidence displayed by private bodies in this regard may be attributed to judicial determinations that have narrowly interpreted the term 'require' and imputed an element of 'reasonableness', so as to set the bar impossibly high.[13] While the Supreme Court's interpretation is yet to be tested in the Constitutional Court, it has made requesters nervous about litigating against private bodies.

Exemptions

There are a few key points to make about the exemptions before going on to consider their application. They are objective grounds, which may be broken down into three categories:

· exemptions that require the information to fall within a specified category;
· exemptions that require particular consequences to flow from disclosure; or
· exemptions with both content and consequence requirements.[14]

They also place on the recipient of the requests the onus to justify that the information is of a type considered by the exemption; that, where necessary, harm will result from disclosure; and that, where discretion is exercised to refuse access, it was appropriately applied. It is important to note that the grounds are limitations that must be read narrowly; ambiguities must be determined in favour of access.[15]

i. Privacy and protection from harm

PAIA provides that access must be refused where it involves an unreasonable disclosure of personal information about a third party, i.e. a breach of privacy,[16] or where disclosure could reasonably be expected to endanger the life or physical safety of an individual.[17] These exemptions require, where an exception to the exemption does not apply, that the public body afford any third parties affected by the request an opportunity to consent to or oppose disclosure.[18]

These exemptions have been the most frequently utilised in requests for apartheid era records. Pigou discusses the use of the exemptions by the Department of Justice (DOJ) to refuse access to TRC records. The privacy exemption was also used by the national archivist to refuse access to listings of security police files, a decision that was upheld on appeal to the minister of arts and culture, Pallo Jordan. The response was perplexing, as SAHA had been provided with a list of security police records in the possession of the South African Police Service (SAPS) in 2002, and the records listed on the document now being refused had been transferred by SAPS to the National Archives in around 2004. SAHA was also somewhat confused given that, at an earlier meeting at the Nelson Mandela Foundation, the national archivist had advised that he held a list of security police files that would be useful for a proposed apartheid victims database. When SAHA appealed on the basis that at least some, if not all, of the information must be 'publicly available', as it had been released pursuant to a request only a few years earlier, it was again refused.

The application of the exemptions raises three key issues. Firstly, the exemptions are being applied to all records, irrespective of whether the document/s had been aired in public hearings or were in the public domain in some other manner (such as the amnesty applications and evidence utilised in hearings related to the Cradock 4), or whether the person who furnished the information was aware that it was of a class that was likely to be made publicly available (such as the amnesty application of Eugene de Kock). The privacy exemption specifically provides for exceptions in these instances,[19] and it is arguable that where information is already in the public domain, it is not reasonable to expect that disclosure could endanger the life or physical safety of an individual.

Secondly, the third-party notification provisions are being inappropriately and inconsistently applied. In matters where the documents have been aired in public hearings or are in the public domain and privacy rights have therefore lapsed, DOJ persists in providing third parties mentioned in such documents with an opportunity to consent to or oppose release. In the case of the Cradock hearing records, notification was taken one step further by DOJ when it sought affidavits from the widows of the deceased, who had no privacy rights to protect (see chapter 2 of this volume) because the information did not relate to them.[20] Any right that they may have held regarding their husbands expired 20 years after their husbands' deaths, which was some four months after the obtaining of the affidavits.[21] In another disturbing case, DOJ sent approximately 22,000 third-party notices to addresses up to ten years old, despite the fact that SAHA specified in its request that it did not want access to personal information.[22] Conversely, upon a request for access to *in-camera* hearing testimonies of the TRC, where DOJ should have issued third-party notices, it failed to do so.

Thirdly, the utilisation of the privacy exemption by DOJ has often been framed in terms of the disclosure of the perpetration of offences, indicating that the persons protected may often be informers or perpetrators. In this context, where some members of the public want to know who informed on, or committed crimes against, them or their families, the privacy of individuals is a difficult issue to balance. The right to privacy does discriminate to a certain extent: a high-profile and influential individual espousing 'say no to drugs' campaigns has been found to have her right to privacy limited when it concerned her treatment for drug addiction.[23]

However, should access to information be used to expose informers, and thereby serve as a form of justice? In 2006, Poland passed a law opening communist era files revealing the names of large numbers of informers. There was debate in the media regarding the integrity of the files and the fact that many people lost their jobs as a result of unsubstantiated allegations.[24] In some cases, the public interest override (discussed later) may compel disclosure if, for example, the record revealed that the informer was involved in a plot to murder. However, simply being an informer without evidence of a resultant link to a criminal offence is not sufficient to satisfy the override. The balancing of these competing interests will never be subject to clear rules: the side upon which the determination falls is largely determined by shifting societal objectives and norms. In terms of protection from harm, the exemption's application in these circumstances commences from an assumption that persons will commit a criminal offence following disclosure; that is, they will threaten the life of the person being protected or commit some violent act against him/her. This is a grave presumption and one that would be difficult to prove if the matter proceeded for judicial determination.

ii. Confidentiality

The confidentiality exemption prevents disclosure where:

- · an agreement of confidentiality binds the parties; or
- · information was supplied in confidence; and
  - disclosure will prejudice the future supply of information and it is in the public interest that information continues to be supplied;[25]

- the person supplying the information does not consent to its disclosure; and
- the information is not already in the public domain.[26]

In 1975 South Africa and Israel entered into a confidentiality agreement regarding the exchange of supplies for the development of South Africa's nuclear weapons programme. The agreement was designed to prevent disclosure of information regarding their relations. It may not be off the mark to speculate that the agreement aimed to avoid scrutiny for engaging in nuclear weapons development without complying with international monitoring requirements, and for breaching international sanctions against trade of goods with South Africa. The agreement is still being relied upon to prevent access to records relating to the now defunct programme. When SAHA gained access to it pursuant to a PAIA request to DOD, it was so heavily masked that it revealed little about the information being secreted, and therefore little grounds upon which to challenge refusals relying on it.

DOJ applied the confidentiality provision to TRC records without distinguishing between the records themselves; that is, whether they record testimony given in public or during *in-camera* hearings, or whether they are applications made with knowledge of the likelihood of their public disclosure. In the request relating to the hearings about the death of the Cradock 4, the department alleged that the records could not be released because, among other things, the amnesty applicants provided the information subject to an agreement of confidentiality. It failed to demonstrate, however, that 'agreements' of confidentiality exist (see the discussion regarding the Promotion of National Unity and Reconciliation Act below and chapter 2 of this volume). DOJ is therefore limited to the second discretionary limb of the exemption. This limb may only apply, however, where information is not in the public domain, which can only be the case where the information was provided through *in-camera* hearings and was not later disclosed at the TRC's discretion in public hearings.[27] It can also only apply where it is likely that the person who provided the information will be called upon to provide further information, and it is in the public interest that he/she does so.

While the public interest in evidence regarding human rights violations committed during apartheid cannot be contested, DOJ has not demonstrated that it has a need for further information from all persons who deposed to affidavits requested by SAHA.[28] In the case of information provided *in-camera*, it is questionable whether the information was supplied in confidence in any event. Sections 28 and 29 of the TRC Act specifically provide that no article or information collected by the TRC investigators or the TRC itself in connection with a hearing should be made public until a public hearing commenced. The persons who provided the information in such forums were witnesses or the deponents of amnesty applications who submitted to the jurisdiction without knowledge of whether their application or testimony would be aired in subsequent public hearings.[29] While a mechanism to apply to provide information in confidence existed, it was in fact the case that, in most instances, the TRC unilaterally determined that the information should be held in confidence at that time.

The exemption raises a number of issues. The confidentiality exemption is being inappropriately used in a blanket fashion to prevent access to records without giving due consideration to their substantive content. The Durban High Court in *The State v Dirk Johannes Coetzee & 5 others*[30] held that the TRC was not permitted to prevent Dirk Coetzee from gaining access to Joseph Tshepo Mamasela's *in-camera* testimony. In refusing the TRC's application seeking a declaration that the head of the investigating unit was not required to release the document, Justice Combrink stated that:

> [W]hat the Commission is enjoined to do by the legislation is to consider each case where a person seeks access to the information obtained by the Commission through its investigating unit and, in the light of the principles of openness and transparency and, having regard to the inherent right of the person seeking the information to a fair trial, decide, after weighing up the interests sought to be reached by this Act and the rights of the individual, make [sic] a value judgment as to whether the information should be made available or not.

The case, while not yet confirmed in a court of higher authority, provides good grounds for challenging DOJ and its blanket application of this and other exemptions to *in-camera* hearings and other records.

The legislation also fails to provide a suitable mechanism for inquiry into an agreement or undertaking to ascertain its legitimacy and ensure that its aims are not to prevent disclosure where the public has a right of access. The requester must therefore challenge the applicability of the agreement to the records in question or argue that the public interest override (considered later) applies without actual knowledge of the records or, in most cases, the content of the agreement. The content of the record should attract confidentiality rather than its classification.

Finally, the exemption fails to provide a mechanism for limiting the duration of confidentiality, except where the information is not subject to a specific agreement and it can be demonstrated that the ongoing provision of information is not required or not in the public interest.[31] The TRC Act is also silent as to the duration of the confidentiality of records. It does provide, however, that the TRC was empowered to authorise that members of the public be given access to documents not produced at a hearing. Pigou notes that the TRC made such a determination regarding *in-camera* hearing records; however, the National Archives and DOJ have viewed the claim as an urban myth without ascertaining its veracity.

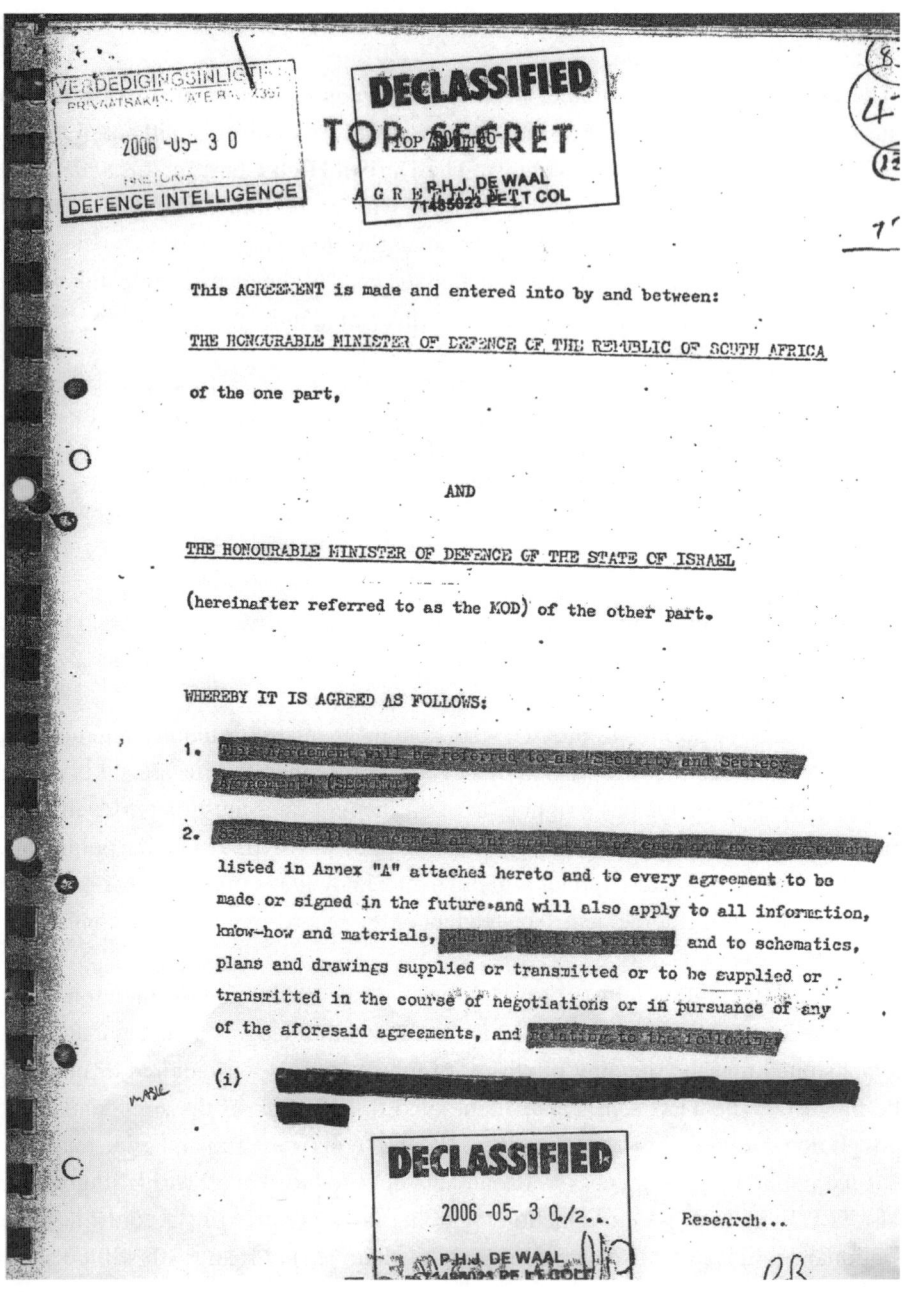

Figure 2: The South African–Israeli agreement (pp 154-157). In 1975 South Africa and Israel entered into a confidentiality agreement regarding the exchange of supplies for the development of South Africa's nuclear weapons programme. The agreement was designed to prevent disclosure of information regarding their relations.

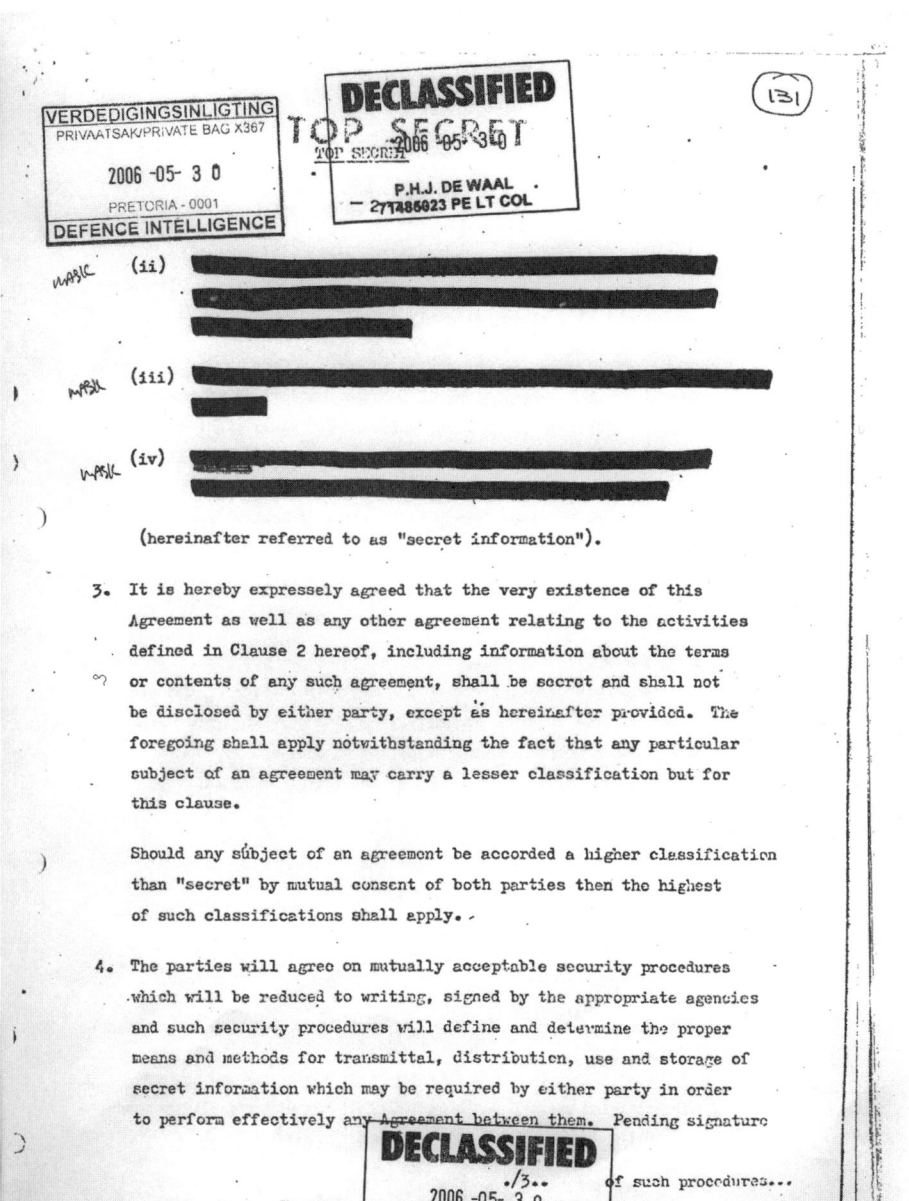

VERDEDIGINGSINLIGTING
PRIVAATSAK/PRIVATE BAG X367
2006 -05- 3 0
PRETORIA - 0001
DEFENCE INTELLIGENCE

TOP SECRET

(131)

(ii)

(iii)

(iv)

(hereinafter referred to as "secret information").

3. It is hereby expressely agreed that the very existence of this
Agreement as well as any other agreement relating to the activities
defined in Clause 2 hereof, including information about the terms
or contents of any such agreement, shall be secret and shall not
be disclosed by either party, except as hereinafter provided. The
foregoing shall apply notwithstanding the fact that any particular
subject of an agreement may carry a lesser classification but for
this clause.

Should any subject of an agreement be accorded a higher classification
than "secret" by mutual consent of both parties then the highest
of such classifications shall apply.

4. The parties will agree on mutually acceptable security procedures
which will be reduced to writing, signed by the appropriate agencies
and such security procedures will define and determine the proper
means and methods for transmittal, distribution, use and storage of
secret information which may be required by either party in order
to perform effectively any Agreement between them. Pending signature

TOP SECRET

./3.. of such procedures...

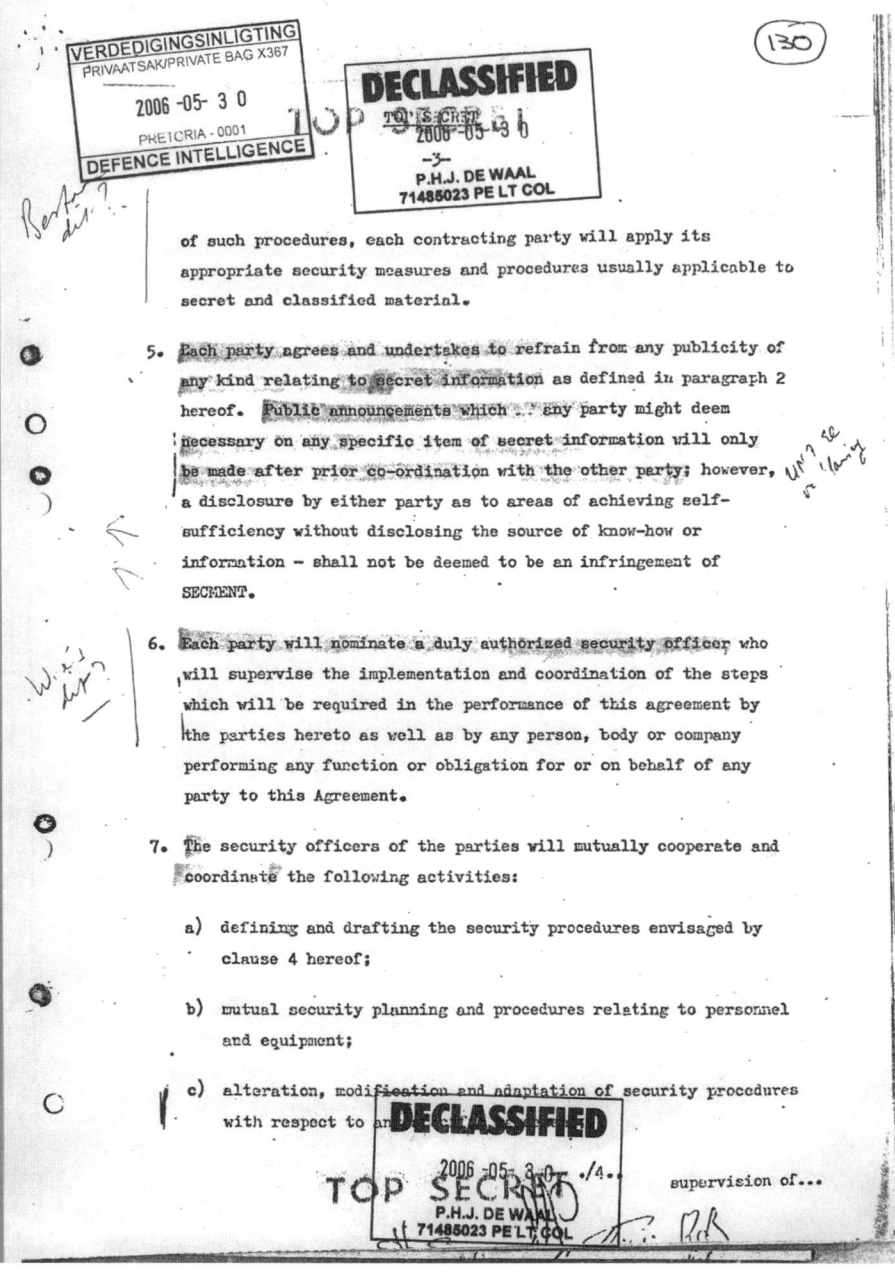

(130)

of such procedures, each contracting party will apply its
appropriate security measures and procedures usually applicable to
secret and classified material.

5. Each party agrees and undertakes to refrain from any publicity of
any kind relating to secret information as defined in paragraph 2
hereof. Public announcements which .. any party might deem
necessary on any specific item of secret information will only
be made after prior co-ordination with the other party; however,
a disclosure by either party as to areas of achieving self-
sufficiency without disclosing the source of know-how or
information - shall not be deemed to be an infringement of
SECMENT.

6. Each party will nominate a duly authorized security officer who
will supervise the implementation and coordination of the steps
which will be required in the performance of this agreement by
the parties hereto as well as by any person, body or company
performing any function or obligation for or on behalf of any
party to this Agreement.

7. The security officers of the parties will mutually cooperate and
coordinate the following activities:

a) defining and drafting the security procedures envisaged by
clause 4 hereof;

b) mutual security planning and procedures relating to personnel
and equipment;

c) alteration, modification and adaptation of security procedures
with respect to an DECLASSIFIED

supervision of...

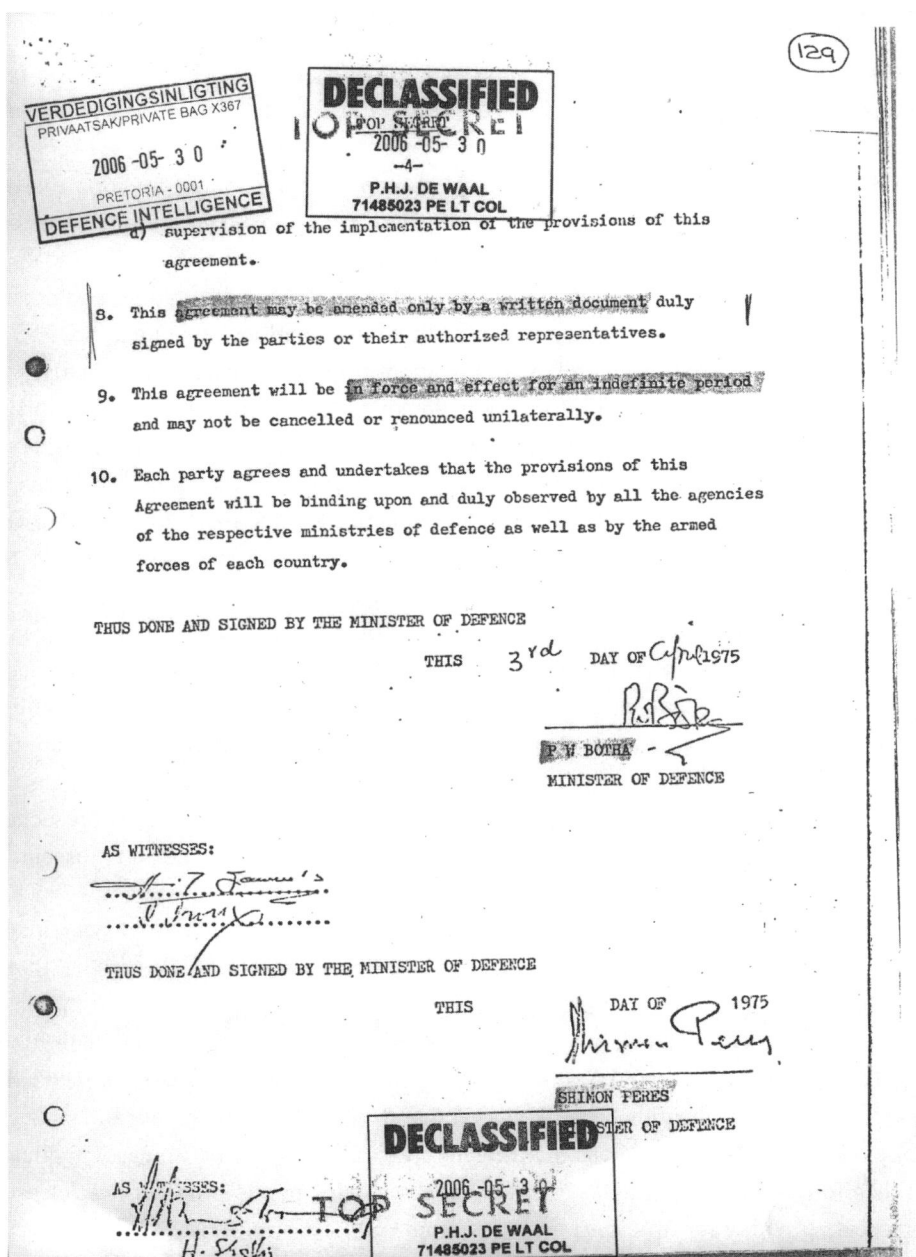

(129)

VERDEDIGINGSINLIGTING
PRIVAATSAK/PRIVATE BAG X367
2006 -05- 3 0
PRETORIA - 0001
DEFENCE INTELLIGENCE

DECLASSIFIED
TOP SECRET
2006 -05- 3 0
-4-
P.H.J. DE WAAL
71485023 PE LT COL

d) supervision of the implementation of the provisions of this

agreement.

8. This agreement may be amended only by a written document duly

signed by the parties or their authorized representatives.

9. This agreement will be in force and effect for an indefinite period

and may not be cancelled or renounced unilaterally.

10. Each party agrees and undertakes that the provisions of this

Agreement will be binding upon and duly observed by all the agencies

of the respective ministries of defence as well as by the armed

forces of each country.

THUS DONE AND SIGNED BY THE MINISTER OF DEFENCE

THIS   3rd   DAY OF April 1975

P W BOTHA
MINISTER OF DEFENCE

AS WITNESSES:

THUS DONE AND SIGNED BY THE MINISTER OF DEFENCE

THIS   DAY OF   1975

SHIMON PERES
MINISTER OF DEFENCE

DECLASSIFIED
2006 -05- 3 0
TOP SECRET
P.H.J. DE WAAL
71485023 PE LT COL

AS WITNESSES:

H. Stelli

iii. Ongoing prosecutions

PAIA provides detailed discretionary grounds of refusal where the information being sought relates to ongoing investigations or prosecutions. In short, it protects police dockets in bail, law enforcement and legal proceedings.[32] DOJ frequently utilises subsection (1)(b)(ii) of the exemption, a discretionary ground that protects information that may affect a particular prosecution, and subsection (1)(b)(iii), a mandatory ground protecting information subject to a criminal investigation (it is the only body to have done so upon a request by SAHA), to protect information subject to ongoing investigations and prosecutions by the National Prosecuting Authority (NPA) into apartheid era violations.

There are four key factors rebutting the application of the exemption. Firstly, while the exemption does not except information already in the public domain like the privacy and confidentiality exemptions, it does require the demonstration of prejudice. Where the allegations and the identity of the person who made them, or the identity of a suspect, have been previously revealed to the public, prejudice cannot arise. Accordingly, where amnesty applications, investigation material, testimonies and any other evidence have been revealed to the public through public hearings, televised broadcasts, provision by the TRC, or in any other form, the exemption should not apply. Secondly, even in the case of *in-camera* hearings, disclosure of information may not necessarily prejudice investigations or prosecutions. It is not guaranteed that allegations of the perpetration of offences will be investigated, or that information not aired at public hearings is not presently known to the public through other forums. Further, it is unlikely to be the case that all information contained in a record is of use in any given investigation or prosecution. Thirdly, the extent to which the NPA is in fact intending to investigate and prosecute the perpetrators of apartheid human rights violations is not clear.

At a conference held by the Institute for Justice and Reconciliation in March 2006, Dr J.P. Pretorius, an advocate in the DOJ Priority Crimes Litigation Unit, stated that the NPA did not have any investigators dedicated to apartheid era offences and that it was likely that not more than half a dozen cases will be prosecuted.[33] Since the finalisation of the TRC's activities, the NPA has only prosecuted three cases of those recommended for investigation or prosecution. The likelihood that the NPA will investigate and prosecute, for example, all of the incidents that Eugene de Kock raised in his amnesty application is therefore minimal.[34] In 2005 the national director of public prosecutions released a prosecuting policy for offences emanating from conflicts prior to May 1994 that allows perpetrators to apply for amnesty under certain conditions.[35] The primary criterion is the full disclosure of all facts and circumstances related to the offence. The policy, however, does not require the disclosure to be made to the public.

Setting aside questions concerning the constitutionality of the policy,[36] the lack of transparency and the imposition of a second executive-based amnesty process, it is clear that the intended outcome of the policy is fewer investigations and prosecutions. The need to ensure the provision of information from witnesses will be reduced and the incentive for perpetrators to come forward increased. The prejudice, therefore, of the disclosure of information provided to the TRC may be lessened. This also has implications for the application of the confidentiality exemption discussed earlier. Fourthly, and in any event, the exemption requires that the information should have 'bearing on an actual and specific prosecution which is "about to commence" or which is pending'.[37] Despite requests for further details, DOJ has rarely been able to confirm that a prosecution is pending or about to commence. Further, the department has not sufficiently demonstrated that the information actually relates to a specific investigation.

Box 6.1: The Department of Justice

DOJ has recently attempted to rework its use of the exemption relating to ongoing prosecutions and preventing the contravention of an offence. In its refusal of access to Eugene de Kock's amnesty application, it stated that:

> The disclosure could reasonably be expected to facilitate a contravention of the law to the extent that the reputations and dignity of the individual names may be impaired thereby as contemplated in section 39(i)(b)(iii)(dd) of PAIA.

SAHA, in its internal appeal to the minister, rejected the ground of refusal, as it utilised an exemption aiming to protect current civil and criminal proceedings in order to prevent what it perceived would be a breach of privacy. An understanding of statutory interpretation informs us that, if we look to the heading of the exemption in question, entitled 'Mandatory protection of police dockets in bail proceedings, and protection of law enforcement and legal proceedings', the provision is intended to be limited to current or proposed civil and criminal proceedings to which the records relate. It is not intended to prevent breach of the law through the act of its disclosure. There must be utilisation of the material contained within the record that will impact upon other proceedings. Furthermore, PAIA considered the possibility of breach of privacy in section 34, which the department had already relied upon, and does not intend to afford two opportunities for recipients of requests to raise the same issue.

iv. South Africa's defence, security and international relations

The Act provides a discretionary exemption preventing disclosure of information if it could reasonably be expected to cause prejudice to the defence, security or international relations of the country, or if the information has been supplied in confidence subject to an arrangement or international agreement or otherwise.[38] The exemption has been applied in two ways: to protect current activities of the state and to protect apartheid era collaborators. Pigou discusses the use of the exemption by the National Archives to protect records documenting its dealings with the TRC archives and its recommendations, where the National Archives refused access to classified records on the basis that they were being transferred 'in an operation that [had] implications for State security, the security of staff and the security of assets'. The minister of arts and culture stated on appeal that:

> [You were] informed that a security threat had been identified (by the National Intelligence Agency [NIA]) directed at the records of the TRC. In order to prevent a breach of security while the TRC records were being relocated the interdepartmental committee, responsible for the arrangements regarding the TRC records, decided that all the TRC related records of the departments serving on the committee would be regarded as confidential until the exercise was completed ... The government is currently engaged in an exercise of policy-formulation regarding the recommendations of the TRC; it is also a matter of public record that legal challenges regarding the finalization of the report of the TRC are presently being considered by the courts. I therefore see no reason to query the opinions of the NIA and to overrule the decisions of the DG [director general] and the National Archives, which are based on the advice they received from the NIA and other departments of government.[39]

SAHA appealed to the High Court. The issue in question was whether the threat to the security of the country was sufficient to warrant refusal. With regard to the records relating to transfer of the TRC archives, the National Intelligence Agency, upon an identical request, granted access to its own correspondence, despite purportedly recommending that all documents be confidential until the transfer took place. In regard to the National Archives' efforts to follow up on TRC recommendations, it was not apparent how disclosing related records, which could cover discussions with other public bodies regarding the development of measures to make apartheid era records accessible, could prejudice national security. The application of this and a number of exemptions over the course of the dispute ultimately appeared to be a tactic to avoid disclosure during a period in which relations with the National Archives were particularly fraught.[40]

The exemption was also relied upon to refuse access to five and mask three of the military intelligence record listings that were withheld from the TRC. DOD argued that the records had only been downgraded to 'secret'.[41] When SAHA appealed, arguing that DOD had not specifically demonstrated how, if at all, the exemption relating to the defence of the Republic applied and that it was inconceivable that the department could not mask exempt information in the listings, DOD argued that the group 6 list contained information relating to 'military tactics or strategy or military exercises or operations undertaken in preparation of hostilities or in connection with the detection, prevention, suppression or curtailment of subversive or hostile activities'.[42] Following SAHA's appeal to the High Court in June 2002, DOD conceded that the list could be released with redactions.

Efforts during this period to access the files referred to in the listings also had mixed results. Access to 22 files relating to anti-conscription activities during the apartheid era was refused on the basis that disclosure would cause prejudice to the defence and security of the Republic,[43] but when SAHA appealed, they were released (with excisions).[44] Again, in 2003 DOD refused access to files contained in group 5 on the basis that they would reveal the location and identities of sources that could endanger their physical safety,[45] military tactics that are still being used[46] and, more generally, intelligence-related information used for the defence of the Republic.[47] In this case, DOD also determined to transfer the entire set of group 4 records to Zimbabwe (discussed later). At the time of writing, the matter was on appeal in the High Court.[48]

In four of six DOD cases that have been appealed (excluding the matter currently before the High Court), SAHA was granted access, albeit in some instances with information redacted. This should lead us to question whether DOD has appropriately applied the exemption in all cases, as it appears to be a default application without consideration of severance. What these cases also reveal is that, like the reliance upon its agreement with Israel, DOD continues to rely on informants secured and relationships established and negotiated by the apartheid government. While these relationships may be legitimate and in the best interests of the Republic, failing the commission of a breach of the law (which may arguably be the case if the agreement or relationship contravenes international sanctions) or a threat to the safety of persons or to the environment, PAIA does not provide a mechanism to interrogate whether this is so.

v. Commercial information and economic interests of the state

These detailed exemptions aim to protect the economic interests and financial welfare of the Republic and the commercial activities of the state.[49] In the instance of information related to commercial activities, it may not be refused if it is already publicly available, the body that owns the information consents, or its disclosure would reveal a serious public safety or environmental risk. In March 2004 SAHA submitted two requests to Eskom for its Service Delivery Framework Agreement with the Department of Minerals and Energy, the Department of Public Enterprises and the South African National Civic Organisation, and a research document titled 'Soweto Socio-economic Research' prepared by EON Consulting.[50] Both requests were refused on the broad basis that disclosure of the records would damage the economic interests of the state.[51]

SAHA was forced to appeal on each of the limbs of the provision. SAHA contended, among other things, that harm was unlikely and could not reasonably be expected, given that some of the subject matter was publicly available, and that, since Eskom has a monopoly on the supply of electricity, it has no competitors that could use the information to the organisation's disadvantage. Of greater importance, however, was the fact that the agreement had been cited many times as authority for actions regarding the provision of electricity, including those with respect to debt write-offs and the installation of pre-paid electricity meters. The documents therefore relate to decisions that are administrative decisions under the Promotion of Administrative Justice Act No. 3 of 2000, which requires affected parties to be afforded an opportunity to comment prior to decisions being taken; failure to disclose may be in breach of these requirements. As a consequence, SAHA alleged that the public interest override compels disclosure in that the agreement and research are likely to reveal limitations on constitutional rights such as health, housing and education where it deals with disconnections to schools, homes and medical centres; the installation of pre-paid meters; and the collection of debt. Eskom subsequently released both documents without masking.

In a later request for access to a report entitled 'Economic Project Evaluation July 2001: A Macroeconomic Impact Study on the Production of Pebble-bed Modular Reactor and Fuel Plant', the company Pebble Bed Modular Reactor (Pty) Ltd (PMBR Ltd) refused the request on the basis that it formed a material part of its business case and the report's release would cause harm to its commercial and financial interests and put it at a disadvantage in contractual and other negotiations, and may prejudice it in commercial competition.[52] Unlike Eskom, PBMR Ltd is competing in the international arena for the sale of nuclear technology and therefore had a legitimate interest in protecting its ability to compete. Nevertheless, the title of the report indicated that it dealt with matters other than internal financial implications.[53] It appeared to contain information regarding the impact of the establishment of the pebble bed modular reactor and fuel plant on the economy and the ability of the company to deliver electricity supply, and therefore must have considered financial impacts greater than the pricing or cost concerns of PBMR Ltd or the ability of the company to compete.[54] Given the limited information available about the report, it is not possible to say with any certainty that this exemption should not have applied. This is particularly so given that the term 'commercial and financial' has a broad scope.[55] SAHA also appealed to the reason of the decision maker in arguing that, in releasing the report, he/she would contribute to a more rational and informed public debate. PBMR Ltd, however, was not convinced and sought further justification. SAHA did not have the resources to litigate.

The utilisation of the exemption has, in these two cases, appeared to be an attempt to camouflage the decision making of parastatals regarding the provision of an essential utility. Earthlife Africa in its case against Eskom has faced similar opposition in relation to minutes of meetings of the Eskom board. In the judgment of the High Court, Acting Justice Fevrier held that the 'expert' testimony of the managing director of the Resources and Strategy Division of Eskom provided sufficient evidence that all the minutes contained trade secrets and information that was confidential, and that Earthlife, despite having no detailed knowledge of the information contained in the records, failed to provide sufficient expert knowledge to rebut.[56] The decision was fundamentally flawed in many respects, particularly in that the onus was placed on Earthlife to disprove the application of exemptions. Nevertheless, the protection afforded the commercial enterprises of publicly owned companies exercising public functions is concerning, particularly given recent developments regarding the failure to meet demand for electricity and the health and environmental concerns regarding nuclear energy proposals.

Challenging cases such as these against profit-making enterprises with resources to litigate is particularly difficult for the people who are most affected. The Fevrier decision has now been overturned by agreement in the Supreme Court, and the parties must send the question of whether the documents contain trade secrets or other commercially sensitive information to two independent experts to report to the court. This is a promising development that has implications not only for considerations relating to trade and commercial secrets, but also for matters in which bodies apply exemptions in a blanket fashion to all records.

vi. Research information of third parties

Section 43 of PAIA protects information about research being or to be carried out by or on behalf of third parties where disclosure would be likely to expose the third party, a person working on behalf of a third party or the subject matter of the research to disadvantage. It also protects research carried out by the public body itself.

In 2004 SAHA submitted six requests to South African Breweries Ltd (SAB) for access to information regarding, among other things, the prevalence of HIV/AIDS among its workforce, access to health services and benefits by the workforce, and HIV/AIDS policies.[57] Although the requests were directed to a private body, the case nevertheless provides a useful example. SAB outsourced the provision of health and counselling services to a third party in order to maintain the confidentiality of workers and ensure that information regarding their HIV/AIDS status was not communicated to co-workers or supervisors. The company argued that to disclose the level of detail requested would prejudice its ability to maintain credibility with its employees in regard to confidentiality, and that disclosing research information or the results thereof would expose numerous parties to disadvantage and prejudice, including SAB, the third party, and employees and their families.

There is certainly legitimacy in this argument: the issue is one that is particularly sensitive and should be treated with great care. However, refusal on the basis of a need to protect research information of the third party is questionable. SAHA was requesting information regarding the prevalence of HIV/AIDS in the company, the number of workers undertaking testing and counselling, the numbers of workers who have left the company or died while in its employ, and the levels of income of workers with HIV/AIDS. While this information is likely to be collected on an ongoing basis, it is not information about research being or to be carried out by or on behalf of a third party, but information collected in the ordinary course of the implementation of SAB policy regarding HIV/AIDS. Further, the information was unlikely to have any commercial value. Currie and Klaaren state that 'disclosure of research that is commercially valuable but which is not ultimately intended for publication arguably does not result in any serious disadvantage to the types of interests protected by the ground'.[58]

Upon reading SAB's three-page response, a sense of concealment is not apparent: SAB was clearly attempting to demonstrate that it had a considered policy that was being implemented and was keen to ensure that worker confidentiality was not breached and thereby workers would not be reluctant to access health services offered. Nevertheless, a reluctance to probe and compare prevalence of HIV/AIDS within the company, the use of health and counselling services, and access to antiretrovirals was apparent, given that the information requested could have been released with masking.

The exemption was similarly used to refuse access to records of the Home Affairs Intervention Team, a body established within government to make proposals and establish mechanisms to rectify the numerous failures of the Department of Home Affairs (DHA) to fulfil its mandate.[59] Both these cases are an attempt to apply the term 'research' to a broad range of activities that the exemption should not contemplate. Upon a plain language interpretation, what the exemption aims to protect is research information that has an intellectual property or monetary value. The 'research' information of the Intervention Team in particular could not have such a value, given that its operations are intended to facilitate the restructuring of a department so that it fulfils its ordinary functions — information that is of no value in terms of its intellectual ingenuity or its sale. It is also interesting that DHA characterised the Intervention Team as a third party, particularly given that the other public bodies with representatives on the team had transferred identical requests to DHA, not to the head of the team itself. In any event, another public body, which the Intervention Team must be, does not fall within the definition of a third party for the purposes of the override.[60]

vii. Operations of public bodies

Section 44 of PAIA aims to protect the operations of public bodies by providing them with the discretion to refuse a request if the records contain, for example, opinions, advice, discussions or deliberations, or a report or recommendation relating to the formulation of policy or the taking of a decision. It also prevents (upon a mandatory ground) disclosure that could be reasonably expected to prejudice the effectiveness of a testing, examining or auditing procedure or of evaluative material.

In 2007 DHA refused access to records regarding its Turnaround Task Team documenting discussion and recommendations for processing asylum seeker applications. The request was refused on the basis that the records would disclose the operations of public bodies (although no further detail was provided). The Turnaround Task Team was set up to deal with the backlog of asylum seeker applications (some asylum seekers, who had applied as far back as 1997, were still waiting for a decision). The Turnaround Task Team determined to set up a refugee reception office at Crown Mines, and purchased additional computers and employed staff for that purpose. The backlog project, as it became known, commenced in 2005.

Given these facts, decisions must have been finalised regarding efforts to 'turn around' the backlog. Pre-decision documents are protected to permit the frank and honest debate necessary to formulate government policy. However, where a decision has been determined, the decision itself must lose its protection, as 'it does not have a deliberative character'.[61] Currie and Klaaren state that 'a pre-decision document that is adopted or incorporated by a final decision or in a finalised policy should therefore lose any protection it may have had and no longer qualifies for this ground of refusal'.[62] Some of the documents contain finalised decisions or opinions, advice, discussions and deliberations that became finalised decisions and therefore cannot be refused. The failure of DHA to provide any detail regarding what records are captured by the request or how the exemption applies to these records made rebuttal lengthy and at times vague.[63]

Public interest override

The definition of public interest tends toward a broad interpretation of matters that are of relevance to the public in that they impact upon their communal interests. The construction of public interest in PAIA, however, is narrow and restrictive: in order to override any exemption, it requires that disclosure would reveal evidence of a substantial contravention of or failure to comply with the law, or an imminent and serious public safety or environmental risk, *and* that the public interest in disclosure outweighs the harm contemplated. As noted earlier, the majority of requests made by SAHA relate to relatively controversial issues. In many cases, the records aim in the first instance to reveal evidence of contraventions of the law; arguments concerning the applicability of the public interest override are easy to construct. The public interest override is a key issue in the majority of requests, not because of difficulty in arguing its application, but because public bodies rarely apply it.

DOJ provides a key example. Almost all of SAHA's requests to the department seek records that make allegations about or reveal the commission of human rights violations. DOJ, in most of these cases, refuses access on the basis of section 34 of PAIA, the protection of privacy. In doing so it states: 'The requested documents contain personal information that implicates various third parties in alleged unlawful activities. Its disclosure could be defamatory to the individuals implicated and could also infringe their dignity which is protected under the Constitution.'[64]

DOJ, however, has never explicitly considered the application of the public interest override, which would apply in the case of the above paragraph in that the record contains information of public interest (i.e. it relates to human rights violations in the apartheid era) and may disclose a contravention of the law. In a meeting with the deputy information officer (DIO) in 2006, SAHA argued that her reasoning would compel disclosure rather than prevent it. When questioned whether she applied the override, she stated that it is the first step she takes. Despite subsequently acknowledging that this in fact should be the final step after giving consideration to the exemptions, the DIO then refused access to Eugene de Kock's application on the same basis without mention of the override.

The issue has also arisen in the military intelligence listings case.[65] When DOD released the group 22 listing, it had been heavily masked on the basis that it cited names of projects and countries, and that disclosure of these names would reveal countries visited by Armscor and thereby their involvement in arms deals when international sanctions were in place against South Africa. DOD stated that, prior to the start of these projects, the parties involved signed international agreements that are still in place. They therefore reasoned that section 37, which prevents disclosure of information subject to confidentiality agreements, prevented access. DOD also masked the names of private firms that dealt with South Africa during this time on the basis that their disclosure might be expected to put such firms at a disadvantage or negatively prejudice future contractual agreements. DOD failed to consider that the engagement by these states and firms was in contravention of international law while international sanctions were in place, and that therefore the first limb of the public interest override was satisfied. In effect, the department was avoiding jeopardising relations developed by the apartheid government. SAHA appealed and, in a rare reconsideration on the grounds of the public interest override, DOD granted access. SAHA requested confirmation that no firms' names had been redacted, as none were revealed in the 'unmasked document', but did not get a further response from the minister.[66]

The contention that the failure to implement the override is experienced across the board can be evidenced by the statistics released by the SAHRC in its yearly reports to Parliament.[67] Across the period 2002–06, 1,997 out of 64,208 reported requests were granted on the basis of the public interest override. The statistics are somewhat skewed, however, by the inclusion of requests reported by SAPS, which constitute 55,027 of the total. Excluding SAPS, the figures show that the override was applied positively in 79 of 9,181 requests; in other words, in less than 1 per cent of cases.[68] While reporting to the SAHRC is fairly minimal, given that bodies that actually report to the SAHRC are more likely to collect accurate statistics, they can provide some measure to show that where the override is applied, it leads to access in only a few cases.

Aside from its limited explicit application, the override raises the following issues. Firstly, the limitation in the first limb excludes records that may reveal the implementation of a practice, for example, that is contrary to government policy and may significantly impact upon access to essential services by the community. Secondly, while the second limb includes the term 'public interest' as a requirement, it fails to actually define it or to provide any means to measure whether it outweighs the harm contemplated by the exemption. And thirdly, the provision imposes the burden of demonstrating that the document would reveal evidence of a contravention of the law or a safety or environmental risk on the requester. It is not feasible to argue that records may provide evidence of a contravention of the law when, in some cases, it is not known which records relate to the request. SAHA has argued that, in accordance with constitutional interpretation,[69] the provision should be read broadly and understood to require requesters to demonstrate that the document may provide any evidence in supporting a contention of illegality or breach of a legal duty. Without judicial precedent, these arguments are simply ignored.

The limited application of the override is an issue that is only remedied through appeals. However, its limited scope could be resolved through amendment to return it to its original formulation in the Open Democracy Bill, where it was a simple public interest test that applied to a broader range of interests, that is, to matters of public interest that do not necessarily relate to contraventions of the law, but are of substantial interest to requesters who aim to ensure that the rights of citizens are being sufficiently represented and upheld.

Box 6.2: Severance

While public bodies have been reluctant to utilise severance, particularly during the first few years following the enactment of PAIA, the key issue seems to be one of consistency. Pollecut notes that DOD mistakenly granted access to a file; SAHA returned the document and its subsequent appeal was refused.[70] Having had the benefit of viewing the file prior to returning it, it was apparent to SAHA that the names that it revealed could have been easily redacted; however, it did not have the resources at that time to litigate.

Some years later, in 2005, DOD released huge volumes of records rather than allowing inspection, because it determined a need to mask the files. The masking undertaken, however, was excessive: the department masked the name of a minister of defence, and the name of an advocate in litigation had been masked, but not the name of the attorney. In a discussion with the Documentation Centre in 2005, DOD acknowledged the problem and laid the blame on the minister for failing to designate sufficient funds to employ and train permanent staff. The National Archives has also adopted an inconsistent approach. In 2003 it masked around 90 per cent of the security legislation directorate files of Michael and Shulamith Muller (making the document worthless in terms of revealing anything substantive about the persons or the monitoring of them),[71] but refused access to security police lists on the basis that the file numbers would disclose information that was subject to the privacy exemption (and what is presumed to be the identity of informers).[72]

There are, however, cases in which large-scale masking is essential. In 2002 SAHA assisted researchers for the Swiss National Science Foundation to obtain access to information regarding Swiss–South African military relations from a number of bodies, including Armscor. After considerable difficulty in eliciting a response — it first ignored the request and then attempted to transfer it, during which time it determined to treat every written inquiry regarding its progress as requests pursuant to PAIA in themselves, then dismissed them as frivolous and vexatious — Armscor released the records, heavily masking the names of third parties. It was apparent to SAHA, however, that Armscor had considered the application of the third-party notification process and determined not to apply it, as it would require Armscor to contact all third parties involved since 1969. In this instance, masking, while subject to challenge on the basis of the public interest override, was accepted due to the practical and legal challenges involved in contacting a large number of third parties.

Enforcement mechanisms

PAIA provides cumulative appeal mechanisms against refusals of access; the application of fees; the failure to respond (i.e. deemed refusal); decisions to extend time periods; and, in the case of affected third parties, the granting of access.[73] Upon any of these events, a requester is entitled to lodge a written internal appeal to the minister of the department or to the head of the public body (provided that the body is not a type (b) public body, that is, a private body exercising a public function). Requesters also have the option of complaining to the public protector or the SAHRC. If unsuccessful, the requester's only recourse is to lodge an application in the High Court for relief.[74]

In her chapter discussing the Nuclear Weapons History Project, Gould notes that when SAHA requested a report by Dr N. von Williegh from the International Atomic Energy Agency (IAEA), the Nuclear Energy Corporation of South Africa (NECSA) irritably responded that it was waiting for clearance from IAEA to release it, and that the Department of Minerals and Energy had instructed that the minister must approve all responses. Despite numerous requests to respond and complaints to the SAHRC and the public protector, no response was received. Due to the classification of NECSA as a type (b) public body, SAHA did not have the right to submit an internal appeal. Its only option was to apply to court to challenge the legitimacy of IAEA's intervention, the minister's need to approve release and the ultimate failure to respond. Given the numerous refusals that were received pursuant to the project and the cost burden of litigation, SAHA was not in a position to take the matter further. The barriers to and limitations of pursuing access through the prescribed appeal mechanisms highlighted by this case have had a significant impact on the right, largely for the following reasons:

· Independent regulators have failed to respond to complaints and have not taken the proactive steps necessary to assist requesters with legitimate disputes.
· The lack of independent regulatory intervention following the internal appeal process

allows decision makers to refuse access or fail to respond with the knowledge that only a select few requesters will proceed to litigation due to prohibitive costs, lack of resources and the failure of independent regulators.

· Where requests do proceed to court, bodies often settle prior to a precedent-setting decision.

Failure of regulatory authorities

The public protector and the SAHRC have legislative obligations in relation to the regulation of PAIA. The public protector is responsible for investigating and mediating complaints of maladministration against public bodies only.[75] The SAHRC is responsible for, among other things, monitoring and education, receipt of manuals and annual statistical reports from public and private bodies, and assisting requesters to exercise their right of access.[76] Section 8 of the Human Rights Commission Act No. 54 of 1994 gives the SAHRC the power to endeavour to resolve by mediation, conciliation or negotiation any dispute or to rectify any act or omission in relation to a fundamental right; any recommendation made as a result is not binding on the public or private body. The intervention by these bodies is intended to provide requesters with a more cost-effective means of resolving disputes.

In June 2003 SAHA was commissioned by the SAHRC to conduct research regarding the role of the commission as a champion of the right of access to information. The research found that persons interviewed for the purposes of the study opined that the activities undertaken to promote the objects of PAIA had not resulted in anything approaching a decisive and cultural shift in the public (or private) sector towards open and transparent governance. This lack of impact must be partly the result of a failure by the SAHRC to take a proactive role in complaints investigation and mediation. The SAHRC failed, until 2007, to follow up on any SAHA complaints in any meaningful way.[77] Despite failing to investigate or finalise complaints, the SAHRC did not include the complaints in its annual report and stated that it had no complaints still under investigation.

The public protector is mandated to have a greater enforcement role, in that he is responsible for investigating and mediating complaints of maladministration, however, his intervention has been similarly weak.[78] Despite provision in PAIA for the public protector to report to the SAHRC, SAHA found in its research regarding the role of the SAHRC in championing PAIA that there was no ongoing contact between the commission and the public protector regarding PAIA cases, and neither reported referring any cases to each other nor receiving such referrals. In 2005 SAHA was advised by the SAHRC that, upon receipt of the complaint about NECSA, it would contact the public protector to determine what steps it would take; if the public protector was not intending to intervene, it would assist in the matter. SAHA was not informed about the precise arrangements, however, neither body took any steps to facilitate negotiation or mediation of the dispute, despite SAHA raising the lack of response two years on.[79]

There are two justifications put forward by the SAHRC for its limited intervention. Firstly, it states that it is severely under-resourced. The PAIA unit established by the SAHRC in June 2002 was severely underfunded from its establishment. The extent of this under-resourcing is demonstrated by the SAHRC in its 2002/03 annual report, in which it states that implementing its obligations to produce a guide to PAIA in the various languages and forms would cost a total of ZAR 2 million, leaving ZAR 0.3 million to conduct education and training, monitor implementation, and provide assistance to requesters. The commission consequently recommended amending the regulations to provide for a 'limited but effective' distribution of the guide.[80] The situation did not improve in the 2003/04 reporting period, when the guide was granted only 1.5 per cent of the SAHRC's total budget, a mere ZAR 2.3 million.

Secondly, the commission argues that the weak enforcement power in PAIA has severely impeded its ability to act. The enforcement power contained in PAIA is weak in that it is a power to recommend to a public or private body that the body make such changes in the manner in which it administers the Act as the SAHRC considers advisable,[81] and it couches the commission's role with caveats in terms of its available resources.[82] It also imposes little obligation upon public and private bodies to engage with the commission regarding complaints, in that it states, 'if appropriate, and if financial and other resources are available, an official of a public body must afford the Commission reasonable assistance for the effective performance of its functions in terms of this Act'.[83]

I make two points to rebut these justifications. Firstly, the PAIA unit is not entirely disconnected from the other units within the commission. The Legal Department, responsible for dealing with complaints and the conduct of mediation, negotiation and litigation, is tasked with intervening in cases and assisting complainants to resolve disputes. The failure of the SAHRC to take an active role in disputes and litigation regarding PAIA cannot therefore be solely one of under-resourcing of the PAIA unit, but must be ascribed to its limited priority in terms of its wide range of legislative obligations. Secondly, the SAHRC has failed to acknowledge its general powers under section 8 of the Human Rights Commission Act; in its 2006/07 report it stated that 'due to [its] lack of powers in [PAIA] to mediate, this is provided only if the two parties agree to such mediation'. The permissive wording in PAIA has allowed the commission to take a very soft approach to promotion and enforcement, with the result that it fails to be a catalyst for the resolution of disputes and access to records.[84]

The work of the SAHRC in promotion and education has increased in recent years (see Box 6.3), raising the potential to elevate the profile of PAIA and DIOs, and achieve greater consensus on not only what is required to implement PAIA, but on the interpretation of provisions. The limited role of the SAHRC in enforcement to date, however, has the effect of lessening this potential; without consequences, some public officers and bodies do not have the impetus to implement or appropriately apply PAIA.

Box 6.3: Deputy Information Officers' Forum

Over the last two years the SAHRC has attempted to raise the profile of the right of access to information held by government bodies by establishing the Deputy Information Officers' Forum. Through yearly meetings and an electronic discussion forum, the project aims to address issues in the implementation of PAIA and the lack of awareness of PAIA obligations by:

· sharing information;
· raising awareness;
· advising DIOs of developments and best practice; and
· building capacity within bodies.

It remains to be seen what impact the forum will have on the implementation of PAIA within bodies and on facilitating access to information.

In addition to the forum, the SAHRC co-hosts the Golden Key Awards, which aim to recognise the exemplary work of particular public and private bodies, DIOs, NGOs, individuals and journalists in using or complying with PAIA. SAHA was awarded the Golden Key Award for the best use of PAIA in 2006.

Deterrent effect of appeal mechanisms

The majority of requests submitted by SAHA are refused or ignored in the first instance. In the absence of facilitative relationships, such as that established with SAPS, where refusals may be negotiated or reconsidered, the only available remedial recourse is through an internal appeal, the intervention of the SAHRC or the public protector, and litigation.[85] The minister or head of a body often refuses the request again on appeal; he/she does so knowing that the majority of requesters are not in a position to litigate due to prohibitive court costs and that independent regulators are unlikely to take steps to intervene. Although SAHA may often rely on pro bono legal assistance, the risk of the imposition of a costs order, as occurred against Biowatch in seeking access to information regarding decision making in granting permits for the production of genetically modified crops,[86] makes litigation an option in only a limited number of cases. This allows bodies not committed to access to disregard their obligations unless court proceedings are instituted.

DOJ provides an example of how the available appeal mechanisms deter bodies from making sound decisions in the first instance. Given that SAHA ordinarily has more than one request with the department at any one time, it is impossible to litigate upon every refusal; the department can therefore wait for litigation before considering the merits of requests.[87] Such conduct is exacerbated when requesters are conducting projects requiring the submission of numerous requests to a number of bodies. When more than one body ignores requests, options for appeal become limited. For example, in the nuclear energy project, SAHA submitted requests to the Department of Minerals and Energy (eight), the NECSA (27) and the National Nuclear Regulator (seven). These bodies simply ignored the requests on first instance and on internal appeal (where submitted), knowing that it would be impossible to litigate in all of these cases. Such cases become particularly difficult when they are deemed refused, as without a response it may be impossible to determine whether the records sought exist or whether legitimate grounds may be relied upon to refuse access. The requester is then left in the position of determining which requests and which bodies may provide the most useful information and the greatest chance of success.

Lack of precedents

SAHA has resorted to litigation in around ten cases, resulting in seven sets of proceedings. In all finalised cases,[88] settlement occurred prior to hearing.[89] While the primary objective of litigation has been to secure access, a key goal has been to secure a judicial precedent that will provide guidance on the interpretation of PAIA. This is particularly so in the cases against DOJ, which repeatedly refuses access to TRC records unless SAHA litigates.[90] The utilisation of litigation, while based on sound strategy and while securing access, has been very costly[91] and has not led to long-term solutions in the form of guiding and binding precedents.[92] This is largely because litigation is being used as a method of negotiation and a means to force bodies to consider the merits of requests, rather than as a means of obtaining clarity on interpretive issues.

Proposals for reform

The lack of an intermediary process between internal appeals and litigation has led to the pursuit of cases by requesters that public and private bodies do not intend to vigorously defend and the failure to pursue information that should be in the public domain. An independent arbiter with the power to make binding orders following the refusal of access at first instance or on appeal would require bodies to consider the merits of requests prior to litigation or institute applications to appeal decisions, leading to greater engagement in the early stages of the request. Requesters would also benefit from a cheap, accessible and binding appeal mechanism.

The Open Democracy Bill, the precursor to PAIA, provided a comprehensive approach to the regulation of access to information, the protection of privacy, whistle-blowing and meetings of open government, and recommended three levels of monitoring and enforcement: an open democracy commission tasked with promotion, education, the provision of assistance and monitoring; information courts tasked with adjudicating disputes, staffed by High Court judges, but operating under rules designed to ensure that they were accessible, cheap, informal and expeditious; and the High Court, to which decisions of the information courts could be appealed. These recommendations were rejected by cabinet.[93]

When it became apparent within the few years following PAIA's enactment that the appeal mechanisms were ineffective,[94] calls were made by a number of organisations, including SAHA, ODAC and the SAHRC, for DOJ to investigate the establishment of an independent arbiter of access to information disputes.[95] The department did not respond. Cabinet had, however, referred the issue of data protection and privacy to the South African Law Reform Commission (SALRC), which, following extensive consultation, drafted the Protection of Information Bill. The Bill, and the discussion paper accompanying it, proposed an information and privacy commission tasked with obligations relating to PAIA and the protection of privacy, including promotion, education, monitoring, investigation, mediation and the issuing of binding determinations. It also proposed that the commission litigate in its own name or on behalf of individuals or classes of individuals for breaches of the Acts.

In its submission to the SALRC regarding the discussion paper, SAHA welcomed its proposal (albeit with a number of concerns regarding the reporting requirements and the lack of power to award compensation and impose fines), but objected to granting the additional powers to the SAHRC. Nevertheless, cabinet had, during this time, established a commission headed by Kader Asmal to investigate Chapter 9 (of the Constitution) and other institutions, in particular whether such institutions required reform and whether they could be amalgamated or streamlined. It reported in September 2007, heavily criticising a number of institutions for failing to take a proactive approach to fulfilling their mandates and recommending that all institutions be collapsed into one human rights commission to be based at the current SAHRC. The commission did, however, make specific note of the SAHRC's failures in regard to PAIA and recommended that two dedicated information commissioners be appointed and ring-fenced funds be injected by Parliament.[96] While the recommendation aims to achieve greater accountability in the administration of PAIA, it is without doubt preferable that a dedicated and independent privacy and information commission, which reports directly to Parliament rather than to DOJ, be established, that will not be subject to any political manoeuvring or affected by any priority decisions. It remains to be seen how the two recommendations, that of the Asmal commission and the SALRC, will be reconciled by Parliament.

The multiple faces of information governance

PAIA does not act in isolation, but in conjunction with what may be hundreds of other enactments. A number of bodies, in particular bodies dealing with the security of the Republic and intelligence gathering, and statutory bodies, have obligations regarding the classification and dissemination of records pursuant to their own legislation. This legislation has an impact on both the procedures followed in responding to PAIA requests and the application of PAIA provisions and exemptions, creating confusion in some quarters regarding inconsistencies among Acts.

PAIA applies to the exclusion of other legislation that prohibits or restricts disclosure if that other legislation is materially inconsistent with an object or specific provision of it; where other enactments provide a greater right of access, resort to PAIA is not necessary. Legislation that restricts the right of access can be, according to Harris and Merrett, broken down into four main categories:

i.   Acts that control official information,
ii.   Acts that restrict information from all sources on specific topics,
iii. Acts that regulate administrative and legal functions, and
iv.   Other acts extending government power.[97]

I would add that these categories are not confined to legislation that necessarily restricts access, but can be extended to legislation that provides for a greater right of access. For example, the National Archives and Records Service Act (NARSA) No. 43 of 1996 provides a greater right of access under category (i) and the National Conventional Arms Control Act No. 41 of 2002 and the Inquests Act No. 58 of 1959 under category (iii).

The minister of justice was obligated by section 86 of PAIA to schedule regulations that would list enactments that provided a greater right of access, but the current minister has not done so. Given the lack of a comprehensive audit of intersecting legislation, and given that there are likely to be a large number of enactments that limit or extend the right of access, it is not within the scope of this chapter to list and discuss them all. What I aim to do, however, is to provide examples of cases where legislation has had an impact on the exercise of PAIA. These examples fall into two categories:

i.   Acts that control information across all public structures or in relation to specific public structures; and
ii.   Acts that relate to specific information held by specific sectors or structures.

Acts controlling access across all public spheres

National Archives and Records Service Act No. 43 of 1996

NARSA requires public bodies to transfer records older than 20 years to the National Archives for public access (with exceptions). This means that any records held by National Archives that are older than 20 years should not be subject to PAIA and should be freely accessible, including cabinet records. Records less than 20 years old should be requested pursuant to PAIA, unless they are cabinet records, in which instance access may only be given by special permission of the national archivist. Prior to the enactment of NARSA and the constitutional right to freedom of information, access to records in the National Archives was only allowed where they were 30 years old, unless the minister of education withdrew the right of access on public policy grounds. The lack of definition of 'public policy' allowed arbitrary restrictions to be enforced, such as the restriction on access to records less than 50 years old of the governor general, the state president, the Public Service Commission, the commissioner of police, Inland Revenue and DHA, and on post-1910 records of the Executive Council, the prime minister, the Department of Foreign Affairs and the Department of Information.[98]

Harris and Merrett note that, even though 2,372 requests out of 2,381 were granted in the period 1980–90, the room for secrecy illustrates that 'the grounds on which public policy restrictions can be applied [should] be established in law'.[99] The enactment of NARSA shortened the access time period; however, it still allows the national archivist to exempt any government body from a provision of the Act (upon authorisation of the National Archives Advisory Board, which is comprised of six persons appointed by the minister of arts and culture and which may be dissolved by the minister on 'any reasonable grounds'), or defer access.[100] While this is a great deal better than the pre-NARSA enactment, the room for secrecy remains; this is concerning, given that the national archivist has been less than active in ensuring that apartheid records are transferred to the National Archives or in facilitating access to such records.

Pigou notes that in 2001 SAHA submitted a request to the National Archives for access to correspondence documenting its dealings with the TRC and other parties in relation to the archive of the TRC.[101] After a number of internal appeals relating to access to 'classified' records, the national archivist, Dr Graham Dominy, stated:

> Your most recent requests for access are being referred for legal advice as there is a lack of clarity between two pieces of legislation, namely the National Archives Act and the Public Access to Information Act (PAIA) [sic] ... Please note that a submission has been made requesting that the National Archives be considered a public body in terms of PAIA. However, the Minister of Justice has not yet approved it. There may therefore continue to be delays in dealing with PAIA requests until this matter has been finalised.[102]

Upon a later request for the Defence and Aid file of the former Directorate of Security Legislation,[103] in which SAHA challenged the national archivist's request for an affidavit of authorisation from a defunct organisation on the basis that it had 'been given access to a number of [the] files in the past without having to make a request in terms of the PAIA', and that 'PAIA is there to be used as a last resort when the file is not open to the public and if access cannot be secured using another piece of legislation',[104] the national archivist stated:

I regret any inconvenience you may have been put to. The relationship between the publication of the National Archives Act and the application of the Promotion of Access to Information Act does have grey areas and we are investigating how to resolve the issues on an on-going basis. Generally, but not in every instance, the Archives Act applies to records that are older than twenty years, and which are in the National Archives, and PAIA applies to more recent records and obviously to accessing records in offices of origin. I have instructed that your complaint be investigated and I will let you know the outcome as soon as possible.[105]

Whether or not the reliance on inconsistency at that time was legitimate is questionable; I would chance that it is a misconstrued attempt to avoid disclosure under PAIA. The National Archives is established pursuant to statute, indicating it may be a 'type (b)' public body;[106] however, it sits within and reports to the Department of Arts and Culture, and is in fact considered part of that department and therefore a branch of a public body in the ordinary sense (and in terms of part (a) of the PAIA definition). In any event, the distinction only affects the appeal process and has, to all other intents and purposes, no practical effect. The body is required to consider access in terms of the prescribed exemptions and exclusions and no other external grounds, and is required to respond within the prescribed time periods.

Contributing to the response of the National Archives may have been the neglect on the part of DOJ to schedule Acts that provide for a greater right of access. Nevertheless, section 86 of PAIA states that, until the amendment of the Act, where any other legislation not referred to in the schedule provides for access to a record of a public or private body in a manner that is not materially more onerous than the manner in which access may be obtained in terms of the Act, access may be given in terms of that legislation. Accordingly, given that the National Archives Act provides for a less onerous right of access, its operation should not be precluded by PAIA. The national archivist noted this in his letter, however, he did not go on to specify where he believed the 'grey areas' lay.[107]

Box 6.4: Cabinet records

An issue of particular concern is that of cabinet records, which are governed by the National Archives Act, but cannot be accessed pursuant to PAIA. In 2007 SAPS refused access to documents on the basis that they were cabinet records to which PAIA does not apply. It took some months, and consultation with the National Archives by SAPS, before SAPS agreed that, given that the records were more than 20 years old, they should in fact be in the custody of the National Archives, and if they were, SAHA would be granted access.[108]

In October 2002 SAHA requested access to cabinet records that were less than 20 years old, in particular those relating to the 1990–94 negotiation period. SAHA reasoned with the national archivist that these records were 'public records of great historical value which should be firmly in the public domain'. Although ordinarily archival legislation allowed for the release of such documents after 20 years, legislation empowered the national archivist to release these documents (as well as State Security Council documents from the 1980s) on a discretionary basis before that time.[109] The request was denied, having been 'duly considered and the relevant bodies ... consulted'. It was explained that 'the National Archives is considering a structured approach to the question and it is not in a position to respond to *ad hoc* requests at this stage'.[110] Over four years later, these records remain closed, and no details of a 'structured approach' to addressing this matter have been publicly divulged.

Protection of Information Act No. 84 of 1982

The Protection of Information Act is an apartheid government enactment that aimed to restrict access to information on public affairs and control the extent to which government employees could disseminate information. The Act was the result of the government's obsession with secrecy:

> Every bureaucrat was graded in terms of a rigorous security clearance procedure, the grading level determining an individual's right of access to information. The procedures meshed with a pervasive system of information grading — commonly referred to as 'classification' — defined by perceived security risks. The Protection of Information Act, and various legislative forerunners, promised severe punitive action against individuals defying the system.[111]

Despite its apartheid origins, the legislation is still in force; that is, the threat of punishment for unauthorised disclosure remains. This means that it is being utilised to both classify and declassify records, and prevent government employees from accessing information for which they do not have the appropriate security clearances and from blowing the whistle on matters of public interest.[112] This has a number of implications for PAIA.

Firstly, Pollecut notes that the declassification of files in the archives is driven by requests. In the absence of an information audit, there has been little, if any, proactive declassification of records. As a result, requests for military and other intelligence records subject to classification under the Protection of Information Act are substantially delayed until declassification is undertaken. Secondly, the Protection of Information Act has been used to prevent access on the basis of classification. Classification was cited as a reason for refusal by the National Archives, in conjunction with the National Intelligence Agency (NIA), following requests for access to TRC records documenting their chain of custody and records related to TRC recommendations discussed by Pigou.[113] These were refused on the basis that they had purportedly been classified as 'confidential' by NIA. It was not clear whether the classification was *ad hoc*, was specifically subject to the classification provisions of the Protection of Information Act, or occurred following submission of the request. Subsequently, the national archivist clarified that he was refusing access in terms of sections 37 and 38 of PAIA.[114] The correct and constitutionally consistent interpretation of the intersection of PAIA with the Protection of Information Act is that PAIA is paramount, and that information should only remain classified where it can be exempted from disclosure pursuant to PAIA.[115] Thirdly, the extension of classification to records that do not relate to national security but to 'sensitive' matters of public interest and therefore to records of the entire public sector may be unconstitutional. According to Klaaren, this is largely because the 'military information security policy has been crudely and inappropriately adapted to cover the entire public sector'.[116] This is shown in the case of the National Archives, which used classification to withhold access to its own records, records that are not traditionally defined as relating to national security.

In February 2003 the then minister for intelligence, Lindiwe Sisulu, established the Classification and Declassification Review Committee (CDRC), which was tasked with developing criteria for the protection of information, which included a review of relevant legislation such as the Protection of Information Act and its implementing policy, the Minimum Information Security Standards. Submissions to the committee by SAHA and other organisations and individuals made a number of recommendations regarding the need for an archival audit and proactive declassification, full access to cabinet records, the release of apartheid operatives from secrecy undertakings, and the replacement of the Protection of Information Act with information protection legislation that is consistent with PAIA and presumes disclosure.[117] Several submissions also argued that apartheid era records should be open; the National Security Archive[118] suggested that the German model, where the East German Socialist Unity Party files were opened, should be adopted and that particular regard should be given to records that relate to human rights abuses.

There were concerns early on about the extent to which the CDRC would bring about any substantial change. Harris, Hatang and Liberman state:

> There is cause for scepticism ... that this initiative will significantly liberalise secrecy policy. It is led by the NIA, which has consistently taken an obstructionist position. Besides its efforts to obstruct the TRC inquiry into project coast ... (i.e. it tried to prevent TRC access as it didn't have the required security clearances), the NIA also illegally took possession of thirty-four boxes of sensitive TRC records, concealed their whereabouts, and then blocked access to them.[119]

Despite the fanfare with which the CDRC was launched, the submission of its report and recommendations received very little public attention, and the momentum of the process appeared to peter out. Indeed, the recommendations were effectively mothballed and only dusted off again during 2006, when the then minister of intelligence, Ronnie Kasrils, decided to revisit the issue by establishing the Intelligence Review Commission.[120] The Protection of Information Act therefore continues to play a role in restricting access to records.

Acts regulating discrete collections
Promotion of National Unity and Reconciliation Act No. 34 of 1996

The Promotion of National Unity and Reconciliation Act (the TRC Act) regulated the confidentiality of information collected by the TRC in the course of its investigations and the conduct of its hearings by the Human Rights Violations, Amnesty and Reparations Committees. In summary, the Act states that records collected during investigations and submitted to the TRC by perpetrators and victims of human rights violations were confidential, but that confidentiality lapsed when a hearing relating to such a violation commenced.[121] Any records of *in-camera* hearings retained confidentiality until the TRC determined otherwise.

I have discussed the application of the PAIA exemption that restricts access to records that are subject to a confidentiality agreement or which were provided in confidence. In these cases, DOJ in effect aimed to rely on the provisions of the TRC Act, in particular section 19(8)(a), which states that applications are confidential. In the Cradock 4 case, while the department made no specific references to subsection (b) of that provision, which states that confidentiality lapsed when an amnesty hearing commenced unless the hearing itself was not public, it stated in its answering affidavit to the High Court that it could not say with any certainty that public hearings were in fact held (although reference to its own website or to the South African Broadcasting Corporation would have provided a simple and quick means of establishing that they in fact were).[122] It then relied upon the provision to apply the PAIA exemption relating to confidential information to refuse access. DOJ similarly relied on the confidential status of *in-camera* hearings (and therefore associated potential breaches of privacy and threats to the life or safety of individuals).

It failed to consider, however, that section 5 of PAIA states that the Act applies to the exclusion of any provision of other legislation that prohibits or restricts the disclosure of a record of a public or private body and is materially inconsistent with an object or a specific provision of the Act. Blanket restriction on access to *in-camera* and public hearings of the TRC constitutes a material inconsistency with the objects of PAIA, which are, among other things, to give effect to the right of access to information by starting from the position that a record should be accessible rather than withheld. As a consequence, each and every record requested must be considered in terms of the application of PAIA, including the exceptions to the confidentiality exemption and the question of whether the information is publicly available,[123] and the applicability of the public interest override.[124]

Inquests Act No. 58 of 1959

The refusal of access to inquest records submitted as evidence in the Cradock 4 hearings also raised the issue of the application of the Inquests Act. DOJ refused access to the inquest judgment and other materials on the bases that the 'information is personal and is protected … and disclosure could be traumatic to the victims' families and offensive to the public'. The Inquests Act provides that the record of an inquest forms part of the records of the magistrate's court in the district in which it was held, and the Magistrate's Court Act No. 32 of 1994 provides that records of that court are available to the public. Accordingly, had the records not been subject to TRC hearings or requested pursuant to PAIA, they would be publicly available. The fact that they were now contained in a collection of materials categorised by their inclusion in another hearing should not have imposed a restriction or a greater burden on access.

National Conventional Arms Control Act No. 41 of 2002

In 2007 SAHA was verbally refused access to the 2003/04 and 2005 annual reports of the National Conventional Arms Control Committee[125] on the basis that the information was confidential. The National Conventional Arms Control Act (NCAC Act) states at section 23 that 'the Committee must … present to Parliament and release to the public an annual report on all conventional arms exports concluded during the preceding calendar year'. Subsection 2 goes on to provide that, subject to the specific details that must be contained within the report, information concerning the technical specifications of conventional arms may be omitted from a report in order to protect military and commercial secrets. Furthermore, subsection 3 states that 'no person may disclose any classified document or the content thereof concerning the business of the Committee except with the authorisation of a competent authority or as required in terms of [PAIA]'.

SAHA consequently appealed on the bases that, firstly, the committee had a positive duty to release to the public an annual report that is only limited to the extent of the content included in the report; and, secondly, the provision made it clear that the annual report cannot be a classified document, as the positive duty to release cannot be overcome by the restriction on disclosing classified information. It is unclear whether the committee had thought so far as to rely upon the exemption contained in PAIA relating to confidential information; however, even if it had, PAIA should not have been used to restrict access, because the NCAC Act provides a greater right.

In light of this, and despite the reference to PAIA in subsection 3, it is questionable whether the document should have been requested pursuant to PAIA in the first place. However, the Ceasefire Campaign, which wished to obtain the report, had made a number of unsuccessful attempts to access it without resort to PAIA. The NCAC Act does not provide any means for individuals outside parliamentary structures to compel release, and therefore PAIA provides the only other viable option. Had the minister of justice amended PAIA to provide for legislation providing a greater right of access, SAHA may have faced the same difficulties with the committee; however, the argument for access would have been simpler had it been forced to litigate.[126]

Other issues

I have discussed the limitations of both PAIA and related legislation that have had a substantial impact on the extent to which SAHA has been able to access information. I would now like to turn to external factors: the destruction of records, record-keeping practices and cultures of transparency or secrecy inherent in public bodies.

Destruction of records: Missing, shredded or gathering dust?

The purge of public records by the apartheid state was one mechanism in a systematic endeavour to selectively write history and influence the memory of oppressed and oppressors alike. The routine destruction of sensitive records began well before the onset of the negotiation period starting in 1990. The destruction of records is routine practice in most governance structures and is accepted as legitimate, as states do not have the resources to retain all records. The TRC, in its final report, noted that 'the selection policies of some countries' national archives secure for archival preservation as little as 1 per cent of all state records', and that the State Archives Service[127] estimates that the policies implemented in South Africa between 1960 and 1994 secured the preservation of approximately 15 per cent of state records.[128]

Despite the requirement to get authority from the Archives Commission from 1926 and subsequently the Director of Archives from 1979 to dispose of records, the security establishment[129] management culture was characterised by 'almost complete autonomy from the intervention of the State Archives Service'.[130] In 1978 all government departments received guidelines for the destruction of classified records outside the operation of the Archives Act, contrary to the State Archives Service standing order.[131] Harris notes that it was clear that state secrecy 'ensured that this programme was neither transparent nor accountable to the public'.[132] In 1990, with the likelihood of transition to democratic rule growing, the National Intelligence Service (NIS) adopted a more proactive approach to disposal by issuing guidelines that required the destruction of paper-based records unless there were very good reasons for retaining them, and mandated that security-relevant records were to be kept on microfilm or in electronic form where they were secure and could be easily erased. This process, sanctioned by cabinet and supported by legal opinions obtained by the State President's Office, NIS and the director general of education, was broadened into a systematic purging of all state records.[133]

The TRC investigation into the destruction of records found that blame could be apportioned to actors on all sides of the political transition: the State Archives Service, the director of archives, the African National Congress (ANC), NIA (and its predecessor, NIS), incumbent heads of the state, the cabinet, the South African Police and the State Security Council. The TRC also found that:

By May 1994, a massive deletion of state documentary memory within the security establishment had been achieved ... The motivation for this purging of official memory was clearly to prevent certain categories of record falling into the hands of the incoming government. The apartheid state was determined in this way to sanitise its image and protect its intelligence sources. It was also apparently intent on eliminating evidence of gross human rights violations.[134]

While the TRC investigation demonstrated that a substantial proportion of public records, particularly those related to more sensitive issues, were destroyed, the limited resources of the TRC and its reliance on the cooperation of departmental officials meant that it was not able to provide a comprehensive account of what remained.[135]

The advent of PAIA provided an opportunity for the findings and recommendations of the TRC to be tested. When SAHA set about requesting records in 2001, it became evident that the well-documented destruction of records was to become an oft-quoted reason for refusal. The greatest evidence of concealment arose in the request for access to the military intelligence lists noted frequently throughout this chapter. This raised grave concerns about the extent of destruction and the secreting of information from the TRC that were likely to seriously skew the recording of events and the findings of the commission. Harris states:

It is not clear what impact this might have had on the Commission's work. Nor is it clear whether this was an isolated incident or part of a broader pattern of obstruction. Nevertheless, it raises serious questions about the degree to which the Commission was permitted access to the records it required in order to fulfil its mandate comprehensively.[136]

This exercise of skewing the recording of history continued well past the transition period. In 2004 DOD informed SAHA and the late Dr John Seiler, the requester whom it was representing that, following a request, it had transferred the entire group 4 collection to its 'country of origin ... in keeping with the archival principle that official governmental records remain the property of the originating country and its people'.[137] It was revealing that the department chose to disclose the transfer two days prior to Christmas, a time when the media and holiday-goers would pay scant attention. In its answering affidavit to SAHA's application in the High Court seeking an explanation and the return of the documents, DOD alleged that it had discovered the origin of the collection in 2002 and, in a discussion among members of the Command and Management Information Systems Defence Intelligence, Military Legal Services, and Policy and Planning, the military legal representative expressed the opinion that the files should be returned to the Zimbabwean government to 'prevent embarrassment' to South Africa. DOD asserted that it 'consulted with the National Archivist',[138] but because the records were official Rhodesian documents obtained 'unofficially' by South Africa, it considered them to be outside the ambit of PAIA and the National Archives Act; an interesting, but entirely misconceived argu-

PRETORIA NEWS
MONDAY SEPTEMBER 3 2007

History archive trust set for war with defence ministry

Organisation seeks court order to obtain military intelligence files

ZELDA VENTER
HIGH COURT REPORTER

The SA History Archive Trust (Saha) is set to battle it out in court with the minister of defence over access to certain information contained in apartheid-era SA Defence Force (SADF) military intelligence files relating to ties between South Africa and various foreign governments.

Saha accused the SANDF of masking the bulk of information and refusing to hand it over to them.

The minister said the files were back in Zimbabwe "where they belong" and that this was done "to prevent embarrassment to South Africa".

Saha, however, is determined to obtain a Pretoria high court order to force the government to hand over the documents.

If they had been sent to Zimbabwe, they should be returned. Saha also wants the court to order that the department declare the names and positions of the officials responsible for sending the documents to Zimbabwe so that it can take legal action against them.

Piers Pigou, Saha's director, said in papers filed before court that the archive was dedicated to recapturing the country's lost and neglected history and recording history in the making.

More than four years ago Dr John Seiler, a former professor of international studies who has since died, applied for access to certain documents from the department in terms of the provisions of the Promotion of Access to Information Act.

The defence department eventually informed Saha that eight of the 22 files requested had been declassified and the rest had to be masked. Pigou said they were told that some of the records were protected and not available for release. The records protected were described as box 260, volume 1-4, American Ambassadors 1966-1977.

Pigou said that two months later the department wrote to them stating that the archive was no longer the custodian of some of the documents pertaining to military information, as these had been "transferred to the country of origin" – Zimbabwe.

He said the department did not give any explanation for not providing the remainder of the documents requested.

Pigou said the grounds for refusing access to the protected records were that the disclosure "could reasonably be expected to endanger the life or physical safety of an individual".

It was also stated that the records contained information relating to military tactics in preparation for hostilities.

Saha expressed its concern that

the records were transferred, despite the request to hand them over before the transfer. The trust also objected that no copies of the documents had been retained.

Pigou said access to information was central to meaningful participation in the democratic process. He also stated that he had reason to believe the documents were not transferred to Zimbabwe, as authorities there claimed they had not received any documents from South Africa.

But Siviwe Njikela, of the SANDF's legal services, stated that the documents were in Zimbabwe because they belonged to that country.

He said the files were official Rhodesian security force records from 1964 to 1979. They had been obtained unofficially by the SADF's military intelligence division in 1980 and kept in the archives for safekeeping.

"At the time the provenance of the Rhodesian files was not realised ... The issue was discussed and all the relevant aspects, including security, were considered. It was decided to return them to Zimbabwe to prevent embarrassment to South Africa should their provenance become known," he said.

Njikela said no court can order the SANDF to have them returned from Zimbabwe.

It is believed that the application will be heard early next year.

Figure 2: Press clipping, *Pretoria News,* 3 September 2007. Copyright: *Pretoria News.*

ment. If records collected through intelligence activities, whether overt or covert, escape the ambit of South African laws, then large collections of intelligence records both of the military and other intelligence-gathering bodies would escape the operation of any South African legislation.[141] The minister also argued that the transfer was in keeping with 'good archival practice', despite the fact that the office of the national archivist of Zimbabwe had not been informed of the transfer and was not aware of where the records were being kept.[140]

The concealing and retention of security police files has also been of fundamental concern. During the TRC investigation into the destruction of documents, the joint investigative team discovered a collection of South African Police records that post-dated 1990 and included:

· 11 back-up tapes of the head office computerised database (the readability of seven of these tapes was confirmed); and

· Security Branch records that fell into three categories:

  - general files, all post-dating 1990;

  - computer data tapes containing data on anti-apartheid organisations, apparently captured in the 1980s; and

  - individual case records.[141]

While access was granted to the lists of provincial records, head office and regional records could not be located.[142] After some time, SAPS advised that the paper records had been found, however, due to a lack of 'intellectual control', it was impossible to retrieve them for public use. SAPS subsequently transferred them to the National Archives for processing.

It became apparent, nevertheless, that select records had disappeared since they had been viewed by the TRC: requests submitted based on the lists of provincial office files released to SAHA in 2002 were refused by the National Archives on the basis that the files in question could not be found.[143] SAHA consequently submitted a request for updated lists of security police files to ascertain what remained,[144] but was refused on the basis that the list contained personal information. During this time, SAHA raised the location of the data tapes again with SAPS, but the latter provided a number of affidavits stating that the records could not be found and staff did not recall having ever seen them. Disturbingly, an affidavit to this effect was provided by Commissioner Roos, who was consulted some three years previously regarding the files, but stated that he 'personally never inspected the files and [was] totally unaware of the existence of the data tapes'.[145] When SAHA requested a meeting with the national archivist regarding the refusal of access to security police lists and the location of the missing security police records and data tapes, he stated that:

> I am informed that the discrepancies you have alluded to relate to the fact that the files we have in the National Archives were sent to us by the National Headquarters of Crime Intelligence. Apparently there are other fragmentary lists from other sources, but the SAPS has assured the National Archives that all files have been transferred.[146]

It is not clear, however, whether the records have actually been indexed since their transfer, nor whether the national archivist in fact knows what he holds, particularly given his reference to being assured by SAPS that the records were transferred.

Box 6.5: NIA and Project Bible

NIA is suspected of concealing records following a request for access to records described as Project Bible. These records were referred to in the ANC's *Daily News Briefing* of 25 November 2003, in which it was stated that former ANC intelligence commander Mo Shaik declared that he had handed over a secret database containing information about 888 suspected apartheid government spies that was compiled as part of the ANC's Project Bible and aimed at combatting government infiltration of the then liberation movement.[147] When the request for these records was refused in the first instance and then on appeal, the minister of intelligence, Ronnie Kasrils, stated that he had 'been assured by the NIA that the information you requested is not in the possession of the NIA',[148] and failed to advise whether it was in fact in his possession or whether SAHA should transfer the request.[149]

The policy and practice of the apartheid state leading up to, and in part following, transition to democratic governance in 1994 resulted in the massive disposal of records characterised as sensitive and of particular importance for and interest to the newly liberated citizenry. However, these case studies provide grounds for questioning the status quo, that is, that the majority of pre-1990 records were subject to furnaces or shredders and were lost to contemporary requesters. While the case studies do not necessarily provide answers, they raise the question: were and are records being concealed, or is a lack of resources responsible for administrative inefficiency and restrictions on access? Information officers are only required by PAIA to provide an affidavit stating what steps they took to locate requested records. They are therefore not required to provide an explanation of why records could not be found or whether they have disappeared, and thereby implicate the body in negligent or wilful destruction. This is a particularly problematic limitation on access, as requesters are often completely reliant upon those to whom requests are made to disclose the existence of records.

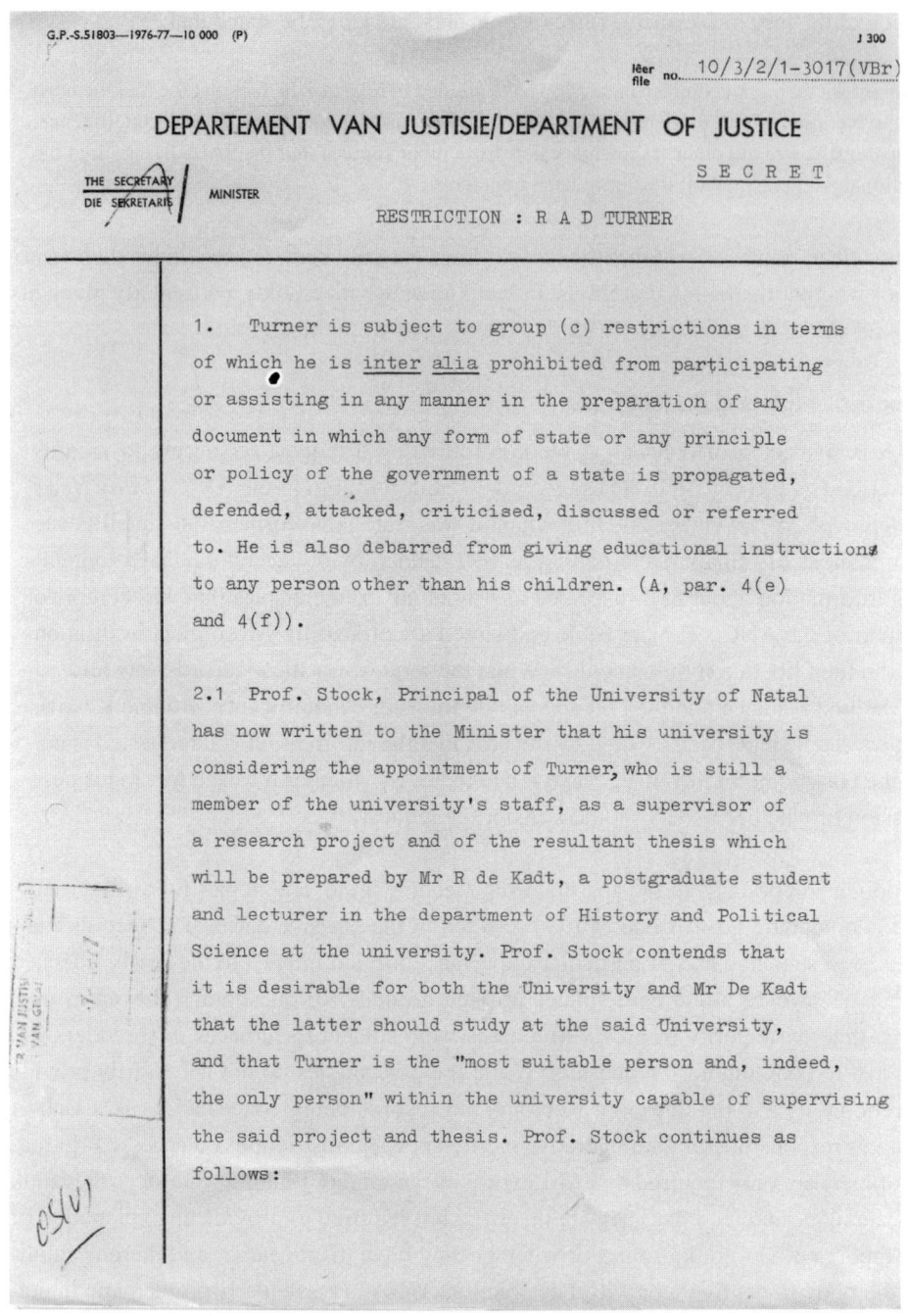

Figure 3: Opening page of 'Secret' document, dated July 1977, from the files of the Directorate of Security Legislation at the Department of Justice regarding a request to allow Dr Rick Turner to supervise a student's research project. Turner, a Durban-based academic whose political involvement had led to various restrictions and banning orders in the 1970s, was assassinated at his home on 8 January 1978 (Archived as SAHA Collection AL2878 – B1.17.1).

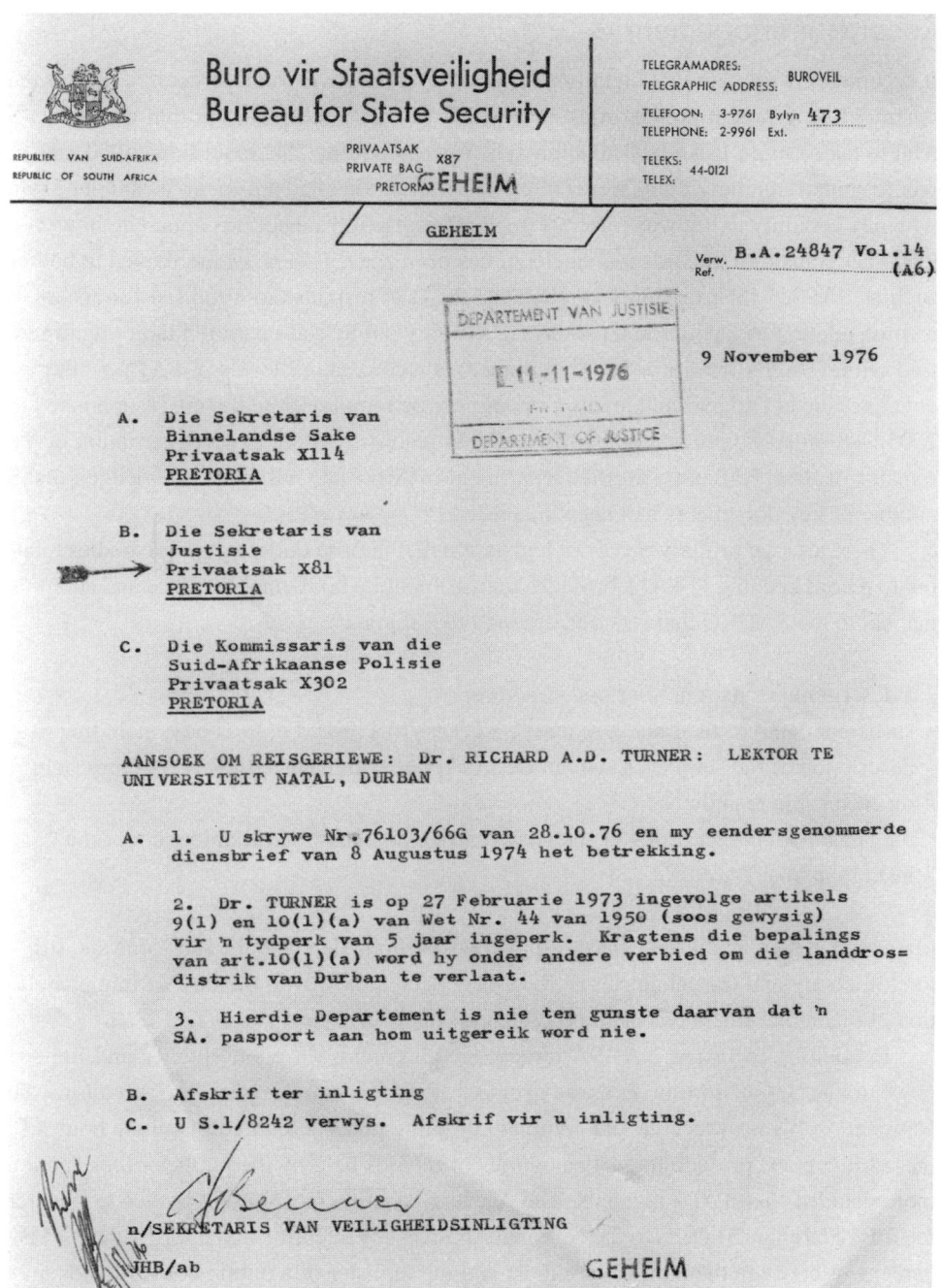

Figure 4: Recommendation marked 'Secret' from the Bureau for State Security (aka BOSS) to the Secretaries of States for Foreign Affairs and Justice and the Commissioner of the South African Police recommending that Dr Turner's application for a passport be refused, which it duly was (Archived as SAHA Collection AL2878 – B1.17.1)

Records management

It is commonly thought that dictatorships or oppressive governance structures such as the apartheid government are rigorous and fastidious record keepers, but that democracies tend to take a more lackadaisical approach. While we know that extensive collections of records regarding individuals were collated by the apartheid government, it cannot be said with any certainty that it was rigorous in all areas of governance. It is apparent, however, that since transition, records management has been poor. This is apparent even in bodies such as SAPS, which fervently implement PAIA; in response to a request for access to records relating to Operation Crackdown, a highly publicised operation targeting organised crime, SAHA was informed that numerous records at all levels of SAPS — that is, area, provincial and national levels — could not be found despite having been created in 2005.[150] Similarly, upon a request for access to records relating to the repatriation of the remains of Saartjie Baartman, the Department of Arts and Culture acknowledged that a number of key documents had been misplaced.[151]

There are two primary pieces of legislation that impose duties on public bodies relating to record keeping.[152] PAIA provides that each public body must produce and submit a manual to the SAHRC that sets out, among other things:

· a description of its functions and structure;
· sufficient detail to facilitate a request for access to a record of the body, including a description of the subjects to which records relate and the categories of records held on each subject; and
· the latest notice regarding the categories of records that are available without the need to invoke PAIA.[153]

Manuals can play a vital role in assisting requesters to understand the functions and structure of a body and the categories of records collected; however, the lack of implementation of this requirement has been problematic (see Box 6.7).

In addition to PAIA, NARSA imposes requirements on public bodies and imparts power to the National Archives as the overseer of records management. The Act allows the National Archives to receive and comment on filing plans submitted by public bodies;[154] these filing plans provide lists of categories of records held by the public bodies and are more detailed than PAIA manuals. The Act also requires most public bodies to transfer records older than 20 years to the National Archives for retention and public access.[155] By agreement between the national archivist and the minister of a public body, records may be withheld from public access or retained by the department despite being created more than 20 years ago.[156]

A more detailed breakdown of records is provided by lists and indexes specific to collections, which may describe individual documents or the subject matter of groups of records. These lists, therefore, go a step further than filing plans in providing guidance on records that are available and may be requested. The use of lists, which ordinarily describe more discrete collections of records, has also saved considerable resources of both requesters and recipients of requests. SAHA has used lists of, for example, security police files (discussed above),[157] Security Legislation Directorate files[158] and Correctional Services files[159] to submit in excess of 360 requests[160] for access to personal files[161] on behalf of individuals or in its own right.[162] Had these lists not been available, requesters would have submitted requests blindly, increasing the number of requests submitted and the burden on recipients of requests to consider them, irrespective of whether or not a file existed. While ideal, it is inconceivable that every public body has the resources to produce and publish lists of records for each of its collections, or that it should be required to do so. As noted in Box 6.7, the inclusion of a full filing plan within the PAIA manuals would significantly facilitate access to records. I would even submit that PAIA's requirement to provide as much detail as required to facilitate requests for information compels such publication.

The extent to which bodies are able to manage record keeping is, in contemporary times, largely determined by the extent to which bodies manage the flow of electronic information. There nevertheless appears to be resistance to the implementation of electronic record-keeping and dissemination practices within government. SAHA reported in 2001 that 'only a sliver of the state's electronic records resources is under any form of archival control' and 'an effective programme for preserving the long-term electronic memory of the state remains out of reach'.[163] In 2005 SAHA reported that, following its commissioned research on access to digital records, a DIO stated that there is no requirement for government bodies to keep electronic records, nor should they be expected to do so.[164] While roughly half of the departments were in the process of implementing or piloting electronic records management systems, in one case this was driven by the information technology section of the department without input from information and records managers.[165] In 2001 the National Archives released guidelines relating to the management of electronic records, and was apparently working with the State Information Technology Agency to develop government-wide standards for electronic record keeping.[166] A regional conference of archivists held in Dar es Salaam in June 2007[167] repeatedly raised the need for the adoption of electronic records management policies; however, the South African National Archives was not represented and appears to have done little since the release of the guidelines in 2001.

What are the remedies to these limitations? The TRC in its final report recommended that 'a comprehensive analysis by independent researchers be undertaken into both the scope and content of the remaining archival holdings of the intelligence services of all divisions of the security forces'.[168] Once completed, the TRC recommended that these documents be subject to existing archival legislation and transferred to the National Archives. Similar specific recommendations were also made with respect to the archival holdings of the apartheid South African Defense Force (SADF).[169] While the TRC limited its recommendations to apartheid records, an information audit covering all historical and contemporary records is necessary, given the poor implementation of records management policies since transition.

This would serve three broad purposes. Firstly, it would assist public bodies to categorise records and publish detailed lists of information that may be voluntarily disclosed without resort to PAIA.[170] While bodies are required to publish such lists in their manuals, the limited detail published at present results in the submission of requests that should require a phone call or email at most. Secondly, it would provide the means to create and provide greater access to finding aids for collections of records held, minimising the resources required to be expended by public bodies in locating records subject to requests. Thirdly, it would also assist public bodies to utilise their own records, in particular historical records, in the formulation of policy. The TRC's recommendation should therefore not be limited to the former security apparatus and the SADF, and should be extended further to apply to all records held by all national, provincial and local governments.

Box 6.6: PAIA manuals

The management of records in the early stage of their life cycle is inextricably linked with and has serious implications for the retention and destruction of records, and therefore goes hand in hand with management of and compliance with an access to information regime. In recognising this, PAIA requires each public body to develop, publish and submit to the SAHRC a manual outlining its operations and categories of records.[171] These manuals can play a vital role in assisting requesters to understand the functions and structure of a body and the categories of records collected. They do have their limitations, however.

PAIA and its regulations fail to provide any direction for compiling the manuals, particularly in relation to the requirement to provide detail on the records held. Despite naming the relevant section 'Index of records', PAIA does not require the body to provide an index of records, but a description of 'subjects' and 'categories'. While it requires a description sufficient to facilitate the submission of a request, the words are imprecise, have been construed broadly and have not always assisted requesters to identify more specifically the types of records sought, their possible location within the body or the activity to which they might relate. The lack of implementation has also been problematic. The publication of manuals has been limited,[172] few are electronically available[173] and they are not regularly updated, despite changes in the allocation of responsibility for PAIA. The manuals have therefore had limited effectiveness in assisting requesters to locate records.

Both Gould and Pollecut note in their chapters in this volume that the use of lists rather than manuals in identifying records played a key role in finding relevant information. Pollecut states that, while in her particular case gaining access to indexes of specific bodies of files transferred the burden of finding pertinent information to the researcher, it also assisted in formulating more specific requests and provided an opportunity to peruse and closely examine records and uncover valuable documentation that may otherwise have been overlooked. Gould queries whether the use of lists by Sasha Polakow-Suransky (see chapter 4, Box 4.1) compared with SAHA's subject-based approach led to the release of records where SAHA was refused on the basis that nothing could be found.

The importance of the availability of more detailed description is demonstrated by requests submitted to SAPS and DHA pursuant to a project examining the history of migration policy and practice in South Africa.[174] Just prior to the commencement of the project, SAHA submitted a request for access to the filing plans of all national government departments to enable requesters to identify potential records relevant to the subject forming the request.[175] The filing plans, compiled by each department and submitted to the National Archives for comment,[176] provide a more detailed breakdown of the categories of records held by the bodies than do PAIA manuals.

In 2006 SAHA obtained access to the SAPS file plan, which it used to draft a request for the inspection of a number of categories of files.[177] A project researcher was therefore able to examine the files and identify records relevant to the research. Consequently, around 5,500 pages were released. While SAPS expended substantial resources and time in preparing the records, it may have expended considerably more had the requests been drafted by subject and not by file location, while SAHA was also likely to obtain a smaller and less relevant collection of records.

By contrast, DHA did not provide access to a file plan, and a large number of requests were submitted that identified the records by subject.[178] It is apparent from the long delays in dealing with the requests and the numerous phone calls seeking clarification regarding progress that the department has struggled to understand what records are sought and move beyond identifying who is responsible for each of the requests.[179] As a result, some 11 months after the submission of the first batch of requests and following the submission of an internal appeal, DHA was only beginning to deal with the substantive issues related to them. Given the obligation to produce a filing plan and submit it for comment to the national archivist, the inclusion of a full filing plan within the PAIA manual would facilitate access.

Culture and transparency

I have said that dictatorships spawn rigid record-keeping practices, and democracies a lackadaisical approach. But to what end? Rigid practices mean greater control; greater control means an increased ability to determine who knows what and when. The secrecy of the apartheid state was no secret. Clandestine operations and informers permeated both sides of the system — the oppressed and the oppressors. It was for this reason that access to information during this period was reserved solely for those who, through covert conduct, sought intelligence necessary to either suppress or resist. This culture of opaqueness and secrecy, after decades, must have become an inherent feature of the way in which government structures and liberation movements operated. What became of this culture, then, when transition to democratic governance was achieved through legislated equality and voting rights? Did the shift in the form of governance lead to a shift in mindset and a commitment to transparency?

I have stated that it was apparent soon after the enactment of PAIA that implementation was severely hampered. In its 2002/03 report, the SAHRC stated that the failure to implement the Act 'can only be attributed to the lack of commitment to the advancement of this important constitutional right'. In its submission to the Human Rights Commission, SAHA and the Public Service Accountability Monitor wrote:

> Effective and meaningful implementation is hampered by the fact that South Africans have been shaped by generations of an absence of the right to information ... Freedom of Information, as an idea and as a culture, has not yet taken root in the country. South Africans have neither the expectations nor the skills to ensure that PAIA is utilised optimally ... By and large existing officials have simply been given additional responsibilities under the Act. Few have experience and expertise in record keeping.[180]

There are four principal features evidencing this lack of shift. Firstly, bodies have failed to establish infrastructure required to implement PAIA obligations. DHA, for example, does not have a PAIA unit or budget, and in every instance relies on Legal Services to provide opinions on access; the deputy directors or their delegates to locate the records (in conjunction with information management, where necessary) and make a decision on access; and the director general to approve that decision. Following the submission of a number of requests over the period 2004–07, DHA lost requests more than once was unable to provide details of the delegated official responsible for processing the requests and was, until late into 2007, unable to provide any substantive responses. Needless to say, SAHA has only had six substantive responses to the 92 requests submitted since 2004.[181]

DOD also suffers from a lack of resources and infrastructure, despite the channelling of requests through its Documentation Centre: with over 5 million records and few permanent staff, it suffers from an overload of requests and an inability to devote considerable resources to conduct more efficient searches. When SAHA, in response to what it perceived to be an inappropriate response to a request, queried why staff do not phone SAHA to discuss problems with requests, the director claimed that, because DOD was not allocated a budget specifically for PAIA requests, staff were required to deal with them outside their normal work hours, and unless SAHA wanted a phone call at six o'clock in the morning, they would not call. The current waiting period for responses to requests is around two years.

Box 6.7: The NIA and South African Secret Service exemption

In 2003 the minister of justice granted an exemption to NIA and the South African Secret Service from compiling a PAIA manual that would set out their functions and categories of records, in terms of section 14 of the Act.[182] The ramifications were concerning: the exemption allowed these bodies to maintain a level of secrecy that PAIA aimed to surmount and would make it difficult for requesters to understand the categories of information that may be available. The exemption has contributed to the difficulties in challenging NIA refusals on the ground that records could not be found or do not exist. When SAHA challenged the refusal of access on the basis that records do not exist, NIA officials stated that the records of NIA's predecessors, the BOSS and NIS, were routinely destroyed through the period 1960–90, and proactive destruction from 1990 until the establishment of NIA left it with little more than boxes of microfilm that have no indexes. In a letter to SAHA dated 17 May 2006, NIA stated:

> BOSS/NIS records were subjected to a routine destruction process which began in 1982 in terms of the National Archives Act. That led to the State Archives Service investigating such destruction not only in the former BOSS/NIS but also in the following bodies: SAPS, SADF (particularly military intelligence), Department of Prison Services, and the Security Legislation Directorate of the Department of Justice. As stated in the TRC Report, Vol. 1 Chapter 9, par. 60-61, implementation of the policy gained a momentum in 1992, but reached its most intense levels in 1993. At the same time the mass destruction of records took place, embracing all media and all structures. The result of the destruction was a massive purging of the NIS's corporate memory.

It is difficult to accept that all former intelligence records were destroyed. While it is clear that large amounts of records were destroyed, the magnitude of the boxes of microfilm is not clear, and the fact that these records are not indexed makes it difficult for both requesters and NIA staff to establish what remains. NIA refuses to provide an affidavit setting out the steps it took to locate records, on the basis that it is exempted from producing a PAIA manual setting out its structure and the categories of its records, and that to reveal the steps taken to search for the records would jeopardise the security of its intelligence. In a meeting in June 2006, NIA argued that the requests are too broad and vague, and requested that SAHA provide it with more specific information to assist it to locate files. However it failed to acknowledge that information in manuals, filing plans and affidavits assists requesters to understand what records it does and does not have and to draft more appropriate future requests.

Given its position concerning the provision of affidavits setting out the steps taken to locate records, it is not apparent to what extent the microfilm records are searched upon submission of a request. SAHA submitted a request for access to intelligence files concerning Hélène Passtoors, an anti-apartheid activist who was detained in South Africa and released pursuant to negotiation between the South African and Belgian governments. SAHA had already obtained large volumes of Security Legislation Directorate and Correctional Services records from the National Archives, but NIA stated that no records could be found.

Secondly, many bodies have not appointed DIOs who are competent to ensure compliance with PAIA. These officials can in effect pose a brick wall, particularly where their superiors continue to refer complaints and appeals to them. For example, DOJ, which has dedicated infrastructure and staff, demonstrates considerable difficulties in compliance, largely due to the incompetence of the official to whom the director general has delegated his responsibility. Pigou outlines numerous disputes, noting that in all cases taken to the High Court and following the intervention of counsel, DOJ settled and granted access with costs. This is largely because the DIO fails to demonstrate the capacity for reasoned thought upon receipt of requests, and uses a template letter to respond in which the subject header is changed and reasons for refusal are removed if not used in a particular letter. As a result, records that are of a substantially similar character to those released through litigation, such as the amnesty applications of Eugene de Kock, continue to be refused. The director general has ignored requests to meet and the minister's office fails to evidence involvement or intervention at any stage of the request process. SAHA submitted a complaint to the SAHRC regarding these issues, and the minister of justice responded defensively and refused to attend a mediation.

Box 6.8: The Department of Labour

In 2005 SAHA requested access to the filing plans of all national departments to assist it to more appropriately frame requests and build on the use of PAIA manuals. The request, once transferred to all departments by the National Archives, had a mixed reception. Some departments provided access to their filing plan, some unsurprisingly advised that their plans were so outdated as to make them unusable and others simply ignored the request. The response of the Department of Labour, however, stood out.

Upon receipt of the request, the department phoned me to query it and asked why I wanted the information. I responded that I was not obliged to provide a reason for the request, but nevertheless was happy to confirm by email that I aimed to use the plan to assist with future requests. A few days later, I received another phone call from the department querying why I wanted the information. I pointed out that I had already discussed this with someone else within the department and I was not obligated to provide the information. The official of the Department of Labour stated that in fact I was. When I stated that the PAIA form, which is prescribed by regulation, does not contain a section that requires me to state the reason for the request, unlike the form for submission to private bodies, and the Act is silent as to this apparent requirement, he responded that 'the form is wrong'. When I asked to whom I was speaking, he stated 'the head of Legal Services'.

Thirdly, a number of bodies demonstrate an unwillingness to engage in any facilitative communication or relationship with frequent requesters such as SAHA. SAHA's relationships with public bodies have evolved over time, leading to an understanding of their respective modi operandi. The evolution of these relationships has, in some cases, led to a greater exchange of information concerning the availability of records and the pressures from various quarters within bodies regarding access. SAHA enjoys a good relationship with SAPS, which has led to increased communication regarding requests, greater access to records and, as a result, greater trust than that enjoyed with other bodies. Indeed, as a result, SAHA has not litigated against SAPS. While SAHA has made considerable effort to establish a similar relationship with the National Archives, suspicion of and disregard for SAHA's motives by the national archivist has led to a fluctuating relationship; SAHA consequently questioned the ability of the national archivist to exercise his powers and to execute his PAIA obligations (see Box 6.10).

Box 6.9: National Archives

The relationship between SAHA and the national archivist from 2001 to 2004 provides an interesting case study of souring relations between a small, vocal and relatively well-resourced NGO and a senior official who did not take well to being challenged, and who apparently believed that SAHA was pursuing a sinister agenda. The events occurring over this period might have been avoided if the relevant state departments and individuals concerned had adopted an open and constructive policy of engagement and a commitment to communicate and seek resolutions to problems. Instead, from SAHA's perspective, the intended spirit of the law was abandoned in favour of resistance and conflict. While I will resist going into too much detail, a few key events are worth noting.

The relationship with the national archivist soured quite early on, when in October 2001 SAHA publicly castigated the National Archives for failing to take decisions on any of the requests submitted by SAHA in May that year.[183] The relationship deteriorated further during 2002 in a public spat and litigation around the missing 34 boxes. The following year, in January 2003, SAHA released a report detailing experience of using PAIA that contained criticism of the National Archives' failure to comply with the Act in terms of timelines and the application of exemptions.[184] As a result, the national archivist submitted a formal complaint to SAHA's board of trustees about its director, alleging that the latter had repeatedly made misleading and negative public statements about the National Archives, and questioning the director's conduct and motives.[185] When the board of trustees concluded that it was satisfied that the director was 'fulfilling his duties and responsibilities to the highest professional standards',[186] the national archivist accused the director of disrespecting due legal process[187] and of being unprofessional and unethical.[188] Once again, the board of trustees defended its director, and now raised its own concerns about the tenor of the accusations made and the fact that allegations were being raised in other government circles. The board challenged the national archivist to 'state [his] views in public so that we can defend the organization against accusations that are damaging to its reputation'.[189]

After a period of silence, the national archivist published an open piece in *This Day* newspaper in which he accused SAHA of an exaggerated response to the 34 boxes case and stated that the tempo of the internal debate has so far done little to encourage balanced and professional discussion of these issues.[190] SAHA's response in the following edition accused the national archivist of obfuscation and maintained that the organisation was simply exercising its rights in terms of PAIA. While the national archivist had accused SAHA of demanding 'instant access', SAHA pointed out that while the legislation required a response within 30 days, it had been waiting for almost a thousand days. SAHA reiterated its fundamental concern that time-consuming and costly litigation could have been avoided if government departments, including the National Archives, had simply done their job.[191]

During this dispute, the national archivist noted in a recommendation to the minister of arts and culture regarding three PAIA requests made by SAHA[192] that:

> many of the delays in responding to [SAHA's] applications have been occasioned by extensive legal research into whether a 'restraint of trade' can be applied in [the director's] case as most of his requests are motivated by an intimate and privileged knowledge of documents in the Archives acquired while in the public service.[193]

The minister of arts and culture at that time was apparently displeased with the national archivist's approach to dealing with these requests. In approving access to records on internal appeal, she noted by hand on the recommendation coming from the director general:

> I really do not appreciate the reason why the CD/NA [i.e. the national archivist] did not get … advice from the very beginning. The PAIA is a serious piece of legislation which requires a legal person to implement … The CD/NA must not put me in such a position.[194]

The national archivist subsequently determined to espouse a policy of non-engage-ment with SAHA.

In July 2003 the National Security Archive in the United States, an independent archive housed at the George Washington University, visited South Africa with the intention of meeting with a number of agencies to discuss mutual issues, and sub-sequently released a report that commented on the difficulties SAHA was facing in accessing information from the National Archives. The national archivist, who did not make himself available to the National Security Archive staff during their visit, was apparently angered that they had reported such comments without his rebuttal. He wrote to the National Security Archive stating that 'I have adopted the policy of no longer responding to the strident and repetitive criticisms of the National Archives by SAHA'.[195]

Although the residue of these disputes remains, efforts to forge a more constructive and collegial approach have been undertaken. This has not, however, resulted in an improved access to TRC records or apartheid era security and intelligence records, or an improved relationship. The national archivist in many cases fails to respond to cor-respondence. In the case of requests that cannot be delegated to his more than helpful staff, the delay in making decisions is still lengthy. We noted above the response of the national archivist to a request for a meeting in July 2007 regarding access to the security police lists and the missing security police files and data tapes that SAPS al-leged were transferred to National Archives in 2003, in which he ignored the request for a meeting and stated that he had been assured by SAPS that he had all the files.

Without political will, or a proactive effort by the national archivist to champion many of the issues around record keeping, the retention of apartheid era records and the transfer to National Archives of records more than 20 years old, in particular cabinet records, a significant shift in the internal cultures of other national bodies cannot be achieved. The national archivist has claimed on numerous occasions that he has no power and that his positioning within the Department of Arts and Culture rather than the Presidency limits perceptions of his authority.[196] While there is some merit in his argument, these oft-repeated excuses are becoming tiresome in the face of numerous complaints, requests to intervene and notifications of concerns about the destruction of significant collections of records. One wonders what in fact he is empowered to do if this is not his domain.

The fourth, and perhaps strongest, indicator of a lack of any shift in culture in public bodies is the utilisation of a long-employed method of deflection by government: silence. The Presidency and the Departments of Minerals and Energy and Trade and Industry have mastered this approach; without making repeated phone calls, it is rare to get any kind of response at all.[197] NECSA and the National Nuclear Regulator (NNR) have also adopted this approach, despite limited attempts to engage through meeting. NECSA was unperturbed by complaints to the public protector and the SAHRC (although this is not surprising, given their lack of action): in its responses it failed to acknowledge its agreement to provide the requested records by the end of 2005, and even went so far as to argue that 'NECSA went beyond the requirements of the Promotion of Access to Information Act'.[198] What it was in fact doing at that time was, some four years after the enactment of PAIA, organising its records in a manner that allowed it to comply with its legislative obligations. When SAHA submitted an additional batch of requests in 2007, it failed to get any acknowledgement at all. NNR adopted a similar approach in failing to respond until Earthlife Africa blew the whistle on a number of issues. In 2006 SAHA was granted access to a limited amount of information pertaining to four requests; however, later requests were ignored, and at the time of writing 22 are outstanding.

Box 6.10: The South African Police Service

SAPS has established a PAIA unit with committed staff and has gone to great lengths to assist requesters. The national DIO is tasked solely with managing the implementation of and compliance with PAIA, and has a dedicated team of staff to assist her. Both she, and Commissioner Geldenhuys to whom she reports, express the importance of ensuring that members of the public have access to information. SAHA has therefore been able to establish a communicative and facilitative relationship that has meant that SAHA has not submitted any internal appeals and has not been required to appeal to the courts.[199] This is largely due to the ability to request the reconsideration of refusals and to negotiate access with officials who are tasked solely with managing requests and who take their obligations seriously in the early stage of the process. While the exemplary performance of SAPS has been limited by its failure to ensure the retention of apartheid era records, in particular data tapes and security police records and the records relating to Operation Crackdown, a strong, dedicated team for facilitating the implementation of PAIA has gone a considerable way toward ensuring that valuable materials are accessed.

These four features — infrastructure, competence of officials, relationships and failures to respond — demonstrate that there has not been a substantial shift in the mindset of those with public power from secretiveness to transparency. Understanding the lack of shift from a long history and culture of secrecy therefore assists us to understand why, in some cases, it seems that implementation of PAIA remains in the starting blocks. This lack of shift must derive from the top, from the ministers and other heads of bodies, from a failure to prioritise compliance, allocate a dedicated budget and appoint qualified staff. It is a sorry (but true) state of affairs when the president of the country himself makes public statements about the need to prevent activist civil society organisations from accessing information and exercising their right to free speech. Without political champions, the importance of access to information in fighting for transparency and democratic governance will not be demonstrated across all layers of the executive.

Conclusion

In concluding, I will start from the end by saying that the culture of secrecy pervading public bodies is the primary limitation on the right of access to information. It informs resource allocations; the enactment of facilitative regulations; the priority accorded to the implementation of procedures to create, manage and retain records and facilitate access; the desire of bodies to be seen to be transparent rather than defensive; the appointment and training of competent staff; and the adoption of narrow interpretations of restrictive provisions rather than broad and blanket applications. It has, therefore, a trickle-down effect that, without intervention not only from the top down but also the bottom up, is and will continue to be the wall between the government and those whom it governs.

The effects of an ingrained culture of secrecy can be seen across two primary areas. While PAIA is lauded as a comprehensive and progressive enactment, it is clear from the case studies considering the application of the definitions, the exemptions and the public interest override that the Act is being used as a method to broaden restrictions on access rather than narrow the extent to which the constitutional right can be limited. This plays out in a number of ways.

It first results in complete silence: a complete failure to actually acknowledge, process or respond to requests. Secondly, it results in a broadening of the interpretation of categories of information to which exemptions apply, and a reduction in the extent to which harm must be demonstrated. This also leads to the limited exercise of discretion in favour of access. Thirdly, it results in the provision of limited information about which records relate to requests and how exemptions apply to them. This blanket application makes the situation particularly difficult for requesters, who are often entirely reliant upon bodies to disclose the existence of records and to determine whether records relevant to their request actually exist and are worth pursuing, whether the exemption/s cited by the body actually apply and whether there are grounds for challenging them. Fourthly, it results in a failure to consider the merits of requests prior to the threat of appeal or litigation.

Another area in which we can see the effects of this ingrained culture is in the application of intersecting legislation, where apartheid enactments influence and restrict access, and enactments providing for greater access rights are ignored. A causal factor influencing the capacity for intersecting enactments to impact upon PAIA in this way is the failure of the minister of justice to issue regulations listing enactments that supersede, and are superseded by, PAIA.

The legislation itself, however, has some fundamental limitations. It fails in some instances to limit the extent to which exemptions may apply. For example, the exemptions regarding confidentiality, do not permit inquiry into the legitimacy of the intent behind the agreements, or limit the duration of the agreement or confidentiality. This may have the effect of permitting parties who wish to avoid disclosure of information that may embarrass bodies or expose them to criticism to withhold such information, even though requesters would otherwise have a right of access to it. It also, as we have seen in the case of the agreement between South Africa and Israel that was entered into in 1975, permits ongoing reliance on agreements without providing requesters with the power to question the extent of their agreements' application or their present applicability. It also limits, to an unnecessary degree, the circumstances in which the public interest override will apply. But, more importantly, it fails to provide adequate enforcement mechanisms that are accessible, efficient and cost-effective; that will provide (where necessary) a means for urgent determinations; and that will provide greater leverage through which to compel bodies to apply PAIA appropriately.

The broader implication, the ability to limit the exercise of a range of other civil and political, social, economic and cultural rights, and merely rely upon oft-repeated rhetoric about resource limitations and quotations of statistics, is not yet realised by the broader public, or even a broader collection of civil society organisations working outside of traditional accountability and transparency rights. This is the challenge for access to information: to bring it to a wider audience and activism, and to push for reform on a larger scale, rather than limit it to the activities of the three organisations in South Africa (at present) who are the primary users of PAIA. The other, equally important implication, the ability to skew the recording of history and its events — and by history here I mean what happened before today — is what I perceive as the key question for archival discourse. The use of access to information mechanisms has a key role to play in combatting the selectivity of archival processes and the hand of the influential in tailoring and tampering with the picture that may be formed by record collections.

So what do we need to fix this right? Legislative amendment, political champions, the systematic declassification of records, an archival audit, an independent and proactive information commission and promotion of the Act across all levels of governance. There is no one answer. As civil society organisations, litigators, activists and requesters, we can only continue to pursue requests, lobby government and promote the importance of the right of access to information.

7

Conclusion: From Gatekeeping to Hospitality[1]

Verne Harris

Framing the enquiry

Frame 1: The nature of the terrain

The essays, case studies and anecdotes that make up this volume occupy a terrain that any concluding piece needs to acknowledge, contextualise and extend. Of course, the attributes of a terrain are, in principle, limitless. In searching for an appropriate closing for this volume — more precisely, in searching for a closing that opens more than it closes — I limit myself to engagement with three in particular.

Firstly, the focus is insistently on the implementation of freedom of information legislation in South Africa in the period 2001–07, against the backdrop of the country's transition from apartheid to democracy. While marking local specificities, here I am more interested in the (more or less) universal dynamics at play.

Secondly, with very few exceptions, the institutional terrain being interrogated is that of the 'public institution'.[2] The records being sought are public records, and the custodians of these records are public officials. This is not surprising. For although South Africa's Constitution draws the private sector firmly into the country's freedom of information regime, the applicability of the Promotion of Access to Information Act (PAIA) to what the Act calls 'private bodies' remains to be tested seriously.[3]

Thirdly, the authors write from the hurly-burly of activism. Theirs is a discourse of resistance to the gatekeepers. For me, this simultaneously expresses the extent to which gatekeeping has become a worrying feature of post-apartheid South Africa and how the country's freedom of information domain forces information requesters to pursue access disputes in court and/or by publicly naming and shaming gatekeepers.

It is always relatively easy to point out where people and institutions are getting things wrong, especially in a domain where, as this volume's contributions suggest, getting it wrong has become almost endemic. Rather than summarise the myriad shortcomings detailed in this volume, I want instead to explore two interrelated questions: why do gatekeepers become gatekeepers; and what would getting it right look like? In other words, what would a gatekeeper become if he or she were to respond to the call of justice?

Already, in what are preliminary moves, I have made a number of assumptions and offered at least one working definition. At least two more are necessary at the outset.

I am assuming 'democracy' as a fundamental frame for the enquiry. Obviously, one could quickly become submerged in debates around what democracy is. At this point, let me simply assert that there are any number of forms to democracy, and that I believe that democracy only has meaning as long as people are contesting its meaning and fighting for it to manifest itself more fully. So the term 'democratising' (a process) means far more to me than 'democratic' (a state).

Which brings me to the concept of justice. I do not believe that anyone can offer a blueprint for identifying it. Following Derrida, I do not believe that justice, ultimately, can be knowable. Like democracy, it must always be coming. It is a phantom; at most 'a relation to the unconditional that, once all the conditional givens have been taken into account, bears witness to that which will not allow itself to be enclosed within a context'.[4] The call of justice resists the totalisation of every such enclosure. It resists, if you like, what is traditionally regarded as the fundamental archival impulse — contextualisation. It is open to the future and to every 'other'. It respects — gives space to, looks again at — 'radical otherness'.[5] In the powerful formulation of Levinas (whose work had a profound influence on Derrida), justice is 'the relation to the other'.[6]

In the last decade of his life, Derrida (drawing on the work of Levinas) developed what he termed an ethics of hospitality.[7] It is predicated on the belief that the call of justice is the most important of all calls, and that the call comes to us in and through 'the other', the stranger. The beginning of ethics is a listening to, a hospitality towards, the stranger. And because for Derrida every stranger is equally important, and 'every other is wholly other', ethics confronts us with an impossible challenge.

Frame 2: The secret

Between 2001 and 2004 I dedicated my professional energies to establishing the South African History Archive (SAHA) as a freedom of information NGO.[8] My team used PAIA (which came into operation in March 2001) to test the parameters of public access to information in South Africa, to force into the public domain records that we believed were being hidden illegitimately and to build up a public archive of such materials accessible to everyone. In the process, I became identified as a troublemaker by many public institutions and, more widely, as a campaigner for transparency. Today, I am a programme manager at the Nelson Mandela Foundation with primary responsibility for Madiba's archive. In this role, I have developed — some would say ironically — an acute awareness of the need to protect 'sensitive' information.

I offer this as anecdotal evidence of how 'positioning' within the structures of society informs the attitudes of individuals to transparency. I could easily pile on the anecdotes at this point, but let me offer just two others to suggest a pattern. Firstly, take the case of Nadine Gordimer's authorised biography.[9] Here an author identified as a lifelong advocate of transparency falls out with her biographer over his reluctance to respect her desire for certain secrets to be kept, and de-authorises the project. Secondly, in 2005 I was privileged to participate in a discussion with two justices of the Constitutional Court. They agreed that it would be detrimental to due process for them to document the internal decision-making processes of the court; although such documentation would provide fascinating and valuable historical evidence, it would at the same time undermine the safe space critical for judges in the sensitive business of determining constitutionality.[10]

All of us believe — and our 'positioning' frames and modulates the belief — in the notion of a legitimate secret. The concept of freedom of information has to live with this notion. Arguably — and I will pursue this argument later — what we call freedom of information, as an endeavour, is precisely about resisting the illegitimate secret.

But what is a 'secret'?[11] I define it as the story that refuses the invitation to be told. The refusal can be made in advance — we identify information (and the story that frames it) that in particular circumstances, or in any circumstances, we will not disclose. Or, in the circumstances that pertain at the time when the invitation comes, we are not comfortable about acceding to the request for disclosure. The refusal can be made consciously — we hold the story in memory, but defer its telling; or unconsciously — the story is held in the play of shadow behind memory, in the hidden place, awaiting our engagement with it, our own telling of it. Of course, there can be no hard boundary between what we call consciousness and the unconscious. As James Hillman puts it, 'whatever consciousness casts light upon at once creates a shadow. The moment we see more clearly, we become more blind and cannot see behind what we see, the other side of what we see'.[12]

Readers might argue that I am losing the institutional frame of my enquiry. The point is a simple one — to understand institutional secrecy, we must begin with the individual. The hidden places are part of the psychic architecture that each one of us carries. Secrecy is the stuff of daily life, individually and collectively.[13] In institutions, we see the same dynamics at play. Behind 'protection' of information, behind every refusal to provide access to a record, I would argue, is a story refusing to be told. The 'classified' record is best understood as the container of stories at one time regarded as ones not to be disclosed except in prescribed circumstances, if at all. And consider the access refusals based either on an organisation not knowing that it possesses a certain record or on the organisation's failure to find such a record. Do these refusals not mark an institutional space that we might legitimately name 'unconscious'?[14]

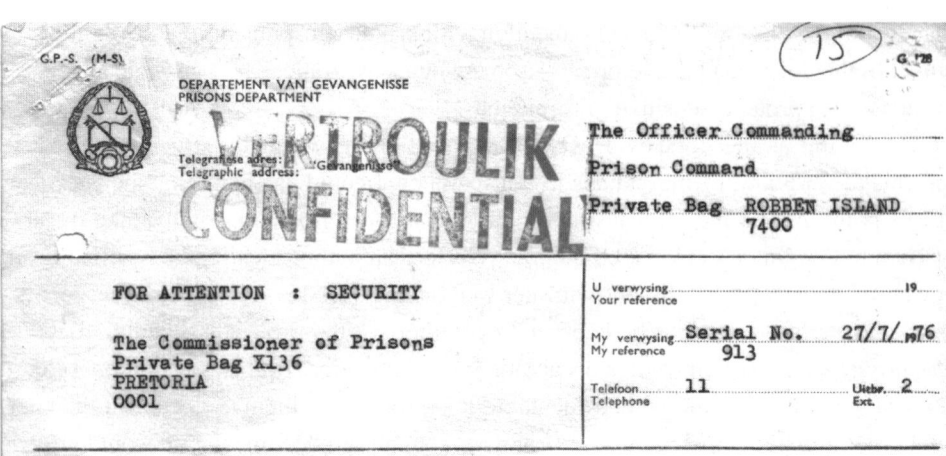

G.P.-S. (M-S) 75 G. 128

DEPARTEMENT VAN GEVANGENISSE
PRISONS DEPARTMENT

VERTROULIK
CONFIDENTIAL

Telegrafiese adres:
Telegraphic address: Gevangenisse

The Officer Commanding

Prison Command

Private Bag ROBBEN ISLAND
7400

FOR ATTENTION : SECURITY

The Commissioner of Prisons
Private Bag X136
PRETORIA
0001

U verwysing 19
Your reference

My verwysing Serial No. 27/7/1976
My reference 913

Telefoon 11
Telephone

Uitbr. 2
Ext.

SERIAL NO. 913 : NELSON MANDELA : LETTER OF COMPLAINT
TO THE COMMISSIONER OF PRISONS

1. Attached please find a copy of a letter of complaint
dated the 12th July, 1976 by the abovementioned
prisoner addressed to the Commissioner of Prisons –
annexure **A**.

2-1. BACKGROUND
Nelson Mandela considers himself as the leader of the
prisoners on Robben Island and to retain and improve
this image amongst his fellow prisoners he, from time
to time, acts as the mouthpiece of the prisoners, by
raising the so-called general complaints directly to
the Commissioner of Prisons or the Honourable Minister –
the highest authority possible.

2-2. Official records are kept of the complaints and requests
by prisoners and the way of disposal and I am quite
satisfied that the head of the prison sees them daily
and that we comply with the provisions as laid down
in Regulation 103.

2/......

Figure 1: Excerpts from a classified record in Nelson Mandela's official prison archive. The record is still not declassified and technically should not be in the public domain. Courtesy of the Nelson Mandela Centre of Memory and Dialogue, Nelson Mandela Foundation.

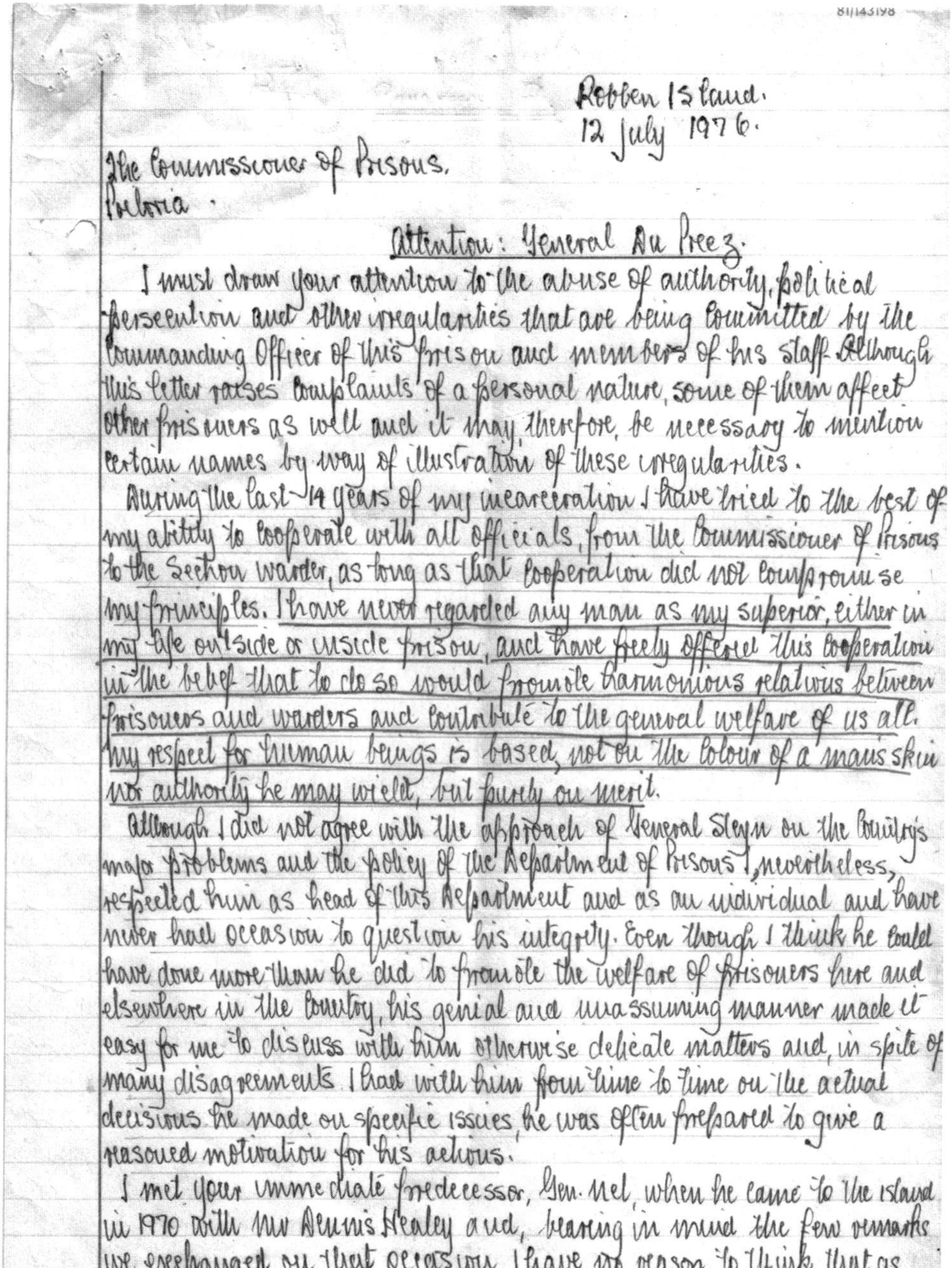

Robben Island.
12 July 1976.

The Commissioner of Prisons.
Pretoria.

Attention: General Du Preez.

I must draw your attention to the abuse of authority, political persecution and other irregularities that are being committed by the Commanding Officer of this prison and members of his staff. Although this letter raises complaints of a personal nature, some of them affect other prisoners as well and it may, therefore, be necessary to mention certain names by way of illustration of these irregularities.

During the last 14 years of my incarceration I have tried to the best of my ability to cooperate with all officials, from the Commissioner of Prisons to the Section warder, as long as that cooperation did not compromise my principles. I have never regarded any man as my superior, either in my life outside or inside prison, and have freely offered this cooperation in the belief that to do so would promote harmonious relations between prisoners and warders and contribute to the general welfare of us all. My respect for human beings is based, not on the colour of a man's skin nor authority he may wield, but purely on merit.

Although I did not agree with the approach of General Steyn on the country's major problems and the policy of the Department of Prisons, nevertheless, respected him as head of this Department and as an individual and have never had occasion to question his integrity. Even though I think he could have done more than he did to promote the welfare of prisoners here and elsewhere in the country, his genial and unassuming manner made it easy for me to discuss with him otherwise delicate matters and, in spite of many disagreements I had with him from time to time on the actual decisions he made on specific issues, he was often prepared to give a reasoned motivation for his actions.

I met your immediate predecessor, Gen. Nel, when he came to the island in 1970 with Mr Dennis Healey and, bearing in mind the few remarks we exchanged on that occasion, I have no reason to think that as head of this Department he fell short of the standard set by his
/predecessor

Figure 2: Another excerpts from a classified record in Nelson Mandela's official prison archive. The record is still not declassified and technically should not be in the public domain. Courtesy of the Nelson Mandela Centre of Memory and Dialogue, Nelson Mandela Foundation.

A final point, to which I shall return before I move to other concepts and assumptions informing this enquiry: the notion of 'contract' is deeply embedded in the concept of secret. Not always, but most often, the boundaries protecting hidden places are contracted. Think about clothing as a simple example. Without being drawn into the larger questions of social and institutional dress codes, I note merely that fundamental to dress is the recognition of the need to keep certain parts of the body hidden in public space, and that contract informs what is regarded as appropriate coverage. Every time we get dressed in the morning, more or less consciously we acknowledge the legitimate secret and engage a web of contracts.

Frame 3: Freedom of information

Up to this point, I have been disclosing what I regard as the primary frames within which I choose to address the question of access to information. Now I want to focus on the concept commonly named 'freedom of information'. I begin with three theses that will form a basis for the subsequent enquiry.

Firstly, no polity can say that it has freedom of information. This freedom, like democracy, like justice, must always be coming. What is critical is the space for contestation, for struggle, for bringing this freedom into play. Secondly, this freedom, this right, is not an absolute one. There are limits. As I have already argued, only a fool would reject the notion of a 'legitimate secret'. On the other hand, this concept is used routinely by the powerful to deny access to information that belongs in the public domain. Thirdly, in terms of meaning, significance and power, it is not information per se that is the key resource at play; rather, the key resource is what I call 'contextualised' information, i.e. archive.

Scholars and commentators from many disciplines and many countries, working with a range of theoretical and epistemological frameworks, have unfolded how the exercise of political power hinges on control of information.[15] My own favourite is Noam Chomsky, whose seering critiques of democracy, in the United States especially, demonstrate how elites depend on sophisticated information systems, media control, surveillance, privileged research and development, dense documentation of process, censorship, propaganda, and so on to maintain their positions.[16] But it is Derrida and Foucault who reach most deeply in exposing the logic, even the law, underlying these phenomena. In Derrida's words: 'there is no political power without control of the archive, if not of memory'.[17] And Foucault, coming from a different direction, but nailing the same law: 'The archive is first the law of what can be said';[18] and when it can be said, how, and by whom. Both of them insist on the archive as a construction: one that issues from and expresses relations of power. Listen to Derrida elaborating this insistence in relation to media apparatuses:

Who today would think his time and who, above all, would speak about it ... without first paying some attention to a public space and therefore to a political present which is constantly transformed, in its structure and its content, by the teletechnology of what is so confusedly called information or communication?[19]

The confusion in this naming of 'information' and 'communication' stems from an under-estimation — sometimes an ignoring — of what Derrida calls 'fictional fashioning': 'No matter how singular, irreducible, stubborn, distressing or tragic the "reality" to which it refers, "actuality" comes to us by way of a fictional fashioning.'[20] Information is always fashioned, always constructed. Derrida clears away the confusion by deploying the term — the concept — 'archive'. In its Derridean deployment, 'the archive' is the law determining meanings and significances — the law, if you like, determining contexts. Here, beneath the surface whirl and clatter of information, is where the instruments of power are forged. Instruments that in their most fundamental of operations create and destroy, promote and discourage, co-opt and discredit contexts. Archivists have conceptualised what they do around their special expertise in context. But it is the archon, the one who exercises political power, who is the purveyor of context and who is the archetypal archivist.

The practical implications of this for those who use freedom of information laws and mechanisms are legion. Seasoned information requesters have learnt to identify the subtler archontic tools — those that reach beyond delaying tactics, various means of obstruction and obfuscation, and crude refusals. For instance, it is relatively easy to overwhelm a requester with irrelevant information, thus diverting the request and obscuring significances.[21] Or information can be released without any indication of the existence of a mass of related information.[22] Or information can be released with vital contextual information masked or severed.[23] The one who controls contexts is the one who controls meanings and significances. This is why, I would suggest, the ruling elites in the United States can afford to permit what is generally regarded as an extremely generous national freedom of information regime. This is why wars undertaken by the US military can now be documented by the media so densely and in such detail: 'embedded' journalists provide the military with a critical means of controlling the construction of archive; such journalists have entered a contract that ties them irrevocably into the military's archontic agenda.

Frame 4: Contest and contract

If the archive is indeed the law determining contexts, and if it is a law informing even the most established of democracies, then how do we measure democracy?[24] To this question, Derrida responds decisively, and not surprisingly, in archival terms: 'Effective democratisation can always be measured by this essential criterion: the participation in and the access to the archive, its constitution, and its interpretation.'[25]

Two points can be made here. Firstly, we diminish freedom of information, we trivialise it, if we remove it from this frame. Secondly, if power is exercised through the con-

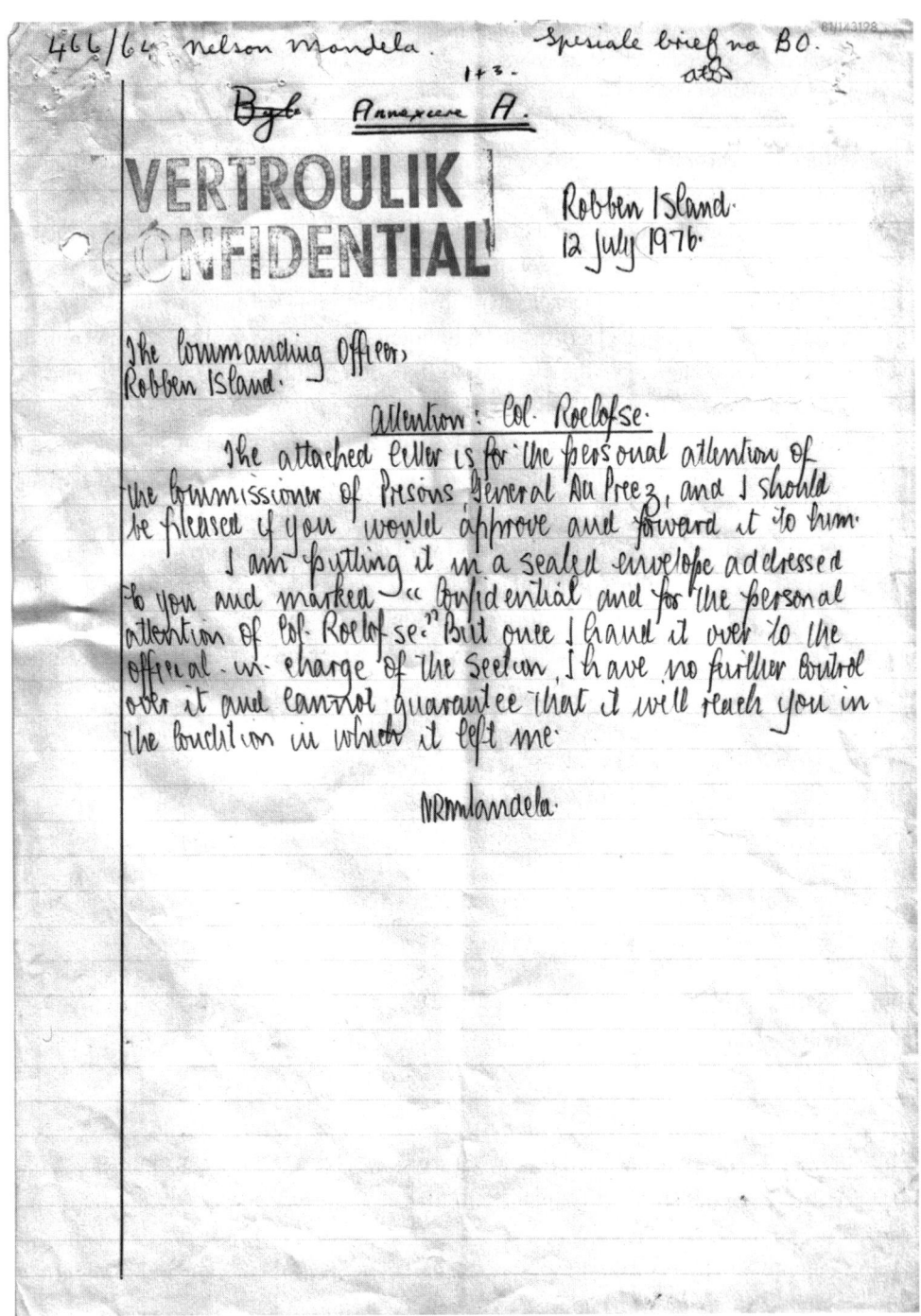

466/64 nelson mandela.   Speciale brief no BO.

1+3.

Bylo   Annexure A.

VERTROULIK
CONFIDENTIAL   Robben Island.
                          12 July 1976.

The Commanding Officer,
Robben Island.

            Attention: Col. Roelofse.

    The attached letter is for the personal attention of
the Commissioner of Prisons, General Du Preez, and I should
be pleased if you would approve and forward it to him.
    I am putting it in a sealed envelope addressed
to you and marked "Confidential and for the personal
attention of Col. Roelofse." But once I hand it over to the
official-in-charge of the section, I have no further control
over it and cannot guarantee that it will reach you in
the condition in which it left me.

            NRMandela.

Figure 3: Another excerpt from Nelson Mandela's official prison archive. Courtesy of the Nelson Mandela Centre of Memory and Dialogue, Nelson Mandela Foundation.

struction of archive, then the locus of participation in the exercise of power is precisely the processes of the archive's construction. And that implies contestation, for society is always an assemblage of competing interests and perspectives. As the British intellectual Richard Hoggart has reminded us, '[a] well-running democracy will constantly quarrel with itself, publicly, about the right things and in the right way'.[26] Even in democracies, of course, there are limits — there must be limits — to contestation. Hoggart points to these with the notion of quarrelling 'in the right way'. Here he suggests the space for contract. Hovering behind the suggestion is the notion of a more or less transcendent social contract. This is a notion that I wish to avoid, as it involves a different set of questions and a different kind of debate. Quarrelling in democracies is regulated by a web of contracts that are expressed in constitutions, laws, codes and agreements. It is the contract constituted by this web that I refer to here and in the remainder of the chapter.

We need to be wary of the penchant of those who hold power in democracies to hold up contract as a substitute for contest. Sometimes the powerful even go so far as to suggest that contestation unravels the contract.[27] These, I want to suggest, are subterfuges — strategies for entrenching power. It is to confuse law, and rights, with justice. Contracts emerge out of contestation. And the very notion of contract assumes potential contest, and puts in place frameworks and mechanisms for managing contestation appropriately. Indeed, ensuring that the contract is respected, adapted to accommodate new realities and new needs, and kept open to the call of justice hinges on our capacity to foster contestation within and around it. So that the contestants — and at times they might be bitter foes — are at the same time partners in a noble endeavour: the endeavour to bring justice.

I have argued that freedom of information must be positioned conceptually within the making of democracy; or, to use Derrida's terminology, within 'the participation in and the access to the archive, its constitution, and its interpretation'. This making — this participating, accessing, constituting and interpreting — takes place in an arena populated by diverse and often competing rights and interests. We oversimplify access to information when we typify it in terms of a transaction between a holder of information and a requester. Access to information involves and implicates the creator of a record, the owner (of the physical record, and of its intellectual content), the holder (or custodian), the controller (because the one who controls access is not necessarily the owner or the holder), the third parties named in the record, the requester, and the public (the public named in the terms 'public institution', 'public record' and 'public interest'). All these players are party to what is always a multiple transaction. The contract identifies these players, defines their rights, and establishes mechanisms for weighing competing rights and resolving conflicts. In South Africa, the contract comprises specific constitutional provisions, PAIA, a body of other laws addressing access to information, an even bigger body of subsidiary regulations and common law.

For many, contract is the beginning and the end of ethical enquiry — getting it right is simply about applying contract correctly. In my experience over three years as an information requester, and in the experience of almost every contributor to this book, public institutions in South Africa almost as a rule adopt this approach to getting it right. Many institutions, of course, are not interested in getting it right. But those that are tend to apply contract in an extremely legalistic mode. Again, I would insist, this is to confuse law with justice. There are different ways of applying contract and there are different ways of interpreting it. Moreover, its provisions can be inadequate, confusing, contradictory, even wrong.[28] And it is not cast in stone; it can be changed. Institutions concerned about 'getting it right' must refuse to stop at contract; they must reach for justice. This imperative acquires special urgency when there are recent histories of systemic disadvantage and oppression.

South African specificities

In the second section of this enquiry, I attempted to demonstrate that secrecy is the stuff of daily life for individuals. It is no surprise, then, that institutions and states are more or less uncomfortable with transparency. And it is no surprise that the apartheid state was particularly uncomfortable with transparency. Indeed, in apartheid South Africa, state secrecy was a standard modus operandi. Interlocking legislation restricted access to and the dissemination of information in vast areas of public life.[29] These restrictions were manipulated to secure an extraordinary degree of opacity in government, and the country's formal information systems became grossly distorted in support of official propaganda. This obsessive secrecy was served not only by legislation, but also by a range of executive tools — many thousands of oppositional voices were eliminated through means such as the confiscation and/or destruction of records, informal harassment, media censorship, various forms of banning, detention without trial, imprisonment and assassination. And a story that still awaits telling is the impact of apartheid on the record-making practices of anti-apartheid individuals and organisations, in particular their reluctance to commit certain types of information to paper and their readiness to destroy records rather than allow them to fall into the hands of state operatives. This history of opacity in large measure explains the liberation movements' and other players' commitment to freedom of information during the formal transition from apartheid. It also underlies the unique features of South Africa's post-apartheid access to information regime.[30]

One of the ironies of the post-apartheid landscape is that, despite possessing a widely admired freedom of information law and despite the country's history of resistance to opacity, South Africa has proved to be a less than fertile environment for freedom of information. The evidence accumulated in the contributions to this volume suggests a wide range of impediments to this freedom: the absence of an information commissioner to resolve disputes quickly and cheaply; the costs of going to court; incompetence; the absence of the necessary political will to make the system work; tardiness in unravelling apartheid era legislation; the deliberate frustration of legitimate interests in public access; and the paucity of resources dedicated to the implementation of legislation. But to understand why we are where we are, I would suggest, we need to identify the cultures that underlie this diverse range of impediments.

In my reading of where we are, South Africa is confronted by a conjunction of cultures antithetical to freedom of information and conducive to gatekeeping. Four cultures, or clusters of culture, can be identified in particular. Firstly, our record-making cultures are poor, and in some sectors getting poorer. In certain reaches of the state, the record-making arena (from paper-based filing systems to databases, from email to financial records) is a Wild West. Secondly, many public institutions are strapped by what Iraj Abedian calls 'a culture of mediocrity and bureaucratic compliance'.[31] This culture expresses itself most frequently in an inertia fed by a deadly combination of incompetence, contempt for administrative justice and fear of displeasing higher authority. Thirdly, our cultures of information access and use are in the early stages of democratisation. The notion of access to information as a fundamental right still feels 'new'. And, fourthly, cultures of secrecy are proving extremely resilient. These latter cultures do not flow only out of the old apartheid state milieus. They also flow out of the anti-apartheid experiences of exile, the underground and mass resistance.[32] South Africa did not experience a revolution. In transitions from oppressive regimes to democracy, the nature of the transition is critical in determining subsequent access environments. A quick overthrow is the best-case scenario (e.g. East Germany). Protracted negotiated settlements give the oppressive regime time to destroy records and provide the space for more or less secret deals that stimulate sensitivity to later disclosures.[33]

Under apartheid, freedom of information was one of many strangers. And it remains so. The call of justice is to embrace this stranger and to offer it whatever hospitality we can muster.

Towards an ethics

Speaking in the decade before the introduction of freedom of information legislation in the United States, T.R. Schellenberg (an American, and one of a handful of canonical voices in international archival discourse) offered the following golden rule for getting access to information right: 'Records should be open for use to the maximum extent that is consistent with the public interest.'[34]

I think there is considerable merit in this rule. Schellenberg privileges information that is more or less contextualised ('records'), he privileges use (rather than the blander 'access') and he privileges public participation (even if only notionally). However, he exhibits no sense of standing above an abyss. He speaks out of a positivist discourse that is assured, unreflective about its assumptions and resistant to the problematisation of conceptual foundations. What for him constitutes a 'record' is self-evident. Records 'open for use' is enough — systemic barriers to access for the marginalised, the weak and the poor fall outside his purview. The fact that 'public interest' is always already being made by a public structured in terms of prevailing power relations does not bother him. He does not sense the structurally determined impossibility of freedom of information — in contrast, say, to Derrida, for whom, in my reading, reasonable access relates to freedom of information as reconciliation relates to forgiveness or as an economy of exchange relates to gift.[35]

But I leave this beginning of a deconstruction in order to move, finally, to a delineation of an ethics that avoids Schellenberg's pitfalls. If the call of justice is indeed the most important call and if the work of providing access to information is justice (and resistance to injustice), then what should our ethics look like? The beginning of an answer takes us into that space we name 'accountability'. For the call of justice demands a response — it demands, in the first instance, a 'yes!' But it also demands a giving of account. We are all accountable to (and responsible for) the call of justice. Discourses of accountability, generally, tend to emphasise the giving of account. I believe that if we are to emphasise any particular dimension, then it should be the listening to a call.[36] As Robert Gibbs argues in his compelling book *Why Ethics?*: 'We begin in a conversation, where two people respond to each other ... Moreover, the listening is primary. My first responsibility arises in listening to another person, not in speaking to her.'[37] For Gibbs, as for Derrida, listening is the beginning of ethics.

My enquiry up to this point has been, precisely, an attempt to listen. In the first instance, I listened carefully to the voices of this volume's other contributors. In absorbing their rich accounts of particular struggles, I have been trying to hear the imperatives that address us in the space we name 'freedom of information'. Within the frames that I deploy (and no doubt they are limited, not least by the specificities of my experience), a just ethics would have to respond to at least eight imperatives:

· to acknowledge the legitimate secret;

· to resist the illegitimate secret;

· to engage (honestly and generously) the contexts that give information its meanings and significances (of course, this is to engage the impossible, for contexts are infinite and ever shifting);

· to understand contract in all its complexity;

· to respect contract;

· to take responsibility for contract (in other words, the imperative is to resist the temptation to take contract as a given, as a stable template; rather, contract must be made permeable, dynamic and hospitable to contestation);

- to redress systemic barriers, imbalances and exclusions; and

- to welcome 'otherness' (in other words, to welcome the energy, the event, the process, the one that comes from outside our capacity to understand and challenges our frames of understanding).

The institution, public or private, that hears these imperatives and seeks to respond to them, in my view, is one that is beginning, at least, to move towards an ethics of hospitality — an ethics that acknowledges the gatekeeper in all of us, while reaching beyond gatekeeping. This — given the dynamics of impossibility always at play — is all that any institution, that any of us, can begin to aim at. Ultimately, it is the freedom longed for, the embrace of *a luta continua*, that defines who we are most fundamentally. It is my hope that this book will contribute to the growth of this ethics (and its enabling cultures) in South Africa. For in it is to be found the future of our hard-won democracy.

Table of Cases

Request number	Recipient of request	Subject	Date of submission	Date of final response	Response
Chapter 2: Accessing the Records of the Truth and Reconciliation Commission					
0013/NAR/2001	National Archives of South Africa	Correspondence file(s) documenting the National Archives' dealings with the TRC and other parties in relation to the records/archive of the TRC	15 October 2001	1 November 2001	Partial release, masked
0015/NAR/2001	National Archives of South Africa	List of video recordings of the TRC hearings in the custody of the National Archives	24 January 2001	12 June 2001	Refused
0022/NAR/2001	National Archives of South Africa	Records documenting National Archives' endeavours to follow up on recommendations relating to archives and record keeping in the TRC final report	24 October 2001	7 June 2002	Refused

0023/DOJ/2001	Department of Justice	List of all TRC records taken into the custody of the Department of Justice	16 October 2001	18 December 2001	Refused
0041/DOJ/2002	Department of Justice	TRC records about Ahmed Timol	2 October 2002	14 November 2002	Refused
0042/DOJ/2002	Department of Justice	TRC records dealing with the life and death of Steve Biko	2 May 2002	29 July 2002	Full release
0047/NAR/2002	National Archives of South Africa	All records documenting the chain of custody of certain TRC records (described in an attached list) from the time they were transferred from the TRC in 1999	21 May 2002	7 June 2002	Refused
0048/DOJ/2002	Department of Justice	All records documenting the chain of custody of certain TRC records (described in an attached list) from the time they were transferred from the TRC in 1999	21 May 2002	12 September 2002	Refused

0051/DOJ/2002	Department of Justice	Transfer list of the TRC records that were transferred from TRC offices to the National Archives	21 May 2002	12 September 2002	Partial release
0073/DOJ/2002	Department of Justice	Minutes of the first three meetings of the commissioners of the TRC	27 August 2002	12 November 2002	Full release
0075/DOJ/2002	Department of Justice	Files on the investigation into the case of the Gugulethu 7	27 August 2002	14 March 2003	Full release, masked
0076/DOJ/2002	Department of Justice	Files on the investigations undertaken in the murder case of Dulcie September	27 August 2002	12 November 2002	Partial release, masked
0009/DOJ/2003	Department of Justice	Submissions to the TRC: Terry Crawford-Brown: 'The armaments industry' and 'The role of business in funding apartheid' Written submission by Eskom K. Naidoo: 'Submission by the National Campaign on the apartheid debt'	9 October 2003	16 October 2003	Full release

0013/DOJ/2003	Department of Justice	TRC section 29 hearing: TRC – Craig Williamson	6 June 2003	8 October 2003	Refused
0014/DOJ/2003	Department of Justice	TRC section 29 hearing: Stanza Bopape	6 June 2003	8 October 2003	Refused
0015/DOJ/2003	Department of Justice	TRC section 29 hearing: Winnie Madikizela-Mandela	6 June 2003	8 October 2003	Refused
0016/DOJ/2003	Department of Justice	TRC section 29 hearing: Joe Mamasela	6 June 2003	8 October 2003	Refused
0017/DOJ/2003	Department of Justice	Khumalo Gang hearing	6 June 2003	8 October 2003	Refused
0003/DOJ/2004	Department of Justice	TRC testimony documents about the Zone 7 or Night Vigil Massacre that occurred in Sebokeng in 1991	12 January 2004	15 April 2004	Full release
0071/DOJ/2004	Department of Justice	TRC records relating to Boiki Thlapi Barikeng Tlhapi	28 June 2004	9 February 2005	Refused
0002/DOJ/2005	Department of Justice	Transcripts of open amnesty hearings relating to the Craddock 4, and related annexures and exhibits	2 June 2004	26 January 2005	Partial release, masked

0028/DOJ/2006	Department of Justice	TRC human rights violations (victims) database (without identifiable personal data)	22 March 2006	21 June 2006	Refused
0030/DOJ/2006	Department of Justice	Transcripts of all hearings convened by the TRC pursuant to section 29 of the Promotion of National Unity and Reconciliation Act of 1995. A list of known 'interviews' was included	22 March 2006	29 October 2006	Refused
0039/DOJ/2006	Department of Justice	Box 151: tracking and status records of the National Investigation Unit of the TRC (containing investigation material relating to the murder of Clare Stewart)	22 October 2006	2 July 2007	Refused
0054/DOJ/2006	Department of Justice	All submissions to the business hearings of the TRC, excluding a listing (provided) of those already available	18 October 2006	14 December 2006	Full release

0059/DOJ/2006	Department of Justice	Confidentiality agreements entered into between the TRC and/or the DOJ and individuals who made submissions or testified at the TRC hearings	3 November 2006	13 December 2006	Refused
0060/DOJ/2006	Department of Justice	Amnesty application of Eugene de Kock to the TRC	10 November 2006	22 January 2007	Refused
Chapter 3: In the Dark: Seeking Information about South Africa's Nuclear Energy Programme					
0088/ESK/2005	Eskom	Economic project evaluation July 2001: A macroeconomic impact study on production of pebble bed modular reactor and fuel plant	17 February 2005	3 May 2005	Refused
0092/ESK/2005	Eskom	PricewaterhouseCoopers March 2000 Eskom generation pebble bed modular reactor due diligence and business case	17 February 2005	21 April 2005	Refused

0093/NNR/2005	National Nuclear Regulator	Any and all records relating to on-the-job accidents and injuries in mines	22 February 2005	Various	Partial release
0094/NNR/2005	National Nuclear Regulator	Any and all records relating to safety violations in mines	22 February 2005	16 August 2006	Partial release
0095/NNR/2005	National Nuclear Regulator	Any and all records relating to mine safety regulations	22 February 2005	Various	Refused
0096/NNR/2005	National Nuclear Regulator	Any and all records relating to cyanide acid and/or sulphuric acid and worker safety	22 February 2005	None	Pending
0097/NNR/2005	National Nuclear Regulator	Report on the Pebble Bed Modular Reactor Company 2000: 'Basic licensing requirements for the pebble bed modular reactor'	22 February 2005	16 August 2006	Full release

0098/NNR/2005	National Nuclear Regulator	Reports on the termination and reapproval of the Vaalputs plant licence relating to the last occasion on which the licence was cancelled and renewed	22 February 2005	16 August 2006	Full release
0099/NNR/2005	National Nuclear Regulator	Any and all records relating to any incident(s) at Pelindaba, Koeberg and Vaalputs since their establishment in which limits on exposure of people or the environment to dangerous substances were exceeded, or in which safeguards against any such exposure proved ineffective or were breached and any injury or illness was sustained as a result of any such incident	22 February 2005	Various	Partial release
0100/NNR/2005	National Nuclear Regulator	List of technical safety reports by the Nuclear Energy Corporation of South Africa and Koeberg	22 February 2005	Various	Pending
0101/NNR/2005	National Nuclear Regulator	Full report of investigation into Ron Lockwood's complaint(s) against Eskom and the modular reactor	22 February 2005	Various	Pending

0271/NNR/2005	National Nuclear Regulator (NNR)	Minutes of any and all meetings of the NNR's board during the months of December 2004, January 2005, February 2005 and March 2005 Any and all records of any communications, whether written or verbal, between the minister for minerals and energy, or representatives of herself, her ministry or her department and any member(s) of the board of the NNR, individually or collectively and whether in that capacity or not, regarding appointment or prospective appointment of Maurice Magugumela as chief executive officer of the NNR Letter of appointment of Maurice Magugumela as chief executive officer of the NNR.	12 May 2005	Various	Refused

Chapter 4: The Nuclear Weapons History Project

0021/DFA/2003	Department of Foreign Affairs	Documents President de Klerk used to make a decision regarding revealing/dismantling the nuclear weapons programme	26 June 2003	21 July 2003	Partial release, masked
0022/DFA/2003	Department of Foreign Affairs	Communications between Israel and South Africa regarding the nuclear programme and/or nuclear weapons	25 June 2003	21 July 2003	Partial release, masked
0023/DFA/2003	Department of Foreign Affairs	Communications between South Africa and the United States regarding dismantling nuclear weapons	25 June 2003	21 July 2003	Partial release, masked
0024/DFA/2003	Department of Foreign Affairs	Communications between Tienie Fourie and South Africa regarding revealing the nuclear weapons programme and/or nuclear weapons and/or IAEA inspections	25 June 2003	21 July 2003	Partial release, masked

0026/ARM/2003	Armscor	Any and all records pertaining to nuclear bombs or weapons constructed. This includes, but is not limited to, inventory and other trackings as well as correspondence (re: said devices)	8 July 2003	8 October 2003	Refused
0028/DTI/2003	Department of Trade and Industry	Any and all records pertaining to nuclear devices exported	9 June 2003	1 September 2003	Refused
0029/DOD/2003	Department of Defence	Any and all records that refer to potential and/or intended targets for nuclear weapons (whether offensive or defensive)	8 June 2003	30 November 2003	Full release
0031/DOD/2003	Department of Defence	Any and all records relating to modifications on Canberra bombers or other devices for the purposes of carrying South African nuclear weapons	8 July 2003	30 November 2003	Refused

0032/PRE/2003	Office of the Presidency	Any and all records that refer to potential and/or intended targets for nuclear strikes (whether offensive or defensive)	15 June 2003	None	Refused
0033/NEC/2003	Nuclear Energy Corporation of South Africa	Report: 'A brief overview of the development of nuclear explosive devices in South Africa. May 1993'	15 July 2003	5 February 2004	No final response
0035/DEN/2003	Denel	Any and all records pertaining to nuclear bombs, weapons and devices constructed. Includes but is not limited to inventory and other tracking, as well as correspondence (re: said devices)	4 July 2003	8 August 2003	Refused
0036/DOD/2003	Department of Defence	Any and all records related to agreements between South Africa and Israel regarding cooperation in nuclear weapons programmes and related areas (certain file numbers provided)	21 July 2003	30 August 2004	Refused

0037/DTI/2003	Department of Trade and Industry	Any and all records relating to agreements between Israel and South Africa relating to technology transfers relevant to nuclear weapons	21 July 2003	None	Refused
0038/DTI/2003	Department of Trade and Industry	Any and all records relating to technology transfers and assistance between South Africa and Germany relevant to nuclear weapons	21 July 2003	None	Refused
0040/ARM/2003	Armscor	Any and all records relating to technology transfers or assistance between South Africa and Germany relevant to nuclear weapons	21 July 2003	8 October 2003	Refused
0041/ARM/2003	Armscor	Any and all records relating to commercial dealings with foreign countries and nuclear weapons	21 July 2003	8 October 2003	Refused
0042/DOD/2003	Department of Defence	Any and all navy records regarding Israel and its use of/interaction with the Simon's Town naval base	6 August 2003	30 August 2004	Refused

0044/DFA/2003	Department of Foreign Affairs	Any and all records pertaining to nuclear testing and Israel	6 August 2003	2 September 2003	Partial release
0046/NEC/2003	Nuclear Energy Corporation of South Africa	Any and all independent auditors' reports regarding the nuclear weapons dismantling process	6 August 2003	5 February 2004	Pending
0054/ARM/2003	Armscor	Any and all records related to the Jericho missile	6 August 2003	8 October 2003	Refused
0056/ARM/2003	Armscor	Any and all records relating to US requirements and/or demands relating to the nuclear weapons programme and/or commercial rockets programme	6 August 2003	8 October 2003	Refused
0066/DEN/2003	Denel	Any and all records relating to communication between the then president of South Africa and Denel regarding termination of the nuclear weapons programme and related destruction of documents and other records	15 August 2003	None	Refused

0014/ARM/2005	Armscor	Records regarding the initiation of nuclear weapons development	20 January 2005	15 April 2005	Refused
0015/ARM/2005	Armscor	Nuclear weapons feasibility study/ studies	20 January 2005	15 April 2005	Refused
0016/ARM/2005	Armscor	Records regarding peaceful nuclear weapons explosions	20 January 2005	15 April 2005	Refused
0018/ARM/2005	Armscor	Records regarding destruction of records about South Africa's nu-clear weapons programme	20 January 2005	15 April 2005	Refused
0025/DOD/2005	Department of Defence	Records regarding destruction of records about South Africa's nu-clear weapons programme	26 January 2005	19 December 2005	Refused
0026/DOD/2005	Department of Defence	1974 military cooperation agree-ment between South Africa and Israel	26 January 2005	23 February 2005	Refused

0075/NEC/2005	Nuclear Energy Corporation of South Africa	Annual budgets of the Nuclear Energy Corporation of South Africa during the life of South Africa's former nuclear weapons programme	15 February 2005	None	Refused
0076/NEC/2005	Nuclear Energy Corporation of South Africa	Records regarding the Vastrap nuclear test site (specific interest in cold testing and site reopening circa 1987)	15 February 2005	None	Refused
0077/NEC/2005	Nuclear Energy Corporation of South Africa	Records regarding dismantling of South Africa's former nuclear weapons programme	15 February 2005	None	Refused

Chapter 5: Unlocking South Africa's Military Archives

0006/DOD/2001	Department of Defence	All SADF records relating to or generated by the Greefswald facility	22 May 2001	17 August 2001	Partial release, masked

Chapter 6: Applying PAIA: Legal, Political and Contextual Issues				
0008/DOD/2001	Department of Defence	Lists of military intelligence records in the custody of the SANDF archives, described as groups 14, 21 and 30 in the published TRC final report (vol. 1), p. 223	22 May 2001	17 August 2001	Partial release, masked
0011/NAR/2001	National Archives of South Africa	List of records of the Security Legislation Directorate in the custody of the National Archives: two series of case files, and one series of subject-based correspondence files. The records are referred to in the TRC final report (vol. 1), pp. 226–27	15 May 2001	1 November 2001	Full release
0013/NAR/2001	National Archives of South Africa	Correspondence file(s) documenting the National Archives' dealings with the TRC and other parties in relation to the records/archive of the TRC	15 May 2001	1 November 2001	Partial release, masked

0021/NAR/2001	National Archives of South Africa	Files of the State Archives Service head office and the Central and Transvaal Archives depots dealing with confidential matters, 1960–80, 8/2	24 October 2001	12 June 2002	Full release, masked
0022/NAR/2001	National Archives of South Africa	Records documenting National Archives' endeavours to follow up on recommendations relating to archives and record keeping in the TRC final report	24 October 2001	7 June 2002	Refused
0001/DOD/2002	Department of Defence	Military intelligence files dealing with anti-conscription groups, Black Sash and Idasa (including, but not limited to those provided in a separate list)	18 January 2002	25 April 2002	Partial release, masked
0003/SAP/2002	South African Police Service	Inventories of pre-1994 Security Branch records referred to in the TRC final report (vol. 1), p. 218, para. 54	13 February 2002	20 March 2002	Full release

0044/SAP/2002	South African Police Service	Inventories of surviving apartheid era security police records from the following offices: Pietersburg office, Rooigrond office and security police head office	13 May 2002	2 December 2002	Refused
0047/NAR/2002	National Archives of South Africa	All records in its possession documenting the chain of custody of the records described in an attached list from the time they were transferred from the TRC in 1999	21 May 2002	7 June 2002	Refused
0052/SAP/2002	South African Police Service	Records of the security police in the North West (Potchefstroom) with the descriptions 'VULA' and 'Third Force', TBZ MR 43/4/79 and S30/2/2(4)	29 May 2002	29 August 2002	Partial release, masked
0053/SAP/2002	South African Police Service	Security police file of an individual	29 May 2002	Transferred to the National Archives on unknown date	No final response

0054/SAP/2002	South African Police Service	Case file: *State versus Dumisa Ntsebeza and four others*, Transkei investigation: PUFLA and PAC, 1976	5 July 2002	26 August 2002	Refused
0079/SAP/2002	South African Police Service	Western Cape SAP file list: file KSD1/1331, S1/57621	28 August 2002	January 2003	Refused
0083/YSK/2002	Iscor	Iscor records relating to labour matters and treatment of workers from 1965 to 1973	21 November 2002	19 December 2002	Refused
0001/SAP/2003	South African Police Service	Security police files and BOSS files, 1971–94	21 January 2003	Transferred to the National Archives on unknown date	No final response
0100/NAR/2003	National Archives of South Africa	Security Legislation Directorate files on Michael Muller and Shulamith Muller Commission of inquiry into M.A. Muller and Pretoria Trade Unions, 1943 Striking off legal register, S. Muller, 1971	10 December 2003	8 November 2004	Full release, masked

0024/SAB/2004	South African Breweries	Documents regarding initiatives to increase the take-up rate in HIV/AIDS disease management programmes	16 March 2004	15 April 2004	Refused
0025/SAB/2004	South African Breweries	Documents regarding participation of workers in HIV/AIDS disease management programmes Levels of income of workers who participate in such programmes Number of workers who undertook voluntary testing for HIV/AIDS and/or associated counselling without proceeding to take part in any programme provided by company	16 March 2004	15 April 2004	Refused
0026/SAB/2004	South African Breweries	Documents relating to workers of the company who have died or left	16 March 2004	15 April 2004	Refused
0027/SAB/2004	South African Breweries	Documents regarding absenteeism	16 March 2004	15 April 2004	Refused

0028/SAB/2004	South African Breweries	Documents regarding workers undertaking voluntary HIV/AIDS testing, associated counselling and treatment	16 March 2004	15 April 2004	Refused
0029/SAB/2004	South African Breweries	Documents regarding payouts for death or illness/disability benefits to employees, beneficiaries and/or former employees	16 March 2004	15 April 2004	Refused
0018/ESK/2004	Eskom	Service Delivery Framework Agreement	9 March 2004	6 April 2004	Refused
0019/ESK/2004	Eskom	Research documents entitled 'Soweto socio-economic research' conducted by EON Consulting	9 March 2004	6 April 2004	Refused
0054/NAR/2004	National Archives of South Africa	Security Legislation Directorate file on the University Christian Movement	27 May 2004	28 May 2004	Full release
0002/DOJ/2005	Department of Justice	Open amnesty hearing transcripts in respect of the Cradock 4, including annexures and exhibits	2 June 2004	26 January 2005	Partial release, masked

0088/ESK/2005	Eskom	Economic project evaluation, July 2001: 'A macroeconomic impact study on production of pebble-bed modular reactor and fuel plant'	17 February 2005	3 May 2005	Refused
0240/NAR/2005	National Archives of South Africa	Lists of security police files and lists of prisoners' files from the Department of Correctional Services	1 May 2005	6 June 2005 19 June 2006	Partial release Refused
0341/NAR/2005	National Archives of South Africa	Filing plans of national government departments	20 July 2005	Various	Partial release
0350/DAC/2005	Department of Arts and Culture	Records of the reference group relating to the repatriation of Sarah (Saartjie) Baartman	20 September 2005	Various	Partial release
0382/SAP/2005	South African Police Service	Records relating to Operation Crackdown, 2000	3 November 2005	25 January 2006	Refused

Endnotes

Preface

1. SFJ is dedicated to preserving and ensuring access to collections of SAHA's records. Through the search, retrieval and preservation of hidden or forgotten narratives, SFJ places an emphasis on giving voice to marginalised histories; it carries the original motivations behind the formation of SAHA in 1988. While retaining traditional archival functions of collection, arrangement and description, preservation, access, and use, it prioritises outreach by weaving the SFJ collections into educational and art-based programmes that aid the development of democracy.

2. In around 1994 SAHA received funding from the Swedish Labour Movement (later known as the Olaf Palme International Centre) and the Canadian-based Catholic Agency for Development and Peace. Following the surety that South Africa would achieve a relatively peaceful transition to democratic rule, many small NGOs in South Africa have been plagued by funding limitations. While SAHA has not escaped funding difficulties (these limitations led to various periods of uncertainty and transition in the organisation), it has been fortunate to benefit substantially from its relationship with the University of the Witwatersrand and funding grants from external agencies. The provision of free physical space, infrastructure and the assistance of Wits University Library staff were, and remain, crucial to the sustainability of the organisation. Additional core funding from Atlantic Philanthropies and the Rosa Luxembourg Foundation; project funding from the Foundation for Human Rights, the Charles Stuart Mott Foundation, the City of Johannesburg, the Plowshares Fund, the Carnegie Corporation and the Ford Foundation; and the support of Australian Volunteers International have maintained the organisation and resulted in staff increases since 2001.

3. K. Allan & I.B. Currie, 2007, 'Enforcing access to information and privacy rights: Evaluating proposals for an information protection regulator for South Africa', *South African Journal on Human Rights*, 23(2).

4. Organisations include Earthlife Africa, the Open Democracy Advice Centre, the University of the Witwatersrand's Forced Migration Studies Programme, the Coalition against Water Privatisation (arising from collaboration with the Anti-Privatisation Forum), the Freedom of Expression Institute, the Legal Resources Centre, Lawyers for Human Rights, the Ceasefire Campaign, the Khulumani Support Group, the Centre for the Study of Violence and Reconciliation, Shadow Films (David Forbes), the Treatment Action Campaign, the AIDS Consortium, the Centre for Health Policy, the WITS AIDS Law Project, the Swiss National Scientific Research Foundation, the Biko Foundation, Jubilee 2000, and various newspaper journalists, including from the *Mail & Guardian* and *The Star*. I have not provided detail of any individuals to ensure protection of their privacy.

5. SAHA has nevertheless had the benefit of pro bono (or discounted) advice, assistance and representation from a large number of attorneys and advocates, including Mark Wesley, Nasreen Rajab-Budlender, Iain Currie (Wits Law School), Jon Klaaren (Wits Law School), Richard Moultrie, Wits Law Clinic, the Legal Resources Centre, Webber Wentzel Bowens and Denys Reitz. SAHA has also had the benefit of assistance from Nicholls Cambanis & Associates, Lisa Thornton Inc., and Cheadle Thompson & Haysom Inc.

6. These are the Gays in the Apartheid Military Project (a collaboration with the Gay and Lesbian Archives), the Truth and Reconciliation Project, the Nuclear Weapons History Project and the Nuclear Energy Project (a collaboration with Earthlife Africa and its Nuclear Energy Costs the Earth Campaign). FOIP

has conducted additional projects including the HIV/AIDS project, the Alternative History Project and the Migration Project (a collaboration with the Forced Migration Studies Programme at Wits University, the Legal Resources Centre and Lawyers for Human Rights).

Chapter 1

1. E. Mureinik, 1994, 'A bridge to where? Introducing the Interim Bill of Rights', *South African Journal on Human Rights*, 10: 31–48.

2. See <http://www.freedominfo.org/documents/global_survey2006.pdf> for the most recent survey of countries with freedom of information laws around the world. See also T. Blanton, 2002, 'The world's right to know', *Foreign Policy*, July/August, <http://www.freedominfo.org/documents/rtk-english.pdf>.

3. A. Arko-Cobbah, 2007, 'The right of access to information: Civil society and good governance in South Africa', June, <http://www.ifla.org/IV/ifla73/papers/135-Arko-Cobbah-en.pdf>.

4. C. Darch & P.G. Underwood, 2005, 'Freedom of information legislation, state compliance and the disclosure of knowledge: The South African experience', *International Information and Library Review*, 37: 76.

5. <http://www.cartercenter.org/resources/pdfs/peace/americas/briefing_group1_politics_economy_eng.pdf>.

6. K. O'Regan, 2000, 'Democracy and access to information in the South African Constitution: Some reflections', paper presented at the conference The Constitutional Right to Access to Information, Pretoria, September, <http://www.kas.de/db_files/dokumente/7_dokument_dok_pdf_4936_2.pdf>.

7. See M. Dimba, 2002, 'A landmark law opens up post-apartheid South Africa', for an account of the civil society campaign in South Africa, <http://www.freedominfo.org/features/20020717.htm>.

8. See ibid. for more details on the process, and also my own short account in R. Calland, 2006, *Anatomy of South Africa: Who Holds the Power?*, Cape Town: Zebra Press, pp. 30–31.

9. OSI (Open Society Institute), 2006, *Transparency and Silence: A Survey of Access to Information Laws and Practices in 14 Countries*, New York: Open Society Justice Initiative, p. 71.

10. See, most recently, A. Florini (ed.), 2007, *The Right to Know: Transparency for an Open World*, New York: Columbia University Press; specifically, chap. 6 of this book: L. Neuman & R. Calland, 'Making the law work: The challenge of implementation', p. 179.

11. Article 19 of the International Covenant on Civil and Political Rights provides for protection of the right to 'seek' information (as a part of a widely constructed right to freedom of expression). In its decision in *Claude Reyes v Chile*, the Inter-American Court of Human Rights, in an important and long-awaited precedent, confirmed that 'seek' means the right to request public information and the concomitant duty of a state to respond to the request.

12. See S. Jagwanth, 2002, 'The right to information as a leverage right', in R. Calland & A. Tilley (eds), *The Right to Know, the Right to Live: Access to Information and Socio-Economic Justice*, Cape Town: ODAC.

13. For a review of many of these issues, see C. Hood & D. Heald, 2006, 'Transparency: The key to better governance?', *Open Government: A Journal on Freedom of Information*, 2(2).

14. My own first-hand account of the case appeared in my column in the *Mail & Guardian*, 'Contretemps:

Opening up rural India', 20–26 February 2004.

15. See <http://www.freedominfo.org/features/20040630.htm> for an account of the pioneering work of MKSS in Rajasthan, India; also, see S. Singh, 'India: Grassroots initiatives', in Florini (2007). Most recently, see ODAC's film *The Right to Know: The Fight for Open Democracy in South Africa*, which charts two sets of community-based requests for information under PAIA, one for information relating to housing policy in Durban, the other for information related to water access policy in rural KwaZulu-Natal.

16. See R. Calland, 'Introduction', in Calland & Tilley (2002).

17. <http://www.cartercenter.org/resources/pdfs/peace/americas/briefing_group1_politics_economy_eng.pdf>.

18. <http://www.cartercenter.org/documents/Atlanta%20Declaration%20and%20Plan%20of%20Action.pdf>.

19. As Allan notes in her chapter, there is also a need for rules around record making, not least because, as technology changes so rapidly, so the old form of 'government by paper record' is disturbed; the paper trail may no longer be there or may no longer be complete; and emails have replaced typed, paper memorandums. In this context, what are the rules of the game in terms of the retention and storage of such records?

20. The survey data are available from ODAC. The results of the comparative study were published in 2006 in OSI (2006).

21. Only Chile (69 per cent) and Ghana (73 per cent), neither of which has specific ATI laws, had higher levels of 'mute refusals' of the 14 countries surveyed (OSI, 2006).

22. OSI (2006, pp. 93–94), which catalogues the dispiriting and outrageous treatment that Ausi received when seeking to use PAIA.

23. Parliament of the Republic of South Africa, 2007, *Report of the Ad Hoc Committee on the Review of Chapter 9 and Associated Institutions*, a report of the National Assembly of the Parliament of South Africa, Cape Town.

24. ODAC submission to the parliamentary Ad Hoc Committee on the Review of Chapter 9 and Associated Institutions, March 2007.

25. *Earthlife Africa (Cape Town) v Director General of the Department of Environmental Affairs and Tourism and Eskom Holdings Ltd*, case no. 7653/03, High Court of South Africa, Cape of Good Hope Provincial Division.

Chapter 2

1. Quoted in *Cape Argus*, 2 April 1998.

2. TRC, 1998, *Truth and Reconciliation Commission of South Africa Report*, Cape Town: The Commission, vol. 6, sec. 4, chap. 3, para. 43.

3. Ibid., vol. 5, chap. 8, para. 100.

4. Ibid., vol. 5, chap. 8, para. 103. It states: 'The Commission recommends that:

• All Commission records be transferred to the National Archives when the codicil to the final report is made public.

- All Commission records be accessible to the public, unless, compelling reasons exist for denying such access, bearing in mind that the individual's rights to privacy, confidentiality and related matters must be respected. In this regard, particular attention needs to be given to the release or withholding of details of human rights violations statements in cases where individuals feel their safety is prejudiced.

- Victims have the right of access to their own files, regardless of whether these are publicly available or not. Victims should be provided with a copy of their file if they so wish.

- To facilitate the above, the Department of Justice provide public notice of the intent to transfer the records of the Commission to the National Archives. The notice should include a statement about the basic access provisions for the records.

  - The following guidelines be used to determine access to Commission records in the National Archives:

    · Because the Commission records are less than twenty years old, access to these records be determined by the National Archivist in terms of section 12(1) of the Archives Act.

    · In case of the record categories identified as requiring protection, the National Archivist refer requests for access to the Department of Justice. In the case of all other record categories, a policy of unrestricted public access should be applied.

    · The following information, which is already in the public domain, be made available as soon as practically possible: transcripts of hearings, reasons for amnesty decisions, public statements issued by the Commission, all other material already available to the public on the Commissions Internet website.

    · The National Archives take over the Commission's Internet website, continue to make existing material — including the report of the Commission — available to the public, locally and internationally, on the website and expand the website in creative ways (taking into account the fact that many Commission records are stored in computer files).

    · The government allocate adequate additional funding to the National Archives to preserve and maintain the records of the Commission. To this end, the National Archives should prepare a comprehensive budget plan on the costs of administering the Commission's records.

    · The government give special support to the National Archives to facilitate the creation of decentralised, nationwide 'centres of memory', at which members of the public who do not have personal access to computers can access details of the proceedings of the Commission, including transcripts and sound and video clips of hearings.'

5. TRC (1998). The final report consisted of five volumes and included a core set of findings and recommendations.

6. The Codicil (i.e. vols. 6 and 7 of the report) comprised further analysis and findings that emanated from the amnesty process, which only concluded in 2002, and some analysis on the interrelationship between the Amnesty and Human Rights Violation Committee process, legal challenges and so forth (vol. 6); and a short précis of each of the roughly 16,000 cases where the TRC had determined that deponents should be classified as 'victims' (vol. 7).

7. 'The TRC codicil and archives/record keeping', *SAHA Update*, 6 May 2003, <http://www.saha.org.za/research/publications/FOIP_TRCCodicil.pdf>.

8. A popular version of the TRC report was developed by the TRC and external consultants in the period

between 1998 and 2002. It reached an advanced stage, and publishing rights were granted to a German publishing house to proceed with translation and publication, which it duly did. The popular version of the TRC report is therefore only available in a German translation.

9. <http://www.doj.gov.za/truth>.

10. The establishment in 2001 of SAHA's FOIP was intended to test the parameters of the new access to information laws i.e. to establish the existence and accessibility of records and seek appropriate procedural and/or legal remedies where necessary. The intention was to access records both on behalf of individuals and organisations, and of SAHA's own volition. As with other aspects of the programme, any records accessed are processed, described and arranged for wider access through SAHA's Struggles for Justice Programme.

11. TRC (1998, vol. 5, chap. 8, para. 103).

12. Correspondence from SAHA to DOJ, 16 May 2002.

13. Request no. 0051/DOJ/2002.

14. Correspondence from DOJ to SAHA, 12 August 2002.

15. 'Out-of-court settlements', *SAHA Update*, 11 May 2003, emailed to SAHA distribution list.

16. Request no. 0013/NAR/2001.

17. Section 27 of PAIA provides that, if a recipient of a request does not respond within 30 days, the recipient is to be regarded as having refused the request.

18. Correspondence from national archivist to SAHA, 1 November 2001.

19. Correspondence from national archivist to SAHA, 6 December 2001.

20. Correspondence from SAHA to national archivist, 12 December 2001.

21. Undated correspondence from national archivist to SAHA, circa mid-December 2001.

22. Request no. 0022/NAR/2001.

23. Officially, this department is known as the Department of Arts, Culture, Science and Technology; however, for the sake of brevity, it is referred to throughout this book as the Department of Arts and Culture (DAC), as it is more popularly known.

24. Correspondence from DAC to SAHA, 7 June 2002.

25. Correspondence from SAHA to national archivist, 24 June 2002.

26. Correspondence from national archivist to SAHA, 27 June 2002.

27. Correspondence from minister of arts and culture to Lisa Thornton Attorneys, 11 October 2002.

28. Memorandum from national archivist to S.W. Bapela, Legal Services Directorate of DAC, attached to correspondence from Bapela to Lisa Thornton Attorneys, 26 November 2002.

29. 'Out-of-court settlements', *SAHA Update*, 11 May 2003, emailed to SAHA distribution list.

30. Correspondence from Lisa Thornton Attorneys to P.D. Burger in the Office of the State Attorney, 25 July 2003.

31. 'DAC progress report re implementation of recommendation of the TRC report', undated.

32. 'TRC and archives', *SAHA Update*, undated, circa late August 2003.

33. Correspondence from Lisa Thornton Attorneys to D.P. Burger, Office of the State Attorney, 1 December 2003.

34. 'Out-of-court settlement with National Archives', *SAHA Update*, 5 March 2004, emailed to SAHA distribution list.

35. Request no. 0023/DOJ/2001.

36. Detail of the destruction of DCC records and security force complicity in this is provided in De Wet Potgieter, 2007, *Total Onslaught: Apartheid's Dirty Tricks Exposed*, Cape Town: Zebra Press, pp. 249–55.

37. Terry Bell, 'Burying the truth, again', *Mail & Guardian*, 5–11 April 2002.

38. Bongani Majola, 'Nothing but the hidden truth', *Mail & Guardian*, 12–18 April 2002.

39. Ibid.

40. Ibid.

41. Verne Harris, 'Where are the TRC records?', *Natal Witness*, 22 April 2002.

42. Terry Bell, '"Missing" truth files are in NIA's hands', *Mail & Guardian*, 10–16 May 2002.

43. Correspondence from Institute of Justice and Reconciliation to Office of the President, 25 April 2002.

44. Correspondence from Lisa Thornton Attorneys to Office of the State Attorney, 18 March 2003.

45. Correspondence from minister of justice to Institute of Justice and Reconciliation, 19 May 2002.

46. Request no. 0048/DOJ/2002.

47. Terry Bell, 'Location of missing TRC files remains a mystery', *Mail & Guardian*, 28 June–4 July 2002.

48. Ibid.

49. Correspondence from NIA to SAHA, 7 June 2002.

50. Bell, 'Location of missing TRC files remains a mystery'.

51. Ibid.

52. Request no. 0047/NAR/2002. See also correspondence from National Archives to SAHA, 13 June 2002.

53. Correspondence from SAHA to National Archives, undated, circa 20 June 2003.

54. Correspondence from National Archives to SAHA, 27 June 2002.

55. Correspondence from SAHA to SAHRC, 20 June 2002.

56. CSVR memorandum to the TRC, 15 June 2002.

57. Correspondence from DOJ to SAHA, 12 August 2002.

58. Correspondence from J.N. Labuschagne, ministerial services in the Department of Justice and Constitutional Development, to SAHA, 7 October 2002.

59. Correspondence from Lisa Thornton Attorneys to minister of arts and culture, 27 August 2002.

60. Terry Bell, 'Media misled over missing TRC files', *Mail & Guardian*, 20–26 March 2003.

61. Graham Dominy, 'TRC files claims devoid of truth', letter to the editor, *Mail & Guardian*, 11–17 April 2003.

62. Terry Bell & Verne Harris, 'Fact and fiction', letter to the editor, *Mail & Guardian*, 17–23 April 2003.

63. Correspondence from Office of the State Attorney to Lisa Thornton Attorneys, 22 January 2003.

64. Email correspondence from Verne Harris to Lisa Thornton Attorneys, 1 February 2003.

65. 'Out-of-court settlements', *SAHA Update*, 11 May 2003, emailed to SAHA distribution list.

66. Bonny Schoonakker, 'Secret files to be opened', *Sunday Times*, 18 May 2003.

67. 'Out-of-court settlements', *SAHA Update*, 11 May 2003, emailed to SAHA distribution list.

68. Christelle Terreblanche, 'Deadline looms for TRC spy files to be handed to the archives', *The Star*, 22 September 2003.

69. Guy Jepson, 'Battle for access to TRC files will be heard in court', *This Day*, 30 October 2003.

70. Patrick Laurence, 'Comrades who wore two masks', *The Star*, 28 May 2003.

71. This included allegations made in Parliament by the leader of the Independent Democrats, Patricia de Lille, who named senior members of the ANC as having worked with the apartheid regime. In addition, former cabinet minister Mac Maharaj accused former national director of public prosecutions Bulelani Ngcuka of being a spy, leading to the establishment of the Hefer Commission, which rejected this contention and raised a number of important concerns and questions around issues of authenticity, custody and access.

72. Christelle Terreblanche, 'Spy lists likely to stay secret', *Natal Mercury*, 22 September 2003.

73. Jepson, 'Battle for access to TRC files will be heard in court'.

74. Graham Dominy, 'A delicate balancing act at the National Archives', *This Day*, 17 November 2003.

75. Verne Harris & Sello Hatang, 'Smoke and mirrors', *This Day*, 24 November 2003.

76. Guy Jepson, 'Archives sticks to its guns over TRC files', *This Day*, 23 December 2003.

77. Terry Bell, 'High Court to rule on "secret" TRC files', *Sunday Tribune*, 18 January 2003.

78. SA Press Association (SAPA), 'Pretoria High Court battle to view secret documents', *Mail & Guardian Online*, 29 January 2004.

79. Guy Jepson, 'Court papers say NIA held sensitive missing TRC files', *This Day*, 2 March 2004.

80. Ibid.

81. Ibid.

82. Ibid.

83. Marlene Burger, 'Fight over apartheid's secret files turns nasty', *This Day*, 29 January 2004.

84. SAPA, 'Pretoria High Court battle to view secret documents'.

85. 'SAHA court action against the Department of Justice', *SAHA Update*, 27 October 2004, emailed to SAHA distribution list.

86. Correspondence from Adv. Vusi Pikoli to Nicholls Cambanis Attorneys, 15 November 2004.

87. See, for example, Marlene Burger & Chandré Gould, 2002, *Secrets and Lies*, Cape Town, Zebra Press, pp. 61-62.

88. Dulcie September was an ANC representative in Paris who was assassinated in 1988.

89. Pro Jack was an ANC leader in the Western Cape who was involved in defence unit structures and was

murdered in suspicious circumstances before the 1994 elections.

90. Alan Kidger was a Johannesburg businessman whose dismembered body was found in the boot of a vehicle in the early 1990s. His death was linked to investigations into the sale of 'red mercury'.

91. General Steyn was tasked by President F.W. de Klerk with investigating allegations that military elements were destabilising the negotiation process, after the Goldstone Commission of Inquiry literally stumbled across documents relating to alleged nefarious activities by the South African Defence Force's Directorate of Covert Collection in November 1992.

92. TRC (1998, vol. 6, sec. 6, para. 10, p. 736). The TRC website is currently hosted by DOJ: <http://www.doj.gov.za/trc>. There is some concern that the site does not host all the transcripts, and a comprehensive audit of what is available has not been undertaken.

93. For example, correspondence from DOJ to Nicholls Cambanis Attorneys, 15 November 2004, Annexure VP1, doc. 503, amnesty application of Johann Philip Verster, p. 102; docs. 512 and 513, amnesty applications of Michael Savory and Jan Lourens, p. 104.

94. PAIA, sec. 34.

95. See, for example, correspondence from DOJ to Nicholls Cambanis, 15 November 2004, Annexure VP1, doc. 974, which relates to seven amnesty applications of security force personnel. According to the annexure: 'There are seven amnesty applications, all of which contain highly personal information about the respective applicants as well as information relating to their alleged unlawful activities, as well as unlawful activities perpetrated by other parties. The information is not in the public domain and the applicants and other parties have not consented to the disclosure of either. The information relating to other parties has also not been tested and/or verified and its disclosure could be defamatory of them and also infringe their dignity which is protectable [sic] under the Constitution.'

96. Doc. 134, Philip Morgan's amnesty application, p. 24; doc. 475, Lionel Snyman's amnesty application, p. 94; docs. 952–57, amnesty applications relating to gun running, pp. 205–7; docs. 958 and 961, amnesty applications of Alec Erwin and Felicity Anderson, pp. 207–10; doc. 1535, amnesty application of Xola Yekwani, p. 300.

97. The amnesty application of Leon Flores is a case in point — refused as doc. 473 on p. 93; access was granted as doc. 519 on p. 105.

98. This report provides an overview of allegations about security force destabilisation activities during the early 1990s and included the names of key security force personnel allegedly involved.

99. This case related to the 1980s murder of four Eastern Cape activists and the subsequent cover-up engineered by members of the Eastern Cape security police.

100. Request no. 0060/DOJ/2006.

101. SAHA complaint to SAHRC regarding DOJ, 25 July 2007.

102. TRC (1998, vol. 6, sec. 4, chap. 1, para. 40; vol. 6, sec. 5, chap. 2, para. 11).

103. Request nos. 0013–0017/DOJ/2003.

104. 'Askari' was the term given to 'turned' liberation movement soldiers who had been captured and 'persuaded' to work for the South African state.

105. Request no. 0030/DOJ/2006.

106. Correspondence from DOJ to SAHA, 18 April 2006.

107. Correspondence from the minister of justice to SAHA, 18 July 2006.

108. Request no. 0059/DOJ/2006.

109. TRC commissioners meeting minutes, 1 July 1998.

110. TRC commissioners meeting minutes, 6 August 1998.

111. CSVR memorandum to the TRC, 15 June 2002.

112. Personal communication with former TRC commissioner Yasmin Sooka.

113. See chapter 6 regarding the TRC Act and the confidentiality exemption for a further discussion of this issue.

114. Undated report from the TRC's Research Department outlining available documents submitted by De Klerk and others to the TRC on 'Secret projects'.

115. Correspondence from DOJ to Nicholls Cambanis Attorneys, 15 November 2004, Annexure VP1, docs. 1734–35, pp. 331–33.

116. Correspondence from NIA to SAHA, 10 June 2004.

117. TRC (1998, vol. 6, sec. 4, chap. 3, para. 42, p. 578).

118. Request no. 0028/DOJ/2006.

119. TRC (1998, vol. 5, chap. 8, para. 103).

120. Request nos. 0041 and 0042/DOJ/2002.

121. Request no. 0075/DOJ/2002: a case about seven activists shot dead by security police in a 'sting' operation in the Western Cape township of Gugulethu.

122. Request no. 0071/DOJ/2004.

123. Request no. 0076/DOJ/2002. Rejected on 6 November 2002 and on appeal in March 2003.

124. Request no. 0039/DOJ/2006.

125. Correspondence from DAC to SAHA, 7 June 2002.

126. Correspondence from SAHA to national archivist, 24 June 2002.

127. Correspondence from national archivist to SAHA, 27 June 2002.

128. See SAHA's internal appeal, request no. 0015/NAR/2001.

129. Correspondence from Lisa Thornton Attorneys to minister of arts and culture, 27 August 2002.

130. Correspondence from DAC to Lisa Thornton Attorneys, 4 September 2002.

131. Correspondence from DAC to Lisa Thornton Attorneys, 12 September 2002.

132. TRC (1998, vol. 5, chap. 8, para. 103).

133. Correspondence from minister of arts and culture to Lisa Thornton Attorneys, 11 October 2002.

134. Request no. 0073/DOJ/2002.

135. Request no. 0003/DOJ/2004, submitted 12 January 2004: 40 mourners at the night vigil of Christopher Ngalember were killed during a hand grenade and AK-47 attack by unknown gunmen believed to be working with elements in the Inkatha Freedom Party and the South African Police.

136. Submissions to the TRC by Terry Crawford Browne, request no. 0009/DOJ/2003, submitted 9 May 2003.

137. Request no. 0054/DOJ/2006, submitted 18 October 2006.

138. Meeting convened by CSVR to discuss the condition of and prospects for preserving and accessing the electronic records of the TRC, 3 October 2006.

Chapter 3

1.   Alec Erwin, minister of public enterprises, to National Assembly in departmental budget vote, 5 June 2006, reported as 'Nuclear power is best for the future', *Cape Times*, 6 June 2006.

2.   Formerly known as the Atomic Energy Corporation (1970–99) and before that the Atomic Energy Board (1949–70).

3.   Formerly known as the Council for Nuclear Safety (1988–99).

4.   To be read with section 32 of the Constitution of the Republic of South Africa, Act No. 108 of 1996. All post-1993 legislation is available at <http://www.polity.co.za/pol/acts>.

5.   NERSA (National Electricity Regulator of South Africa), 2006, *Investigation into the Electricity Outages in the Western Cape, November 2005–March 2006*, Pretoria: NERSA.

6.   Pelindaba is the headquarters of the parastatal South African Nuclear Energy Corporation (known as NECSA, previously the Atomic Energy Corporation). Located on a property to the west of Pretoria, and technically within the North-West province, most of South Africa's official nuclear research occurs here. The complex houses a research reactor (SAFARI-1), and during the apartheid years also saw the building of plants for the conversion of uranium into a gas, enrichment, nuclear fuel fabrication and the earlier stages of the development of nuclear weapons. Pelindaba is also home to a controversial nuclear waste dump (Radiation Hill). It is the likely site for the manufacture of fuel for the pebble bed nuclear reactor, and a highly contested plant to smelt nuclear waste.

7.   Richard Rhodes, 1986, *The Making of the Atomic Bomb*, New York: Simon & Schuster; Kai Bird & Martin Sherwin, 2005, *American Prometheus: The Triumph and Tragedy of J. Robert Oppenheimer*, New York: Alfred A. Knopf.

8.   Gar Alperovitz, 1995, *The Decision to Use the Atomic Bomb*, New York: Alfred A. Knopf.

9.   Richard Rhodes, 1995, *Dark Sun: The Making of the Hydrogen Bomb*, New York: Simon & Schuster, p. 130.

10. R.A. Cooper, 1923, paper presented to the Chemical, Metallurgical and Mining Society of South Africa, October, referred to in L. Taverner, 1956, 'An historical review of the events and developments culminating in the construction of plants for the recovery of uranium from gold ore residues', *Journal of the South African Institute of Mining and Metallurgy*, 57(4), November, reproduced in Associated Scientific and Technical Societies of South Africa, 1957, *Uranium in South Africa 1946–1956*, Johannesburg: Associated Scientific and Technical Societies of South Africa, vol. 1, p. 1.

11. Dr C.F. Davidson, chief geologist of the Atomic Energy Division of the Geological Survey of Great Britain, quoted in Taverner (1956, p. 5).

12. Taverner (1956, p. 5).

13. R.B. Hagart, 1957, 'National aspects of the uranium industry', *Journal of the South African Institute of*

Mining and Metallurgy, 57(9), April, p. 567. The AEB was established by the Atomic Energy Act, No.35 of 1948.

14. David Fig, 1999, 'Sanctions and the nuclear industry', in Neta C. Crawford & Audie Klotz (eds), *How Sanctions Work: Lessons from South Africa*, Basingstoke: Macmillan, p. 80.

15. B.J. Vorster, speech to Parliament, *Hansard*, 20 July 1970.

16. *Washington Post*, 16 February 1977.

17. Zdenek Červenka & Barbara Rogers, 1977, *The Nuclear Axis: Secret Collaboration between West Germany and South Africa*, London: Julian Friedmann.

18. For details, see Fig (2205,p. 57)

19. The site was chosen by excluding land located in 'growth axes' or within 50 km of 'white' municipalities, but ended up within 24 km of a Nama settlement at Paulshoek. See map in AEC (Atomic Energy Corporation of South Africa Ltd), 1984, *Vaalputs: National Radioactive Waste Disposal Facility*, Pretoria: AEC, p. 2, reproduced in Fig (2005, p. 62).

20. S.W.P. de Waal (manager: licensing, AEC) to Dr H.B.F. Minnaar (manager: risk analysis, AEC), 25 September 1996 (AEC ref. VB0035) and attachment, in NNR (National Nuclear Regulator), 1996, *Vaalputs Licence Compliance Inspection,* report, 8–11 September, Pretoria, SAHA ref. 0098/NNR/2005.

21. EMG (Environmental Monitoring Group) & Western Cape ANC Science and Technology Group, 1994, *The Nuclear Debate: Proceedings of a Conference on Nuclear Policy for a Democratic South Africa*, Cape Town: EMG/ANC, p. 5.

22. DME (Department of Minerals and Energy), 1998, White Paper on the Energy Policy of the Republic of South Africa, Pretoria: DME, sec. 7.2.iv.

23. Ibid.

24. Ibid., secs. 7.2.iii & 7.2.v.

25. DME, 2003, press release, 16 October.

26. This became very clear at a briefing conducted for ANC members of the parliamentary Portfolio Committee on Environment and Tourism, Gordon's Bay, 16–18 September 2006.

27. The courts recognised that the record of decision that allowed the development to go ahead conditionally had been reached unfairly.

28. The decision was made by Eskom in late 2006 and announced by Minister Erwin on 12 February 2007. See Hilary Joffe & Mathabo le Roux, 'Second (sic) nuclear power plant to ease SA's power crisis', *Business Day*, 13 February 2007. While Erwin announced that Eskom would 'decide on a preferred bidder in the first quarter of 2007', Westinghouse stands the best chance of winning.

29. Michael Schmidt, 'Should South Africa re-arm with nukes?', *Weekend Argus*, 16 September 2006.

30. Heindrich Wyngaard, 'Vakbonde looi Erwin oor bout: "Sabotasie", bontpratery en iemand JOK' ('Trade unions challenge Erwin about bolt: "Sabotage", double dealing and someone is LYING', *Rapport*, 6 March 2006, p. 6.

31. NERSA (2006, pp. 12–16, 20–22).

32. *Engineering News*, 4–10 August 2006, pp. 16–17.

33. This was because any 'installation or site' declared a key point was out of bounds for public protests, occupations, etc. State of emergency legislation allowed for detention without trial, the military could assume policing functions, and all public gatherings needed police permission. By the early 1970s it was illegal for more than 11 people to gather together in public, and this figure dropped further during states of emergency.

34. 'More controversy at South African nuclear facility', *African News Dimension*, 24 October 2006.

35. Kate Allan, 2005, 'Burning bodies: The peril of poor record-keeping practices in South Africa's nuclear industry', paper disseminated at the conference Updating International Nuclear Law, Salzburg, 20–23 October, p. 2, <http://www.saha.org.za/research/publications/FOIP_IntNuclConf_Allan.pdf>.

36. Yolandi Groenewald, 'How did Victor Motha die?', *Mail & Guardian*, 25 February–3 March 2005, p. 3; Shaun Smillie, 'Nuclear death probe: But family in the dark', *The Star*, 12 August 2005, p. 5.

37. Yolandi Groenewald, 'Surprise cheque for Motha family', *Mail & Guardian*, 15–21 April 2005, p. 5.

38. W. Murray Coombs, 2005, *Review of the Medical Files for Occupational Exposure to Radiation of Ex-NECSA Employees: Report for Earthlife Africa*. Pretoria: Health Gap Network, February, pp. 9–10.

39. Allan (2005, p. 5).

40. See S.P. de Waal (interim CEO, NECSA) to Advocate N.P. Thejane (senior investigator, Public Protector's Office), 14 November 2005.

41. A letter from the public protector dated 17 November 2005 stated that NECSA had advised him that in a meeting 'held on 7 October 2005 in which your organization was represented, it made an undertaking to provide you with the medical records by December 2005 … Kindly confirm whether such an agreement was concluded between yourselves and NECSA so that we can reassess our intervention'.

42. Earthlife Africa Johannesburg NECTEC, 'Fear of whitewash as NECSA slams door on civil society', press release, 21 September 2005; SA Press Association, 'Nuclear health study looks like a whitewash', *Mail & Guardian*, 23–29 September 2005.

43. Malepa Holdings, <http://www.malepa.co.za>, accessed 29 October 2006.

44. By the end of February 2007, this had still not occurred.

45. Janneker's statement reported in *African News Dimension*, 24 October 2006.

46. SA Press Association, 'Government denounces Pelindaba "nuclear threat"', *Mail & Guardian*, 28 April–4 May 2005.

47. SA Press Association, 'Incitement law will "chill freedom of expression"', *Mail & Guardian*, 3–9 May 2005.

48. National Environmental Management Act No. 107 of 1998. See section 31(5)(b), which ensures that whistle-blowers who disclose evidence of environmental risk in good faith are protected from being dismissed, disciplined, prejudiced or harassed on account of having furnished such information (Jan Glazewski, 2000, *Environmental Law in South Africa*, Durban: LexisNexus Butterworths, p. 185).

49. Request no. 0088/ESK/2005; for the response, see letter from Eddie Laubscher (senior professional advisor, Eskom) to Sello Hatang (SAHA), 14 April 2005.

50. Banie van Vollenhoven (PBMR Ltd) to Rolf Sorenson (SAHA), 22 April 2005.

51. The appeal was submitted on 31 August 2005.

52. Request no. 0092/ESK/2005.

53. S.J. Lennon (managing director: resources and strategy, Eskom) to S.K. Hatang (SAHA), 8 September 2005.

54. K. Allan (SAHA) to Mashile Phalane (NECTEC coordinator, Earthlife Africa Johannesburg), 14 September 2005.

55. G.N. Mojapelo (deputy information officer, DME) to R.K. Sorenson (SAHA), undated (February 2005?).

56. P. Mlambo-Ncguka (minister of minerals and energy) to the Motha family (relatives surviving the death of Victor Motha, a former NECSA worker), 17 November 2001.

57. Nuclear Regulation Act No. 47 of 1999.

58. Request nos. 0093–0096/NNR/2005.

59. Request no. 0097/NNR/2005.

60. Request no. 0098/NNR/2005.

61. Request no. 0099/NNR/2005.

62. Request no. 0100/NNR/2005.

63. Request no. 0101/NNR/2005; also see reports on the Lockwood case in 'Koeberg's secret medical files', *Noseweek*, 53, February 2004; and 'The long goodbye: Eskom drag their feet over sick radiation worker', *Noseweek*, 54, March 2004, pp. 18–19.

64. Request no. 0271/NNR/2005.

65. M.T. Magugumela (CEO, NNR) to K. Allan (SAHA), 8 May 2006.

66. Prof. K. Bharuth-Ram (chair, NNR board) to M. Phalane (NECTEC coordinator, Earthlife Africa Johannesburg), 24 May 2006.

67. Council for Nuclear Safety, 1996, *Vaalputs Licence Compliance Inspection, 8–11 September*, Centurion: CNS.

68. Ibid., p. 8.

69. 'Vaalputs: South Africa's nuclear crypt', unattributed article written in 2001, downloaded from NECSA website, <http://www.necsa.co.za> , on 27 December 2006.

70. See 'Submission to the National Nuclear Regulator Act internal review process, 11 July 2006' issued by Earthlife Africa Johannesburg, South African Catholic Bishops' Conference, National Union of Mineworkers, COSATU and SAHA.

71. NNR did not respond to the remainder of the requests.

Chapter 4

1. These documents have been released by the Washington, DC-based National Security Archive and are available online at <http://www.gwu.edu/~nsarchiv/NSAEBB/NSAEBB181/index.htm>.

2. Hannes Steyn, Richart van der Walt & Jan van Loggerenberg, 2003, *Armament and Disarmament: South Africa's Nuclear Weapons Experience*, Pretoria: Network Publishers. See also Waldo Stumpf, 1995, 'Birth and death of the South African nuclear weapons programme', presentation given at the conference 50 Years

After Hiroshima, organised by Unione Scienziati per il Disarmo, Castiglioncello, Italy, 28 September–2 October, <http://www.fas.org/nuke/guide/rsa/nuke/stumpf.htm>.

3. See David Albright & Mark Hobbs, 1993, 'South Africa: The ANC and the atom bomb', *Bulletin of Atomic Scientists*, 49(3), April, <http://www.bullatomsci.org/issues/1993/a93/a93AlbrightHibbs.html>; David Albright, 1994a, 'South Africa and the affordable bomb', *Bulletin of Atomic Scientists*, 50(4), July/August: 37–44; Peter Liberman, 2001, 'The rise and fall of the South African bomb', *International Security*, 26(2), Fall: 45–86; David Fischer, 1994, 'South Africa', in Mitchell Reiss & Robert Litwak (eds), *Nuclear Proliferation after the Cold War*, Washington, DC: Woodrow Wilson Center Press, chap. 9. A chronology of key events related to the nuclear weapons programme is available from the Centre for Nonproliferation Studies at <http://cns.miis.edu/research/safrica/chron.htm>.

4. Steyn, Van der Walt & Van Loggerenberg (2003).

5. Ibid.

6. Ibid., p. 6.

7. Request no. 0014/ARM/2005.

8. Request no. 0015/ARM/2005.

9. Correspondence from T.T. Goduka, deputy information officer, Armscor, to SAHA, 13 March 2005 (including as attachments affidavits from the author and Gideon Smith, general manager: acquisition, Armscor).

10. L.J. van der Westhuizen & J.H. le Roux, 1997, *A Will to Win*, Bloemfontein: Institute for Contemporary History, University of the Orange Free State, p. 174.

11. Van der Westhuizen & Le Roux (1997, p. 175).

12. Steyn, Van der Walt & Van Loggerenberg (2003, p. 43).

13. The reference is to AS: Minutes Archive Group, file 1/7/1/142, memorandum no. 18 re Project Mantel, dated 2/10/1990, in Van der Westhuizen & Le Roux (1977, p. 181).

14. Liberman (2001, p. 49).

15. Author's interview with Andre Buys, former general manager of Armscor's Circle nuclear weapons plant, University of Pretoria, 14 August 2006.

16. Van der Westhuizen & Le Roux (1997, pp. 171–84; made available to the public).

17. In particular, detailed information is provided by David Albright, 1994b, *South Africa's Secret Nuclear Weapons*, Institute for Science and International Security report, May, <http://www.isis-online.org/publications/southafrica/ir0594.html>.

18. According to Buys during an interview with the author, University of Pretoria, 14 August 2006.

19. Author's interview with Andre Buys, University of Pretoria, 14 August 2006.

20. Fischer (1994, pp. 215–16).

21. Ibid.

22. Request no. 0027/DOD/2003.

23. Request no. 0029/DOD/2003.

24. Request no. 0032/PRE/2003.

25. Memorandum from the chief of staff, SADF, to the chief of the SADF, SADF document no. HS/11/4/34, 'The Jericho weapon system', 21 March 1975.

26. Ibid.

27. Ibid.

28. Liberman (2001, pp. 56–57).

29. 'Bonn's capital share and influence in the nuclear co-operation with South Africa', *Sechaba*, November/December 1975.

30. 'Foreign countries helped SA develop nuclear arms', *The Citizen*, 25 March 1993.

31. Paul Stober, 'De Klerk's three nuclear lies', *Weekly Mail & Guardian*, 11–17 February 1994.

32. Tim Kennedy, 1995, 'As South Africa integrates, Israel cutting military ties', *Washington Report on Middle East Affairs*, July/August: 31, <http://www.washington-report.org/backissues/0795/9507031.htm>.

33. Request no. 0022/DFA/2003.

34. Request no. 0044/DFA/2003.

35. Affidavit of Johan Kellerman attached to correspondence from D. Moerane-Khoza, deputy information officer, DFA to SAHA, 21 July 2003.

36. Uri Machamai, 1989, 'Israel and South Africa have carried out nuclear tests in the region of the South Pole', *Yediot Ahronot*, 4 October.

37. Request no. 0028/DTI/2003.

38. Request no. 0037/DTI/2003.

39. Request no. 0038/DTI/2003.

40. Request no. 0036/DOD/2003.

41. Request no. 0042/DOD/2003.

42. Request no. 0026/DOD/2005.

43. Correspondence from the minister of defence to SAHA, 29 October 2004.

44. Minutes of the meeting between SAHA and DOD, 19 May 2006.

45. This request will be discussed again in chapter 6.

46. This issue will be discussed further in chapter 5.

47. Request no. 0040/ARM/2003.

48. Request no. 0041/ARM/2003.

49. Request no. 0054/ARM/2003.

50. Agence France Presse, 'Israel helped SA develop N-arms', *Arab News*, 21 April 1997.

51. Request no. 0026/ARM/2003, for 'Records pertaining to nuclear bombs or weapons constructed. This includes, but is not limited to, inventory and other trackings as well as correspondence (re said devices)'; request no. 0054/ARM/2003, for 'Records related to Jericho Missile'; request no. 0055/ARM/2003, for 'Records relating to mid-range missiles and nuclear weapons'.

52. Request no. 0033/NEC/2003, for 'Report: A brief overview of the development of nuclear explosive devices in South Africa'.

53. Request no. 0031/DOD/2003, for 'Records relating to modifications on Canberra bombers or other devices for the purposes of carrying South African nuclear weapons'.

54. Request no. 0035/DEN/2003, for 'Records pertaining to nuclear bombs, weapons and devices constructed. Includes but is not limited to: inventory and other tracking as well as correspondence (re said devices)'.

55. This explains why, at the time of the termination of the programme, there were only six devices.

56. Von Williegh (1993, p. 3).

57. Steyn, Van der Walt & Van Loggerenberg (2003, p. 42).

58. Ibid.

59. Request no. 0044/DFA/2003.

60. Request no. 0016/ARM/2005.

61. Request no. 0076/NEC/2005.

62. Anita Allen, 'South Africa's nuclear reaction', *Saturday Star*, 6 March 1993, pp. 10, 11.

63. Kathy DeLucas, 'Blast from the past: Los Alamos scientists receive vindication', Los Alamos press release, 11 July 1997, <http://www.fas.org/news/safrica/97-087.html>.

64. Request no. 0021/DFA/2003.

65. Request no. 0024/DFA/2003.

66. Request no. 0022/DFA/2003.

67. Fischer (1994, pp. 216–17).

68. Author's interview with Professor Andre Buys, University of Pretoria, 14 August 2006.

69. Fischer (1994, p. 219).

70. 'Why South Africa gave up the nuclear option', speech by Ambassador Mackerdhuj to the Second UN Conference: Towards a World Free from Nuclear Weapons, Nagasaki, Japan, 1995.

71. Request no. 0046/NEC/2003; request no. 0056/ARM/2003; request no. 0077/NEC/2005; request no. 0066/DEN/2003.

72. Request no. 0023/DFA/2003.

73. Request no. 0066/DEN/2003; request no. 0018/ARM/2005; request no. 0025/DOD/2005; request no. 0075/NEC/2005; request no. 0077/NEC/2005.

Chapter 5

1. Mikki van Zyl, Jeanelle de Gruchy, Sheila Lapinsky, Simon Lewin & Graeme Reid, 1999, *The aVersion Project: Human Rights Abuses of Gays and Lesbians in the SADF by Health Workers during the Apartheid Era*, report, Cape Town: Gay and Lesbian Archives, Health and Human Rights Project, Medical Research Council, National Coalition for Gay and Lesbian Equality, October, interview IV, trans. by Mikki van Zyl.

2. SAHA (South African History Archive), 2002, *SAHA Annual Report 2002*, Johannesburg: SAHA.

3. Anonymous, 1986/87, 'The abuse of psychiatry in the SADF: "I am first a soldier and then a psychiatrist"', *War Resister*, 47, December–January: 11.

4. Vol. 47 of *War Resister* was where the initial information surfaced, but all editions of this publication offer insights into the brutality conscripts faced, if not from superior officers, then from their fellow conscripts who were encouraged to act out the most extreme ill treatment of 'weaker' conscripts and black South Africans. Copies of *War Resister* can be found in the Committee on South African War Resistance (COSAWR) archive BC 1005, M3 Resister 1–67 (Journal of COSAWR) based at the University of Cape Town Archives. See also Van Zyl et al. (1999, pp. 31–32) and the original *War Resister* publications in the COSAWR collection.

5. Bill Frost (ed.), n.d., *Behavioral Psychology: History, Techniques and the Role of Hypnotherapy*, last modified 31 December 2004, <http://freespace.virgin.net/changing states/behavioural_approaches.html>.

6. Apart from hearings at which individuals would present their accounts of abuse, the TRC had what was referred to as institutional or sector hearings. The health sector hearing was the first and was held over two days, 17–18 June 1997.

7. Health and Human Rights Projects, 1997, 'Professional accountability in South Africa', final submission to the TRC, prepared for the hearings on the health sector, June, p. 1.

8. For personal accounts of treatment meted out to homosexuals at this time, see Van Zyl et al. (1999). Also, for initial documentation, see GALA (Gay and Lesbian Archive)/SAHA (South African History Archive), 2003, *Gays in the Apartheid Military*, report, Johannesburg, September, <http://www.saha.org.za/research/publications/FOIP_6_3.pdf>.

9. After the first democratic elections in South Africa, the SADF became the SANDF.

10. A particular drawback of the TRC was that many institutions called upon to make presentations were in the process of transformation. This affected the input in several ways. New personnel could not be expected to respond to allegations of human rights abuses that took place during apartheid, when they were the enemy, so to speak. So SAMS personnel presenting at the TRC saw themselves as being part of the new defence force, the SANDF, instead of the old defence force, the SADF.

11. TRC (Truth and Reconciliation Commission), 1997, Human Rights Violations, Health Sector Hearings, Cape Town, 17 June, transcript, <http://www.doj.gov.za/trc/special/health/health01.htm>.

12. Ibid.

13. Ibid.

14. TRC (1998, vol. 4, chap. 5, 'Institutional hearing: The health sector').

15. Ibid., para. 43, p. 125.

16. Ibid., para. 147, p. 157.

17. Ibid., para. 149, p. 157.

18. Van Zyl et al. (1999).

19. Ibid., interview IV, pp. 1–2.

20. Michael King, Glenn Smith & Annie Bartlett, 2004, 'Treatments of homosexuality in Britain since the 1950s – an oral history: The experience of professionals', *British Medical Journal*, 328: 429.

21. Anonymous (1986/87).

22. See SAHA's inventory of materials released under PAIA, ref. AL2878, sec. B1.1.

23. SAHA's records were assembled in terms of its mandate to document the struggles for justice in South Africa, particularly in relation to apartheid.

24. There are numerous publications on South Africa's militarisation, but a rounded and thorough exposition can be found in Jacklyn Cock & Laurie Nathan (eds), 1989, *War and Society: The Militarisation of South Africa*, Cape Town: David Philip.

25. DOD, n.d., *PAIA Manual*, Pretoria: DOD.

26. Michel Pickover & Verne Harris, 2001, 'Freedom of information in South Africa: A far off reality?', May, <http://www.saha.org.za/research/publications/FOIP_1_4_PickoverHarris.pdf>.

27. A battery of legislation, including the Defence Act, the Internal Security Act, the National Key Points Act and the Protection of Information Act contributed to the overwhelming secrecy that led to classification of many records. See Benita Whitcher, 2003, *The Anti-censorship Programme: Opinion on Legislation Affecting Freedom of Expression in South Africa*, Freedom of Expression Institute report, <http://www.fxi.org.za/PDF's/ACP/Annexure+1+Main+Report1.pdf> for an up-to-date look at some of this legislation, which is still on the statute books. The Protection of Information Act is currently under review.

28. SAHA believes that resources should be made available to declassify records proactively, i.e. not just when requests are made. However, the DOD archives budget does not allow for this.

29. There was a hiccup that is discussed in detail below regarding a request for perusal that turned out to be a costly exercise.

30. My notes for the *SAHA Annual Report 2004* record: 'Limited staff are available to undertake the declassification of records requested, meaning long waits between the request and the release of the records. Although it is encouraging to know that researchers are making considerable use of PAIA, it is also disheartening to be told that our requests are 24th in line and that it will take months for them to be released!' (SAHA [South African History Archive], 2004, *SAHA Annual Report 2004*, Johannesburg: SAHA, <http://www.saha.org.za/research/publications/SAHA_ann_rep_2004.pdf>).

31. For a more detailed report on the response at this time see Verne Harris, 2001, *Freedom of Information Watch*, SAHA report, October, <http://www.saha.org.za/research.htm>.

32. PAIA, sec. 45.

33. See GALA/SAHA (2003, Appendix 2).

34. Request no. 0006/DOD/2001.

35. Some of these documents were copied and are housed at the archive. See SAHA, ref. B1.2.3.1.3. Also see GALA/SAHA (2003, Appendices 2 & 4).

36. See GALA/SAHA (2003, Appendix 2).

37. P.W. Botha was minister of defence before he became the prime minister in the period 1978–83, then state president.

38. The total was 4,100 pages, to be exact: copying cost ZAR 2,460 and search and preparation ZAR 2,115. Implementation problems were noted in SAHA (South African History Archive) & Public Service Accountability Monitor, 2003, 'Proposed amendments to the Promotion of Access to Information Act: A

joint submission by the South African History Archive and the Public Service Accountability Monitor', August, <http://www.saha.org.za/research/publications/FOIP_3_1.pdf>, which covered the reluctance to sever exempt material from documents requested and to provide the remainder of the documents with exempt parts masked, and the inordinate complexity and cost of enforcing compliance.

39. The Protection of Personal Information Draft Bill suggests that section 34 will have to be revised. For a more detailed examination of the need to harmonise PAIA and legislation on the protection of personal information, see Mandela House/SAHA (South African History Archive), 2006, *Report on a Workshop on the Protection of Personal Information Draft Bill, Mandela House, 13 May 2006*, Johannesburg: Mandela House/SAHA, 29 May, < http://www.saha.org.za/research/publications/FOIP_4_3.pdf>.

40. Black Sash file no. T1/204.

41. Copies of these directives are held by SAHA:

- A1.10 SADF policy file: discipline: homosexuality/lesbianism (1982–83);

- A1.11 SADF correspondence file: promiscuity: homosexuality (1986);

- A1.12 SADF correspondence file: discipline: promiscuity: homosexuality (1986);

- A1.13 SADF correspondence file: discipline: promiscuity: homosexuality (1982–83);

- A1.14 SADF policy: discipline: promiscuity: homosexuality, headquarters: South African National Defence Force policy directive (1983).

42. For example, MV-B 62/1, group 2, box 60, 27/01/67–29/09/71, 'Personeel beserings' contains records on the Medical Board, pensionable disabilities, and referrals to the Department of Social Welfare and Pensions and the Military Pension Board.

43. Although not part of the current brief, an analysis of the requests for exemptions and postponements could provide insight into how decisions were generally made on these issues. Difficulties in matching the applications with the response because of masking could, however, be an obstacle.

44. After 1994, the northern Transvaal became the Northern Province and, more recently, Limpopo province.

45. Van Zyl et al. (1999, Appendix G: Reprint *War Resister*, 47, pp. 131–32).

46. Section 34(1) provides for the mandatory protection of privacy of a third party who is a natural person.

47. This request is discussed in more detail in chapter 6.

48. SAHA ref A1.1 (529G/TRG/1), 'Opleidings, voorskrifte en instruksies Greefswald'.

49. Aubrey Levin,1975, "'n Ontleiding van die gebruik van dwelmmiddels en sekere gevolge daarvan met klem op cannabis sativa by 'n monster jongmans opgeroep vir militiere diensplig' (An analysis of the use of drugs and certain sequelae thereof with emphasis on cannabis sativa, in a sample of young men conscripted for military service), DM thesis, University of Pretoria.

50. Levin also confirms this in his evidence to the TRC.

51. Greefswald file no. 3MH/104/10/14/1/1, housed at SAHA: Ref A1.1 (529G/TRG/1), 'Opleidings, voorskrifte en instruksies Greefswald'.

52. This was probably around the time that the official memos on homosexuality began circulating.

53. <http://dme.gov.za/publications/pdf/guidelines/miss.pdf>. According to a parliamentary media briefing of

the Justice, Crime Prevention and Security Cluster in February 2006, the envisaged replacement of this document with the National Information Security Regulations (NISR) is currently being addressed. The NISR derives its legitimacy from the National Security Intelligence Act. See also Verne Harris, 'Sex, spies and psychotherapy', *Natal Witness*, 17 June 2002.

54. SADF memo, 'Policy directive on homosexuality', H SAW/1/13/82, available at SAHA, special projects A1 Gays in the Apartheid Military, A1.5.

55. MVB, group 2, box 61, vol. 2, 21/2/72–27/6/74, 'Rade: Wenke en uitvindings'. A copy of this file can be accessed at SAHA.

56. Ibid.

57. MVB MV42/11, group 2, box 48, 'SAW: Burgermag 12/3/69–15/5/70, Beserings en eise teen opsigte van lede van die burgermag'.

58. MV/42/3, vol. 13, 23/12/74–8/7/74, 'Administrasie: Navrae en klagte'.

59. MVB, group 2, box 46, vol. 6, 26/4/71–1/7/71, 'SAW: Burger mag: Aansoek om vrystelling en uitstel van diensplig'. This is a thick file consisting mainly of applications for exemption, the vast majority of which were unsuccessful. Levin, the surgeon general and a Dr Beyers interviewed a conscript's mother regarding an exemption on the basis of medical fitness. It reflects a degree of insensitivity in the response, but otherwise says very little. It was a case that had been taken up by MP J.A.L. Basson.

60. See KD/328/2/1, box 42, vol. 1, 'Sielkundige operasies binneland'. Documents in this file illustrate clearly how involved the institution of chaplain general was in the army's objectives. The purpose of the Sielkundige (psychological) Action Committee includes: collecting information and research to do with psychological action and the threats through the church in South Africa; the initiating, implementing and coordinating of psychological action projects; and implementing and coordinating performance of the recommendations of the committee.

61. One letter from chaplain general to the Cultural Action Committee talks of how important it is to stress the 'service of God' (KD/305/5/3/4/1, box 21, vol. 1, 'Totale nasionale strategiese beplanning').

62. Two files were not declassified, but may yet become available, as they first need to be masked.

63. Peter Moll, 1984, 'A theological critique of the military chaplaincy of the English-speaking churches', M.A. thesis University of Cape Town, interview with army chaplain John Anderson, Mayibuya Centre, reference MCH274.

64. KD 203/4/9504 is a valuable file. One example of such a warning is MI/TF/203/4/9504, 9/05/78.

65. KD/203/4/9504, vols. 1, 2 & 3, 21/3/78–24/12/79, 29/1/80–23/1/81 contain correspondence from the head of the army providing the chaplain general with military intelligence information on anti-conscription groups. The literature of these groups (mostly translated into Afrikaans) is included, as is information on churches and their decisions around the issue.

66. KD/102/6/1/1/2, 12/09/77–22/12/82, 'Aanstelling met kommissierang'.

67. The NGK was often referred to as the Nationalist Party at prayer. It propagated the theology that apartheid was the will of God. Despite army chaplains from other denominations serving in the SADF, this pro-apartheid theology was obviously central in its chaplaincy.

68. Files in the SAHA collection under B Non-project records B1.1.2.3.1.1.11, End Conscription Campaign, vol. 9, 1985–86; B1.1.2.3.1.1.5, End Conscription Campaign, vol. 17, 1984–86.

69. MWB MV/61/4, group 2, box 87, 12/2/67–29/5/72, 'Opleiding: Gewetensbesware'.

70. KD521/3/1/2/9, 1/5/77–6/10/77, 'Kommitees, kommissies en rade deur H SAW angetstel: Notules and sakelyste: SAW personeel adviesraad'.

71. GG/104/10/1B GG/521/3/1/2/8. Interestingly enough, this document did not turn up in the surgeon general files we requested

72. T1/202/2/3B.

73. Legally this was true. It was only in 1998 that the common law crimes of sodomy, unnatural sexual offences and section 20A of the Sexual Offences Act were struck down. Later in the same year, the Constitutional Court declared that laws that criminalised sex between men were unconstitutional.

74. HSP/S/521/3/1/2/9.

75. The document did not explain why they were a security risk or how the issue was linked to Jehovah's Witnesses. Homosexuals were considered a security risk because it was against the law to be a practising homosexual: perhaps if the enemy were aware of your sexual orientation they could use blackmail to gain information by threatening to expose this sexual orientation.

76. 'Item 14 (confidential) – treatment of homosexuals in the SADF'.

Chapter 6

1. SAHA requested 'lists of military intelligence records in the custody of the SADF (South African Defence Force) archives (described as groups 14, 21 and 30 in the published TRC Final Report, Volume 1, page 232)'. It was granted access to the three lists requested; however, at a subsequent meeting the SADF informed SAHA that there were in fact 41 lists in total.

2. Evidence wa ka Ngobenei, 'Army file shock for the TRC', *Mail & Guardian*, 12–18 October 2001.

3. Evidence wa ka Ngobenei, 'Lekota to probe what is fact and fiction', *Mail & Guardian*, 19–25 October 2001.

4. Minister of Defence Mosiuoa Lekota announced to the media that a full enquiry into assertions that the military had sabotaged the TRC's inquiries would be launched; the 'inquiry' was never reported on again.

5. Request no. 0083/YSK/2002.

6. ODAC (Open Democracy Advice Centre), 2005, *ODAC Annual Report 2005*, <http://www.opendemocracy. org.za/documents/AnnualReport2005.doc>.

7. *Mittalsteel South Africa Ltd (formerly Iscor Ltd) v Hlatshwayo 2007 (1) SA 66 (SCA) and Mittal Steel South Africa Ltd v Hlatshwayo [2006] SCA 94 (RSA).*

8. Request nos. 0034–0036/BOS/2007.

9. It was later confirmed through company searches at the Companies and Intellectual Property Registration Office and information provided pursuant to requests submitted to the South African Human Rights Commission (0091/HRC/2007) that Leading Prospect Trading was a wholly owned subsidiary of Bosasa and operated from the same address.

10. Section 8(1) of PAIA states that:

For the purposes of this Act, a public body referred to in paragraph (b)(ii) of the definition of 'public body' in section 1, or a private body,

> i) may be either a public body or a private body in relation to a record of that body; and

> ii) may in one instance be a public body and in another instance be a private body, depending on whether that record relates to the exercise of a power or performance of a function as a public body or as a private body.

11. Letter from Bosasa Operations (Pty) Ltd to SAHA, 25 October 2007.

12. Section 50 of PAIA provides that a requester must be given access to any record of a private body if that record is required for the exercise or protection of any rights.

13. See *Clutcho (Pty) Ltd v Andrew Christopher Davis 2005 (3) SA 486 (SCA)* and *Unitas Hospital v Maria Magdalena van Wyk 2006 SCA 32 (RSA)*.

14. I. Currie & J. Klaaren, 2002, *The Resolve: KPMG Commentary on the Promotion of Access to Information Act*, Cape Town: Siber Ink, pp. 99–105.

15. Ibid.

16. PAIA, sec. 34(1).

17. PAIA, sec. 38(1). The section also goes on to state that access may be refused where disclosure would impair or prejudice the security of, for example, buildings, computer systems, transport or any other property, or any methods, systems, plans or procedures for the protection of an individual in a witness protection scheme, the safety of the public or the security of property. There are no exceptions to the exemption.

18. PAIA, secs. 47–49.

19. The exceptions are contained in section 34(2).

20. Request no. 0002/DOJ/2005.

21. The definition of personal information in section 1 excludes information about an individual who has been deceased for more than 20 years.

22. Request no. 0028/DOJ/2006. The request was for access to the TRC victims database.

23. *Campbell v MGN [2004] UKHL 22.*

24. See <http://news.bbc.co.uk/1/hi/world/europe/5205280.stm> and <http://www.novinite.com/view_news.php?id+72601>.

25. PAIA, sec. 37(1).

26. PAIA, sec. 37(2).

27. Sections 28 and 29 of the TRC Act specifically provided that, as a general rule, no article or information collected by the TRC investigators or the TRC itself in connection with a hearing should be made public. However, in terms of sections 28(5) and 29(5), the production of any article or the furnishing of any document during a public TRC hearing removed the blanket confidentiality previously conferred by the TRC Act. Such documents were considered to have been made public.

28. The capacity of the National Prosecuting Authority to prosecute and therefore to require further information will be discussed further when considering the exemption relating to ongoing prosecutions.

29. See Currie & Klaaren (2002, p. 56) for a discussion of this point.

30. Case no. 137/96, High Court of South Africa, Durban and Local Coast Division.

31. While there is a 20-year limitation on information that may prejudice international relations, there is no such expiration period in relation to contracts between states.

32. PAIA, sec. 39.

33. The Truth and Reconciliation Commission: Ten Years On, conference held by the Institute for Justice and Reconciliation, Cape Town, 20–21 April 2006.

34. Eugene de Kock raised in excess of 60 incidents.

35. NPA (National Prosecuting Authority), 'Prosecuting policy and directives relating to the prosecution of offences emanating from conflicts of the past and which were committed on or before 11 May 1994', Annexure A, effective 1 December 2005.

36. The constitutionality of the policy is being challenged by the Centre for the Study of Violence and Reconciliation and a number of other individuals who were victims of apartheid conflicts. The proceedings were launched in July 2007: *Nkadimeng & Others v The National Director of Public Prosecutions and Others*, case no. 32709/07, High Court of South Africa, Transvaal Provincial Division. The High Court awarded in favour of the applicants on 12 December 2008. The National Director of Public Prosecutions and the Minister of Justice has sought leave to appeal. At the time of writing their application was pending.

37. Currie & Klaaren (2002, p. 165).

38. PAIA, sec. 41.

39. Letter from the minister of arts and culture, 11 October 2002. The minister stated that her decision was based on sections 41(1)(a) and 44(1)(a) and (b) of PAIA.

40. Agreement dated 30 April 2003.

41. PAIA, sec. 41(1)(a)(i). They were also refused on the basis that they contained personal information of third parties (PAIA, sec. 34).

42. PAIA, sec. 41(2)(a).

43. PAIA, secs. 41(1)(a)(i) and (ii); request no. 0001/DOD/2002.

44. 'Court action on military intelligence records', *SAHA Update*, 6 August 2002.

45. PAIA, secs. 38(a) and 41(2)(f).

46. PAIA, secs. 41(1)(a)(i) and 41(2)(a). This exemption is a mandatory provision based on content alone; if the information discloses military tactics, it is presumed that its disclosure will cause prejudice; see Currie & Klaaren (2002, p. 175).

47. PAIA, secs. 41(1)(a)(i) and 41(2)(d).

48. *The South African History Archive v the Minister of Defence*, case no. 5109/06, High Court of South Africa, Transvaal Provincial Division.

49. The exemption is too detailed to provide a comprehensive overview here. Please see PAIA, sec. 42.

50. Request nos. 0018–0019/ESK/2004.

51. PAIA, sec. 42.

52. Request no. 0088/ESK/2005.

53. Macroeconomics, by definition, implies a study of 'the part of economics concerned with large-scale or general economic factors, such as interest rates and national productivity', as opposed to microeconomics, which is 'the part of economics concerned with single factors and the effects of individual decisions' (*The Concise Oxford Dictionary*, tenth edition, 2001).

54. In particular, it argued that PAIA and the Promotion of Administrative Justice Act No. 3 of 2000 compelled disclosure, relying upon a court ruling that the environmental assessment procedures for approval of the pebble bed modular reactor were flawed because the public was not provided with sufficient information about the reasons for the decision to enable it to properly comment prior to the decision being made. See *Earthlife Africa (Cape Town) v Director General of the Department of Environmental Affairs and Tourism and Eskom Holdings Ltd*, case no. 7653/03, High Court of South Africa, Cape of Good Hope Provincial Division.

55. See Currie & Klaaren (2002, p. 140) for a discussion of this point. Currie and Klaaren argue that the broad scope of the term requires a 'robust' application of the limb requiring harm.

56. *Earthlife Africa v Eskom Holdings Ltd*, case no. 27514/04, High Court of South Africa, Witwatersrand Local Division.

57. Request nos. 0024–0029/SAB/2004.

58. Currie & Klaaren (2002, p. 181).

59. Request no. 0017/DHA/2007.

60. See PAIA, sec. 1.

61. Currie & Klaaren (2002, p. 185).

62. Ibid.

63. At the time of writing, this and other DHA requests were to be pursued in the High Court. When SAHA indicated its intention to appeal this and other matters in the High Court, the DHA started releasing records in a piecemeal fashion.

64. Letter from Ms Raswiswi, DOJ, to SAHA, 21 December 2006, regarding request number 0060/DOJ/2006 (DOJ reference number 7/6/9 Allan K [9]).

65. Request no. 0008/DOD/2001.

66. DOD did, however, continue to mask the names of individuals who were connected to ongoing projects.

67. These can be found at <http://www.sahrc.org.za>.

68. In 2005/06 the following bodies reported applying the override: DHA (3), Limpopo Department of Health and Social Development (15) and City of Johannesburg (2); in 2004/05: Department of Public Works (1) and Department of Water Affairs and Forestry (1); in 2003/04: DHA (2), Limpopo Department of Health and Social Development (1), Gauteng Gambling Board (1) and Armscor (9); in 2002/03: Department of Labour (14), Department of Water Affairs and Forestry (2), Free State Department of Public Works, Roads and Transport (1), North West Department of Roads and Public Works (1), City of Cape Town Administration (1) and Eskom (1).

69. In arguing as such, it has relied on *Minister of Land Affairs v Slamdien (1999) 4 BCLR 413 (LCC)*, para.

13 and *S v Makwanyane (1995) 3 SA 391 (CC)*, paras. 100–9 and 132–34.

70. Greefswald Works Committee, GG521/3/5/2/2, January–November 1977.

71. Request no. 0100/NAR/2003.

72. Request no. 0240/NAR/2005.

73. PAIA, sec. 74.

74. PAIA, sec. 78.

75. See sec. 182 of the Constitution of the Republic of South Africa, Act No. 108 of 1996, and sec. 6 of the Public Protector Act No. 23 of 1994.

76. See PAIA, part 5.

77. In 2005 SAHA submitted a complaint to the SAHRC regarding the failure of NECSA to respond to requests; however, despite a meeting with the SAHRC in October 2005, the commission did not contact SAHA regarding the complaint until January 2007, at which time it simply attached a letter from NECSA and asked for a response. When SAHA rejected NECSA's version of events, SAHRC failed to take the matter further. Similarly, upon a complaint regarding DOD, SAHRC wrote to the minister, but failed to pursue a response or participate in the litigation that SAHA ultimately commenced. It also failed to become involved in two other cases referred to it: Richard Young's litigation regarding the arms deal (request no. 0083/YSK/2002) and SAHA's case against DOJ and the National Archives regarding access to the 34 boxes of sensitive TRC materials.

78. SAHA also submitted the SAHRC complaint regarding NECSA to the public protector, who requested an explanation from NECSA and, in response, NECSA merely reiterated a conversation that had taken place at a meeting. The public protector took no steps following SAHA's response that set out the multiple failures to comply with not only NECSA's own guarantees in relation to medical record requests, but with requests for non-medical records, some of which had been outstanding for over two years.

79. It appears that the public protector determined to investigate the matter, but then referred it to SAHRC following receipt of SAHA's letter disputing NECSA's version of events and requesting that he take further steps. There was a delay of one year, however, between the public protector's and the SAHRC's correspondence to SAHA.

80. SAHRC (South African Human Rights Commission), 2003/2004/2005, *South African Human Rights Commission Annual Report* for 2002/2003, 2003/2004 and 2004/2005.

81. PAIA, sec. 83(3)(d).

82. Section 83(2) of the Act states that the commission 'must, to the extent that financial and other resources are available', conduct education programmes. It goes on in section 82(3) to state that the commission 'may, if reasonably possible, on request, assist any person wishing to exercise a right contemplated in this Act'.

83. PAIA, sec. 83(5).

84. It must be noted that, for the first time, the SAHRC has indicated its willingness to litigate or intervene as *amicus curiae* in litigation in response to a comprehensive complaint about DOJ, and has at the time of writing requested that the department first provide a response to the complaint.

85. The distinction between types of public bodies further limits the efficacy of appeal mechanisms. Internal appeals cannot be submitted to type (b) public bodies. Accordingly, requesters refused in the first instance

are required to proceed directly to litigation. This has been a considerable barrier in the nuclear energy project, where the majority of bodies were type (b) bodies.

86. *Biowatch v The Director of Genetic Resources and others*, case no. 25005/2, High Court of South Africa, Transvaal Provincial Division.

87. PAIA does not impose penalties that would deter such conduct. Any penalty orders would be at the discretion of the court, requiring the requester to first get to a hearing and decision, obtain a favourable order, and argue that there is sufficient reason for the imposition of a penalty order in addition to the granting of costs.

88. At the time of writing, one matter was pending: *SAHA v Minister of Defence and others*, case no. 5109/06, High Court of South Africa, Transvaal Provincial Division.

89. The case against DOJ for access to records of the TRC hearings relating to the murder of the Cradock 4 was settled five minutes prior to the hearing commencing; see chapter 2.

90. In the Cradock 4 case, SAHA sought access to amnesty applications discussed in public hearings that had lost their confidential status under the Promotion of National Unity and Reconciliation Act. Amnesty applications such as these were granted in the 34 boxes case. Following settlement, SAHA submitted a request for access to Eugene de Kock's amnesty application, only to be refused at first instance and on appeal, despite having been granted a portion of it in the Cradock 4 case and despite the fact that most of the application has lost its confidential status through public hearings.

91. SAHA has had the benefit of pro bono assistance in many of its cases and has been granted costs pursuant to settlement agreements in all cases; however, the expenditure of SAHA's resources and the time of its staff are not compensable.

92. There have been a number of cases taken up by other independent requesters and organisations, such as the Open Democracy Advice Centre and Biowatch, which have progressed to judgment. Irrespective of the success of the requesters in these cases, some of which have provided useful guidance on issues such as the distinction between public and private bodies and the right of access to information of private bodies, they have not necessarily provided interpretation of frequently utilised exemptions such as those relating to privacy and confidentiality. A key case that is likely to provide some useful guidance is currently on appeal in the Supreme Court from a flawed judgment of the High Court, i.e. *Earthlife Africa v Eskom Holdings Ltd,* case no. 27514/04, High Court of South Africa, Witwatersrand Local Division.

93. As were the portions of the Bill dealing with issues other than access to information (although whistle-blowing legislation was later enacted).

94. PAIA also required the submission of statistics to the SAHRC regarding requests. The aim behind the publication of statistics compiled by public and private bodies concerning requests received and granted, as a method of passive enforcement, was not achieved due to the limited availability of resources for compiling statistics and therefore the small number of bodies that submitted them. While such methods can be of value in jurisdictions with entrenched democracies and cultures of transparency, such as Canada, in emerging and somewhat fragile democracies such as South Africa they are insufficient.

95. RULA (Research Unit for Law and Administration) & SAHA (South African History Archive), 2002, *Proposed Amendments to the Promotion of Access to Information (PAIA): Report on a Workshop Convened at the University of the Witwatersrand, 4 October 2002*, <http://www.saha.org.za/research/publications/FOIP_3_2.pdf>.

96. Parliament of the Republic of South Africa, (2007).

97. Verne Harris & Christopher Merrett, 2007, 'Toward a culture of transparency: Public rights of access to official records in South Africa', in Verne Harris, *Archives and Justice: A South African Perspective*, Chicago: Society of American Archivists, p. 271.

98. Ibid., p. 279.

99. Ibid.

100. NASRA, secs. 5(2)(d) and 11(2)(c), respectively.

101. Request no. 0013/NAR/2001.

102. Letter from national archivist to SAHA, 6 December 2001.

103. Request no. 0054/NAR/2004.

104. Letter from SAHA to national archivist, 14 July 2003.

105. Letter from national archivist to SAHA, 1 August 2003.

106. Section 1 of PAIA defines public bodies as:

   (a) any department of state or administration in the national or provincial sphere of government or any municipality in the local sphere of government; or

   (b) any other functionary or institution when-

   (i) exercising a power or performing a duty in terms of the Constitution or a provincial constitution; or

   (ii) exercising a public power or performing a public function in terms of any legislation.

107. The national archivist subsequently verbally informed the former director of SAHA, Verne Harris, that he had been designated an information officer rather than a deputy information officer, which means that he reports directly to the minister of arts and culture in regard to PAIA. The only regulation that has been issued in this regard relates to the Office of the Auditor General: see 'Promotion of Access to Information Act: Public body determined by part of another public body: Office of the Auditor General', *Gazette* 25100, *Regulation Gazette* 7692, 20 June 2003.

108. Letter from SAPS to SAHA, 4 October 2007.

109. Correspondence to National Archives from SAHA, 9 October 2002.

110. Correspondence from National Archives to SAHA, 25 November 2002.

111. Verne Harris, 2007a, '"They should have destroyed more": The destruction of public records by the South African state in the final years of apartheid, 1990–1994', in Verne Harris, *Archives and Justice: A South African Perspective*, Chicago: Society of American Archivists.

112. The Protected Disclosures Act No. 26 of 2000 provides a limited mechanism for employees to blow the whistle. A discussion of its impact and intersection is beyond the scope of this chapter. For further reading, see J. Klaaren, 2002, *The Gap Report: Issues regarding Disclosure of Information by Public Officials*, June, <http://www.saha.org.za/research/publications/FOIP_2_4_Klaaren.pdf>, accessed 27 September 2007.

113. Request nos. 0021/NAR/2001, 0022/NAR/2001 and 0047/NAR/2002.

114. These exemptions aim to protect confidential agreements or undertakings of confidentiality and protection of persons or state property. The SANDF similarly refused access to records on the grounds that they were classified. After SAHA submitted an appeal on the basis that PAIA does not recognise the fact

of classification as a legitimate reason for refusing access and that records classification is effected in terms of the Protection of Information Act, which is subordinate to PAIA, and after several discussions with SANDF, the latter agreed that the refusals must be grounded in the exemptions contained in PAIA rather than classifications. See Verne Harris, 2003, *Promotion of Access to Information Act: The Case of the South African History Archive*, January, <http://www.saha.org.za/research/publications/FOIP_update_jan2003.pdf>.

115. Klaaren (2002).

116. Ibid., p. 5.

117. 'SAHA submission to the Classification and Declassification Review Committee', 23 April 2003. See also the submissions of the South Africa Democracy Education Trust Regional Committee, Western Cape, undated; the late Dr John Seiler, dated 24 April 2004; and the National Security Archive (Washington, DC).

118. The National Security Archive is a non-government archive based in Washington, DC at the George Washington University.

119. Verne Harris, Sello Hatang & Peter Liberman, 2004, 'Unveiling South Africa's nuclear past', *Journal of Southern African Studies*, 30(3): 16.

120. See <http://www.intelligence.gov.za/Ministerial%20Review%20Commission/index.asp>, accessed 27 September 2007. The commission has not yet published a final report.

121. See TRC Act, secs. 19 and 33.

122. *Forbes & SAHA v The Minister of Justice and the National Archives of South Africa*, case no. 17095/05, High Court of South Africa, Transvaal Provincial Division.

123. In a request for records of *in-camera* hearings (no. 0030/DOJ/2006), SAHA argued on internal appeal that a number of testimonies were in fact aired in later public hearings and therefore no longer attract confidentiality.

124. A determination made in the Durban High Court regarding the attempted use of section 29 of the TRC Act to prevent the disclosure of the testimony of Joseph Mamasela found that the Act did not contemplate the exercise of blanket restrictions on access by the TRC, but that it should be read to ensure openness and transparency in dealing with past violations, in conjunction with ensuring that the rights of accused persons to fair trials are not contravened (*The State v Dirk Coetzee and five others*, case no. 137/96, High Court of South Africa, Durban and Local Coast Division). See the discussion regarding the confidentiality exemption for more information.

125. Request no. 0017/DFA/2007 for the 2003 and 2004 reports, and no. 0001/NCA/2007 for the 2005 report.

126. Ultimately, access without redaction was granted to the joint 2003/04 report, and at the time of writing the 2005 report had not yet been presented to Parliament and was therefore not available.

127. The State Archives Service was the national archives repository until 1996. It became the National Archives and Records Service of South Africa with the advent of the National Archives and Records Service Act No. 43 of 1996.

128. TRC (1998, vol. 1, chap. 8, para. 84).

129. Comprising the National Security Management System, the National Intelligence Service (formerly the Bureau of State Security and currently NIA), the security police and the SADF.

130. Harris (2007a).

131. Ibid.

132. Ibid.

133. Ibid. See also TRC (1998, vol. 1, chap. 8, para. 93). Despite a successful challenge by Lawyers for Human Rights (*Lawyers for Human Rights v the State President, the Minister of National Education, the Director of Archives and the Director General of NIS*, case no. 19304/93, Supreme Court of South Africa, Transvaal Provincial Division), opposition by the State Archives Service and a subsequent media statement issued by the minister of justice to the effect that 'Cabinet is of the view that state documentation should be dealt with in terms of the Archives Act', disposal continued (TRC, 1998, vol. 1, chap. 8, para. 94).

134. TRC (1998, vol. 1, chap. 8, para. 93). The TRC found that, not only did the destruction have a severe impact on South Africa in terms of its social memory and heritage, but in terms of the commission's own work. It stated that 'the destruction of state documentation probably did more to undermine the investigative work of the Commission than any other single factor' (Ibid., para. 13).

135. The TRC recommended that 'a comprehensive analysis by independent researchers be undertaken into both the scope and content of the remaining archival holdings of the intelligence services of all divisions of the security forces' (Ibid., para. 62). Once completed, the TRC recommended that these documents be subjected to existing archival legislation and be transferred to the National Archives (Ibid.). See also section 5 of chapter 7 of the TRC Codicil to the final report presented to the president in March 2003, which became volume 6 of TRC (1998): it recommends that the National Archives should be given the necessary resources to take transfer of, process professionally and make available to the public the TRC's own records, including its victims database and website. Similar specific recommendations were also made with respect to the SADF's archival holdings (Ibid., para. 67).

136. Harris (2003).

137. Letter from secretary for defence to SAHA, 23 December 2004.

138. Section 13(2)(a) of the National Archives and Records Service Act requires that the national archivist provide written permission to destroy, erase or otherwise dispose of a public record, unless the relevant minister issues a final ruling upon irresolvable differences between the national archivist and the National Archives Advisory Council (established pursuant to section 6 to, among other things, advise and consult with the minister of arts and culture, the national archivist, the South African Heritage Resources Agency and the public protector).

139. SAHA (South African History Archive), 2006, 'SAHA rejects claim intelligence records outside ambit of PAIA', *News Archive* 2006, posted 15 December, <http://www.saha.org.za/saha.htm?saha/noticeboard_archive.htm@05>.

140. Email from the National Archives of Zimbabwe, 30 January 2006. This was divergent practice from a prior transfer of records by the minister of arts and culture when he returned records to Namibia that were created in Namibia, but removed by occupation forces prior to independence. In that instance, the South African government retained a copy and ensured that the records would be made available for scientific research in the National Library of Namibia. The national archivist of Namibia stated in his press release that negotiations regarding military and police files were continuing. SAHA continues to seek a declaration that the conduct was in contravention of the constitutional right of access to information and the provisions of PAIA in that the state did not preserve the records while the request was pending, and demanded the return of the records. Section 21 of PAIA states that the 'information officer must take

steps that are reasonably necessary to preserve the record … until the information officer has notified the requester concerned of his or her decisions in terms of section 25'. Section 13(2) of the National Archives Act provides that 'no public record under the control of a governmental body shall be transferred to an archives repository, destroyed, erased or otherwise disposed of without the written authorisation of the National Archivist issued subject to section 6(4)(e) of this Act and a final ruling by the Minister when irresolvable differences arise between the National Archivist and the Council'.

141. TRC (1998, vol. 1, chap. 8, para. 53).

142. Request nos. 0003/SAP/2002 and 0044/SAP/2002.

143. Request nos. 0044/SAP/2002, 0052/SAP/2002, 0053/SAP/2002, 0054/SAP/2002, 0079/SAP/2002 and 0001/SAP/2003.

144. Request no. 0240/NAR/2005.

145. Affidavit of Commissioner Andre Roos dated 25 July 2006 attached to a letter from SAPS dated 14 August 2006.

146. Letter from national archivist to SAHA, received 23 July 2007.

147. ANC (African National Congress), *Daily News Briefing*, 25 November 2003; mailing list at <http://lists.anc.org.za/mailman/listinfo/ancdnb>.

148. Letter from minister of intelligence to SAHA, 1 March 2005.

149. The Department of Intelligence is obliged to transfer the request to the body that is in possession of the record, pursuant to section 20 of PAIA.

150. Request no. 0382/SAP/2005.

151. Request no. 0350/DAC/2005.

152. There are a number of other pieces of legislation that deal with records management by specific bodies, such as the Defence Act No. 42 of 2002, which requires DOD to manage its own archives. A discussion of the impact of various other pieces of legislation upon PAIA will be dealt with later.

153. PAIA, sec. 14.

154. Sections 5 and 13 of NARSA set out the National Archives' general powers regarding records in the custody of government bodies.

155. National Archives Act, sec. 11.

156. Ibid., sec. 11(2)(b).

157. Request no. 0003/SAP/2002.

158. Request no. 0011/NAR/2001.

159. Request no. 0240/NAR/2005.

160. A total of 248 of these requests were submitted to NECSA for access to personal medical records.

161. Requests for personal files are requests for files relating to or about an individual, such as files kept by the former security police or the Directorate of Security Legislation.

162. SAHA is permitted by PAIA to submit requests for personal files in its own right when the persons to whom the files relate have been deceased for over 20 years.

163. Michele Pickover & Verne Harris, 'Concerns raised over Access to Information Act', *Mail & Guardian*, 11–17 May 2001.

164. I. Forest, 2005, *Report on the Survey of Public Bodies Conducted on Behalf of the South African History Archives relating to the Promotion of Access to Information Act 2 of 2000 and Born Digital Electronic Records*, <http://www.saha.org.za/research/publications/FOIP_1_5_SAHA.pdf>, accessed 20 July 2007.

165. Ibid.

166. Pickover & Harris, 'Concerns raised'.

167. East and Southern African Regional Branch of the International Council of Archives General Conference on Empowering Society with Information: The Role of Archives and Records as Tools of Accountability, Tanzania, June 2007.

168. TRC (1998, vol. 5, chap. 8, para. 62).

169. Ibid. (vol. 5, chap. 8, para. 67).

170. Section 14 of PAIA requires public bodies to publish a list of categories of records that may be voluntarily disclosed in their manuals.

171. Section 14. The manual must set out, among other things: a description of the body's functions and structure; sufficient detail to facilitate a request for access to a record of the body concerned, including a description of the subjects dealt with by records and the categories of records held on each subject; and the latest notice regarding the categories of records that are available without the need to invoke PAIA.

172. See the report highlighting the results of the 2004 Open Society Justice Initiative monitoring project 14 country study on the state of access to information, which was conducted in South Africa by ODAC, <http://www.humanrightsinitiative.org/programs/ai/rti/international/laws_papers/intl/justice_initiative_transp_&_silence_report_2006.pdf>.

173. The SAHRC is not required to make them electronically available to the public. At the time of writing, the commission was aiming to make all public body manuals available electronically. As it received over a million manuals from private bodies, these will not be made available online.

174. The project was a collaborative endeavour between SAHA and the Forced Migration Studies Programme at the University of the Witwatersrand, aiming to access records related to historical and contemporary migration issues.

175. Request no. 0341/NAR/2005.

176. NARSA imposes requirements on public bodies and imparts power to the National Archives as the overseer of records management. The National Archives Act allows the National Archives to receive and comment on filing plans submitted by public bodies that provide detailed lists of categories of records. The Act also requires most public bodies to transfer records older than 20 years to the National Archives for retention and public access (section 11). By agreement between the national archivist and the minister of a public body, records may be withheld from public access or retained by the department despite being created more than 20 years ago (section 11(2)(b)).

177. Request no. 0055/SAP/2006.

178. Request nos. 0061-0102/DHA/2006, 0013-0036/DHA/2007 and 0085-0090/DHA/2007.

179. At a meeting in July 2007, SAHA provided the example of SAPS's approach to assisting with the project, and requested DHA to provide the file plan so that it could identify records for perusal. DHA provided

access to the file plan in July 2007, two years after the request was submitted. By that time, all requests pursuant to the migration project had already been submitted. At the time of writing, all but four of the requests had not received substantive responses.

180. SAHA Public Service Accountability Monitor (2003).

181. Request nos. 0341/NAR/2005, 0013/DHA/2007, 0014/DHA/2007, 0015/DHA/2007, 0017/DHA/2007 (including 0041/PSA/2007), 0030/DHA/2007, 0032/DHA/2007, 0088/DHA/2007 and 0089/DHA/2007.

182. Christelle Terreblanche, 'NIA seeks right not to share its secrets', *Cape Times*, 18 June 2003. 'Promotion of Access to Information Act: Exemption from compilation, publication and making available of manual: South African Secret Service', *Gazette* 25102, *Regulation Gazette* 7694, 20 June 2003; 'Promotion of Access to Information Act: Exemption from compilation, publication and making available of manual', *Gazette* 24697, *Regulation Gazette* 7627, 11 April 2003; 'Promotion of Access to Information Act: Exemption from compilation, publication and making available of manual', *Gazette* 24706, *Regulation Gazette* 7630, 11 April 2003.

183. Verne Harris, 'State info not easily available', *Mail & Guardian*, 12–18 October 2001.

184. Harris (2003).

185. Correspondence from national archivist to SAHA, 13 January 2003.

186. Correspondence from SAHA trustees to national archivist, 5 March 2003.

187. The national archivist claimed that no inference could be drawn, because he made no specific reference to some of the allegations contained in the SAHA report, and pointed out that these matters were subject to pending litigation in the High Court and therefore sub judice. SAHA subsequently pointed out that simply repeating criticisms that are subject to court proceedings cannot be read as prejudicial to the outcome of those proceedings.

188. Correspondence from national archivist to SAHA, 7 March 2003.

189. Correspondence from SAHA trustees to national archivist, 14 May 2003.

190. Graham Dominy, 'A delicate balancing act at the National Archives'.

191. Verne Harris & Sello Hatang, 'Smoke and mirrors'.

192. Request nos. 0011, 0021 and 0022/NAR/2001.

193. During this time, the national archivist also attempted to avoid the disclosure of files that SAHA had identified by file number by arguing that he did 'not interpret the PAIA as allowing for random trawling (taking up valuable staff time and energy) through large volumes of documents for nebulous purposes. I believe that my request that [this] application should be more closely defined is reasonable and within the letter and spirit of the Act … a legal opinion may be needed'. It was also brought to SAHA's attention that, following the submission of the request, the national archivist was intending to destroy human resources records relating to individuals contained within those files, despite the restriction on doing so under PAIA. He ultimately conceded that he must retain them until the request was dealt with (request no. 0021/NAR/2001).

194. Response dated 11 October 2002, and relating to file nos. 0011, 0021 and 0022/NAR/2001.

195. The national archivist wrote to the director of the National Security Archive in Washington, DC on 18 November 2003 following the release of the National Security Archive's report on its visit to South Africa. In it he also complained about the allegations made by the author of the report and argued that the failure

to verify the allegations was unethical and unprofessional. The National Security Archive had made efforts to verify the claims by meeting with the national archivist; however, he did not respond to any attempts to arrange a meeting. The National Security Archive consequently met with other officials at the National Archives.

196. The TRC, in acknowledging the limitations of the National Archives' location within the Department of Arts and Culture, urges in volume 6 of its final report that the government take steps to ensure the positioning of the National Archives within the state to support its function as the auditor of government record keeping. The commission advocates for either independent agency status or positioning within the Office of the President or that of the deputy president.

197. The Department of Minerals and Energy did not respond to seven out of ten requests and the Department of Trade and Industry did not respond to four out of eight requests.

198. Letter from CEO of NECSA to SAHRC, 20 November 2006.

199. SAHA did submit an appeal in one matter (0382/SAP/2005); however, it withdrew the appeal following discussion with SAPS.

Chapter 7

1. This piece draws heavily on a paper I presented to a University of the Witwatersrand research workshop in October 2004. Segments of the paper were later drawn on for my book: Verne Harris, 2007b, *Archives and Justice: A South African Perspective*, Chicago: Society of American Archivists. These segments are cited in the notes.

2. By 'public institution' I mean one that is at least partially funded by public monies; is service driven rather than profit driven; and is positioned structurally within the state (in the broadest sense of the term). This understanding of the term is not far removed from the definition of 'public body' contained in PAIA.

3. With 'private bodies', the right of access is more limited — a 'need to know' rather than a 'right to know' applies. This, and the prioritisation of public records by the NGOs driving the use of PAIA, has delayed a serious testing of the Act's much-vaunted applicability to the private sector.

4. Jacques Derrida & Maurizio Ferraris, 2001, *A Taste for the Secret*, Cambridge: Polity Press, p. 17.

5. Ibid., p. 21.

6. Quoted in ibid., p. 56.

7. Catherine Malabou & Jacques Derrida, 2004, *Counterpath*, Stanford: Stanford University Press, p. 17.

8. In truth, while I have moved on in terms of employment, my dedication to SAHA has never ended. It is no accident that I was SAHA's acting director for four months in 2005.

9. Ronald Suresh Roberts, 2005, *No Cold Kitchen*, Johannesburg: STE.

10. Justice Albie Sachs reflected on this question during the conference National System, Public Interest, Nelson Mandela Foundation, Johannesburg, April 2007.

11. In this paragraph I draw heavily from text in Verne Harris, 1999, 'The archive and secrecy in South Africa: A personal perspective', *Janus*, 1: 7–12.

12. James Hillman, 1967, *Insearch: Psychology and Religion*, Woodstock: Spring Publications.

13. Here, clearly, I draw on both Freud and Jung.

14. There are numerous examples of matters where the body has little knowledge of the records: the National Intelligence Agency admits that it holds undisclosed amounts of unindexed microfilm; the Department of Defence has millions of records with only rudimentary finding aids that requesters are now assigned the responsibility of perusing; and the National Archives, as far as can be ascertained, has a collection of security police records that have not been processed and for which no finding aids are available to the public. I think that we are also confronted by the institutional unconscious in cases where access to records is refused simply because the institution is ignorant of what the records contain. Fear of what they might contain determines the refusal. This, in my view, underlies what feels like a paranoia in relation to the archive of South Africa's Truth and Reconciliation Commission (TRC) — a paranoia fed in part by the assumption that a 'classified' record must contain extremely sensitive information.

15. This paragraph has been published in Harris (2007b, pp. 245–46).

16. See, for instance, Peter Mitchell & John Schoeffel (eds), 2002, *Understanding Power: The Indispensable Chomsky*. New York: New Press.

17. Jacques Derrida, 1995, *Archive Fever: A Freudian Impression*, Chicago: University of Chicago Press, p. 4.

18. Michel Foucault, 1992, *The Archaeology of Knowledge and the Discourse on Language*, New York: Pantheon, p. 129.

19. Derrida in Jacques Derrida & Bernard Stiegler, 2002, *Echographies of Television*, Cambridge: Polity Press, p. 3.

20. Ibid.

21. For example, when the Open Democracy Advice Centre assisted an activist to access records related to the local council's plans for the development of an informal settlement, the Ethekwini Metropolitan Council, after significant delays, released hundreds of pages of records, which the requester had to trawl through. Ultimately, the volume of records made it impossible for the requester to obtain answers to the questions leading to his request.

22. For example, in 2004 SAHA requested access to 'medical records' of former and current nuclear energy plant workers, which the Nuclear Energy Corporation of South Africa (NECSA) granted. They were provided to Dr Murray Coombs for assessment, who reported that the records were not complete. NECSA in response advised that it had only provided access to records categorised by it as 'medical records', and determined not to provide records that related to the medical history of the individuals, but were contained in personnel and other files.

23. For example, the National Archives released to SAHA a report relating to its implementation of TRC recommendations, but failed to provide any contextual information such as the date of creation, the origination and the status of the document. SAHA went to court, and in an out-of-court settlement the National Archives provided the contextual information specified by SAHA.

24. A version of the following two paragraphs was published in Harris (2007b, pp. 246–47).

25. Derrida (1995, p. 4).

26. Quoted in Christopher Merrett, 2001, 'A tale of two paradoxes: Media censorship in South Africa, pre-liberation and post-apartheid', *Critical Arts* 15(1–2), p. 64.

27. The national archivist's assaults on SAHA over the period 2002–03 provide a useful example: see Box 6.10 in chapter 6.

28. See Kate Allan's discussion in chapter 6 of this volume regarding the inadequacy of the public interest override, the need for an information protection commission and the call for replacement of the Protection of Information Act.

29. These included, among others, the Archives Act, Criminal Procedure Act, Disclosure of Foreign Funding Act, Inquests Act, Internal Security Act, Nuclear Energy Act, Official Secrets Act, Petroleum Products Act, Protection of Information Act and Statistics Act.

30. PAIA is one of a growing family of freedom of information laws in the world, but two of its attributes set it apart. Firstly, it is rooted in a constitutional requirement; and, secondly, it applies not only to information held by the state, but also to information held by so-called 'private bodies'.

31. *Mail & Guardian*, 7–13 September 2007, p. 25.

32. Some of the indicators of these cultures are discussed by Allan in chapter 6.

33. In 2003 the proceedings of the Hefer Commission provided a fascinating window into how this sensitivity is playing out in South Africa. See Verne Harris, 2003, 'After the Hefer circus', *Natal Witness*, 29 December, which was reproduced in Harris (2007b, pp. 418–20).

34. T.R. Schellenberg, 1956, *Modern Archives: Principles and Techniques*, Melbourne: F.W. Cheshire, p. 226.

35. For sustained accounts of my reading of Derrida, see Harris (2007b, pp. 39–54 and 69–84).

36. For an elaboration of this in the context of records and archives, see Harris (2007b, pp. 253–65).

37. Robert Gibbs, 2000, *Why Ethics?: Signs of Responsibilities*, Princeton: Princeton University Press, p. 30.

Bibliography

AEC (Atomic Energy Corporation of South Africa Ltd). 1984. *Vaalputs: National Radioactive Waste Disposal Facility*. Pretoria: AEC.

Albright, David & Mark Hobbs. 1993. 'South Africa: The ANC and the atom bomb.' *Bulletin of Atomic Scientists*, 49(3), April. <http://www.bullatomsci.org/issues/1993/a93/a93AlbrightHibbs.html>

—. 1994a. 'South Africa and the affordable bomb.' *Bulletin of Atomic Scientists*, 50(4), July/August: 37–44.

—. 1994b. *South Africa's Secret Nuclear Weapons*. Institute for Science and International Security report. May. <http://www.isis-online.org/publications/southafrica/ir0594.html>

Allan, Kate. 2005. 'Burning bodies: The peril of poor record-keeping practices in South Africa's nuclear industry.' Paper disseminated at the conference on Updating International Nuclear Law, Salzburg, 20–23 October. <http://www.saha.org.za/research/publications/FOIP_IntNuclConf_Allan.pdf>

Allan, K. & I.B. Currie. 2007. 'Enforcing access to information and privacy rights: Evaluating proposals for an information protection regulator for South Africa.' *South African Journal on Human Rights*, 23(2).

Alperovitz, Gar. 1995. *The Decision to Use the Atomic Bomb*. New York: Alfred A. Knopf.

Anonymous. 1986/87. 'The abuse of psychiatry in the SADF: "I am first a soldier and then a psychiatrist"'. *War Resister*, 47, December–January.

Arko-Cobbah, A. 2007. 'The right of access to information: Civil society and good governance in South Africa.' June. <http://www.ifla.org/IV/ifla73/papers/135-Arko-Cobbah-en.pdf>

Associated Scientific and Technical Societies of South Africa. 1957. *Uranium in South Africa 1946–1956*, vol. 1. Johannesburg: Associated Scientific and Technical Societies of South Africa.

Bird, Kai & Martin Sherwin. 2005. *American Prometheus: The Triumph and Tragedy of J. Robert Oppenheimer*. New York: Alfred A. Knopf.

Blanton, T. 2002. 'The world's right to know.' *Foreign Policy*, July/August. <http://www.freedominfo.org/documents/rtk-english.pdf>

Burger, Marlene & Chandré Gould. 2002. *Secrets and Lies*. Cape Town: Zebra Press.

Calland, R. 2002. 'Introduction.' In R. Calland & A. Tilley (eds). *The Right to Know, the Right to Live: Access to Information and Socio-Economic Justice*. Cape Town: ODAC.

—. 2006. *Anatomy of South Africa: Who Holds the Power?* Cape Town: Zebra Press.

Červenka, Zdenek & Barbara Rogers. 1977. *The Nuclear Axis: Secret Collaboration between West Germany and South Africa*. London: Julian Friedmann.

Cock, Jacklyn & Laurie Nathan (eds). 1989. *War and Society: The Militarisation of South Africa*. Cape Town: David Philip.

Coombs, W. Murray. 2005. *Review of the Medical Files for Occupational Exposure to Radiation of Ex-NECSA Employees: Report for Earthlife Africa*. February. Pretoria: Health Gap Network.

Council for Nuclear Safety. 1996. *Vaalputs Licence Compliance Inspection, 8–11 September*. Centurion: CNS.

Currie, I. & J. Klaaren. 2002. *The Resolve: KPMG Commentary on the Promotion of Access to Information Act*. Cape Town: Siber Ink.

Darch, C. & P.G. Underwood. 2005. 'Freedom of information legislation, state compliance and the disclosure of knowledge: The South African experience.' *International Information and Library Review*, 37: 76.

Derrida, Jacques. 1995. *Archive Fever: A Freudian Impression*. Chicago: University of Chicago Press.

— & Maurizio Ferraris. 2001. *A Taste for the Secret*. Cambridge: Polity Press.

— & Bernard Stiegler. 2002. *Echographies of Television*. Cambridge: Polity Press.

Dimba, M. 2002. 'A landmark law opens up post-apartheid South Africa.' <http://www.freedominfo.org/features/20020717.htm>

DME (Department of Minerals and Energy). 1998. White Paper on the Energy Policy of the Republic of South Africa. Pretoria: DME.

DOD (Department of Defence). n.d. *PAIA Manual*. Pretoria: DOD.

EMG (Environmental Monitoring Group) & Western Cape ANC Science and Technology Group. 1994. *The Nuclear Debate: Proceedings of a Conference on Nuclear Policy for a Democratic South Africa*. Cape Town: EMG/ANC.

Fig, David. 1999. 'Sanctions and the nuclear industry.' In Neta C. Crawford & Audie Klotz (eds). *How Sanctions Work: Lessons from South Africa*. Basingstoke: Macmillan.

—. 2005. *Uranium Road: Questioning South Africa's Nuclear Direction*. Johannesburg: Jacana.

Fischer, David. 1994. 'South Africa.' In Mitchell Reiss & Robert Litwak (eds). *Nuclear Proliferation after the Cold War*. Washington, DC: Woodrow Wilson Center Press.

Florini, A. (ed.). 2007. *The Right to Know: Transparency for an Open World*. New York: Columbia University Press.

Forest, I. 2005. *Report on the Survey of Public Bodies Conducted on Behalf of the South African History Archives relating to the Promotion of Access to Information Act 2 of 2000 and Born Digital Electronic Records*. <http://www.saha.org.za/research/publications/FOIP_1_5_SAHA.pdf>

Foucault, Michel. 1992. *The Archaeology of Knowledge and the Discourse on Language*. New York: Pantheon.

Frost, Bill (ed.). n.d. *Behavioral Psychology: History, Techniques and the Role of Hypnotherapy*. Last modified 31 December 2004. <http://freespace.virgin.net/changing states/behavioural_approaches.html>

GALA (Gay and Lesbian Archive)/SAHA (South African History Archive). 2003. *Gays in the Apartheid Military*. Report. Johannesburg. September. <http://www.saha.org.za/research/publications/FOIP_6_3.pdf>

Gibbs, Robert. 2000. *Why Ethics? Signs of Responsibilities*. Princeton: Princeton University Press.

Glazewski, Jan. 2000. *Environmental Law in South Africa*. Durban: LexisNexus Butterworths.

Hagart, R.B. 1957. 'National aspects of the uranium industry.' *Journal of the South African Institute of Mining and Metallurgy*, 57(9), April.

Harris, Verne. 1999. 'The archive and secrecy in South Africa: A personal perspective.' *Janus*: 7–12.

—. 2001. *Freedom of Information Watch*. South African History Archive report. October. <http://www.saha.org.za/research.htm>

—. 2003. *Promotion of Access to Information Act: The Case of the South African History Archive*. January. <http://www.saha.org.za/research/publications/FOIP_update_jan2003.pdf>

—, Sello Hatang & Peter Liberman. 2004. 'Unveiling South Africa's nuclear past.' *Journal of Southern African Studies*, 30(3): 457–75.

—. 2007a. '"They should have destroyed more": The destruction of public records by the South African state in the final years of apartheid, 1990–1994.' In Verne Harris. *Archives and Justice: A South African Perspective*. Chicago: Society of American Archivists.

—. 2007b. *Archives and Justice: A South African Perspective*. Chicago: Society of American Archivists.

— & Christopher Merrett. 2007. 'Toward a culture of transparency: Public rights of access to official records in South Africa.' In Verne Harris. *Archives and Justice: A South African Perspective*. Chicago: Society of American Archivists.

Health and Human Rights Projects. 1997. 'Professional accountability in South Africa.' Final submission to the Truth and Reconciliation Commission, prepared for the hearings on the health sector. June.

Hillman, James. 1967. *Insearch: Psychology and Religion*. Woodstock: Spring Publications.

Hood, C. & D. Heald. 2006. 'Transparency: The key to better governance? *Open Government: A Journal on Freedom of Information*, 2(2).

Jagwanth, S. 2002 'The right to information as a leverage right.' In R. Calland & A. Tilley (eds). *The Right to Know, the Right to Live: Access to Information and Socio-Economic Justice*. Cape Town: ODAC.

Kennedy, Tim. 1995. 'As South Africa integrates, Israel cutting military ties.' *Washington Report on Middle East Affairs*, July/August. <http://www.washington-report.org/backissues/0795/9507031.htm>

King, Michael, Glenn Smith & Annie Bartlett. 2004. 'Treatments of homosexuality in Britain since the 1950s – an oral history: The experience of professionals.' *British Medical Journal*, 328.

Klaaren, J. 2002. *The Gap Report: Issues regarding Disclosure of Information by Public Officials*. June. Accessed 27 September 2007. <http://www.saha.org.za/research/publications/FOIP_2_4_Klaaren.pdf>

Levin, Aubrey. 1975. "'n Ontleiding van die gebruik van dwelmmiddels en sekere gevolge daarvan met klem op cannabis sativa by 'n monster jongmans opgeroep vir militiere diensplig.' DM thesis, University of Pretoria.

Liberman, Peter. 2001. 'The rise and fall of the South African bomb.' *International Security*, 26(2), Fall: 45–86.

Malabou, Catherine & Jacques Derrida. 2004. *Counterpath*. Stanford: Stanford University Press.

Mandela House/SAHA (South African History Archive). 2006. *Report on a Workshop on the Protection of Personal Information Draft Bill, Mandela House, 13 May 2006*. Johannesburg: Mandela House/SAHA. <http://www.saha.org.za/research/publications/FOIP_4_3.pdf>

Merrett, Christopher. 2001. 'A tale of two paradoxes: Media censorship in South Africa, pre-liberation and post-apartheid.' *Critical Arts* 15(1–2): 50–68.

Mitchell, Peter & John Schoeffel (eds). 2002. *Understanding Power: The Indispensable Chomsky*. New York: New Press.

Moll, Peter. 1984. 'A theological critique of the military chaplaincy of the English-speaking churches.' M.A. dissertation, University of Cape Town.

Mureinik, E. 1994. 'A bridge to where? Introducing the Interim Bill of Rights.' *South African Journal on Human Rights*, 10: 31–48.

NERSA (National Electricity Regulator of South Africa). 2006. *Investigation into the Electricity Outages in the Western Cape, November 2005–March 2006*. Pretoria: NERSA.

Neuman, L. & R. Calland. 2007. 'Making the law work: The challenge of implementation.' In A. Florini (ed.). *The Right to Know: Transparency for an Open World*. New York: Columbia University Press, chap. 6.

NNR (National Nuclear Regulator). 1996. *Vaalputs Licence Compliance Inspection*. Report. Pretoria. 8–11 September.

ODAC (Open Democracy Advice Centre). 2005. *ODAC Annual Report 2005*. <http://www.opendemocracy.org.za/documents/AnnualReport2005.doc>

O'Regan, K. 2000. 'Democracy and access to information in the South African Constitution: Some reflections.' Paper presented at the conference The Constitutional Right to Access to Information, Pretoria, September. <http://www.kas.de/db_files/dokumente/7_dokument_dok_pdf_4936_2.pdf>

OSI (Open Society Institute). 2006. *Transparency and Silence: A Survey of Access to Information Laws and Practices in 14 Countries*. New York: Open Society Justice Initiative.

Parliament of the Republic of South Africa. 2007. *Report of the Ad Hoc Committee on the Review of Chapter 9 and Associated Institutions*. A report of the National Assembly of the Parliament of South Africa, Cape Town.

Pickover, Michele & Verne Harris. 2001. 'Freedom of information in South Africa: A far off reality?' May. <http://www.saha.org.za/research/publications/FOIP_1_4_PickoverHarris.pdf>

Potgieter, De Wet. 2007. *Total Onslaught: Apartheid's Dirty Tricks Exposed*. Cape Town: Zebra Press.

Rhodes, Richard. 1986. *The Making of the Atomic Bomb*. New York: Simon & Schuster.

—.1995. *Dark Sun: The Making of the Hydrogen Bomb*. New York: Simon & Schuster.

Roberts, Ronald Suresh. 2005. *No Cold Kitchen*. Johannesburg: STE.

RULA (Research Unit for Law and Administration) & SAHA (South African History Archive). 2002. *Proposed Amendments to the Promotion of Access to Information (PAIA): Report on a Workshop Convened at the University of the Witwatersrand, 4 October 2002*. <http://www.saha.org.za/research/publications/FOIP_3_2.pdf>

SAHA (South African History Archive). 2002. *SAHA Annual Report 2002*. Johannesburg: SAHA.

— & Public Service Accountability Monitor. 2003. 'Proposed amendments to the Promotion of Access to Information Act: A joint submission by the South African History Archive (SAHA) and the Public Service Accoutability [sic] Monitor (PSAM).' August. <http://www.saha.org.za/research/publications/FOIP_3_1.pdf>

—. 2004 *SAHA Annual Report 2004*. Johannesburg: SAHA. <http://www.saha.org.za/research/publications/SAHA_ann_rep_2004.pdf>

SAHRC (South African Human Rights Commission). 2003. *South African Human Rights Commission Annual Report, 2002/2003*. Pretoria: SAHRC.

—. 2004. *South African Human Rights Commission Annual Report 2003/2004*. Pretoria: SAHRC.

—. 2005. *South African Human Rights Commission Annual Report 2004/2005*. Pretoria: SAHRC.

Schellenberg, T.R. 1956. *Modern Archives: Principles and Techniques*. Melbourne: F.W. Cheshire.

Singh, S. 2007. 'India: Grassroots initiatives.' In A. Florini (ed.). *The Right to Know: Transparency for an Open World*. New York: Columbia University Press.

Steyn, Hannes, Richart van der Walt & Jan van Loggerenberg. 2003. *Armament and Disarmament: South Africa's Nuclear Weapons Experience*. Pretoria: Network Publishers.

Stumpf, Waldo. 1995. 'Birth and death of the South African nuclear weapons programme.' Presentation given at the conference 50 Years After Hiroshima, organised by Unione Scienziati per il Disarmo, Castiglioncello, Italy, 28 September–2 October. <http://www.fas.org/nuke/guide/rsa/nuke/stumpf.htm>

Taverner, L. 1956. 'An historical review of the events and developments culminating in the construction of plants for the recovery of uranium from gold ore residues.' *Journal of the South African Institute of Mining and Metallurgy*, 57(4), November.

TRC (Truth and Reconciliation Commission). 1997. Human Rights Violations, Health Sector Hearings, Cape Town, 17 June. Transcript. <http://www.doj.gov.za/trc/special/health/health01.htm>

—. 1998. *Truth and Reconciliation Commission of South Africa Report*. Cape Town: The Commission.

Van der Westhuizen, L.J. & J.H. le Roux. 1997. *A Will to Win*. Bloemfontein: Institute for Contemporary History, University of the Orange Free State.

Van Zyl, Mikki, Jeanelle de Gruchy, Sheila Lapinsky, Simon Lewin & Graeme Reid. 1999. *The aVersion Project: Human Rights Abuses of Gays and Lesbians in the SADF by Health Workers during the Apartheid Era*. Report. Cape Town: Gay and Lesbian Archives, Health and Human Rights Project, Medical Research Council, National Coalition for Gay and Lesbian Equality. October.

Von Williegh, N. 1993. 'A brief overview of the development of nuclear explosive devices in South Africa.' Atomic Energy Corporation of South Africa. May.

Whitcher, Benita. 2003. *The Anti-censorship Programme: Opinion on Legislation Affecting Freedom of Expression in South Africa*. Freedom of Expression Institute report. <http://www.fxi.org.za/PDF's/ACP/Annexure+1+Main+Report1.pdf>

Index

This index lists terms, concepts, subjects, Acts, organisations, institutions and personal names. Figures are indexed and are indicated in italics. Prepositions in subheadings are not used for alphabetical ordering.